James Gibbons

Our Christian Heritage

James Gibbons

Our Christian Heritage

ISBN/EAN: 9783742856623

Manufactured in Europe, USA, Canada, Australia, Japa

Cover: Foto ©Lupo / pixelio.de

Manufactured and distributed by brebook publishing software (www.brebook.com)

James Gibbons

Our Christian Heritage

OUR CHRISTIAN HERITAGE.

BY

JAMES CARDINAL GIBBONS,

Archbishop of Baltimore.

AUTHOR OF "THE FAITH OF OUR FATHERS."

BALTIMORE:
JOHN MURPHY & COMPANY.

LONDON: R. WASHBOURNE.
1889.

COPYRIGHT, 1889,
BY
JAMES CARDINAL GIBBONS.

TO THE

MEMORY OF

John Carroll,

THE PATRIARCH OF THE AMERICAN CHURCH,

AND TO THE

Prelates and Clergy

OF THE UNITED STATES,

HEIRS OF HIS FAITH AND HIS MISSION,

THIS VOLUME

IS AFFECTIONATELY INSCRIBED

ON THE ONE HUNDREDTH ANNIVERSARY

OF THE

CREATION OF OUR HIERARCHY.

PREFACE.

The great majority of readers in this bustling age profess to have no leisure, and certainly evince no inclination to peruse bulky volumes, no matter how superior their merit may be.

It is chiefly to this busy restless class that the writer addresses himself and he craves their earnest attention. That his appeal may be more favorably received, and may meet with the success which he hopes for, he has endeavored to compress within as small a compass as possible, a variety of subjects which he considers of vital consequence to all men who take a serious view of the solemn duties and of the sublime destiny of human life.

He has reasons to fear that in aiming to be brief, he may have occasionally been wanting in clearness and precision. Nor is he without grave misgivings that owing to the incessant interruptions occasioned by the imperative work of the ministry, some of the questions he has discussed, may not have been treated with the fulness which their importance demands. He confesses in truth that this consideration had for some time, deterred him from venturing to submit these pages to the judgment of a discerning public.

He hopes, however, that the few scattered fruits which the reader will gather from this little garden, may whet his appetite for a more abundant feast, and may allure him to enter other fields where his hunger for truth and righteousness will be fully appeased.

BALTIMORE,
November 6th, 1889.

CONTENTS.

		PAGE
Introduction,		1

CHAPTER I. Was the World Created, or is it Eternal and Self-Existing? 16
    II. The Existence of God Attested by all Nations, Ancient and Modern, ... 24
    III. Conscience bearing Witness to God, . . 51
    IV. The Omnipresence of God, ... 61
    V. Lessons drawn from the Recognition of God's Presence, ... 69
    VI. The Providence of God, ... 77
    VII. Popular objections against Divine Providence, 90
    VIII. The Dignity and Efficacy of Prayer, . . 110
    IX. Refutation of Objections against Prayer, . 130
    X. Gratitude to God, ... 148
    XI. Man possesses Moral Freedom, . . . 163
    XII. How to Exercise our Free-Will, . . . 181
    XIII. The Immortality of the Soul, . . . 198
    XIV. The Eternal Exclusion of the Reprobate from Heaven not Incompatible with Divine Justice and Mercy, ... 216
    XV. The Divinity of Christ attested by Himself and His Disciples, ... 229
    XVI. Our Lord's Divinity Confirmed by His Miracles, and especially by His Resurrection, 240
    XVII. The Divine Mission of Christ Demonstrated by the Marvellous Propagation and Perpetuity of the Christian Religion, . . 252
    XVIII. Pagan System of Worship. Origin and Destiny of Man as viewed by Pagan Philosophy, ... 273

CHAPTER.		PAGE
XIX.	Origin and Destiny of Man as viewed by Modern Unbelief, ...	281
XX.	Christian Idea of God. Origin and Destiny of Man as viewed by Christian Revelation,	290
XXI.	Christianity and Modern Science. There is no Conflict between Science and Religion,	301
XXII.	The Church is the True Friend and Promoter of Science, ...	309
XXIII.	Influence of Paganism upon Morals, . .	322
XXIV.	Influence of Christianity upon Morals, .	331
XXV.	Condition of Woman under Pagan Civilization, ...	349
XXVI.	What Christianity has done for Woman, .	358
XXVII.	Paganism and Christianity compared in the Practice of Social Virtues—Abortion, Infanticide—Neglect of the Poor and the Sick in Heathen Countries—Compassion of Jesus Christ for Suffering Humanity Imitated by the Primitive Church—Her Abhorrence of Fœticide—Her Care of the Poor and the Sick in Primitive Times,	374
XXVIII.	Benevolent Institutions Founded and Fostered by Christianity in Modern Times,	384
XXIX.	Warfare in Pagan and Christian Times— Christianity has Diminished the Number, and Mitigated the Atrocities of Wars,	396
XXX.	The Influence of Paganism on Human Slavery,	416
XXXI.	The Influence of Christianity on Human Slavery, ...	425
XXXII.	The Dignity, Rights and Duties of the Laboring Classes, ...	438
XXXIII.	Religion the Essential Basis of Civil Society,	456
XXXIV.	The Religious Element in our American Civilization, ...	472
XXXV.	The Dangers that Threaten our American Civilization, ...	484

OUR CHRISTIAN HERITAGE.

INTRODUCTION.

This book is not polemical. It does not deal with the controversies that have agitated the Christian world since the religious convulsion of the sixteenth century. It does not, therefore, aim at vindicating the claims of the Catholic Church as superior to those of the separated branches of Christianity—a subject that has already been exhaustively treated.

It has nothing to say against any Christian denomination that still retains faith in at least the divine mission of Jesus Christ. On the contrary, I am glad to acknowledge that most of the topics discussed in this little volume have often found, and still find able and zealous advocates in Protestant writers.

And far from despising or rejecting their support, I would gladly hold out to them the right hand of fellowship, so long as they unite with us in striking the common foe. It is pleasant to be able to stand sometimes on the same platform with our old antagonists.

Nor were these pages written in the fond hope of influencing *professional* free-thinkers, agnostics, and other avowed enemies of Christianity, who will not learn lest their knowledge might compel them to do well, who trade in blasphemy, who glory in their infidelity, and who earn for themselves a cheap reputation by coarsely caricaturing every doctrine and tradition that Christians hold dear. Every scoffer at religion is the Thersites of the Christian camp. Such characters are found in every age; and they were aptly described over eighteen centuries ago by the Apostle as "ungodly men denying the only Sovereign Ruler, and our Lord Jesus Christ, blaspheming whatever things they know not; and what things soever they naturally know, like dumb beasts, in these they are corrupted; feasting together without fear, clouds without water which are carried about by the winds, autumnal leaves without fruit, raging waves of the sea, foaming out their own confusion, wandering stars to whom the storm of darkness is reserved forever."[1]

These men profess to have discovered in the revealed Scriptures, contradictions and absurdities and legislative enactments unworthy of the wisdom and justice of a Divine Lawgiver. They judge every thing from their own narrow standpoint without regard to the circumstances of time and place in which the Scriptures were written. They will offer more objections to Christianity in an hour than

[1] *Jude* I.

could be reasonably answered in a month. While avowing their ignorance of many of the physical laws that govern the universe and that regulate even their own bodies which they see and feel, they will insist on knowing everything regarding the incomprehensible Deity and His attributes. In a word, they will admit mysteries in the material world that surrounds them; but mysteries in the supernatural world, they will not accept. They will deny any revealed truth that does not fall within the range of human experience and that is not in accordance with the discovered laws of nature. But to reject a dogma on such grounds cannot be approved by philosophy or sound sense.

Had a man living in the last century, been told that the day was near at hand when one could travel with great rapidity by steam over land and water; when a message could be conveyed in a few seconds around the globe; when lightning would be so chained and subdued as to be made to diffuse a soft and steady light in our streets and parlors; when we could whisper to a friend a hundred miles away and our voice even be recognized by him, he would have laughed at prophecies so bold, and declared them the ravings of a visionary. He would, by the light of his experience and common sense, have pronounced such things physically impossible. And yet we are all witnesses of these phenomena which are daily occurring around us.

Now, if new and startling secrets are daily revealed in the material world, surely it is rash to reject a fact of Christian faith on the sole ground that it *appears* to be out of harmony with recognized laws, or is not confirmed by the experience or observation of mankind.

A man should have some acquaintance with the unseen world before undertaking to pass judgment on the phenomena that govern it:

> "There are more things in heaven and earth, Horatio,
> Than are dreamt of in your philosophy."

This little volume is affectionately addressed to a large, and I fear an increasing class of persons who, through association, the absence of Christian training, a distorted education, and pernicious reading, have not only become estranged from the specific teachings of the Gospel, but whose moral and religious nature has received such a shock that they have only a vague and undefined faith even in the truths of natural religion underlying Christianity.

These deserve more pity than blame. They have never shared in the Christian heritage of their fathers, or they were robbed of it before they had the moral and intellectual vigor to resist the invader, or they quietly surrendered their inheritance before they could appreciate its inestimable value. They do not boast of their spiritual darkness and moral obliquity. They make no parade of their irreligion. They feel unhappy in their deprivation.

Some of them not questioning our sincerity, nor quite denying the objective truth of our Christian profession, contemplate us with secret envy. But as they fancy that the atmosphere of faith would be oppressive to them, because it involves sacrifices hard to flesh and blood, they make no efforts to acquire it. Their disease is partly mental doubt, but still more moral cowardice.

Others of them honestly imagine that, in accepting and professing the truths of Christianity, we are in a state of happy delusion, and they pity us.

There are others, I think, who as honestly persuade themselves that we do not believe what we preach; and they very naturally despise us.

The men of whom I speak, have but a dim and hazy view of the first principles of religion.

To lead them back to the Christian fold by starting with an appeal to the divine claims of Christ, to the value of the soul, the voice of conscience, the importance of salvation, the glory of heaven or the sufferings of the reprobate, is to assume as granted facts which they do not accept. It is like commencing the house at the roof instead of at the foundation. As grace is founded on nature, so the knowledge of supernatural religion must rest on natural religion. We waste our time in trying to build up the edifice of faith in men in whose souls the foundations of natural truth have been undermined.

What is to be gained in exhorting men to worship the Trinity until the misgivings they have about the existence of a personal God are removed?

What will it profit us to admonish them to submit to the inscrutable decrees of Providence, if they do not admit a superintending Providence, but look upon all events that happen as the result of physical laws or of blind chance?

There is little to be gained in quoting Scripture to men who imagine that many facts of Scripture are controverted by the deductions of science.

In vain do we strive to persuade men to be solicitous about the salvation of their souls, so long as they are seduced into the belief that they have no soul or spiritual being, and maintain that their mental conceptions are mere modifications of the brain.

Before we can persuade them to listen with docility to the voice of conscience, we must first convince them that conscience is the voice of God, and not, as they imagine, the prompting of a timid nature, or the outcome of education.

Before we can succeed in urging men to keep the Commandments, the distinction between virtue and vice, which is well-nigh obliterated from their hearts, must be made clearly manifest.

And we are preaching to deaf ears in rebuking sin and in exhorting men to resist their evil inclinations, till we get them to admit that man enjoys moral freedom, and disabuse them of the false notion that sensual desires were given us to be gratified, and that it is neither expedient nor possible to resist what a cotemporary writer calls "the divine rights of passion."[1]

[1] *Robert Elsmere.*

In a word, it is time thrown away to expatiate on the happiness of eternal life before hearers who do not believe in immortality, but who regard death as the term of man's existence.

The class of men of whom I am writing, will bluntly say to us: We are longing for light, but we hesitate to become Christians, not so much because your religion claims to be supernatural, as because we *suspect* it to be irrational. We reject your authority as teachers; we reject Christian revelation; we take nothing for granted; we appeal to the court of reason and historical evidence. Let us try to meet them on their own ground, and accept the appeal.

I have, therefore, endeavored in these pages to show that these fundamental truths underlying Christianity, such as the existence, the providence, and the omniscience of God, the immortality of the soul, the existence of free-will, and the essential distinction between moral good and evil, are all susceptible of being demonstrated by our unaided reason, while they are made still more luminous by the light of Christian Revelation.

This little book may be a serviceable manual not only in the hands of those outside the fold of Christianity, but of Christian believers as well; as it will furnish them with a reason for the hope that is in them, and supply them with arguments to meet the sophistries of professed free-thinkers, and to enlighten the sincere inquirer after truth.

II.

There are some writers in our country over whom the arts and literature and the material splendor of Pagan Greece and Rome exercise a special fascination, and who seem to long for the return of the old civilization of those countries. They are full of admiration for the marble palaces of the "City of the Cæsars," but they close their eyes to the midnight orgies, the scenes of crime, debauchery, and revelry that were enacted within them. The colossal power of Rome is suggested to their mind by the contemplation of the Coliseum and the Arch of Titus; but they overlook the fact, that the Coliseum was erected by the sweat and blood of Jewish captives, and that the triumphal arch commemorates not only the glory of Rome, but the exile and degradation of a conquered nation as well. They are fond of holding up to public view the domestic and civic virtues of a Lucretia, a Cornelia, and a Marcus Aurelius, and the military prowess of the Scipios and the Fabii; but they keep in the background the unnatural crimes and abominations of the Neros, the Caligulas, the Domitians, and other Pagan rulers who were a disgrace to humanity.

There are even others, few thank God in number, who thinking that Christianity has outlived its day and is unsuited to our times, would fain supplant it by Buddhism, which they regard as less exacting in its tenets and as appealing to the highest aspirations of man's nature.

Our Buddhist brethren in Japan, encouraged by their admirers in America, have actually established in Kioto a periodical advocating the religion of Buddha, which they propose to circulate among us with the view of converting us to their faith.[1]

I may dismiss this subject with the simple observation that there is no good feature in Buddhism which is not eminently found in the Christian religion. There is no want of the soul which Christianity does not satisfy; there is no civilization that it does not enlighten and purify. It is broad and elastic enough to embrace all nations, and minute enough to occupy itself with every individual soul. It is a perennial tree, which flourishes all the world over, while Buddhism is an exotic that has never thrived outside of its native soil of Asia.

While these pages are passing through the press, we are informed by the daily papers that an anti-Christian Sunday-school has been opened in a public hall in Baltimore, and that weekly sessions are regularly held there. We learn from the same source that some Protestant clergymen of our city have urged the Mayor to suppress this infidel school. Waiving the question of right which the civil authorities may have to interfere in matters of this kind, I do not believe that any radical cure of this religious distemper can be effected by repressive measures. It is not by coercion, but by the voluntary surrender of the citadel of the heart, that man

---

[1] See New York *Sun*, September 16, 1888.

is converted. Coercion only drives the poison into the social body, where it secretly ferments. Our divine Saviour never invoked the sword to vindicate His doctrines. He rebuked His disciple, when he once drew the sword in defence of His Master, and commanded him to put it back into its scabbard. "The weapons of our warfare," says the Apostle, "are not carnal,"[1] but spiritual; they are the weapons of argument, of persuasion and charity. The only sword I would draw against the children of unbelief, is "the sword of the Spirit, which is the word of God;" and the only fire I would light against them, is the fire of divine love which our Lord came to enkindle in the hearts of men. In a word, I would convince them that Christianity "is profitable for all things, having the promise of the life that now is," as well as "of that which is to come."[2]

With the aim to show what blessings Christianity has conferred on the human race, even in a temporal point of view, the latter part of this volume contains a series of chapters exhibiting the superiority of Christian over Pagan civilization.

If we institute a comparison between the relative influence of Paganism and Christianity in promoting the welfare of the individual, the family, and society, we have no doubt that the investigation will result overwhelmingly in favor of the latter.

It is only by placing the two systems in juxta-position that we adequately realize the degradation

[1] II. Cor. X.
[2] I. Tim. IV.

from which we have been rescued and the privileges we enjoy.

The Pagan had only a vague and indistinct conception of the Supreme Being. His worship was, for the most part, idolatry. Not only every striking creation in nature, but even every crime and passion had its tutelary divinity; so that the object of his worship was, at the same time, an incentive to the gratification of his desires.

He knew not whence he came nor whither he was going. His vision of the future was bounded by the horizon of the tomb. His philosophers and teachers were unable to shed any clear and unerring light on this subject. Their discussions invariably ended in speculation and doubt.

To solid peace and contentment, he was therefore a stranger; for how can an intelligent being yearning for immortality, be truly happy who has received no clear revelation of a life to come?

His wife was the toy of his caprice, the slave of his passions. He regarded marriage as a temporary compact to be easily dissolved at will.

He had the power of life and death over his children. He had a very convenient expedient for limiting the number of his offspring, by strangling them in their infancy or casting them into the streets. There was no law to restrain him, or it was so feebly enforced as to be practically inoperative.

If the Roman could murder his child without dread of the law, he could with equal impunity starve his slave. He had commonly less consideration for his aged and infirm servant than we have for our beast of burden. The disabled or veteran steed no longer able to work, we compassionately turn out to pasture; the superannuated slave was sent to perish on the banks of the Tiber.

As for asylums and hospitals, he knew nothing about them. They had no existence whatever, and the rich vocabularies of Greece and Rome had not even a word to express such terms. It was reserved for Christianity not only to create such institutions, but even to coin the words that convey their meaning.

Throughout all heathendom, slavery was universal. In the Roman Empire there were usually three slaves for every freeman. And as manual labor was restricted to the slaves, it was branded with the stamp of degradation, and deemed a pursuit unworthy of a freeman.

It must be conceded that war is always an expensive luxury and generally a great calamity. Now, prior to the advent of Christianity, war was the rule, peace the exception among the nations of the earth. During the six hundred and fifty years intervening between the first successor of Romulus and Augustus Cæsar, Rome was engaged in continuous war at home or abroad, with the exception of a six years' interval of peace.

The evils flowing from habitual warfare were aggravated by its fearful atrocities. Vengeance without mercy was meted out to the vanquished, who were either put to the sword, or became the slaves of the conqueror.

This is the moral bondage from which we have been delivered; this is the darkness from which we have been rescued by the admirable light of the Gospel.

What are the blessings that Christian civilization confers on the individual, the family, and society?

It has delivered us from idolatry and led us to the worship of the one, true, and living God. Our Saviour came down from heaven to shed light on that illimitable world which lies beyond the tomb, and to reveal to us a new life which begins with death. He has made known to us our origin and destiny and the means of attaining it.

He has brought not only light to our intellects, but also peace to our hearts, that peace which springs from the knowledge of the truth and the hope of eternal life.

He has given benediction to the home by proclaiming the unity, the sanctity, and the indissolubility of marriage. The wife is no longer the slave, but the partner of her husband; she is no longer a tenant at will, but the mistress of her household; she is no longer confronted by a usurping rival, but she is the undisputed queen of the domestic kingdom.

The father has no longer the power of life and death over his child. So sacred and inviolable is human life that the killing of even the unborn babe, is regarded as murder by the ethics of the Gospel.

The aged poor are no longer at the mercy of heartless masters. They are not cast aside like a worn-out machine. Their life is sacred like that of infants, and they are comfortably provided for in institutions now spread throughout Christendom.

The tender and compassionate spirit of Christ has caused orphan asylums and hospitals to spring up and bloom in every land. There is no phase of human misery and suffering that does not find solace and relief in these establishments.

Human slavery has, at last, melted away before the effulgent rays of the Gospel. To borrow with a slight paraphrase the words of a distinguished writer, we can say with truth that a slave stands redeemed, regenerated, and disenthralled, as soon as he plants his foot on the sacred soil of Christendom.

The Gospel proclaims the dignity of labor. Judged by its standard, every honest employment is honorable, how menial soever it may be.

Christianity has been a peacemaker to the nations. By her beneficent influence she has made wars far less frequent than they used to be under Pagan régime. During the empire of ancient Rome, there was a century of warfare for every year of peace. The history of our Republic records but one decade of military conflict in the hundred years of its existence.

Christianity has not only diminished the number, but has also mitigated the horrors of military campaigns. Society would stand aghast to-day if death or slavery were meted out to the vanquished. Our own country furnishes one of the most beautiful examples on record to illustrate this truth.

How rapidly have the sectional hate and fierce

animosities engendered by our late Civil War been allayed! In both Houses of Congress and several of our State Legislatures are found to-day representatives who fought against each other, but are now framing laws for the welfare of our common country.

"Now, look here, upon this picture, and look on this." In passing from Pagan to Christian civilization, we have emerged from darkness to light, from a state of puny childhood to full-grown, sturdy manhood, from Egyptian bondage to the liberty of the children of God!

Let us not grow weary of the salutary restraints of Christian life. Let us not cast wistful glances towards Egypt from whose bonds we have been rescued, nor long for its flesh-pots. Let us glory in our Christian heritage; and, above all, let us not be guilty of the mockery of leading Pagan lives while making profession of Christianity, recalling to mind what the Apostle said to our gentile forefathers! "Ye were once darkness; but now light in the Lord. Walk as the children of light."[1]

---

[1] *Eph.* V.

CHAPTER I.

WAS THE WORLD CREATED, OR IS IT ETERNAL AND SELF-EXISTING?

"The heavens show forth the glory of God, and the firmament declareth the work of His hands."[1]

Represent to yourself a gorgeous palace of the most symmetrical proportions. Magnificent chandeliers are suspended from the ceilings, lighting up every apartment of the spacious edifice. The walls are decorated with the most exquisite paintings, and the floors are adorned with luxurious carpets of the most varied and attractive design. You see, moreover, set before you a sumptuous table laden with a rich variety of meats and vegetables and delicious fruits and choice wines. And the whole scene is enlivened by the sound of charming music.

If such a structure were presented to your view, after being cast on a desert island, where no visible trace of man was to be found, would you not at once conclude that it was the work of an experienced architect, and that a wise and provident master

---

[1] *Ps.* XVIII., 1.

superintended the affairs of the household? Though you searched in vain for the owner, you would know for a certainty that he was not far off.

Now contemplate the great temple of nature, so vast in proportions, so perfect in design, so elaborate in detail, so beautiful to the eye, that we never grow weary of beholding it. Look at the glorious luminary which sheds its flood of light throughout this temple by day, and the myriads of lamps suspended from the blue dome of heaven by night. Gaze on the magnificent and ever-varying pictures embellishing this temple, and moving before us in panoramic view—pictures that serve as models to works of art; for the works of art approach nearer to perfection, the more closely they copy the models of nature. It is the triumph of human genius to be true to nature.

See the rich, flowery carpet which is spread before you. Admire also the fecundity of the earth, which yields all kinds of fruits for the nourishment of man. She presents to us her varied stores with so much regularity, that her unceasing bounty is no longer considered a marvel; but rather it would be a marvel, if she once failed in her supplies.

And, then, what sweet music comes from those winged songsters that people our woodlands! But sweeter still and more soothing is that silent melody produced in our heart by the harmony of nature:

> "Look how the floor of heaven
> Is thick inlaid with patines of bright gold:
> There's not the smallest orb which thou behold'st

>But in his motion like an angel sings,
>Still quiring to the young-ey'd cherubims:
>Such harmony is in immortal souls;
>But while this muddy vesture of decay
>Doth grossly close it in, we cannot hear it."[1]

And while the palace made with hands decays with time; while its lamps must be replenished with oil; while its pictures fade, and its carpets become moth-eaten;—this palace of nature is renewing its beauty every day. Its countless lamps are as bright now as when they were fixed in their azure roof; its pictures are ever-changing and ever-new; its carpet is as fresh and downy and bright to-day as when it was trodden upon by Adam.

Who can look on the works of creation, without exclaiming with the Psalmist: "Thou, O Lord, didst found the earth, and the heavens are the works of Thy hands," and without feeling in his inmost soul that an invisible Power is ruling over this beautiful temple of nature? When Robinson Crusoe observed a human footprint on the sand, in the island of Juan Fernandez, he justly concluded that some man had trodden there. And how can we behold the works of creation without tracing the footprint of the Almighty! It is marked on every star of the firmament, on every leaf of the forest, every sand on the sea-shore. How true are the words of Wisdom: "All men are vain, in whom there is not the knowledge of God; and who by these good things that are seen could not understand

---

[1] *Merchant of Venice.* Act V., Sc. I.

Him that is, neither by attending to the works, have acknowledged who was the workman. . . . For by the greatness of the beauty, and of the creature, the Creator of them may be seen, so as to be known thereby" (chap. xii).

Indeed, every man whose intellect is not perverted, is forced to acknowledge that a world in which such beauty and harmony and order are displayed, must be the work of a supremely intelligent Being. All men, even the most uncultivated, have a sense of the beautiful; they have certain fixed and uniform canons of taste more or less developed; they have in their mind an ideal by which they can at once determine whether, or not, a certain work is marked by order and regularity. The most ignorant peasant will recognize order in the disciplined march of an army, and disorder in the pell-mell rout of a mob. The sense of order is, therefore, common to us all, and we see it everywhere displayed in the universe.

Now this order presupposes an adaptation of means to an end. This adaptation implies a wonderful conception and foresight, and this conception and foresight manifest an intelligent Creator. There is no other reasonable way of accounting for the order existing in the universe. It cannot be the result of chance, as some ancient philosophers imagined. Chance, as we commonly understand the term, implies a cause which does not foresee the effect that follows from it. Chance involves the absence of uniformity and continuity. But in the world of nature, we observe laws that are constant and invariable in their operations. We see a regular succession of day and night, and a uniform revolution of the seasons.

The theory which attributes to chance the order and harmony pervading the world, is thus eloquently refuted by Cicero, when, in the words of the Stoic Cleanthes, he mentions the causes which have led all men to believe in the existence of "some celestial and divine power. . . ." "The strongest of these causes," he says, "is the regular motion of the heavens, the gradation, diversity, beauty, and harmony of the sun, the moon, and all the stars—to behold which is of itself sufficient evidence that they are not the work of chance. If, when we enter a house, a school, or a hall of justice, we at once trace the order, method and discipline therein observed to some cause, and conclude that there is some one who commands and to whom obedience is paid; how much more, when we see the wonderful motions and revolutions of such a prodigious number of heavenly bodies, continuing with unimpaired regularity for endless ages, ought we to be convinced that those movements are governed and directed by an intelligent Being!"[1]

For like reasons the formation of the world cannot, as Epicurus and some modern materialists have surmised, be ascribed to the fortuitous accretion of eternally-existing atoms. For, the arrangement of the universe is marked, as we have seen, by conspicuous order and beauty, revealing a marvellous Intelligence. The material substance of which the

[1] *De Natura Deorum*, L. II., C. V.

world is composed, is utterly devoid of intelligence; and the atoms, or elements of matter, cannot possess any rational power which is not inherent in the whole mass. We might as well suppose that the sublime poems of Homer or of Milton were produced by the accidental grouping together of letters of the alphabet, as that the universe was constructed by the chance accumulation of atoms. This supposition would destroy the first principles of reason. For it would be tantamount to admitting the existence of an effect, denying at the same time the existence of a cause capable of producing it.

The constant and regular motion of the planetary system also demonstrates the existence of a Supreme Being. The countless stars of the Firmament above us, as well as the planet on which we dwell are in perpetual motion. Now everything which is in motion must be impelled ultimately by a Power distinct from and superior to it. Hence there exists a Power or Being distinct from, and superior to created things.

If, on reaching the uninhabited island to which I referred before, you discovered there in the midst of the solitude, a railroad engine complete in all its parts, though you could find no trace of man, you would, at once, reasonably conclude that some skilful mechanic had wrought it. And we see before us this grand and complex engine of the Universe so vast in proportions, so perfect in detail;—an engine not standing still, but in perpetual motion. This earth which we inhabit, though it forms but an insignificant part of the whole machinery of nature, is revolving around its own axis at the rate of a thousand miles an hour, and is rushing through space with the surprising velocity of 68,400 miles an hour; yet so smoothly does it make its revolutions, that so far from experiencing any jarring sensation, we are quite unconscious of its motion.

And there are myriads of other planets constantly moving like our own, each in its own sphere, and with so much order as never to diverge from their proper course, and never to occasion the slightest collision.

Is it not strange that any sane man, much more that any scientist could venture to ascribe the motion of the heavenly bodies to any power or intelligence intrinsic to them? The planets are composed of inert matter, and are purely passive in their operations. They have no more intrinsic intelligence or independent force than the clod on which I tread.

But it will be said that they move and are controlled by the laws of attraction and repulsion. Very well. But whence come these laws? A law *presupposes* a Lawgiver. And the Framer of the law is greater than the subject of the law. The existence of the laws of attraction and repulsion in matter demonstrates three important truths: 1°. the existence of a Lawgiver; 2°. of a Lawgiver distinct from and superior to matter; 3°. of a Being anterior to matter: for, matter never existed without laws, and He who controls it by laws, must have existed before it; otherwise He could not have given it laws at the instant of its creation.

If we admire Newton who discovered some secret laws of nature, how much more should we admire the divine Lawgiver whose wisdom framed these laws! If we praise an Herschel, a Secchi, and other astronomers, because they could calculate with precision the exact moment when a planet would reach a certain point in the heavens, how much more praise is due to the unerring Engineer who directs the course of the planets!

When we see a magnificent army march in review before us, and pass through a series of the most complicated evolutions with the utmost precision, we give expression to our admiration, and we applaud the General whose eagle eye surveys these movements, and whose voice directs them. And should we not pour forth our admiration for the Lord of hosts, when we see marshalled before Him the army of heaven whose concerted movements are viewed by His sleepless eye, and directed by His sovereign will, and whose shining armor is but the reflection of His own transcendent splendor!

We may appropriately conclude this chapter in the words of Sir Isaac Newton: "The origin of the material world must be ascribed to the intelligence and wisdom of a most potent Being, always existing and present everywhere, who controls according to His good pleasure, all parts of the universe much more effectually than our soul controls by its will the movements of the body united to it."[1]

---

[1] *Optics*, B. III.

CHAPTER II.

THE EXISTENCE OF GOD ATTESTED BY ALL NATIONS, ANCIENT AND MODERN.

When we take into consideration the luminous evidences of a Creator furnished by the order and motion of the planetary system, we are not surprised to find that mankind in every age and country, and in every condition of life, have recognized the existence of a Supreme Being. The most illustrious historians and writers of antiquity, as Aristotle declares, have testified to the belief of the human race in a Divinity. Herodotus and Plutarch among the historians; Plato, Aristotle, Cicero, and Seneca among the philosophers; Homer, Hesiod, Virgil, and Ovid among the poets, vouch for the truth of this assertion.

"If you traverse the earth," says Plutarch, "you may find cities without walls, or literature, or laws, or fixed habitations, or coin. But a city destitute of temples and gods—a city that employeth not prayers and oracles, that offereth not sacrifice to obtain blessings and avert evil, no one has ever seen, or ever shall see."[1]

[1] *Contra Coloten.*, C. XXXI.

In the opening chapter of Herodotus, Solon addresses Crœsus in these words: "We ought to consider the end of everything in what way it will terminate; for the Deity, having shown a glimpse of happiness to many, has afterward utterly overthrown them." The whole work is pervaded by a recognition of a higher Power to whom religious worship was due.

"The earth," says Plato, "the sun and stars, and the universe itself, and the charming variety of the seasons, demonstrate the existence of a Divinity. Moreover, the barbarous nations unite with the Greeks in proclaiming this truth." Again he asserts: "No man has persisted from youth to old age in the opinion that there are no gods."[1]

"According to the avowal of the whole human race," says Aristotle, "God is the Cause and Principle of things."[2]

"There is no one so savage," observes Cicero, "as not to have his mind imbued with a sense of the Divinity. Among so many kinds of beings, there is no animal but man, that has any notion of God. And among men themselves, there is no race so wild and untamed, as to be ignorant of the existence of God, though they may be ignorant of His attributes."[3]

"We are accustomed," says Seneca, "to attach great importance to the universal belief of mankind. It is accepted by us as a convincing argument. That there are gods we infer from the sentiment engrafted in the human mind; nor has any nation ever been

[1] *De Legibus*, Lib. XI.   [3] *De Natura Deorum.*
[2] *Metaphysics*, II., 11, 820.

found, so far beyond the pale of law and civilization as to deny their existence."[1]

One day, after explaining the anatomy of the human body, Galen exclaimed: "I have offered to the Eternal a sacrifice more pleasing than goats or oxen."

Lucretius, an avowed atheist, extols his master Epicurus, as being the *first* who dared to raise his voice against religious worship.

The ancient Egyptians are among the most memorable for antiquity, and among the most conspicuous for mental culture of all the nations of the earth. That they also, in the early period of their history, recognized and adored one true God, is evident from the following doxology found among their oldest monuments:

> "Hail to Thee, say all creatures;
> Salutation from every land;
> To the height of heaven, to the breadth of the earth;
> To the depths of the sea,
> The gods adore Thy majesty.
> The spirits Thou hast made, exalt Thee,
> Rejoicing before the feet of their Begetter.
> They cry out welcome to Thee,
> Father of the father of all the gods;
> Who raises the heavens, who fixes the earth.
> Maker of beings, Creator of existences,
> Sovereign of life, health, and strength, Chief of the gods;
> We worship Thy Spirit who alone hast made us;
> We whom Thou hast made, thank Thee, that Thou hast given us birth;
> We give to Thee praises for Thy mercy towards us."[2]

[1] *Epis.*, CXVII.
[2] See Hoare's *Religion of the Ancient Egyptians*.

Chevalier justly observes: "The higher we ascend towards the origin of the Egyptian nation, the clearer we find in their primitive purity, the principles of the natural law at first revealed to man by God Himself; the adoration of the one, only God, Creator of the world and of man."

Well, then, may we borrow Cicero's[1] eloquent language on a different though kindred subject, and exclaim: "Why should we entertain a doubt as to the certainty of the existence of a God—a truth which reason and history and all peoples, which the Greeks and the Barbarians, which all ages, which the greatest of philosophers and poets, which the wisest founders of commonwealths, have always admitted! What! shall we wait until the dumb beasts themselves join with men in proclaiming that truth, and not be content with the concurring testimony of mankind!"

Modern nations are not less unanimous than were the peoples of antiquity, in the confession of a Supreme Being. The human family, estimated now at nearly fourteen hundred millions, may be classified in a religious point of view, into the following generic bodies: Jews, Christians, Mohammedans, Buddhists, Brahmins, Parsees, and worshippers of Fetichism.

The number of Christians of all denominations is computed at four hundred millions, and the number of Jews at nearly eight millions. That Christians and Jews worship one God, there is no doubt. The

---

[1] *De Divinatione*, L. I., C. 89.

Mohammedan population amounts to about one hundred and twenty millions. What has been said of Christians and Jews, may also be affirmed of Mohammedans, as is evident from the Koran which contains their rule of faith and morals.

Buddhists, with the followers of Confucius, and Shintos, form the popular religious sects of the great Empires of China and Japan, and are estimated at four hundred and eighty millions.[1] The lower classes generally belong to the first, and the upper and more intelligent classes, to the second of these sects. The alleged moral corruption and religious indifference of the Buddhists, have led some writers into the impression that they are atheists. But the closer investigation of the Abbé Huc, of Du Halde, Baron Hübner, in his *Ramble Round the World*, and other authors, has considerably modified this unfavorable judgment, and has shown that, underlying gross superstitions, there exists some belief in the Divinity, adulterated, however, by false systems degenerating into Polytheism and even Pantheism. In conversation, one day, with the Abbé Huc, a lama, or priest of Buddha, made the following remarks: "You must not confound," said he, "religious truths with the superstitions of the vulgar. The Tartars, poor simple people, prostrate themselves before whatever they see. But there is

---

[1] It is difficult to estimate the relative number of these three sects. Sir Monier Williams, professor of Sanscrit in the University of Oxford, subscribes to the opinion that all the Buddhists of the world do not exceed one hundred millions.

only one sole Sovereign of the universe, the Creator of all things, alike without beginning and without end."[1] The belief of this lama may be accepted as a fair standard of the faith of the Buddhist priests, and, to a great extent, of the Buddhist people of the Chinese empire; for we are justified in gauging the religion of a nation by that of its priests. At all events, the Buddhists' recognition of a Deity may be inferred from the numerous temples they have erected, and from the fact that they have priests, sacrifices, and religious ceremonies, and believe in a judgment to come and a future state of rewards and punishments—which cannot be reconciled with atheism.[2] Mr. St. George Mivart in his *Lessons from Nature*, makes the following judicious reflection: "I know that Buddhism, though 'a religion,' is sometimes asserted to be atheistic; but the Buddhistic conception of a *power*, or *principle* apportioning after death rewards and punishments according to a standard of virtue, necessarily involves the existence of an *entity*, which as being most powerful, intelligent, and good, is virtually and logically, a *personal* God, whatever be the name habitually applied to it."[3] So we may conclude with Dr. Cairn, President of the University of Glasgow: "Buddhism, though apparently, is not really an atheistic system."[4]

[1] *Travels in Tartary*, Vol. I., p. 126 *et seq.*
[2] Alzog's *Univer. Church Hist.*, Vol. I., p. 76 *et seq.;* also Hübner's *Ramble*, pp. 492-93.
[3] *Lessons from Nature*, p. 362.
[4] Buddhism, in the *World's Cyclopedia of Science* (John B. Alder, N. Y.), Vol. I., p. 575.

That the upper classes of Chinese are theists, there can hardly be a reasonable doubt. In the year 1600, the Emperor declared in an edict, that the Chinese adore not the material heavens, but the Master of heaven.[1] The Emperor Kang-hi, in the latter part of the 17th century, wrote the following inscription on the façade of a Christian church in Pekin: "To the true Principle of all things."

On the first column:—	*On the second column:—*
"He is infinitely good and infinitely just. "He enlightens, He sustains. "He rules with supreme authority and with sovereign justice."	"He had no beginning, and will have no end. "He has created all things from the beginning. "It is He that governs them, and He is their true Lord."

A learned and experienced Chinese missionary, in a letter addressed, in 1730, to the Director of the Academy of Sciences, in France, says: "It has always appeared to me that those who have accused the lettered Chinese of atheism, have had no other motive than the interest of the cause they sustained. I never saw a Chinese who was a practical atheist. I may add that the number of those who wish to pass for atheists, is very small."[2]

To-day, the number of sceptics, among educated Chinese, is more considerable. But their scepticism is not more practical now than it was in the last century. "I read in a book of an American Pro-

---
[1] De la Luzerne, *Existence de Dieu*, p. 137.
[2] *Lettres Edifiantes*, Tome 21, p. 493.

testant missionary, that the literates of China ordinarily return, at the hour of death, to the belief and practices of Buddhism; and Catholic missionaries have confirmed this assertion."[1] The traveller from whose book we quote these words, Baron von Hübner, mentions facts[2] that fully bear out the above statements, and prove that belief in God underlies the practical conduct of the educated Chinese, or followers of Confucius.

As to the members of the third religious sect which makes up the remainder of the Chinese population,—the Shintos—it is admitted, on all sides, that they are theists. The first commandment of their religion is expressed in these words: "Thou shalt honor the gods, and serve thy country."

Brahminism, whose votaries number about one hundred and twenty millions of souls, is the prevailing religion of Hindostan. The Brahmins recognize one Supreme Being, as appears from the Vedas, which is their Sacred Scripture. Towards the end of the last century, Sir William Jones published a digest of the doctrines found in the Vedas, from which I quote the following passages: "What the sun and light are to this visible world, the Supreme Good and Truth is to the intellectual and invisible universe; and, as our corporeal eyes have a distinct perception of objects enlightened by the sun, thus our souls acquire sure knowledge by meditating on the light of truth which emanates

[1] Hübner's *Ramble*, p. 494.
[2] *Ibid.* p. 491 *et seq.*

from the Being of beings; that is the light by which alone our mind can be directed in the path of beatitude. . ." "Without hand or foot, He runs rapidly and grasps firmly; without eyes, He sees; without ears, He hears all. He knows whatever can be known, but there is none who knows Him. Him the wise call the Great, Supreme, Pervading Spirit."

The following is an authorized prayer addressed to God by Brahminical priests: "I adore that Being who is not subject to change or disquietude, whose nature is indivisible, whose spiritual substance admits not of component parts; that Being who is the Origin and Cause of all beings, and who surpasses them in excellence, who is the Support of the universe."[1]

The Parsees, who are chiefly found in Persia and India, are estimated at about one million. That they believe in Monotheism, is manifest from the Zend-Avesta, which they revere as their Sacred Scripture. Their religious worship embraces the service of priests, the use of temples, altars, a liturgical language, and a copious Ritual. The worship of the Parsees is less tainted with Pantheism and Polytheism, than that of the Gentile religions to which reference has been made.[2]

The Supreme Being is called in the Zend-Avesta, "the living God, the Good Spirit, the Sublime Truth, the Creator of life, the Essence of Truth,

[1] *Lettres Edif.*, Tome 10, p. 15.
[2] Thébaud's *Gentilism*, p. 183.

the Primordial Spirit, the Creator of all that is good, the Author of the world and of law, the most powerful of beings. It is He that has marked out for the sun and stars their road in the heavens. It is He that brings on the increase and decrease of the moon. It is He that has created the earth."[1]

The negro races of Africa and the aboriginal pagan tribes of Oceania, may be roughly computed at 230 millions. Archbishop Vaughan of Sydney, whose sacred office threw him into close personal relations with the natives, and whose wide experience and habits of observation attach great weight to his opinion, emphatically declares that the aborigines of Australia believe in a Supreme Being.[2]

With the exception of some tribes that have embraced Mohammedanism, and a small number converted to Christianity, the mass of the African race practise Fetichism, which is the lowest and most degrading form of idolatry. Their religious practices are stained by divinations, witchcraft, sorcery, and the sacrifice of human victims. But, while gross superstitions and ferocious ceremonies pollute their worship, they are not without some vague idea of a Superior Power. Chapman relates that during a storm the Bechuanas (South African tribe) cursed the Deity for sending thunder,[3] which shows that, if they did not pay due reverence to the Divinity, they, at least, acknowledged His existence.

[1] *Ibid.*, p. 184.　　[3] *Travels in Africa*, Vol. I., p. 45.
[2] *Science and Religion.*

Among the negroes of West Africa, Brue mentions a "prophet" who pretended to be inspired by the Deity in such a manner, as to know the most hidden things.[1] This circumstance proves, at all events, that both the impostor and his dupes recognized a Supreme Power. Counterfeit coin never circulates unless where genuine coin is found.

The Rev. Joseph Zimmerman, of the Society of African Missions, who, in 1882, was on a visit of charity to the United States, informed me that the inhabitants of the Kingdom of Dahomey, where the Fathers of his congregation have been laboring for twenty-five years, recognize the existence of a Supreme Being, whom they call Oloron, the Creator of heaven and earth. These Fathers have also missions among the Yoruba tribes, on the coast of Benin, and among the Ashantees, the Hanssa, and others, and they never met a single tribe which had not some notion of a Supreme Being, though their worship is not paid to Him, but to inferior divinities.

The information given by this missionary, is confirmed by the valuable testimony of David Livingstone, the great African explorer. He frequently refers to the religious belief of the tribes through whose territory he passed. After commenting on their absurd rites and superstitious practices, he summarizes their faith in the following words: "The uncontaminated Africans believe that Morungo, the Great Spirit, who formed all things, lives above the

---

[1] Astley's *Collection of Voyages*, Vol. II, p. 83.

stars; but they never pray to him, and know nothing of their relation to him, or of his interest in them. . . . They believe also that they shall live after the death of the body, but have no distinct idea of the condition of the departed spirits."[1]

There is no race of modern Pagans of whose religious character we are enabled to form a more correct idea, than of the aboriginal tribes of the American continent. Travellers, historians and missionaries have given us ample information on this subject. The North American tribes, once so numerous, now threatened with extinction, had no temple but the dome of heaven, no preacher but the voice of reason and conscience, no Sacred Books to read but the works of nature. Yet these works of nature proclaimed to them, as they did to David, "the glory of God, and the firmament declared the work of His hands." "They had," as Bancroft tells us, "an undeveloped conception of the Divine Power,"[2] whom they addressed by the beautiful and appropriate name of the Great Spirit, and of a continued existence after death, whose happiness, according to their crude notions, consisted in the unrestrained freedom they would enjoy in hunting through their native forests.

"The Aztecs of Mexico" (and the same remark applies also to most of the aborigines of South America) "recognized the existence of a Supreme

---

[1] *The Life and Labors of Livingstone*, p. 280.
[2] *Hist. of the U. S.*, Ch. III. See, also, Schoolcraft, *Archives of the Indian Tribes in the U. S.*, in 6 vols., Vol. II.

Creator and Lord of the Universe. They addressed Him, in their prayers, as '*the God by whom we live,*' '*Omnipresent,* that knoweth *all thoughts and giveth all gifts,*' '*without whom man is as nothing,*' '*invisible, incorporeal, one God, of perfect perfection and purity.*' Their temples, or houses of God, as they are called, were very numerous."[1]

But, like all nations not illumined by the light of revelation, the religious system of the aboriginal tribes of America was stained by gross idolatry, witchcraft and divination, and was rendered hideous by ferocious human sacrifices and other abominable rites.

From the foregoing facts, it is evident that mankind, both past and present, have recognized the existence of a Supreme Being, of a Divinity superior to all others, though their conception of Him became corrupted, and degenerated into Polytheism and idolatry, so revolting to our reason.

Homer has expressed the thoughts of every sensible Pagan in the following lines:

"A golden chain let down from heav'n and all,
Both gods and goddesses, your strength apply:
Yet would ye fail to drag from heav'n to earth,
Strive as ye may, your mighty master Jove:
But, if I choose to make my power be known,
The earth itself and ocean I could raise,
And binding round Olympus' ridge the cord,
Leave them suspended so in middle air:
So far superior my pow'r o'er gods and men."[2]

[1] Prescott's *Conquest of Mexico*, Book I., Chap. III.
[2] *Iliad*, B. VIII., Derby's translation.

"Men had, indeed," as Cicero observes, "false notions regarding the Deity, but they all acknowleged a divine nature and energy."

The gross Polytheism of the Gentile world, and the perverted ideas which even the Pagan philosophers had of God, conclusively demonstrate the necessity of the new Revelation through Jesus Christ, our Saviour. For, while the light of reason is capable of leading us to the recognition of a First Cause, the stronger light of Revelation is needed to guard us against the illusions of our passions which cloud the intellect, and to show forth, in clearer view, the sublime perfections and beautiful attributes of our Creator.

While we have to deplore the fact that some of the most advanced thinkers and scientists of this century occasionally run counter to the teachings of Holy Scripture, and manifest a lamentable spirit of religious indifference; and, while some of the principles which they espouse have a tendency to materialism, Pantheism, and even Agnosticism; yet it is consoling to reflect that no modern leader in the Republic of letters or science, in Great Britain, America, Germany, or France, has ever carried his scepticism and intellectual license so far as absolutely to deny the existence of a Supreme Being.

Mr. Darwin, who may be considered as a leading representative of modern science, and whose peculiar theory of evolution has led some to suspect him of atheism, more than once avows his belief in a Divine Creator. In the last chapter of his work

On the Origin of Species, he says: "I see no good reason why the views given in this volume, should shock the religious feelings of any one."[1] He could not, of course, have made this assertion if he had believed that his theory involved a denial of the Creator. After developing his system maintaining that all animals and plants are descended from a few, or a single prototype, he adds: "There is grandeur in this view of life with its several powers *having been originally breathed by the Creator, into a few forms, or into one.*" In another work he says: "The question . . . whether there exists a Creator and Ruler of the universe . . . has been answered in the affirmative by the highest intellects that have ever lived."[2]

Mr. Huxley expressly says that he is not a fatalist, nor a materialist, nor an atheist. He simply declares that the ultimate Cause of existence is beyond the reach of his mental powers. He relegates God to the region of the unknowable. He considers the attempt to prove that there is no God the greatest absurdity. He says that God's existence can neither be affirmed nor denied. Mr. Huxley is, therefore, an agnostic.[3]

Professor Tyndall seems to hold the same view as Mr. Huxley. "Science," he says, "knows nothing of the origin or destiny of Nature. Who or what made the sun, or gave his rays their alleged power? Who or what made and bestowed upon the ultimate

---

[1] Page 421.   [2] *Science and Culture,* p. 247.
[3] *Descent of Man,* Part I., Ch. II.

particles of matter their wondrous power of varied attraction? Science does not know; the mystery, though pushed back, remains unaltered." He adds: "There are more things in heaven and earth than are dreamt of in the present philosophy of science." He evidently yearns for an invisible Power independent of, and beyond, the region of matter. If Mr. Tyndall's science is unable to solve the mystery of Nature's origin and destiny, of course, it cannot lead him to the negation of God. Where his science cannot enter, it has nothing to reveal.[1] And in propounding these questions about creation, the sun, and the authorship of matter and its properties, does he not suggest the inference that the creation of the sun and the laws governing matter are due to a cause antecedent and superior to them?

The late Ralph Waldo Emerson, who is a recognized type of our American progressive school of thought, disclaims any affiliation with those who reject the Creator. "Unlovely," he says, "nay, frightful is the solitude of the soul which is without God in the world. . . . To see men pursuing in faith their varied action . . . what are they to this chill, houseless, fatherless, aimless Cain, the man who hears only the sound of his own footsteps in God's resplendent creation."[2] In the following lines he expresses a loving trust in Providence: "A little consideration of what takes place around us every day, would show us that a higher law than that

[1] *Fragments of Science*, pp. 644–5.
[2] *The Preacher*.

of our will regulates events; that our painful labors are unnecessary and fruitless. . . . A believing love will relieve us of a vast load of care. O my brother, God exists!"[1]

Oliver Wendell Holmes, not less conspicuous than Emerson for intellectual vigor, thus professes his faith in God:—

> "Lord of all being! throned afar,
> Thy glory flames from star to star;
> Centre and Soul of every sphere,
> Yet to each loving heart how near!
>
> * * * * * * * *
>
> Grant us Thy truth to make us free,
> And kindling hearts that burn for Thee,
> Till all Thy living altars claim
> One holy light, one heavenly flame.
>
> O Lord divine that stooped to share
> Our sharpest pang, our bitterest tear,
> On Thee we cast each earth-born care,
> We smile at pain, while Thou art near."[2]

Happily, no American writer of note has sullied his pages with a denial of God. Our country is not a favorable field for the growth of atheism.

Max Müller, the learned German Professor in the University of Oxford, describes in a happy vein, the sense of the Divinity stamped on the human heart: "As soon," he says, "as a man becomes conscious of himself, as soon as he perceives himself as distinct from all other things and persons, he at the same

[1] *Essays.*
[2] *Poems.*

time, becomes conscious of a higher Self, a higher Power, without which neither he nor any thing else would have any life or reality. We are so fashioned, and it is no merit of ours, that we feel on all sides, our dependence on something else, and all nations join in some way or other, in the words of the Psalmist: 'He hath made us, and not we ourselves.'"[1]

Goethe and Schiller occupy a foremost rank in the nineteenth century, in Germany, as men of genius and literary culture, as Max Müller does in scientific attainments. Goethe observes: "It is a belief in the Bible,"—and consequently in God—"the fruits of deep meditation, which has served me as the guide of my moral and literary life. I have found it a capital safely invested, and richly productive of interest."

Schiller thus proclaims his belief: "There is a God. There lives a holy Power. And how much soever the human will may waver, the Supreme Intelligence soars high over time and space. And though all things move round in perpetual change, there abideth forever a Spirit unchangeable and serene."[2]

M. Pasteur, one of the most distinguished scientists of France and of all Europe, delivered in April, 1882, before the French Academy, an address in which he eloquently proclaims the existence and majesty of an Infinite Power, amid the enthusiastic plaudits of

[1] *Ps.* XCIX., 3.
[2] *The Words of Faith*, Vol. I.

his fellow academicians. An address from such a source, and so heartily endorsed by the most eminent body of savants perhaps in the world, happily proves that in the council of great minds, God shall never be dethroned.

Even Voltaire, who may be called the father of modern French infidelity, manifests his abhorrence for atheists, whom he scourges with his trenchant satire: "I would not like," he says, "to have anything to do with an atheistic prince whose interest it would be to pound me in a mortar; for, pounded I certainly would be. If I were a sovereign, I would not wish to be surrounded by atheistic courtiers whose interest it was to poison me. I would be compelled to take antidotes every day. It is, therefore, absolutely necessary for princes and people that the idea of a Supreme Being, Creator, Governor, Rewarder, and Avenger, should be deeply engraved on the mind."[1]

No man, indeed, who has ever soared to eminence in literary, scientific, or military life in this, or any preceding age, has ever avowed himself an unbeliever in the Deity. You will never find an Abercrombie, or a Sir Humphrey Davy, or a Faraday, or a Benjamin Franklin, or even a Hume, or a Galen led astray by atheistic sophisms. Faraday, one of the greatest chemists and natural philosophers of the present age, observes that the notion and rights of God are as certain as physical truths.

---

[1] *Diction. Philos.*, Art. Athéisme.

"My rule," says Franklin, "is to go straight forward in doing what appears to me to be right, leaving the consequences to Providence."

David Hume, though a religious sceptic, makes the following emphatic avowal: "The whole frame of nature bespeaks an intelligent Author, and no rational inquirer can, after serious reflection, suspend his beliefs for a moment, with regard to the primary principle of genuine theism and religion."[1]

When Napoleon was dying at St. Helena, he held a religious conference with his chaplain, in presence of Dr. Antommarchi. The physician's face seemed to Napoleon to bear an expression of incredulity, though his suspicion was without foundation. "Doctor," exclaimed Napoleon, "can you not believe in God, whose existence everything proclaims?"—"Sire," replied the Doctor, "I never doubted it."[2]

Bismarck in a letter to his wife, written from Weisbaden in July, 1851, speaks of having met one of his early friends, and tells her how in the course of a conversation he came to realize the vast difference between his present ideas and those which he held as a youth of one-and-twenty:—

"What transformations has my view of the world undergone in the course of fourteen years, each of which I always took to be the right form! And how much is small to me now which then seemed great; how much worthy of reverence which I then

[1] *Nat. Hist. of Religion*, IV., 435.
[2] *Las Casas*, Vol. IV., pp. 393–4.

scorned! . . . I do not understand how a man who reflects about himself and yet knows, or will know nothing of God can, for very disgust and *ennui*, endure this life. I know not how I formerly bore it." And in February, 1888, in a speech in the German Reichstag, Bismarck used these words: " Germans fear God and nothing else."

Atheists real or pretended there are, indeed, to be found. I do not even deny, though it is difficult to prove, that savage tribes exist who are so warped in their intellect, as never to have formed any conception of a Supreme Being. But their number is too insignificant to affect the force of the argument derived from the universal consent of mankind. We might as well suppose that a one-eyed Polyphemus, or the hundred-handed Briareus, or the Siamese twins, or a race of Liliputians, could be taken as types of man's physical stature and formation, as to consider a handful of atheists, or a savage group, as standards of man's moral and religious nature.

Nor are atheists less feeble in argument, than contemptible by paucity of numbers. The specious sophistry of an Ingersoll,[1] borrowed though it be from the armory of more formidable unbelievers,

---

[1] I do not know whether Mr. Ingersoll's infidelity is confined to the God of the Bible, or whether it extends to the God of nature. Thomas Paine is often, though incorrectly, classed as an atheist. For, though in his *Age of Reason*, he blasphemes the Christian religion, he avows his belief in God and in a future life.

may impose on the unthinking multitude; his captivating rhetoric may excite their tumultuous applause; his blasphemous irony may arouse our righteous indignation; but it will never disturb the religious convictions of any sensible man.

We have seen, then, that the human race of every type, Caucasian, Mongolian, and Malay, the American Indian and African Negro;—mankind in every age, in every quarter of the globe, and in every condition of life, from the lowest barbarism to the highest civilization, have believed in the existence of a Supreme Being, no matter by what name He may have been called:—

> "Father of all! in every age,
> In every clime adored,
> By saint, by savage, and by sage
> Jehovah, Jove, or Lord."[1]

How are we to account for this faith common to all men? Atheists, while admitting the fact, ignore its true cause; and, after taxing their ingenuity, they have suggested four reasons to explain this general sentiment of the human family regarding the Deity:

1°. Lucretius and other Pagan writers attribute this belief to ignorance. If this theory were true, then it would follow that, as soon as a man became enlightened by study and observation, he would cease to recognize a Creator. But we know, on the contrary, that the greatest philosophers of ancient and modern times, have avowed their belief in God.

[1] Pope.

The more profoundly men have studied the works of nature, the more clearly they have traced the hand of the Creator. "It is true," says Bacon, "that a little philosophy inclineth men's minds to atheism, but depth in philosophy bringeth men's minds about to religion."[1] It is only the sciolist and shallow thinker that is led astray from God. "The undevout astronomer is mad."[2]

2°. Other atheists ascribe the universal recognition of a God to the prejudices of early education. They say that, if men admit the existence of the Deity, it is because they have imbibed this notion in their youth from their parents, nurses, and teachers. They confound the cause with the effect. The lessons imparted to children are not the cause, but the consequence of the general sentiment of mankind. Men do not believe in a Divinity, because they have been so taught in their youth. On the contrary, the existence of God has been inculcated on them in youth, because it is a doctrine universally diffused among the human family. By age and experience we are disabused of many erroneous impressions acquired in youth, such as a vain credulity regarding ghosts, Arabian Nights' stories, and other popular tales. But age and experience, which dissipate these illusions, tend to strengthen our belief in God.

3°. Others assert that the belief in a Sovereign Being has its origin in a sense of fear. When men

[1] *Essay XVII., of Atheism.*
[2] Young.

saw the vivid flashes of lightning, or heard the sound of thunder, or felt the shock of an earthquake, or witnessed any other alarming phenomenon; or, when they were conscious of some enormous crime, their imagination aroused by secret dread, conjured up some invisible power whom they wished to propitiate.

This fallacious explanation scarcely needs refutation; for, then, the removal of the cause of fear would efface the belief in God. We know, on the contrary, that sensible persons retain their belief in God after these alarming phenomena have no longer any terrors for them, and after they commence to have a well-grounded hope that their crime is forgiven.

I maintain, on the other hand, that it is the sense of God which has aroused their fear, and not their fear which has fabricated a God. Fear, so far from making men theists, tends rather to make them atheists, if atheists they can be. For criminals are logical enough to know that, if God exists, He is a just and righteous God. And, in order to drive from their hearts the fear of divine vengeance, they try to dispel from their mind the consciousness of an avenging Deity. If men had no dread of God's justice, they would not question His existence. "The fool hath said *in his heart:* there is no God." The wish is father to the thought. They would like to persuade themselves and others that there is no God. But all in vain. His presence ever haunts them.

If God were the offspring of man's perturbed

imagination, then the human race, with the exception of a handful of atheists, would be all cowards. But we know that millions exist in every age, who, believing in God, are actuated towards Him more by sentiments of love than of fear.

4°. Finally, there are others who try to account for the belief of mankind in a Supreme Being, by saying that the idea of a God was invented by kings and legislators, in order that the law might have a higher sanction, and the sovereign might receive from his subjects greater reverence, as the representative of divine Power. This theory is easily disposed of by the fact that the idea of a God is anterior to all society and all legislation, because it is the foundation of both. "The establishment of public worship," as Montesquieu judiciously observes, "has without doubt contributed more than anything else to humanize peoples, and to strengthen societies. The existence of a Supreme Being, Sovereign Arbiter of all things, is one of the first truths which present themselves to the mind of every intelligent creature who wishes to make use of his reason." . . . Religion, therefore, is antecedent to the establishment of civil society, and of all human compact."[1]

Solon and Lycurgus, Minos and Numa, and other law-framing sovereigns, in founding their legislation on the solid basis of religion, presupposed the existence of the Divinity, and addressed themselves to peoples who had already acknowledged His existence.

[1] *Origine des Lois*, L. I., Ch. I.

We read of peoples subsisting without fixed laws and government. We are acquainted with none which have existed without some form of religion. History records the destruction of empires and dynasties, and the subversion of laws. But, on the ruins of prostrate laws and dynasties, the belief in God has stood triumphant. This fact conclusively shows that God is not the invention of legislators.

How, then, are we to account for this moral unanimity of mankind in acknowledging a Supreme Being? There is but one rational solution to be given, which may be thus briefly expressed: God enlightens with the light of reason every man that cometh into the world. Guided by that light, we recognize the Creator from the contemplation of His works. We naturally and without effort of mind, associate the Architect with the temple of nature luminously standing before us, just as the human voice sounding in our ears, is associated in our mind with a speaker hidden from our view. How can our soul listen in silent wonder to the heavenly music of the spheres, without admiring the divine Composer? We cannot separate the Builder from His work. We cannot admire the masterpiece without bestowing a thought on the great Artist. The connection is inseparable. The invisible Author is "clearly seen, being understood by the things that are made."[1]

By the same light of reason, we see also within

---

[1] *Rom.* I., 20.

us a moral law written on our hearts. We perceive an essential difference between right and wrong, good and evil, virtue and vice. From the recognition of this universal law, we inevitably infer a universal Lawgiver. We hear a voice within us judging us, commending or condemning us; and from the imperious judgment pronounced upon us, we conclude that there exists a Sovereign Judge.

And thus God reveals Himself to us as our Creator, as our Lawgiver, as our Judge. As our Creator, He manifests Himself to us by His works. As our Lawgiver, He speaks to us by His law written on our hearts. As our Judge, He speaks to us by the voice of conscience. We apprehend Him by our reason, our moral sense, and our conscience. And, therefore, as long as man continues to exercise his intellectual and moral faculties, so long will he profess his faith in the existence of a living God.

CHAPTER III.

Conscience bearing Witness to God.

In the concluding lines of the preceding chapter, I said that not only is there a law written in the hearts of all men; but there is, also, a secret voice in every human breast interpreting, expounding, and enforcing that law. Whether he be young or old, civilized or savage, learned or unlearned, Jew or Gentile, Christian or infidel,—who can say that he has never heard this silent preacher? Tell me, do we not hear this interior monitor every day, every hour, every minute? At one time, we hear him exhorting, entreating, commanding, impelling us to virtue. At another, he is restraining, checking, holding us back, cautioning us against the precipice of sin that lies before us. Now he thunders in our ears words of reproach and condemnation. He fills us with bitterness and remorse, and calls us wicked and ungrateful servants. Again, we hear him praising and commending us, diffusing joy, consolation, and peace through our soul, and saying to us: "Well done, good and faithful servant."

Mark the essential difference that exists between this invisible preacher and the ordinary minister of God's word. The earthly preacher addresses the same remarks to all his hearers, without knowing for certain whether or how far his strictures may be applicable to any of them. He cannot read the hearts of men, and therefore he cannot tell whether his listeners merit his censures or not.

But the invisible herald to whom our heart is laid open, addresses special warnings to each individual soul; and the admonition or condemnation that he pronounces, is adapted to each one in particular.

This moral governor of whom I am speaking, demands that his jurisdiction over us be absolute and supreme, and that we render to him entire obedience. He is imperious in his dictates. He admits no rival or associate judge. His decision is to us final and irrevocable. There is no appeal from it. Neither Pope nor Bishop can dispense from it. And it is this same voice that will judge us on the last day. "The Gentiles, who have not the (Mosaic) law, do by nature the things that are of the law . . . who shew the work of the law written in their hearts, their *conscience* bearing witness to them, the thoughts mutually accusing, or even defending one another on the day when God shall judge the secrets of men by Jesus Christ."[1]

Now, who is this judge? It is *conscience*. Con-

---

[1] *Rom.* II., 14-16.

science is the practical judgment we form upon the moral rectitude or depravity of our acts. It is the expression of that Divine Justice by which society is upheld and bound together. It is the living witness and interpreter of that natural "law written in our hearts" which is the basis of all human legislation. It is the echo of the voice of God.

To my mind conscience affords a conclusive proof of the existence of a Supreme Being, and bears the impress of the divine attributes. Much as I am impressed with the sense of God's existence by the works of nature which surround me, by "the heavens which declare His glory and the firmament which announces the works of His hands," I am still more deeply penetrated with His presence by the voice of conscience speaking within me.

Modern science claims to deal with concrete facts rather than with abstract ideas. We have here a concrete fact, known experimentally by every one, pervading human nature and asserting its influence everywhere. Within us a mysterious power compares our acts with a law superior to our will, and condemns them when they are not in accordance with that supreme rule of conduct. To be applied and to become a standard of right and wrong, that law must be more than an abstraction. It must remain engraven in our heart at least as a psychological fact. An attempt to explain its presence by education, tradition or culture, would be fruitless; for we judge the opinions of the world and the justice of human laws by referring them to that standard. It is, therefore, in our hearts more or less distinctly expressed before we accept as our own the conclusions of other men. It stands on a higher plane; since, by reference to it, we judge all moral doctrines. A law requires a lawgiver. Without a lawgiver it cannot be conceived. A law constantly acting, universally asserted, inwardly enforced, supposes a living, omnipotent, omnipresent lawgiver. The power that asserts and applies it to individual cases, must be superior to us. What else can it be but the voice of God? The sound of this voice is heard indeed in the depths of my being, it is in me; but it must come from a living principle higher than myself. It prompts me to do what my inclinations shrink from, and forbids me to do what I am naturally desirous of performing. I cannot be at the same time and in the same relation, both master and subject. That voice is a ray of the Uncreated Light illumining my path and directing my steps. It fulfils the office of St. John the Baptist. It is "the voice of one crying in the wilderness: Prepare ye the way of the Lord. Make straight His paths."

Conscience tells me that God is a *just Judge*, and that His "judgments are true." He is a Judge who cannot be corrupted by bribes, nor intimidated by threats, nor blinded by flattery; for though the world should admire and applaud my conduct, I feel that I have done amiss so long as the court of conscience rules against me; and though the world condemn me, I feel that I am right if I have the testimony of a good conscience.

The rulings of conscience, as well as the law which they interpret and apply, prove that the Lawgiver is essentially *good* and *benevolent*. For if I secretly deposit an alms in the box of a poor blind man, without the knowledge of any human spectator, why do I feel a joy and satisfaction similar to that which a child experiences on performing an act that wins the approbation of good parents? Is it not because I see the smiling image of my Heavenly Father and hear His approving voice in the depths of my soul?

I learn from my conscience that God is *holy*. For if I commit a grievous sin of thought, why have I that sense of shame and confusion akin to the mortification I should feel in the presence of an upright person to whom my sin had been revealed? Is it not because I recognize the One that sees me as the God of holiness who "loveth righteousness and hateth iniquity?"

Conscience enlightens me on the existence of a God who is *all-seeing*, and to whom I am responsible for my deliberate acts. There is no moral action of mine on which He does not pronounce a decision. There is no crime I commit against which He does not give an immediate sentence. His court is never adjourned. He never nods on the bench.

If I shed my neighbor's blood in secret, why am I alarmed? Why, like Cain, do I "become a fugitive and a vagabond upon the earth?" Why, like him, do I fear that "every one that findeth me shall kill me?"[1] Why do I flee when no man pursueth? I do not dread the civil law. I do not fear man. He is ignorant of my crime. It is a secret in my own breast. Does not my terror, therefore, spring from the conviction, that the avenging God sees me? And in order to quiet the voice of Divine Justice thundering in my breast, may I not, as thousands have done before me, throw myself on the mercy of human justice and confess my crime?

Go where I will, fly where I will, this Judge is ever with me, holding up the scales of even-handed justice. How profoundly was the Royal Prophet impressed with the presence of the Divine Judge when he cried out after his crime: "Lord, Thou hast proved me and known me. Thou hast known my sitting down and my rising up. Thou hast understood my thoughts afar off. My path and my line Thou hast searched out. . . . Whither shall I go from Thy Spirit, or whither shall I flee from Thy face? If I ascend into heaven, Thou art there: if I descend into hell, Thou art present. If I take my wings early in the morning, and dwell in the uttermost parts of the sea, even there also shall Thy hand lead me, and Thy right hand shall hold me. And I said: Perhaps darkness shall cover me, and night shall be my light in my pleasures. But darkness shall not be dark to Thee, and night

---

[1] Gen. IV., 14.

shall be light as the day. The darkness thereof and the light thereof are alike *to Thee.* . . Thy eyes did see my imperfect being, and in Thy book all shall be written."[1]

Again, how forcibly does the voice of conscience remind me that God is a *providential* Governor, that He takes a fatherly interest in us, and that He is swayed by our prayers! This consoling truth forces itself on all men; not only on the religious and virtuous, but on the infidel and libertine in the hour of danger and distress. At that supreme moment they all instinctively cry to God for help.

Toward the close of the late war, I happened to be on board of a steamer that was plying from New Orleans to New York. The passengers comprised both army officers and civilians of various denominations, some perhaps professing no religion at all. Many of them gave themselves up to boisterous mirth, and indulged freely in intemperance and profanity. The voyage was most propitious till we came abreast of the Jersey shore where, about midnight, a serious accident occurred to the machinery, and converted the fleet sailer into a huge, helpless log drifting about at the mercy of a rough sea. Toward morning, a steamer, seeing our distress, hastened to our relief, and attempted to tow us to the Chesapeake Bay. But when we were nearing Cape Charles, the sea became very stormy, a strong wind beating landward. To add to our

---

[1] *Ps.* CXXXVIII.

danger, the hawser that bound us to our consort broke, and our rudder became unmanageable. As soon as the passengers were made fully aware of their critical situation, all indecent language ceased; and the same lips that, a short time before, were polluted by ribaldry and profanity, were now devoutly invoking the assistance of a kind and merciful Providence. How true it is that infidels are scarce in the hour of danger! In the moment of dire distress and in the face of death, their number can be counted on one's fingers.

The voice of conscience, it is true, may be silenced and the spiritual sense blunted by a life of habitual sin and a neglect of divine inspirations, just as our sense of hearing is impaired by the ceaseless hum of the factory. But like Banquo's ghost, it will never down. Let a serious moment come in which we incline our ear to its whisper, and the Divine Voice will reassert itself and claim a hearing. While the voice of God is inaudible amid the tumult of the passions, it becomes more distinct in the soul by religious education, good companionship, and especially by prayer and meditation. For just as our sense of hearing is rendered more acute by attention and exercise, so do we catch the faintest whisperings of God's voice in our soul by habitual communion with Him. If men will make any pecuniary sacrifice; if they will travel from city to city consulting eminent physicians, in order to recover their lost or impaired hearing, that they may again enjoy the familiar conversation of friends and relatives, should not we be still more zealous to improve our spiritual hearing, that we may the better enjoy sweet converse with God?

O blessed are we if we listen devoutly to the Divine Voice, and if we can say with Samuel: "Speak, Lord, for Thy servant heareth!"[1] Blessed are we if, with Saul, we can say: "Lord, what wilt Thou have me do?"[2] Then, indeed, like the Patriarchs of old, we may be said to walk with God. Then is "the kingdom of God within us;" for, surely, God's kingdom is there where He triumphantly reigns. And where does God rule so absolutely as over a soul obedient to His voice? Then how clear becomes the path of life before us! How distinct and well-defined is the knowledge of our duty! Then, by a certain interior illumination, we can decide for ourselves a complicated moral question more readily than a learned theologian can by a process of reasoning.

How instinctively we then shrink from the faintest shadow of sin! We can detect the enemy though he appear before us in the most specious garb of innocence. Or if we occasionally lapse into a fault (for lapse we sometimes shall), God's reproach will be so tender and our own sorrow so genuine and spontaneous as to leave no sting behind.

And if the Divine Voice is so mild in His reproaches, how sweet are His words of approval!

---

[1] *I. Kings* III., 10.
[2] *Acts* IX., 6.

Then shall we comprehend the force of the Apostle's words when He says: "This is our glory, the testimony of our conscience." We shall drink in the joy, the delight, the melody of the Divine Voice resounding within us. Our understanding, our will, memory, and imagination will, like a joyous and united family of children, dwell securely under this paternal Voice so gentle yet so strong, so exacting yet so endearing.

CHAPTER IV.

The Omnipresence of God.

"God is near you," writes Seneca to Lucilius, "is within you. A Sacred Spirit dwells within us, the observer and guardian of all our evil and our good. There is no good man without God."[1] "What advantage is it that anything is hidden from man? Nothing is closed to God. He is present to our mind and enters into our central thoughts."[2]

Such are the luminous expressions of a Pagan writer taught by the light of reason, unless indeed, as some think, he was instructed by St. Paul; or, at least, that he read his Epistles. And the learned Canon Farrar places several passages of Seneca's writings side by side with those of the Apostle, to show the close resemblance between them not only in sentiment, but even in expression.

God is present everywhere in three ways: by His essence, by His knowledge, and by His superintending power.

[1] Letter 41st to Lucilius.
[2] Letter 83rd.

1°. God must be present wherever His action is; for because of His infinite perfection, His substance and His action are one and the same. Now, God's action is everywhere, for in all places we find its effects; viz., the works of creation.

As the motive-power is present with the thing moved, and fire with the material which it consumes; and the wind with the ship that it propels; so is God ever necessarily present with His works. One might as well expect an engine to run without steam, wood to burn without fire, a ship to sail without wind, as to conceive any creature to exist in the absence of the Creator; for, the relation of a mover to motion, or of fire to heat, is not more intimate than is God's relation to everything that exists. The Apostle says: "In Him we live and move and have our being."[1]

There is, therefore, an essential difference between a human architect and the Divine Architect. When a house is constructed, it stands without the aid of the builder; but the works of God must always lean on God for support. They cannot subsist without Him, because they depend on Him as much for their conservation as they did for their creation; so that every fresh moment of their existence may be said to imply a renewed act of creation.

Cast your eyes upward, and contemplate the starry firmament. Consider that immense space above and around you between heaven and earth.

---

[1] *Acts* XVII., 28.

THE OMNIPRESENCE OF GOD. 63

Cast your eyes downward, and behold in imagination the bottom of the deep underlying countless fathoms of water. I tell you that there is not an inch of space in the heavens above, or in the earth beneath, or in the waters under the earth that is not filled with God's presence. "Do not I fill heaven and earth, saith the Lord?"[1] In the sublime words of Isaias, "Thus saith the Lord: Heaven is My throne, and the earth My footstool."[2] Though God fills all space, He is circumscribed by none. He is not divided nor dismembered; He is not partly here and partly there, but entire everywhere. Hence, Solomon exclaims: "Heaven and the heavens of heavens cannot contain Thee."[3] "He is higher," says Job, "than heaven. He is deeper than hell. The measure of Him is longer than the earth and broader than the sea."[4] Stretch forth your hand, and He is there. He is present with you at every step you take. He envelops the seat that you occupy. He dwells within your beating heart. You are more thoroughly penetrated by the Divine Presence than is the sponge by the water that it soaks. You are more completely surrounded by Him than is the fish by the waters of the sea, or the bird by the air which it cleaves in its flight.

2°. God is intimately present with you not only by His essence, but also by His omniscient intelligence, which beams upon you more luminously

---

[1] *Jer.* XXIII., 24. [2] *III. Kings*, VIII., 27.
[3] *Isaias* LXVI., 1. [4] *Job* XI., 8, 9.

than the noon-day sun in his cloudless splendor. God cannot exist without seeing all things, since infinite knowledge is one of His essential attributes. If any one object were unknown to Him, His knowledge would be finite. The past, the present, and the future are all manifest to Him; or, to speak more correctly, He has no past or future. He lives in the eternal present.

The congregation assembled at the Sermon on the Mount is as present before Him as a congregation assembled at this moment. A man wedged in a crowd could barely see the part of the procession passing immediately before him on Inauguration Day; but a spectator on Washington's Monument could, at one and the same moment, see the whole line from end to end. In like manner, we behold the events of life only as they pass in review before us. The past and the future are separated from us by an impenetrable barrier. But God, who dwelleth on high, beholdeth at the same instant the beginning and the end of all things. "He telleth the number of the stars, and calleth them all by their names."[1] There is not a star in the firmament of heaven, there is not an atom in the air, there is not a leaf in the forest, there is not a grain of sand on the sea-shore, nor a creeping insect in the bowels of the earth, that is not observed by your Heavenly Father. Even "the very hairs of your head are all numbered."[2].

[1] *Ps.* CXLVI., 4.
[2] *Matt.* X., 30.

There is no secret measure discussed in the cabinets of kings and rulers, there is not a word uttered by the children of men, there is not a thought concealed in the human heart, that is not visible to the searching eye of God. "Shall a man lie hid in secret places and I not see him, saith the Lord?"[1] "There is no creature invisible in His sight: but all things are naked and open to His eyes."[2] "The eyes of the Lord in every place behold good and evil."[3] All the ways of men are open to His eyes. The Lord is the Searcher of spirits. How eloquently does the Royal Prophet give expression to this great truth in the following words: "Lord, Thou hast known my sitting down and my rising up. Thou hast understood my thoughts afar off. My path and my line Thou hast searched out. And Thou hast foreseen all my ways.... Behold, O Lord, Thou hast known all things, the last and those of old.... Thy knowledge is become wonderful to me: it is high, and I cannot reach to it. Whither shall I go from Thy Spirit? or whither shall I flee from Thy face? If I ascend into heaven, Thou art there. If I descent into hell, Thou art present. If I take my wings in the morning and dwell in the uttermost part of the sea, even there also shall Thy hand lead me, and Thy right hand shall hold me."[4] The carnal man may, indeed, succeed in concealing his crimes from the eyes of men. He may say with the fornicator

[1] *Jer.* XXIII., 24.   [3] *Prov.* XV., 3.
[2] *Heb.* IV., 13.   [4] *Ps.* CXXXVIII.

in the Scripture: "Who seeth me? Darkness compasseth me about, and the walls cover me, and no man seeth me: whom do I fear? The Most High will not remember my sins. And he understandeth not that His eye seeth all things, . . . and he knoweth not that the eyes of the Lord are far brighter than the sun, beholding round about all the ways of men and the bottom of the deep, and looking into the hearts of men, into the most hidden parts. For all things were known to the Lord God before they were created: so also after they were perfected, He beholdeth all things."[1]

Do not imagine that this universal knowledge involves any labor or study on the part of God. As the sun, at the same instant and without fatigue, gilds the clouds, illumines the mountain-peak, and reveals the pebbles at the bottom of the stream, so without effort of will does God observe the great and small things in heaven and on earth.

3°. Not only is God everywhere present by His essence, not only does His infinite knowledge penetrate into our inmost thoughts, but He exists also in all places by His superintending power. "He is not far from every one of us."[2] We can perform no work, we can utter no word, we can conceive no thought without the concurrence of God. His presence is so necessary for our very existence that were He to withdraw His protecting hand from us for one instant, we should be utterly annihilated. He

---

[1] *Ecclus.* XXIII., 25–29.
[2] *Acts* XVII., 27.

is as necessary for our life as the air we breathe, or as the watery element is for the fish that move through it. Not even a bird "shall fall on the ground without your Father."[1]

But while God exists in all His creatures by His essence, knowledge, and power, He is present with the chosen members of the human family in a still more intimate manner. He dwells in them by His friendship, grace, and love. It is of this mysterious indwelling that the Prophet Jeremias speaks when he says: "Behold the days shall come, saith the Lord, and I will make a new covenant with the house of Israel and with the house of Juda: not according to the covenant which I made with their fathers. . . . But this shall be the covenant that I shall make with the house of Israel: I will give My law in their bowels, and I will write it in their heart: and I will be their God, and they shall be my people."[2] I will not again call Moses to Me on the mount, but I will descend into the valley of your heart, and "all thy children shall be taught of the Lord, and great shall be the peace of thy children."[3] I will no longer fix My seat in Jerusalem alone, but I will establish My throne in every devout soul. There will I lovingly dwell. And My eyes shall be open and my ears attentive to the prayers of him that shall pray to Me within this living sanctuary.

It is of this Divine Presence that the Apostle

[1] *Matt.* X., 29.
[2] *Jer.* XXXI., 31–33.
[3] *Isaias* LIV., 13.

speaks when he says: "Know ye not that you are the temple of God, and that the Spirit of God dwelleth in you? But if any man violate the temple of God, him shall God destroy. For the temple of God is holy, which you are."[1]

It is of this sacred indwelling that our Lord speaks when He says: "If any one love Me, . . . My Father will love Him, and We will come to him, and will make our abode with him."[2]

It was thus that God abode with Abraham, Isaac, and Jacob; with Moses, Josue, and David, with His Prophets and Apostles, whom He so often addresses in these words: "Behold, I am with you." I am with you by My knowledge to witness and approve; by My power to defend and encourage; and by My grace to sanctify.

---

[1] I. Cor. III., 16, 17.
[2] John XIV., 23.

CHAPTER V.

Lessons drawn from the Recognition of God's Presence.

There are some persons who affect not to see any relation between faith and morals, between intellectual conviction and practical duties. They are fond of using this popular maxim: It matters not what I believe, provided I am an honest man. But this maxim is more plausible than solid. Religion without fixed belief is sentimental, emotional, and vapory; it evaporates at the first breeze of temptation.

The superstructure of moral integrity must rest on the solid basis of dogmatic truth and intellectual conviction. How can I love God, unless I believe in Him as the Author of my being and the Source of every blessing that I receive?

How can I love my neighbor, unless I recognize him as my brother, descended from the same primeval parents, and redeemed by the same Precious Blood of Jesus Christ?

How can I be always honest and equitable toward him, unless I am convinced that there is a Supreme

Judge who will hold me responsible for every violation of my just obligations?

How can I be induced always to tell truth even against my personal interests, unless I am persuaded that, for every lying word of which I may be guilty, I shall have to render an account on the Day of Judgment?

How can I be moved to avoid secret sins and to curb my passions, unless I am confronted with the thought that the all-seeing eye of God, who loves righteousness and hates iniquity, is upon me?

How could consecrated virgins immolate themselves on the altar of charity, daily make their rounds through the hospital, unless they were conscious that the eye of God is upon them, saying to them what He said to Abraham: "Fear not, for I am with you, and I will be your reward exceeding great."

There never was a martyr or hero that was not a man of strong faith and earnest convictions.

I do not know of any revealed truth that can exercise so dominant an influence on our moral conduct as the belief in the abiding presence of God. The more we are penetrated with this thought, the more perfectly shall we possess interior freedom, indifference to human judgment, and a habitual disposition to rectitude of conduct.

I shall draw four obvious inferences from the truths I have laid down.

1°. God seeth me. He readeth the hidden thoughts of my heart, and He is a God who hateth iniquity. Should not this salutary reflection deter me from sin? Who, I ask, would conceal his impiety under the veil of hypocrisy, if the fact were brought home to him that there are no successful hypocrites with God? Who would presume to nurse a spirit of resentment, did he reflect that his inmost thoughts are known to One who calls the revengeful man a spiritual murderer? Who could, with an easy conscience, indulge in unchaste desires, did he bear in mind that his heart is open to the eyes of the Lord, who condemns lascivious affections not less than illicit actions? Who would stealthily defraud his neighbor, did he remember that the eye of the great Detective is upon him, and that He will exact even to the last farthing? Who would not tremble to tell a deliberate lie, did he remember that he lies before the God of truth? "Thou hast not lied to men, but to God,"[1] said Peter to Ananias. Who would bear false witness against his neighbor, did he reflect that the Supreme Judge is at that moment passing sentence upon him and recording his condemnation in the Book of Life?

God seeth me! How many thousands has this simple reflection preserved from sin! How many others has it drawn out of the vortex of crime! It was this thought that made Joseph exclaim: "How can I sin before my God?"[2] It was this truth that filled the guilty David with compunction when

[1] *Acts* V., 4.
[2] *Gen.* XXXIX., 9.

he cried out: "Lord, whither shall I go from Thy Spirit, or whither shall I flee from Thy face? . . . I said: Perhaps darkness shall cover me. But darkness shall not be dark to thee, and night shall be light as day."[1]

2°. God is nigh unto us; He is in our heart. Is not this sentiment calculated to inspire us with courage and confidence in time of temptation or persecution? When oppressed by interior trials, let us call on the strong God within us: "O God, come to my assistance! O Lord, make haste to help me!"—and how violent soever the temptation, our victory is assured. We can say with confidence: "The Lord is my light and my salvation,— whom shall I fear? The Lord is the Protector of my life,—of whom shall I be afraid? . . . If armies in camp should stand together against me, my heart shall not fear,"[2] for He is with me.

When assailed by enemies from without, when our actions are impugned and our motives misrepresented, how reassuring it is to know that there is a God looking on who will vindicate our innocence in His own good time; who will bring to light the hidden things of darkness, and make manifest the counsels of the heart; who will one day reverse the false judgments of men! "They shall fight against thee," says the Lord to Jeremias, "and shall not prevail; for I am with thee, to save thee

[1] *Ps.* CXXXVIII., 12.
[2] *Ps.* XXVI., 1, 3.

and to deliver thee."[1] He does not say: I *shall be* with thee, but *I am* with thee, to denote that His presence is constant and abiding without any interval of absence.

It was the consideration of the presence of the Holy One that sustained the chaste Susanna when solicited to commit a secret crime. She was asked by two wicked men to yield to their desires under penalty of being falsely accused of a similar offence before a public tribunal. And those men were to be her accusers and her judges, and they were held in great esteem before the people. What a trying situation! "I am straitened," she says, "on every side: for if I do this thing, it is death to me; and if I do it not, I shall not escape your hands. But it is better for me to fall into your hands without doing it, than to sin in the sight of the Lord."[2] She was falsely accused and condemned to death. "Then Susanna cried out with a loud voice and said: 'O eternal God, who knowest hidden things, who knowest all things before they come to pass, Thou knowest that they have borne false witness against me.'" But God, whom she feared to offend, did not abandon her in her distress. Her innocence was proclaimed by an inspired youth, the Prophet Daniel, who appeared as she was being led to execution. The trial was renewed. The perjury of the witnesses was clearly shown, and her

---

[1] *Jer.* XV., 20.
[2] *Dan.* XIII., 22, 23, 42, 43.

accusers suffered the very death that they had attempted to inflict upon the innocent Susanna.

3°. The presence of God should inspire us with profound reverence in prayer. If I am penetrated with the thought that the Almighty reads my heart, and listens to the faintest echo of my voice, that without Him I could not give utterance to speech, I shall not fail to observe exterior decorum and interior recollection in my devotions. Then, indeed, whether I pray in church or in my room, I shall be filled with the sentiments of the Patriarch Jacob when he exclaimed: "Indeed, the Lord is in this place and I knew it not. . . . This is no other than the house of God and the gate of heaven."[1] Wherever God is, there is His mercy; and wherever His mercy is, there is the gate of heaven.

4°. Charles Reade in one of his works gives us a vivid description of the mental tortures endured by a young man condemned to solitary confinement. One night seemed to him an age; his hair turned prematurely grey. He was devoured by his own thoughts, and driven almost mad. He had no one to whom he could speak, and he heard no voice save the echo of his own, which terrified him. Contrast with this man St. Paul, the first hermit, who lived in the third century. He spent ninety years of voluntary solitude in the desert, and those ninety years seemed no longer to him than did so

---

[1] *Gen.* XXVIII., 17.

many hours to the young man of whom I have spoken. The roar of the elements, the chirping of the birds, and the hum of the insects, were the only sounds that reached his ears. And yet he was happy—and why? Because he communed with God, and God communed with him. He enjoyed the delight of God's abiding presence.

Cardinal Wiseman's exquisite story of Fabiola contains an instructive dialogue between Syra, a Christian slave, and Fabiola as yet a Pagan. After Syra had expounded to her mistress the sublime doctrine of God's omnipresence and omniscience, Fabiola exclaimed in alarm: "If all you say is true; if I am under the perpetual gaze of an eye of which the sun is but a shadow; for this Eye penetrates beyond matter into my secret thoughts, is not the apprehension of this truth sufficient to tempt me to suicide?"

If the sense of God's presence is a terror to evildoers, what delight, consolation, and joy is it to the devout man to bask in the sunshine of His protecting providence! Under that sweet care, he feels that he is in the company of his Father, his Friend, and his Benefactor.

As God is nigh unto us, so should we draw near to God in thought, affection, and desire. Then, indeed, we shall never be alone. "Never less alone than when alone." Then will the solitude of our room be instinct with divine life, and we shall "taste and see that the Lord is sweet."[1] We shall

---

[1] *Ps.* XXXIII., 9.

say with St. Peter on Mount Thabor: "Lord, it is good for us to be here."[1] We shall have a foretaste of the joy experienced by the Apostles on beholding their transfigured Lord. We shall be lifted up from earth to the clear atmosphere of God's presence. And after walking with God, like the Patriarchs, in the light of faith, we shall one day behold Him in the light of glory. "We now see through a glass darkly; but then face to face. Now I know in part; but then I shall know even as I am known."[2]

---

[1] *Matt.* XVII., 4.
[2] *I. Cor.* XIII., 12.

CHAPTER VI.

THE PROVIDENCE OF GOD.

There is a' Providence. To say: There is a God, is to say: There is a Providential God; for, we cannot conceive a Creator, who would be indifferent to the works of His hands.

The world with all that it contains, which was created by Divine Power, is also governed by Divine Wisdom. God is mindful of all His creatures. He never wearies watching over them. He controls all beings by laws adapted to their nature, and directs them to their respective destinies.

God's Providence extends not only to every creature that exists, but to every event that happens in the world. He holds in His hands not only the destiny of nations, but also that of individuals. He numbers not only the stars of heaven, but the very hairs of your head. He guides not only every planet that courses through space, but every bird that cleaves the air: "Not one of them shall fall on the ground without your Father."[1] He sustains the worm that crawls on the earth, as

[1] *Matt.* X., 29.

well as the glowing seraph that adores in heaven. His omnipotent wisdom and providence are displayed in the one, as well as in the other. In a word, there is no creature, how vile soever; there is no event or circumstance how insignificant soever, which is beyond the domain of God's providence.

Nothing is beneath His personal supervision. If the creation of the smallest insect does not detract from His Majesty, surely His superintending providence over it, does not compromise His dignity. The whole world is to be accounted as nothing in comparison with God. If, therefore, the care of little things would be unworthy of God, so also would be the care of the universe itself.

But if God governs the brute creation and all animal life and even inanimate nature, He rules mankind by a special providence; and it is with God's government of man that we are chiefly concerned. How can we doubt this special providence when we reflect that our Creator has made us to His own image and likeness, that He has given us an immortal soul, that He has endowed us with the Godlike faculties of intelligence and free-will, that He has made us the lords of His earthly creation, and that He has destined us for imperishable bliss in the life to come! Man is the only earthly creature who is made partaker of these sublime gifts.

Yes, God has not only created us, but He created us for a definite purpose, a certain end. His relations toward us began indeed actually with our creation, but did not end there. His wisdom and goodness required that He should perfect the work He had begun, by leading us onward to our destination; and as this destiny will be attained only in the life to come, and as this life will be eternal, it follows that God's providence will accompany us throughout the present life, and extend even beyond it.

Every moment of our life implies, as it were, a new and supplementary act of creation. As none but a Divine Power could give us life, so none but a Divine Providence can sustain and perpetuate it. Every breath we breathe, every pulsation of our heart, is a fresh manifestation of divine energy and clemency. He is more necessary for our existence than the air we breathe, or the sun that enlightens us.

If I want to set before you a pattern of tender affection and provident care, I naturally select a good father in his relations toward his child, as the embodiment of these virtues. A kind father instinctively loves his child. From the moment of birth, the infant is the object of parental solicitude. To clothe and feed and shelter it, is a labor of love. What is it that stimulates the father's zeal in his daily avocations? What is it that enables him to endure heat and cold, fatigue and privation, with patience and fortitude? It is his love for his child and the desire to provide for its future wants. So closely is he identified with his offspring, that he accounts himself happy or miserable just in proportion as his child succeeds or fails in life. And so strictly in accordance with man's nature is this parental affection, that its exercise occasions no surprise, while the absence of it would brand the father as a moral monster. But why do I speak of man alone? Are not the instincts of parental love so deeply rooted even in the brute creation, that the fierce tigress will protect her offspring at the risk of her own life?

Now, what is the earthly parent but the representative of our Heavenly Father, "of whom all paternity in heaven and earth is named?"[1] God is the type and model of all earthly parents. The more devoted a father is to the true interests of his offspring, the more closely he resembles the Divine Pattern.

Can we, therefore, expect to discover in an earthly parent any benevolent characteristics not found in the Almighty Father of all? Shall the poor copy possess virtues not existing in the great Original? Can you imagine that God gave you life without intending to provide all that is necessary to sustain it? Is He like a cruel tyrant who punishes his subjects through mere caprice? Or shall we compare Him to those unnatural monsters said to devour their own offspring as soon as they are born? Or shall we compare our Heavenly Father to the god of the African Fetich-worshippers, who is hidden beyond the clouds, and who takes no interest in them? This is not the God in whom we believe. If there is any love, any provident care, any tender devo-

---

[1] *Ephes.* III., 15.

tion in an earthly father, they are but the faint ray of the sunshine that beams upon us from the heart of our heavenly Father.

It is too well known that many parents fail to make wise and suitable provision for their offspring on account of their inexperience and limited knowledge of parental duty, or on account of circumscribed means, or owing to indifference or misplaced affection. But our Heavenly Father does not labor under any of these defects. *He* cannot be charged with ignorance, since our life, past, present, and future, is clearly seen by Him. He cannot be suspected of inability to provide for us, as nothing is impossible to Him. Nor can He be charged with indifference toward us, since He is essentially good and benevolent. A God of infinite knowledge, He is acquainted with all our wants: a God of omnipotent power, He is abundantly able to supply them: a Father of tender compassion, He yearns to make us happy.

He knows our wants in fact, infinitely better than we know them ourselves. How often have we longed for something with sleepless anxiety; and God, knowing full well that if we had succeeded in obtaining it, it would prove to us a curse instead of a blessing, mercifully withheld from us the object of our desires. He dealt with us like a prudent father who refuses to give his child a dangerous toy which might prove injurious to it.

Nay, besides a father's care, God has more than a mother's undying love for us. "Can a woman,"

He says, "forget her infant, so as not to have pity on the son of her womb? and if she should forget, yet will I not forget thee."[1] If I were to ask you: At what period of your life did your mother concentrate her affections on you with the greatest ardor and watch you with undivided attention, you would say that her care was the most unremitting, when you were in the helpless and confiding state of infancy. And yet that is the very period of your life of which you have no personal recollection whatever, so that you are correctly led to this conclusion by your knowledge of a mother's nature.

If you ask me: When is God's providence most strikingly manifested toward me?—I answer: When you are most profoundly impressed with a sense of your own misery, and when you lean most trustingly on Him. When the hidden things of darkness shall be brought to light, when God's dealings with you shall be revealed, you will then discover that never was His providence more lovingly displayed than in those incidents of your life that had entirely escaped your memory.

Cast your eyes about you. See the great palace of nature constructed for you by your Heavenly Father. Observe with what order and regularity this palace is superintended. It is so carefully renovated every day, from its bright green floor to its azure roof, that it never shows signs of decay or old age.

See how diligently every member of this vast

---

[1] *Isaiah* XLIX.

household is provided for, from the huge elephant of the forest and the leviathan of the deep to the flying bird and the crawling worm. Imagine the quantity and variety of food that is necessary to sustain so immense a family. O Heavenly Father, Thy commissariat never fails. Thou makest ample provision for all. "Thou openest Thy hand and fillest with blessing every living creature."[1]

Now, if God takes such care of the palace that He built for your temporary dwelling; if He provides for the innumerable living creatures created to minister unto you, how can He neglect you, His son, whom he appointed lord of His earthly manor, and heir of His future kingdom.

But rather let me present to you these thoughts clothed in the beautiful language of our Saviour: "Be not anxious for your life, what ye shall eat, nor for your body, what ye shall put on. Is not the life more than the food, and the body more than the raiment?" "Behold," He says, "the fowls of the air, for, they neither sow, nor do they reap, nor gather into barns: yet your Heavenly Father feedeth them. Are not you of much more value than they?"[2] Man, restless man, sows and reaps and gathers into barns. He toils from early dawn till evening, and yet he is uneasy about the future. The birds neither plant, nor reap, nor hoard up, nor do they make much provision for the future; yet they sing their evening song of thanksgiving to their Creator,

[1] *Ps.* CXLIV.
[2] *Matt.* VI., 25, 26.

perch on the branch, and take their rest at night, without the slightest misgiving or anxiety about the morrow; for, they know by that instinct which God has planted in their tiny breasts, that the Divine Hand which feeds them to-day, will feed them to-morrow also. Now, if God feeds the bird of the air which is created for your use and pleasure, and which will live but a few days, how much more you who were created to live for ever, and to be a co-heir with Christ in His eternal kingdom!

"And for raiment why are ye solicitous? Consider the lilies of the field, how they grow: they labor not, neither do they spin, yet I say to you that not even Solomon in all his glory was arrayed as one of these. And if the grass of the field which is to-day, and to-morrow is cast into the oven, God doth so clothe, how much more you, O ye of little faith?"[1]

I appeal to your personal experience. Look back on the years that have passed with their daily and hourly vicissitudes, their long chain of varying incidents. How can you calmly reflect on those years without being impressed with the conviction, that your steps have been guided by a special Providence that "reacheth from end to end mightily, and ordereth all things sweetly,"[2]—*mightily*, indeed, by the force of His power and the strength of His love; *sweetly* by His tender regard for your liberty. Consider how carefully God has provided for all your

[1] *Ibid.*
[2] *Wis.* VIII.

wants and satisfied your reasonable desires. What day have you ever spent without the necessaries and even the comforts of life? Or if sometimes you have been disappointed in your wishes, if you have suffered privations, did not the great Dispenser compensate for the loss of temporal gifts, by holding out to you blessings of a higher order?

If, then, the Almighty has been so thoughtful of you in the past, why doubt His ability or His goodwill to provide for you in the future? It is time enough to distrust the vigilance of Divine Providence when He begins to neglect us. If you had supported and educated a child with paternal solicitude up to the present moment, and had never given her any cause of complaint, would you not have just reason to complain of her distrust and ingratitude, were she to express to you her doubts of the continuance of your benevolent dispositions toward her? If this child would be judged blameworthy, how much more reprehensible would you be in manifesting a want of trust in God for the time to come; for, "if ye then being evil know how to give good gifts to your children, how much more will your Father who is in heaven give good things to those who ask Him?"[1]

And has not His providence been as manifest in the guidance of your soul to its eternal destiny, as it has been in making provision for your temporal wants? How many secondary agents has He employed as

[1] *Matt.* VII., 11.

ministers of His providence in conducting you on the narrow path of righteousness? He has given you parents to guide you in your tender years. He has sent you teachers to instruct you in more mature life. He has set before you the lives of men that have figured prominently in the world, that the example of the good might shine like the stars of the firmament inviting you to follow the path which they trod; whilst that of the wicked might serve as beacon lights cautioning you to shun the rocks on which their souls were shipwrecked.

But while making use of these subordinate agents, God has never surrendered His personal supervision over you. He has written His law on your heart that you might be ever mindful of your moral responsibility. He interprets that law by His secret voice, that you might never be without a teacher. He has filled your soul with remorse when you have done ill; and He has cheered you by the testimony of a good conscience when you have done well. He has stimulated you to virtue by the hope of reward, and He has warned you against vice by the fear of future retribution. He has given you days of abundance, that you might find favor in His sight by your compassion for those that are in want; and He has, perhaps, sent you days of privation, that you might become more conformable to the spirit of His Son, who was so poor that He had not whereon to lay His head. He has given you peace and prosperity, that you might pour forth your gratitude to the Giver of all good gifts. And

He has so guided your steps even amid adverse circumstances, as to impress them into your service, and compel them to subserve your spiritual interests; like a skilful pilot who, by judicious tacking, causes almost contrary winds to fill his vessel's sails, and waft her to her destined port.

What, then, are those visitations of health and sickness, of joy and sorrow, prosperity and adversity, but the handmaids of Providence, yea, the frowns and caresses of God, leading you on like a gentle mother to your destination? And thus the testimony of your experience and observation confirms the voice of Revelation, "To them that love God" (and adore His providence), "all things work together unto good."[1]

How sad and wretched is the life of the man who believes not in God's superintending providence! Like Cain, he is a wanderer and an outcast on the face of the earth. There is no brightness above him, no sunshine on his path, no joy within his breast. Everywhere are chaos and desolation. The music of the spheres affords no melody to his soul. All is discord to him, because he is out of harmony with God and His works. He sees no beauty in the flower at his feet, no brightness in the stars, no glory in the firmament. "He hears only the sound of his own footsteps in God's resplendent creation. To him it is no creation; to him, these fair creatures are hapless spectres: he knows not what to make

[1] *Rom.* VIII., 28.

of it. To him heaven and earth have lost their beauty."¹ The past is to him a bad dream; the present, an oppressive weight; the future, a spectre of annihilation. He is without God in this world, and without the hope of Him in the next. O how dreary is such a life, because it is without a purpose! No wonder that so many unbelievers in a Providential God have, like Lucretius, put an end to their miserable lives; and that so many others, like the demons,² find no satisfaction save that of infecting others with their horrible despair, and of communicating to them their gospel of hate and unbelief?

How blessed, on the contrary, is the man who is always conscious of the overshadowing influence of Divine Providence! He never feels lonely, because he is never alone. Like the infant nestling on his mother's breast, he has an abiding sense of security and confidence. He is ever basking in the sunlight of God's presence. Or if at times the face of God appears dark and lowering, he still recognizes it as the face of his Father. He knows that "whom the Lord loveth, He chastiseth, even as a father, the son in whom he delighteth."³ The world is not an enigma to him. It is a mirror reflecting his Father's face. It is an open Bible in which he reads God's dealings with His creatures.

No event disquiets or startles or alarms him, or shakes his faith, because he knows that everything that occurs from the fall of an empire to the flight

---

[1] Emerson's *Preacher*.   [3] *Prov.* III., 12.
[2] *Matt.* XII, 43 *et seq.*

of a bird, is controlled by the moral Governor of the world. With the Royal Prophet, he can therefore say : "The Lord is my Shepherd : and I shall want nothing. He hath set me in a place of pasture, He hath brought me up on the waters of refreshment, He hath converted my soul, He hath led me on the paths of justice for His own name's sake. For though I should walk in the midst of the shadow of death, I will fear no evils, for Thou art with me."[1]

---

[1] *Ps.* XXII.

CHAPTER VII.

Popular Objections against Divine Providence.

This chapter will be chiefly devoted to the consideration and refutation of some of the most popular objections advanced against the providence of God.

1°. You will say: In the physical world, there are desert wastes, barren mountains, and poisonous plants; and in the animal world, there are many noxious reptiles and savage beasts which "go about seeking whom they may devour." How can these blots on creation, these constant sources of danger in the physical and animal world, be reconciled with the wisdom, power, and goodness of a God who ought to exclude from His works all that is defective and hurtful to man for whom these things were created?

I shall first give a general answer to this objection: There are no defects in the works of God. They exist only in your imagination. To form a correct judgment on this subject, you should be acquainted with all the purposes for which each object was created. But this knowledge you have not acquired. There are heights and depths in the plan of creation which you can never reach nor fathom.

Nature has not yet revealed to us all her secrets, and probably she never will. Every fresh discovery hitherto made of nature's laws has afforded new evidence of the fact, that God creates nothing in vain. The more profoundly naturalists will study the secrets of the vegetable and animal kingdoms, the more clearly they will see revealed the marvellous wisdom and foresight of the Creator, and the usefulness of every creature that vegetates, moves, or exists on the face of the earth.

The researches of science confirm the declaration made by God after the creation, that all things which were created "were very good."[1] There is not a leaf of the forest, nor a beast of the field, nor a creeping insect, that does not in some way manifest the creative power, the sublime wisdom, and the infinite goodness of God, and that does not contribute at least indirectly to man's use and benefit.

To descend to particulars. There are, indeed, desert wastes. But even deserts are made serviceable to man. "But for the deserts of Asia," as Maury observes, "there would be no cultivation in India; for north-east trade winds would prevail all the year. It is the dry season in India when the north-east trade winds (called there the north-east monsoons) blow. They come over the land, and

---

[1] Gen. I., 31.

are as empty as the east wind of Arabia; for they have no moisture in them.

"But for *Sahara* to draw the winds in upon the land from the sea, or to deflect them in their course, there would be neither Nile nor Niger. The periodical overflowing of the Nile is the escaping to the sea of the annual flood caused by the rains into which the vapor that the monsoons of Africa bring with them from the sea, is condensed. For by the month of June, the African deserts are heated up sufficiently to bring in the rain winds.

"The rainy season then commences and lasts till late in autumn. By that time, the flood which the water-sheds of Abyssinia poured into the Blue Nile has got down into Egypt. Thus that country is supplied with its annual overflow and made fruitful. Such is the use of deserts in the physical economy; and such the machinery by which the earth is watered and dry lands made fruitful."[1]

There are, also, mountain-ranges. But are they not essential to complete the gorgeous picture of nature spread before us? The beauty of a landscape is more conspicuous when the prominent features are relieved by a suitable back-ground. In the grand tableau of nature, the smiling valley presents a more luxuriant aspect when contrasted with the bleak mountain towering afar off. The fertile plains of Italy appear to greater advantage when the snow-capped Alps loom in the distance.

[1] *Physical Geography*, p. 80.

OBJECTIONS AGAINST PROVIDENCE. 93

A verse, or sentence of Scripture read by itself apart from the context, often sounds paradoxical and sometimes even inconsistent with our idea of morality. But read in connection with the context, its truth and beauty appear manifest. It is the same with God's works. Viewed piece-meal, they may appear rude and unsightly; but observed in connection with the surrounding scenery, each part elicits our admiration. We must study the book of nature as we study the Book of Scriptures; not in detached portions, but each in connection with the whole.

These mountain fastnesses serve not only to please the eye, but also to satisfy the wants of man. There is not an acre of useless land on God's beautiful earth. The mountains that cannot produce grain will reward the hardy son of toil by yielding gold or silver or iron or coal; or they will supply him with timber and rocks for his habitation and fuel. They will afford him grateful shade in summer's heat and a shelter from the blasts of winter.

The poison contained in a noxious weed may and does become by the aid of science an antidote to disease. Thus the hemlock, though classed among poisonous plants, is now employed in effecting wonderful cures.

And if God has created venomous reptiles, it should be borne in mind that their sting is given them as a weapon rather of defence than offence. They rarely attack unless provoked; and some of the most deadly snakes give an example of chivalry to man by sounding the alarm before they attack an enemy. Serpents, moreover, according to naturalists, serve the useful purpose of destroying animals, or consuming vegetables, or absorbing vapors that would be very injurious to man.[1]

A modern writer of distinction, the Duke of Argyll,[2] from the consideration of even the virus of a snake, draws a profound lesson regarding the marvellous power and wisdom of our Creator in adapting the means to the end with precision so unfailing. What is poison? It is a secretion of certain chemical constituents whose properties bear special reference to the organism of the animal that it is intended to destroy. How minute, how subtle must be the knowledge of animal structure in the Divine Mind when He adjusts in one animal a liquid particle which, in a few moments, is capable of inflicting death on another by curdling the blood, benumbing the nerves, and rushing in upon the citadel of life!

And if God has given to the beasts a fierce and savage nature, His dominion over them is manifested by His assigning to them a fitting habitation, far from human abodes, in the wild, uncultivated forests to which He confines them, saying: "Hitherto you shall come, and shall go no further." If He has made them terrible in their strength and rapacity, He has endowed man with sagacity and power to subdue them. If they prey on other animals, this fact

[1] *Le Livre de la Nature*, par M. Desdouits, Tome II.
[2] *The Reign of Law.*

shows forth one of nature's laws; viz., that individuals of one species must suffer, so that the race of another may be perpetuated; and that one family of beings must be sustained by the sacrifice of some particular members of another.[1] Thus extinction on the one hand, and excess on the other are prevented; and equilibrium in the animal kingdom is maintained.

It might also be remarked that this apparent want of harmony in God's creation is accounted for both by Revelation and by the oldest traditions of the human race. Sin entered into this world, and as a consequence the path of man is beset with trials and hardships. Yet even these results of an original transgression have become, through God's providence, the means of developing in man wonderful resources. For it is certain that, in our present condition, these very trials and hardships usually call forth an energy, foresight, and inventive power that otherwise might have remained inactive.

2°. You will, perhaps, object in the second place by saying: There is a marked inequality in the condition of the human family. Talents and wealth, honors and pleasures are very unequally distributed among mankind. Is not this inequality incompatible with our idea of the providence of God, whose primary attribute is justice, and who ought, therefore, to mete out to all an equal measure of His gifts?

---

[1] S. Thomas, pars I, Quæst. XXII, Art. 11.

The equality you demand is not only inexpedient, but absolutely impracticable. It destroys the very concept of order, such as is understood by all true philosophers. St. Augustin, one of the greatest among the Doctors of the Church, tells us that *inequality* is essential to order. "Order," he says, "is a setting of things equal and unequal each in its fitting place."[1]

It is essential for the well-being and maintenance of society that there should be various degrees of wealth, station and talent. Social life is perpetuated by the free and constant intercourse of human beings with one another. This intercourse is prompted and stimulated by the mutual dependence that a man has on his fellow-man. The rich rely on the poor for labor. The poor depend on the rich for remuneration. The strong sustain the weak. The weak lean on the strong and are grateful for their support. Those in authority frame and administer laws. Those under authority observe them. Men of talent write for the instruction and entertainment of the masses. The masses read, admire, and are instructed. And thus are fostered in the community a spirit of industry, benevolence, magnanimity, gratitude, vigilance, veneration, and the other natural and social virtues that constitute the bond of society and the main-spring of human authority. Without inequality, there can be no

[1] Ordo est parium, dispariumque sua cuique loca tribuens dispositio." *De Civ. Dei.*, Lib. XIX, c. 13.

emulation; and without emulation, there is no progress.

A man's wealth is profitable to him only because he can offer it as a compensation for the labor of others. But if all were equally wealthy, of what use to them would be their wealth? It would be rather a burden; and, though it may seem a paradox, it is strictly true, that equality of riches would make all men poor. "If all," says Livy, "were equally rich, all would perish of hunger. Who, then, would plough the field, who would sow the seed, who would press the vines?"[1]

A man's dignity is estimated by his relations with those of inferior grade. There would be no superiors if there were no inferiors. There would be no kings if there were no subjects. There would be no generals if there were no privates. Robinson Crusoe was "monarch of all he surveyed," and yet he was the most wretched of men, because he had none but his good man Friday to serve him or to pay court to him.

Imagine all the members of the human family possessed of the same talents, the same personal beauty, the same physical strength. Such a rigid uniformity would take away all pleasure from life, would destroy all laudable ambition and honorable emulation, would paralyze the vital energies, and engender universal stagnation.

The social body, like the animal body, cannot be

[1] Lib. II.

all head with no subordinate members. It must have not only a brain to direct and eyes to survey, but also feet to move, hands to work, and a back to bear the burden.

> "What if the foot, ordained the dust to tread,
> Or hand, to toil, aspired to be the head?
> What if the head, the eye or ear repin'd,
> To serve mere engines to the ruling mind?
> Just as absurd for any part to claim
> To be another in this gen'ral frame:
> Just as absurd to mourn the tasks or pains
> The great directing Mind of All ordains."[1]

What kind of a world would this be if all trees were oaks, if all rocks were marble, if all beasts were lions, if all birds were eagles, and all fish were whales? Our beautiful globe would become more intolerable than a Siberian desert. As the beauty of the material world consists in its admirable variety, so the charm of the moral world lies in these social distinctions that God has created.

Hence we may judge of the madness and impiety of Socialism and Communism, which would level all social distinctions and distribute to all an equal measure of earthly goods. This pernicious school would paralyze industry, and rob honest toil of its well-earned remuneration

It must also be observed that the degree of happiness or misery resulting from inequality in the

---

[1] Pope's *Essay on Man*.

distribution of earthly gifts, is grossly exaggerated. Place in one scale a king with his pomp, his wealth, and his indulgence, and in the other a peasant with his obscurity, his privations, and his life of toil; and you will find that the scale will often turn in favor of the peasant. If you believe that exalted station renders men contented, you take counsel of your imagination rather than of the experience of mankind.

> "Order is heav'n's first law; and this confest,
> Some are, and must be, greater than the rest;
> More rich, more wise; but who infers from hence
> That such are happier, shocks all common sense." [1]

You see the monarch in his splendid palace, seated on a throne, surrounded by obsequious courtiers; he wears a brilliant crown, but you do not perceive the thorns concealed beneath it.

> "Within the hollow crown
> That rounds the mortal temples of a king,
> Keeps death his court; and there the antic sits
> Scoffing his state, and grinning at his pomp." [2]

You get a glimpse of the sumptuous table of Heliogabalus, laden with viands and delicious, costly wines; but you do not consider the want of appetite that renders insipid the most palatable food. You are a stranger to the complicated diseases engendered by surfeiting and intemperance.

[1] Pope.
[2] *Richard II.*

You are, perhaps, tempted to envy the rich man his sensual gratifications, but you do not see the worm of conscience gnawing at his heart, or feel the sense of loathing that oppresses him after a night of debauch. If your lot is cast in the humbler walks of life, you have a lightsome heart, you are not weighed down by the heavy burden of cares of state. If your fare is plain, you may have the sweetest of all seasoning, a good appetite. If you voluntarily renounce carnal indulgence, you have the testimony of a good conscience. Many a man in high station sighs for the sweet tranquillity and solid peace of those that walk contentedly in the obscure paths of life.

3°. I admit now, you will say, that there must be some inequality in the condition of human life, and that the degree of happiness or misery arising from this unequal condition, is exaggerated. But honors and riches, you will tell me, are blessings of God, though they are often misused. Why, then, do the wicked so frequently possess them while the righteous are so often oppressed by contempt, poverty, and suffering? Why is the just Abel ruthlessly slain, while the fratricide Cain is permitted to roam the earth? Why is Achab exalted on a throne, while Job is festering on a dunghill? Why is Herod seated in a palace, while John is immured in a dungeon? Why is Nero commanding an empire, while Paul is languishing in chains? Surely, if God would show partiality

to any, it ought to be extended to His friends and not to His enemies.

To judge correctly of God's providence, we must bear in mind: first, that man's soul is immortal; secondly, that his duration will be eternal; and thirdly, that the day of final reckoning will come at the term of his mortal life. Why, then, impeach the wisdom and justice of God's providence, if He defers rewarding His servants till the end of their mortal life? "One day with the Lord is as a thousand years, and a thousand years as one day."[1] And what are even a thousand years compared with eternity?

What soldier ever complained of the privations he endured or of the perils to which he was exposed, when he knew that the eyes of his commander were upon him, and that he would be promoted at the end of the campaign in proportion to his zeal and devotedness to his country? Or what hero felt aggrieved because he was not rewarded for his valor in the heat of battle? He would prefer to wait till his return home, when he would be welcomed by the deafening plaudits of his countrymen, and receive an adequate reward from a grateful sovereign.

And shall we have less faith in the word of God than a soldier has in the promise of his king? Why should we repine at the tribulations we now endure in the battle-field of life, since they are the

---

[1] II. Peter III., 8.

raw material for future glory? And why should we murmur that we are not rewarded here? It is better to wait till the warfare of life is over, when our fellow-citizens will greet us in our future home and the Great King will give us an unfading crown.

Yet we are like children bent on the enjoyment of a holiday. Their mental vision does not extend beyond the horizon of that single day. Their thoughts are concentrated upon it. The wished-for morning comes; but as they are preparing to start on their pleasure-trip, they see with dismay that the sky is overcast. Soon a few drops fall; and then comes the steady, pattering rain to dispel their hopes, and convert their anticipated day of pastime to one of gloom. Their father pities them and tries to console them; but he inwardly rejoices at the rain because it revives his drooping corn, and gives him the hope of a rich harvest that will enable him to sustain his family during the long winter months. So the rain was a blessing, though the children saw in it only an unmixed evil.

Let us not be as short-sighted as those children. Let us look beyond the horizon of the tomb. Let us remember that "our present tribulation, which is momentary and light, worketh for us above measure exceedingly an eternal weight of glory."[1] Let us learn like Moses " rather to be afflicted with the people of God, than to have the pleasure of sin

---

[1] *II. Cor.* IV., 17.

for a time. Esteeming the reproach of the Christ greater riches than the treasure of the Egyptians: for he looked to the reward."[1]

Nay more, we may with reason claim that the lot of the virtuous even here below is far better than that of the wicked. The true delights of a rational nature are theirs; for virtue bestows on them that full and placid joy of soul which strengthens and ennobles even in the midst of want and affliction. Their life, too, is secure against all that can embitter and debase it; for, as even the pagan Seneca remarks, "The strife of wild passions causes no havoc there."[2] Not so the life of the wicked. It is a stranger to that true joy of soul which is the warm sunshine of life. Amid its golden bowls and gorgeous spectacles, and grand palaces, it may appear fair of mien; but within it is wretched with bitter remorse and dire dread of the near future.

But although God usually reserves for the life to come the full manifestation of His providence, He is sometimes pleased to vindicate His justice even in the present life, by the signal chastisement of iniquity and by the reward of suffering virtue. This fact may be illustrated by the two examples following:—

Antiochus, surnamed *Epiphanes*, or the *Illustrious*, whose history is related in the Second Book of Machabees, and in the writings of Polybius, was a monster of impiety and tyranny. His usurpa-

---

[1] *Heb.* XI., 25, 26.
[2] *De Providentia*, C., 6.

tions, his wanton cruelties, his insatiable rapacity and horrible sacrileges, were speedily followed by a manifest visitation of divine retribution. While hastening to destroy the inhabitants of Jerusalem, after having already profaned its Temple, he is suddenly stricken with an incurable malady and afflicted with excruciating pains. His body, even before death, emits a stench intolerable to the army; and he dies a raving maniac in a strange country, execrated by his enemies, despised by his own people, and regretted by none.

As an offset to this summary chastisement, witness the history of the Patriarch Joseph. Were not his very trials the steps by which he ascended to eminence, and by which he became the providential deliverer of his people? Were they not the key-stone in the triumphal arch of earthly fame, erected by the hand of God, to record his name and his virtues to all future generations?

His first great sorrow is connected with his final triumph by an unbroken chain of incidents which, to the human eye, would seem to be unmitigated calamities. If he had not been sold, he would not have been exiled. If he had not been exiled, his virtue would not have been sorely tried. If he had not been tempted, he would not have been imprisoned. If he had not been imprisoned, he would not have been brought to the notice of Pharaoh. And if he had not come to the knowledge of Pharaoh, he would never have been exalted. In the persecutions he endured from his brethren and in all the afflictions that followed, Joseph clearly traces the hand of an overruling and tender Providence. "You thought evil against me," he says to his brethren, "but God turned it into good, that He might exalt me as at present you see, and might save many peoples."[1]

Do not tell me that such and such events are the result of pure accident. What are accidents to us, are links in the chain of God's designs upon us. Abraham sends his servant to Mesopotamia to procure a suitable wife for his son Isaac. The servant prays that the first maid whom he might meet at the well, should be his young master's chosen bride. Eliezer meets Rebecca at the well. The meeting is apparently accidental; but, in the providence of God, Rebecca was destined to be the wife of Isaac and the mother of His chosen people.

4°. But, perhaps, as a last objection, you will say: If God has such an eye to my wants, if His providence intervenes in each and all the events of my life, may I not take the world as it comes, sit down quietly, fold my arms, and do nothing? Why should I make any provision for the future, and not rather await patiently the action of a provident Ruler? Trusting that God will replenish my coffers, am I not even justified in squandering what I have acquired? Is it not my duty when sick to refuse the aid of a physician? And if placed in imminent danger, should I not decline to rescue

---

[1] *Gen.* L., 20.

myself from my perilous position? This would be pure fatalism, which is condemned alike by reason and revelation.

God forbid that, whilst admonished to avoid the extreme of solicitude, you should fall into the other of indifference! For if, on the one hand, God condemns excessive care and anxiety, He reproves on the other, an improvident and indolent life. If He claims your gratitude by reminding you of the care He takes of you, He arouses your zeal by asking you to co-operate with Him. God helps those that help themselves. He "reacheth therefore from end to end mightily, and ordereth all things sweetly."

It is true that He feeds the birds of the air, but it is equally true that He does not furnish the bird with her breakfast in her nest. She must go out early and seek for it.

It is true that He makes the crops to grow for the use of man, but it is also true that man must break and cultivate the soil. He must sow and reap and gather into barns, and grind the grain before it is fit for use.

It is true that He makes the trees to grow in the forest and that, from decayed vegetation, He has gradually formed beds of coal in the bowels of the earth. But those trees must be cut down, and those deposits of coal must be mined with immense labor before they can be used for fuel.

He tells us, it is true, that all healing is from God.[1] But He adds immediately after, that in time

---

[1] *Eccles.* XXXVIII. 2.

of sickness, we should call in a physician.[1] It is in accordance with the designs of Providence that He employs ourselves and other secondary agents to lead us to our end. Hence, we must use every legitimate means at our disposal in the accomplishment of our destiny, and look upon them all as the instruments of Providence. If we neglect these means, we resist God by the perverse use of our will.

In short, your Heavenly Father wishes you to be industrious, without too much solicitude; to be active and diligent without yielding to excessive care and anxiety. He desires you to labor to-day as if all depended on your own right arm, and to trust to to-morrow as if all depended on the mercy of God. Use to-day, for it is yours. Trouble not yourself about the morrow, for it belongs to God. It is still in the womb of time, and may never be born for you.

> "In human hearts what bolder thought can rise
> Than man's presumption on to-morrow's dawn?
> Where is to-morrow? In another world.
> For numbers this is certain. The reverse
> Is sure to none. And yet in this Perhaps,
> This Peradventure, infamous for lies,
> As on a rock of adamant, we build
> Our mountain hopes, spin our eternal schemes,
> As we the Fatal Sisters could outspin,
> And big with life's futurities, expire."[2]

But would not the goodness of Providence be

---

[1] *Ibid.*, Verse 11.
[2] Young's *Night Thoughts.*

more strikingly manifested, if God gave us an insight into the future? Forewarned we should be forearmed. We should be enabled to ward off the dangers that threaten us, or to encounter them with vigilant energy.

The hypothesis which is the basis of this objection is self-contradictory. Either the event whose occurrence we anticipate with dread will happen or it will not. In the former case it would be impossible to avert the threatened evil, and a certain knowledge of the impending danger would only augment our solicitude; in the latter case, it would unnecessarily add to our unhappiness.

If the bare possibility of some future calamity excites our dread, how much would our alarm be increased by the certain foreknowledge of its occurrence!

If the burden of each passing hour is hard to be borne, how overwhelming would be the accumulated cares of the future superadded to the present!

Providence, therefore, doles out to you each day its special trials, and mercifully casts the veil over those that are to come, lest the contemplation of so many tribulations might appal you.

> "Heaven from all creatures hides the book of Fate,
> All but the page prescrib'd, their present state:
> From brutes what men, from men what spirits know:
> Or who could suffer being here below?
> The lamb thy riot dooms to bleed to-day,
> Had he thy reason, would he skip and play?
> Pleased to the last, he crops the flow'ry food,
> And licks the hand just raised to shed his blood.

O blindness to the future! Kindly given,
That each may fill the circle marked by Heav'n." [1]

The whole may be summed up in the golden words of our Saviour: "Be not solicitous for to-morrow; for the morrow will be solicitous for itself. Sufficient for the day is the evil thereof." [2]

---

[1] Pope.
[2] *Matt.* VI., 34.

CHAPTER VIII.

THE DIGNITY AND EFFICACY OF PRAYER.

"Prayer moves the Hand that moves the universe."
GURNALL'S *Christian Armor.*

"Hast thou not learn'd what thou art often told,
A truth still sacred, and believed of old,
That no success attends on spears and swords
Unblest, and that the battle is the Lord's?"
COWPER.—*Expostulation.*

"More things are wrought by prayer
Than this world dreams of."
TENNYSON.—*Morte d'Arthur.*

Some years ago, in a Southern city, I was requested by a Catholic lady to call on her husband, who was suffering from a fatal malady, though his mind was entirely clear. This gentleman had been brought up by his father in the school of Voltaire and his associates, whose infidel teachings he had imbibed, and he avowed himself not only an unbeliever in the Catholic faith, but even a skeptic, as far as all revealed religion was concerned.

Knowing the bent of his mind on the subject of

religion, I endeavored, at some length and by every argument at my command, to remove his objections to Christianity, and to prepare him for the rational acceptance of our holy religion.

After listening to me with great patience and close attention, he courteously, but frankly, informed me that my remarks had made no impression on him whatever, and that between him and me there was an impassable gulf, which no reasoning of mine could bridge over.

Although mortified and discouraged by his candid reply, I did not despair, but resumed the conversation, which was, in substance, as follows:

"You certainly acknowledge," said I, "the existence of a Supreme Being, the Author of creation, and the living Source of all life?"

"Every man," he replied, "that uses his brains, must concede that truth."

"You will further admit," I continued, "that, as the Author of all being is omniscient, He knows our condition; as He is omnipotent, He has the power to succor us; and, as He is infinitely good, He is not indifferent or insensible to the wants of His creatures, especially of those whom He has endowed with an immortal soul and an intelligent nature. He does not cast them off from His thoughts, as the loosened fragment is thrown off from a planet and hurled into space. He, from whom all paternity is derived, must have, in an eminent and perfect degree, those paternal feelings which a father has for his child."

"That truth," he answered, "irresistibly follows from our conception of a Being supremely intelligent, powerful and beneficent."

"Is it not reasonable to suppose," I added, "that a Creator so benevolent and paternal, will be moved by our entreaties, and that He will mercifully hearken to our petitions?"

"I cannot deny," he said, "the reasonableness of your conclusion."

"Then, you admit," I observed, "the utility of prayer, and I ask you to promise me to offer up to this Supreme Providence this short supplication: O God, give me light to see the truth, and strength to follow it!"

He gave me an earnest assurance that he would repeat this prayer day after day, with all the fervor of his heart.

Some days later, I received a pressing message from my invalid friend to visit him again, as soon as possible. I did so, and, on entering his room, I was sensibly impressed with the glow of enthusiasm which shone in his face, and which had succeeded his former forlorn and despondent expression. Before I had time to address him, he burst forth into an eloquent profession of faith in the divinity of the Christian religion, and spoke in language at once so simple and connected, so luminous and penetrating, that I have never lost the impression which his words made on me. He begged, then and there for the grace of baptism, if he were deemed worthy of it. Some weeks afterward he died, fortified and consoled by the sacraments of the Church.

Here is a striking instance of the power of prayer and of the direct interposition of God in the conversion and illumination of a soul without the help or agency of man. One ray of divine light had effected what no force of reasoning could accomplish. In his tribulation, he sought God and found Him, and with Him he found light and peace and rest.

The yearning voice issuing from this man's heart, was but the echo of the voice of humanity. It was the expression of a sentiment indelibly engraved on the soul of mankind. This divine spark may lie smouldering for years, buried under the accumulated weight of pernicious maxims and worldly preoccupations; but it needs only calm introspection and a ray of divine grace to rekindle it into a flame.

As the world has never yet beheld, and never will behold, a nation of atheists, so will the sun never shine on a nation that does not worship God. And prayer is an essential element of divine worship. No people have ever existed, whether ancient or modern, savage or civilized, Jew or Gentile, Pagan or Christian, that have not poured forth supplications to the Deity.

Just as the first cry of infancy is a wail of sorrow, and the last expression of expiring old age is a sigh of grief, even so do we hear the voice of prayer at the very source of human life; and its plaintive notes have never ceased, but grow louder and louder as the stream of life advances, and this voice will continue till the human stream has run its course, and is swallowed up in the ocean of eternity.

The forms, indeed, of worship and supplication have differed widely among men, but the language of the heart has always been the same.

The Holy Scripture, which contains the history of God's people from the days of Adam till after our Saviour's Resurrection, records their abiding faith in the efficacy of prayer. And the most ancient authors of Greece and Rome attest the belief of the Pagan world in the duty of propitiating the Deity by prayers and sacrifice. The language of Homer represents the sentiments of all ancient heathen writers:

> "The gods (the only great, and only wise)
> Are moved by offerings, vows and sacrifice;
> Offending man their high compassion wins,
> And daily prayers atone for daily sins."[1]

The practice of prayer is not less strongly commended by the philosopher Pythagoras:

> "In all thou dost, first let thy prayers ascend,
> And to the gods thy labors first commend:
> From them implore success, and hope a prosperous end."[2]

How are we to account for the practice of prayer, so widespread, so uninterrupted, so deeply-rooted in our nature? This universal aspiration springs from a sense of our misery and utter dependence, and from

---

[1] *Iliad*, B. IX.
[2] *Golden Rule* (Rowe's Trans.).

an innate conviction of God's infinite power and mercy. Let us analyze our soul by the light of reason and faith:

1st. As to our intellect: its light, in the best of us, is very dim, and that light is obscured by passion and prejudice, by pride and presumption. Our judgment is so easily biassed and warped, especially where our personal interests or predilections are concerned. The famous Electoral Commission is well remembered. It was organized with the view of determining which of the two candidates was duly elected President, in 1876. The members of the Commission were chosen from the Senate, the House of Representatives, and the Supreme Court of the United States—the most grave and exalted deliberative bodies in the country. Seven members of the Commission belonged to one political party, and eight members to another, each member invariably voting for his party candidate. Was this the result of accident, or of honest conviction, or political bias? Let the reader decide for himself. If neither the restraints of senatorial and judicial decorum, nor the momentous issues involved, nor the spectacle of a whole nation anxiously awaiting the decision, could divest the illustrious court of partisan bias, how are we to escape the dangers of a perverted judgment, when we have no monitor to guide us save the voice of duty, which is often silenced by the clamors of self-interest? How many of us are like that blind man, mentioned in the Gospel, after his sight was partially restored by our Saviour: "I see men," he says, "as it were trees, walking."[1] We magnify the things around us, we exaggerate the importance of passing petty events, and we are blind to the great, everlasting truths, confronting us like the stars of heaven in their imperishable splendor. There is no truth, no matter how evident and luminous, which men have not denied or doubted, even though it be the existence of God, or their own very existence. There is no error, how monstrous and absurd soever it may be, which men have not espoused; they have bowed down and worshipped as gods the work of their own hands.

2d. Our heart is as much influenced by outward impressions as the thermometer is affected by the fluctuations of the weather. What is man's unregenerate heart but a tumultuous sea continually tossed about by the winds of conflicting passions? To-day, it is transported by impetuous, capricious, criminal, ambitious desires, which rapidly succeed one another, like wave rushing on wave. To-morrow, it is disquieted by vain, frivolous fears and anxieties, tormented by the dread of some impending calamity, or oppressed by the weight of cares, despondency, sorrow, and tribulation. At intervals, it enjoys a treacherous calm, lulled to sleep and fancied security by the soft breath of some unlawful gratification. Then, again, it is agitated by the furious storms of anger, bitterness, jealousy, hatred, revenge, and remorse.

---

[1] *Mark* VIII., 24.

3d. Our will is so weak and vacillating. We are so prompt and generous in forming good resolutions, and so remiss in keeping them; so courageous when no enemy is at hand, so cowardly when the tempter confronts us. We glide so readily down the slippery path of vice, we ascend with such faltering steps, the steep hill of virtue and self-denial. What is the history of each day, but a record of pledges broken, of vows to God unredeemed, and of humiliating defeats on the battle-field of this world!

Where shall I find light for my intellect, comfort for my heart, strength for my will? In vain shall I look for them in the writings or conversation of men who eliminate the Providence of God from the moral government of the world, and who, consequently, reject prayer from their system of philosophy, who declare that man is all-sufficient for himself. These men may dazzle me by their glittering generalities, but they convey no truth to my mind; they may captivate me by their specious declamation, or entertain me by their curious speculations, but they do not heal the wounds of my heart. They may arouse in me a momentary enthusiasm and excite some emotional feelings, but they give no energy to my will, they do not inspire me with heroic or generous resolutions, because they furnish me with no exalted motives of action. I rise from the perusal of their works with a bewildered mind, a sadder, though not a wiser man.

This light and consolation and strength are to be found only in God, the Source of all intelligence, the

Father of all consolation, the Lord of strength, and prayer is the great channel through which this spiritual illumination, comfort, and strength are communicated to us.

In prayer we are led like Moses up the holy mountain, away from the noise and bustle and tumult of the world. There God removes the scales from our eyes; He dispels the clouds of passion, or prejudice, or ignorance by which our mind was obscured; He enlarges our mental vision. A flood of heavenly light is shed upon us, which enables us to penetrate the hidden things of God. Hence, the Psalmist says: "Come ye to Him and be enlightened."[1]

Standing on that mountain, we see the shortness of time. How it passes before us like a fleeting shadow! We contemplate the immeasurable length of eternity. We are penetrated with a profound sense of the majesty and greatness of God, and of the littleness of man; or, if we observe anything good and noble in man, it is because, like the atom in the sunbeam, he basks in the sunshine of divine grace.

We see how paltry and contemptible are all things earthly, and like St. John, we get a glimpse of the Heavenly Jerusalem. In prayer, we are struck by the hideousness of sin, when it is presented before us in its naked deformity, stripped of its specious attractions and false charms. We become enamoured of virtue when we discover how graceful and beautiful a queen she is. So attractive

---

[1] *Ps.* XXXIII., 6.

are the charms of virtue as she reveals herself to us in prayer, that we can say of her in the words of Wisdom: "I preferred her before kingdoms and thrones, and esteemed riches nothing in comparison of her. Neither did I compare unto her any precious stone: for, all gold, in comparison of her, is as a little sand, and silver, in respect to her, shall be counted as clay. I loved her above health and beauty, and chose to have her instead of light; for her light cannot be put out. Now all good things came to me together with her, and innumerable riches through her hands."[1]

Sometimes God is even pleased to reveal to His saints in prayer a knowledge of His mysteries without noise of words or the labor of study. It was in response to prayer that God revealed to Daniel the mysteries of the future.[2] It was during the ecstasy of prayer, that He revealed to St. Paul the mysteries of the kingdom of heaven: "I know a man in Christ above fourteen years ago. . . . He was caught up into Paradise, and heard secret words which it is not granted to man to utter."[3]

St. Thomas Aquinas was perhaps the most profound thinker the world has produced since the dawn of Christianity. His vast mind ranges over the entire field of philosophy and theology. His writings are an inexhaustible storehouse to which the secular, as well as the ecclesiastical student, has recourse in every age. This great divine, being

---

[1] *Wisd.* VII., 8-11.   [3] *II. Cor.* XII., 2-4.
[2] *Dan.* II., 19.

asked whence he drew his knowledge, declared that he learned more in silent meditation than in the study of books.

It is true, indeed, that God vouchsafes to very few those extraordinary illuminations with which He favored the Prophet Daniel, the Apostle of the Gentiles, and the Angel of the Schools, because these gifts are not essential to man's happiness. But He will give to all of us in prayer that which is essential, the light necessary to deliver us from the illusions of our senses, our imagination, and false judgment; He will grant us that practical wisdom which is needed to guide us in the duties of our daily life. If, like Moses, we consulted God's mercy-seat every morning, and offered to Him the sacrifice of supplication, we would stumble into fewer pitfalls in the course of the day. We are often surprised and worsted by the enemy, as Josue was deceived by the Gabaonites, because, like him, we "consulted not the mouth of the Lord."[1]

In prayer, our heart is inflamed with devotion and dilated with joy, because we feel that we are in the presence of the God of all consolation, whose Spirit, like the sun, warms while it enlightens. In prayer, the agitation of the heart is quieted, because, in communion with our Maker, grace is imparted to us not only to subdue our inordinate ambition, but even to moderate our laudable and legitimate desires and aspirations. St. Ignatius dearly loved

---

[1] *Josue* IX., 14.

the illustrious Society of Jesus which he had founded. Being once asked whether he could survive its extinction, he replied: "I would need but a quarter of an hour's meditation to reconcile me to its dissolution."

Those earthly things which we so eagerly crave, appear small and trivial when calmly weighed in the scales of the Sanctuary, and the sufferings and trials we endure seem short and momentary when measured with the line of eternity.

It is as easy for our Lord, in answer to our supplication, to heal the hidden wounds of our soul, as it was to cure the corporal maladies of those that appealed to Him. It is as easy for Him to calm our tumultuous passions, as it was to say to the winds and waves: "Peace, be still." When Peter was afraid of sinking on the lake of Galilee, he cried out: "Lord, save me,"[1] and our Saviour enabled him to walk on the waters and reach the boat in safety. And, if we implore our God with the faith of the Apostle, and in the fervent words of the Psalmist: "Out of the depths I have cried to Thee, O Lord," we shall walk triumphantly on the troubled waters which threaten to engulf us.

We are told by St. Luke that, while Jesus was praying in the garden of Gethsemani, "there appeared to Him an angel from heaven strengthening Him."[2] What a touching symbol was this heavenly messenger of the angel of consolation whom God

[1] *Matt.* XIV., 30.
[2] *Luke* XII., 43.

sends to us in prayer, to pour a soothing drop into our bitter chalice!

In communion with God the energies of our will are invigorated, and our moral courage is strengthened. Observe with what confidence the child, when conscious of danger, rushes into the arms of its mother. There it reposes as in an ark of safety. Within its mother's warm embrace, its courage is renewed, and its heart loses its fears. And so, when we flee with confidence to the arms of our Heavenly Father, we go forth from His presence renewed in strength and resolved to do what human weakness could not of itself accomplish.

With the Apostle of the Gentiles, the man of prayer can exclaim: "I can do all things in Him who strengtheneth me." [1]

Before entering the Cenacle, in Jerusalem, to pray, the Apostles were weak, timid, vacillating men. In the supreme hour of trial, they all fled from their Master, leaving Him in the hands of His enemies. Their leader, when questioned by a maid, denied with an oath that he knew his Master. But, after spending ten days in prayer, these same Apostles are filled with the Holy Ghost and armed with superhuman courage. They boldly proclaim themselves the disciples of Him whom they had before forsaken or denied, and they go "from the presence of the council rejoicing that they were accounted worthy to suffer reproach for the name of Jesus." [2]

[1] *Phil.* IV., 13.
[2] *Acts* V., 41.

It was after fervent prayer that Judith undertook the hazardous mission of entering the camp of Holofernes, and rescuing the children of Israel from impending danger. It was after prayer and fasting, that Esther, at the risk of her life, saved the Jewish race from the sentence of death pronounced against them by King Assuerus. It was prayer that inspired the foundation of every religious Community that has existed in the Church, and these Communities have usually encountered at their birth, poverty, privations, and formidable opposition.

The same spirit of prayer which has inspired apostolic men and women in every age to undertake herculean works in the cause of religion and humanity, has also nerved the soldier with martial prowess and endued him with superhuman courage. He knew that "the race is not to the swift, nor the battle to the strong,"[1] and that God is called "the Lord of hosts," or armies, as well as "the God of peace," because it is He that gives victory to the warrior, as well as peace to the troubled spirit. Josue and Gedeon and Judas Machabeus were men of military renown, and they accomplished deeds of valor superior to human strength, because they were men of prayer and invoked the Lord of hosts.

Who was more daring and courageous in war than David? David, who, when a boy, strangled a lion and a bear; who, when yet a young man, slew the giant Goliath; David, of whom the daughters of Israel sang: "Saul slew his thousands, and David

---

[1] *Eccles.* IX., 11.

his ten thousands;"[1] David, who conquered the Philistines, the Amalecites, the Syrians, the Moabites, and the Ammonites, and who crowned his victories by conquering his resentment and sparing the life of his unrelenting persecutor Saul.

And who surpassed David in piety and the spirit of prayer? He habitually invokes the God of battles before engaging in war. He blesses the Lord who nerved his arm for the contest: "Blessed be the Lord my God, who teacheth my hand to fight, and my fingers to war."[2] And when his enemy is overcome, he humbly ascribes the victory not to his own prowess, but to the Lord of hosts.

Many Christian heroes have emulated the devotion of the pious King of Juda. From a host of Christian warriors, I may select one representative, John Sobieski. In 1683, the city of Vienna was besieged by a Turkish army numbering 300,000 men. After a siege of forty-five days, the city was on the eve of surrendering, and a secret message was sent to Sobieski, urging him to hasten to the relief of the beleaguered city. His troops together with the German allies numbered about 70,000 men. Before descending from the heights of Calemberg, the army of Sobieski assembled to pray, the leader himself serving the Mass. So successful was the attack that the besiegers were utterly routed, leaving 20,000 Moslems dead outside of the walls. The next day, the *Te Deum* was sung in thanksgiving

[1] *I. Kings* XVIII., 7.
[2] *Ps.* CXLIII., 1.

EFFICACY OF PRAYER. 125

for the victory, Sobieski intoning the anthem. His letter to the Pope announcing the victory, was a modest paraphrase of the memorable words of Cæsar: "I came, I saw, God conquered."

Happening to be in Paris at the opening of the Franco-Prussian war, I was grieved to hear some of the French soldiers so far forgetful of the faith and chivalry of their heroic forefathers as to avow that their god was the mitrailleuse. They soon discovered to their cost that their idol proved as impotent and treacherous to them, as Dagon was to the Philistines. The German Emperor, on the contrary, was accustomed to invoke the aid of Heaven on the eve of an engagement, and to thank God for victories won. On the evening before the battle of Sedan, the chant that filled the air from every German camp, was not the song of ribaldry, but the glorious hymn, "Now let us all thank God."[1]

The light, comfort, and strength which prayer imparts to our intellectual and moral nature, is not the only benefit resulting from this exercise; its blessing is still more enhanced by the assurance of our Saviour that God will grant us what we fervently ask, provided that the object of our petition redounds to our spiritual welfare. If a man of unbounded wealth, of large benevolence, and unimpeachable veracity, pledged himself to do you a great favor, how gladly would you have recourse to him! But here you have the Giver of all good gifts, the Father of all

[1] Nun danket Alle Gott.

consolation, the God of truth, promising in the most explicit manner to grant you all your reasonable petitions: "Ask," He says, "and it shall be given you: seek, and you shall find: knock, and it shall be opened to you. For every one that asketh, receiveth: and he that seeketh, findeth: and to him that knocketh, it shall be opened. Or what man is there among you of whom if his son shall ask bread, will he reach him a stone? Or if he shall ask him a fish, will he reach him a serpent? If you then, being evil, know how to give good gifts to your children; how much more will your Father, who is in heaven give good things to them that ask Him?"[1]

Again, He solemnly inculcates the duty and advantage of prayer: "Amen, amen, I say to you: If you ask the Father anything in My name, He will give it to you." He even reproaches His disciples for their neglect to pray: "Hitherto you have not asked anything in My name: Ask, and you shall receive, that your joy may be full."[2]

The obligation to pray becomes still more imperative and its neglect is more inexcusable, when we consider the sovereign majesty of Him whom we address, and the facility with which we can have recourse to the throne of grace.

To have a private audience with a distinguished crowned head is always deemed a great honor and a privilege, although certain formalities must be observed before the audience can be obtained. You are

---

[1] *Matt.* VII., 7–11.
[2] *John* XVI., 23, 24.

required to appear in court-dress; you must send in your card, or present a letter of introduction, stating who you are and the object of your visit; you must await the monarch's good pleasure in the ante-room, till he appoints the time and place for the interview. He can spare you but a few moments, he may be secretly wearied by your presence, and he will dismiss you with a formal bow and a faint smile, whilst you esteem yourself exceptionally favored if he bestows some gift upon you. And so elated are you by the interview that you devour every word uttered by royalty as eagerly as Lazarus desired to be filled with the crumbs which fell from the table of Dives, and you treasure up the gift he bestowed with as much care as you would preserve a saintly relic.

But how much greater is the honor to be admitted into the presence of the King of kings and Lord of lords, to converse familiarly with Him, and to present to Him your petitions!

And to be favored with an interview with the Divine Majesty you have not to appear in court-dress. The garment He desires you to wear is the robe of innocence, or the sackcloth of humiliation; and the ornaments most precious in His sight are the jewels of faith, humility, and devotion. These sparkle in the light of the Sun of justice; these delight the heavenly King, for "all the glory of the king's daughter is within."[1] You are not obliged to

---

[1] *Ps.* XLIV.

be furnished with a letter of introduction, for no one knows you as well as your Creator. You are not compelled to wait till the place of interview is appointed, for He is everywhere. He restricts you to no time, because He is never engaged, or preoccupied, but always at home, always ready to receive and hear you: "The eyes of the Lord are upon the just; and His ears unto their prayers."[1] And when you enter His holy presence, you need not have your petition engrossed on vellum or satin, expressed in choice language and well-rounded periods. Those eloquent and impressive prayers of which we sometimes read in the papers, reach no farther, I fear, than their authors intended them to go. They tickle men's ears, but do not pierce the clouds. To such prayers we can apply the words which God saith in Job: "Who is he that wrappeth up sentences in unskilful words?"[2] The prayers which move the heart of God are those which flow directly from the soul, such as the prayer of the publican when he cried out: "O God, be merciful to me a sinner!"

You are not ordinarily required to clothe your prayers in any words at all. It is sufficient to express them in thought; for thoughts are acts in the sight of God, who is the searcher of the hearts and the reins of men. Nay, there are times when your prayer may be most acceptable in the sight of God, though your mental conceptions may assume

[1] *Ps.* XXXIII., 16.
[2] *Job* XXXVIII., 2.

no definite shape, and though they formulate no particular need.[1]

To sum up: Prayer is the most exalted function in which man can be engaged, because it exercises the highest faculties of the soul,—the intellect and the will; it brings us into direct communication with the greatest of all beings,—God Himself; it is the channel of Heaven's choicest blessings; it excludes no one, it embraces all in the circle of its benedictions; it gives us access to our Heavenly Father at all times, in all places, and under all circumstances. In a word, prayer renders us co-operators with our Creator in the moral government of the world, since many of the events of life are shaped in accordance with our pious entreaties. Conceive, then, the dignity of God's saints. The affairs of life are decreed from all eternity; and the eternal decrees themselves are in a measure, regulated by the prayers of His servants. "Prayer moves the Hand that moves the universe."

[1] *John* V., 2-4.

CHAPTER IX.

REFUTATION OF OBJECTIONS AGAINST PRAYER.

This chapter will be devoted to the consideration and refutation of some of the most popular objections against Prayer.

1st. Some men have condemned the practice of prayer as vain,[1] on the assumption that there is no Providence.

If the assumption were correct, their conduct would be logical. But this objection need not detain us, as the existence of a Providence, and the reality of a divine government has been already demonstrated in a preceding chapter.

2d. All prayers have reference to some future event. In all our petitions, we ask God to grant us some temporal or spiritual favor, or to avert some calamity. Now, all future events are foreordained by the eternal decrees of the Divine Legislator and regulated by His immutable laws. Therefore, our prayers cannot alter these laws, and hence they seem to be useless. How can we expect God to change these laws for our good pleasure,—not once, but

---

[1] *Malach.* III., 14.

at every instant, throughout the world? Would not a favorable response to our prayers disturb at every moment the stability of order, existing in the physical and moral world? Would not science be an impossibility, based as it is on fixed and uniform laws?

Of what use, for instance, were the prayers of Moses for Josue and the Israelites, when they fought against the Amalecites? Of what benefit were the prayers of the primitive Christians for Peter's deliverance from prison?[1] Would not these events have turned out precisely as they did, whether Moses and the first Christians had prayed or not?

Of what use were Samuel's prayers for thunder and rain?[2] Of what avail were the prayers of St. Paul for the safety of the passengers during a storm in the Mediterranean?[3] Was it any advantage to Ezechias to pray for the recovery of his health?[4] The wishes of the suppliants were all fulfilled, it is true; but were the results due to their prayers? Are not rain and storms and fevers controlled by fixed and immovable laws? And how can Providence interpose, in answer to our prayers, to alter or modify those laws which His wisdom has framed? In a word, is it not vain to ask of God grace to avoid sin, since our salvation or condemnation is already determined in the eternal decrees of God?

ANSWER: The efficacy of prayer does not infringe on the eternal decrees of God, and is entirely com-

[1] *Acts* XII., 5.
[2] *I. Kings* XII., 18.
[3] *Acts* XXVII.
[4] *IV. Kings* XX., 1-6.

patible with the immutability of His laws. I will quote the lucid exposition of St. Thomas on the subject: "In proclaiming," he says, "the utility of prayer, we are not to be understood as putting any restraint on human acts, subject to Divine Providence, nor are we supposing any change in the ordinances of God. Divine Providence has determined in advance, not only the effects which are to be produced, but also their order, and the causes which are to produce them. Among these causes are included human acts. Man, therefore, must do something, not, indeed, to change by his acts the arrangement of God, but to concur in producing certain effects in accordance with the divine dispensation. Just as it is with regard to physical causes, so is it, too, with regard to prayer. The aim of prayer is not to alter the designs of God, but to ask that we may obtain what God has determined to grant to us by our prayers. In the words of St. Gregory: 'Men pray that they may merit to obtain from the Almighty what He has decreed from all eternity to grant to their prayer.'"[1]

This explanation strikes at the root of the objection. It shows that prayer is efficacious without disturbing, for a moment, the order existing in the world; that God has no after-thoughts; that He is never surprised by our petitions, and never compelled to review or correct our account in the Book of Life. The dawn of creation, the present moment,

---

[1] *Summa Theol.*, II^a. II^{ae}., Quæst. LXXXIII., Art. 2.

and the day of judgment, are all imultaneous with God. Though in point of execution, my prayer is posterior to God's absolute decrees, yet before God it is anterior to them.

God from all eternity knew that I would, for example, pray to-day for a special grace to avoid sin. In answer to my prayer He decreed from all eternity to give me to-day this special grace. The reason, therefore, why I receive this grace to-day is, indeed, because God has so decreed, but He has so decreed because I have prayed. In other words I do not pray in order to alter God's designs, but I pray in order to execute them. By prayer I fulfil the condition under which He has promised to bestow His gifts upon me. "Your Father, who is in heaven, will give good things to them *that ask Him.*"[1]

They who invoke the immutability of God's universal laws, lose sight of the great law of prayer itself. They forget that prayer holds a conspicuous place in the harmony of creation. They forget that it is a powerful leaven in shaping and moulding the mass of human actions, and an essential element and factor in framing His eternal decrees. As well might we suppose that the Signal Service Corps would take no account of the winds in forecasting the state of the weather, as that God would take no note of the spirit of prayer in determining our moral condition, and our future destiny.

Euler, the famous mathematician, expresses him-

---
[1] *Matt.* VII., 11.

self lucidly on this point: "Religion," he says, "prescribes to us the duty of prayer, in giving us the assurance that God will listen to our supplications, provided they are conformable to the rules which He has laid down for us. Philosophy, on the other hand, teaches us that all the events of life happen in accordance with the course of nature established from the beginning, and that nothing can happen which has not been foreseen and decreed. But, I answer, that, when God established the course of nature, and arranged all the events that were to occur, He evidently had regard to all the circumstances which accompanied each event, and particularly to the dispositions and prayers of each intelligent being, and that the arrangement of every event has been placed in perfect accord with all these circumstances. When a Christian, therefore, addresses to God a prayer worthy of being heard, it must not be imagined that this prayer has just come to the knowledge of God. He has already heard it from all eternity, and if, as a compassionate Father, He has judged it worthy of being granted, He has arranged the world expressly in favor of this prayer, so that its accomplishment might be the succession of the regular course of events."[1]

Let us now apply these principles to the special objections which I have adduced. From all eternity, God decreed that Josue and his hosts should conquer the Amalecites in answer to the prayer of his

---

[1] *Lettres à une Princesse d'Allemagne.*

servant Moses, and that Peter should be rescued from prison in response to the prayer of the first Christians. The petitions of the Jewish Lawgiver and of the early Christians, were a potent element in deciding the earthly career of the Hebrew people and the Prince ot the Apostles. From all eternity, God decreed to send rain in answer to Samuel, to rescue the voyagers in view of the prayer and merits of St. Paul, and to prolong the life of Ezechias in compliance with his petition.

Hence, we see the fallacy of Mr. Tyndall's assertion that science regards a prayer for rain as involving a miracle just as much as a prayer for water to run up-hill;[1] for, should we ask for a stream to run up-hill, we would beg for a phenomenon clearly contrary to nature's laws; but when we pray for rain, we ask for an atmospheric change which is habitually occurring throughout the world without any disturbance of the established laws of nature.

But, if the laws of nature are immutable, are they emancipated from divine control? Does God allow them to run their course blindly, like the vessel which is launched at the river's source, and which rushes headlong without a pilot? By no means. It should be borne in mind, as Mr. Ward observes, that, though "it is true, on the one hand, that the laws of external nature are strictly invariable (waiving the case of miracles, which are not here discussed), it is equally true, on the other hand, that

---

[1] *Fragments of Science*, p. 39.

those laws are premoved and directed by God at every moment, according to the dictates of His uncontrolled and inscrutable will."[1] God is not self-excluded from interference in the movements of His own works. He has not surrendered the reins of government in the moral and physical world. His knowledge, power, and influence are all-pervading. *He is behind the veil of nature, working always.* When God wished to chastise Egypt, He caused a burning wind to blow for a whole day and night. The next morning the wind spread the locusts over all Egypt, and He then made a very strong westerly wind to blow, which cast the locusts into the Red Sea.[2] Here we have a series of inanimate and irrational creatures, acting in phenomenal sequence, following the law of their nature, but directed to a specific purpose by a supreme, intelligent Being.

How true are the words of the Prophet: "The Lord's ways are in a tempest, and a whirlwind, and clouds are the dust of His feet. He rebuketh the sea, and drieth it up; and bringeth all the rivers to be a desert. Basan languisheth and Carmel, and the flower of Libanus fadeth away. The mountains tremble at Him, and the hills are made desolate; and the earth hath quaked at His presence."[3] Yes, He is behind the veil of nature, working always!

3d. But does not prayer paralyze human energy and encourage indolence, by resigning everything to God and neglecting the natural means of safety?

---

[1] *Dublin Review*, 1867.   [2] *Nahum* I., 3–5.
[3] *Exod.* X., 13–19.

Lord Palmerston is reported to have put this objection in a terse and plausible form, in reply to a delegation that asked him to recommend a day of public prayer and fasting, to avert the cholera: "Gentlemen," he said, "never mind prayer and fasting, but cleanse your drains."

This objection is more specious than solid. It supposes, what is not true, that natural remedies are to be disregarded, because supernatural aid is invoked. The advocates of prayer teach that every human means is to be resorted to, that all the appliances of science and the rules of prudence are to be employed to avert calamities, for, "God helps those that help themselves."

There are four ways in which the deputation referred to might have been answered. 1st. An unbelieving scientist would reply with Palmerston: "Cleanse your drains, let prayer alone." 2d. A superstitious Christian (if such is to be found) would say: "Never mind the drains, but attend to your prayers." 3d. A fatalist would advise the deputation to do nothing at all, as, do what they would, their fate was sealed. 4th. A Christian philosopher would enjoin, as St. Charles Borromeo did during the plague of Milan, that prayers be offered up to God, but he would, also, direct that the drains be cleansed and the doctors consulted; for he knows that God ordinarily works His wonders through the established laws of nature, and it is not His will that the laws of hygiene and the science of medicine should be disregarded.

Lord Palmerston was right in advising that the drains be cleansed; but he was wrong in discouraging the invocation of the Deity, since prayer enters largely into the divine economy. The superstitious Christian would be doing right in counselling supplications to the Divinity, but in discouraging natural remedies he would be tempting God. The fatalist, in rejecting both human and divine assistance, pursues a course condemned alike by reason and revelation. The Christian philosopher, in enjoining prayer *and* the remedies approved by science, acts in accordance with sound sense and the ordinances of God.

4th. But, perhaps, you will say with Rousseau:[1] "I commune, indeed, with God; I adore Him; I am sensibly touched by His benefits; I bless Him for His gifts; but why should I petition Him?" In representing my wants to God, would I not be calling in question His infinite knowledge and insulting His uncreated wisdom? Do I pretend to enlighten Him of whom our Saviour says: "Your Father knoweth that you have need of all these things?"[2]

Our object in petitioning God is not, of course, to enlighten Him in regard to our condition, but to manifest our filial piety towards Him and our entire dependence on Him, and to acknowledge Him as the Author of every good gift. The obligation to implore God's mercy, is quite as imperative as the duty of worshipping and thanking Him. Experience

---

[1] *Profession de foi du vicaire Savoyard.*
[2] *Matt.* VI., 32.

OBJECTIONS AGAINST PRAYER. 139

shows that those who never ask favors of God, seldom bless Him, or give Him thanks, and often end by forgetting their Benefactor, if they do not even go so far as to deny His Providence altogether.

The practice of supplicating God fosters a spirit of devotion, filial gratitude, humility, and dependence, and keeps alive those hallowed relations which, as loving children, we ought to maintain with our Eternal Father. O say not, then, that prayer is a mark of spiritual bondage! On the contrary, the more frequently we commune with God in prayer, the more we exercise our glorious prerogative as children of God; for surely, the children enjoy more familiar intercourse with the father of the family than do the servants of the household. Wretched, indeed, should be those children who would live under their parents' roof, without ever holding any conversation with them,—and tenfold more wretched are they who abstain from all communion with their Heavenly Father.

Our purpose in laying our wants before God, is not to excite His benevolence, which needs no incentive, but to discharge a duty, to fulfil the law of prayer, and to comply with a condition to which He has annexed some of His gifts.

There are, indeed, some blessings which the Divine Bounty bestows upon all without being solicited; for, He "maketh His sun to rise on the good and the bad, and raineth on the just and the unjust." But there are, also, many favors which are attached to prayer; for our Saviour says: "*Ask* and it shall be given you: *seek* and you shall find: *knock* and it shall be opened," evidently implying that there are certain gifts which we shall not receive, if we do not ask for them.

When our Lord says: "Your Father knoweth that you have need of all these things," His aim is certainly not to dissuade us from asking God (for, in the same discourse, He is encouraging prayer), but to inspire us with unbounded confidence in Divine Providence.

5th. Supplication, I now admit, forms an integral and essential element of divine worship. But, as "we know not what we should pray for as we ought,"[1] is it not sufficient to make our petition in general terms, or are we enjoined to descend to particulars?

Most assuredly: for the duty of prayer is prompted by a sense of our wants. But who is concerned about his general wants? It is our daily and particular necessities that excite our solicitude, and, taught by our Master, we ask "this day our daily bread." Hence, if we habitually restricted ourselves to vague petitions, we would soon cease to pray at all. As the bond of domestic union and friendship is maintained, not by indefinite sentiments of benevolence, but rather by specific acts, so is our devotion to our Heavenly Father quickened and fostered by asking Him for daily needs. And, although we know not of ourselves what is expedient to ask, "the Spirit (of God) helpeth our infirmity," by inspiring us with holy desires.

---

[1] *Rom.* VIII., 26.

6th. Again, it will be objected, perhaps, that many persons have been justified in giving up the practice of prayer, because they have often failed to obtain the particular object of their petition. A Maryland physician informed me that, in the course of one of his professional visits, he expressed to the mother of the family the hope that God would spare the life of her sick child. "I have never," she replied, " bent my knee in prayer for the last two years, when I lost my other child, for whose recovery I earnestly, but vainly, prayed."

And did not the death of the late President Garfield, notwithstanding the prayers that were offered for his recovery, tempt many persons to doubt the efficacy of prayer? Did they not say in their heart, as a certain lady said to myself: "I have prayed for the life of the President, and prayed in vain. My family prayed for him; our congregation prayed for him; the city of Baltimore prayed for him; the State prayed for him; the nation prayed for him, and prayed in vain. How can you reconcile the futility of the nation's appeal to heaven with the promise of our Saviour when He says: 'If you shall ask the Father anything in My name, He will give it to you.'"[1]

Having put the objection as strongly as possible, I answer, nevertheless, that the words of our Saviour are most true, and are to be received with unshaken faith. No good prayer ever goes unanswered. If a

---

[1] *John* XVI., 23.

single drop of water, or breath of air is never annihilated, still less is the faintest aspiration of prayer uttered in vain that ascends from a fervent heart to the throne of grace.

And now, in reply to your difficulty, I affirm that God answers our prayers in one of two ways, either directly or indirectly. Sometimes He grants us the direct and specified object of our petitions; sometimes He denies us what we particularly ask for, but He grants us something equivalent to, or even better than that for which we seek. Just as a prudent father withholds from his child a dangerous toy, and bestows on him, instead, something harmless or useful, so our Heavenly Father gives what to Him seems best, and our wisdom is but folly compared with the wisdom of God.

First. In regard to the President: If God, in response to our prayers, did not save his life, He has done more,—He has saved the life and preserved the peace of the nation, and the life of the nation is of more value than the life of any individual.

Secondly. He was pleased to prolong the President's life for nearly three months after he had received the fatal wound. Had he died immediately from the wound, what terrible consequences might have ensued! So intense at the moment was public feeling; so strong (though most unjust) was the suspicion aroused against the leaders of a certain political party; so bitter was the animosity engendered by those suspicions, that, if the President had immediately succumbed, it would have needed but a spark to ignite the flame. The first assassination might have been followed by others, and anarchy and confusion and sedition might, for a time, have reigned supreme.

But God mercifully prolonged his life till the excitement subsided, when cool reason could regain her throne, and men could plainly see that the crime was the work of one man alone, having no collusion with others.

Thirdly. As another fruit of our prayers, God inspired the country with a more intense abhorrence of assassination, and a greater reverence for the Chief Magistrate of the nation.

Fourthly. As another result of our prayers, during the trying ordeal through which we were passing, party spirit yielded to the nobler and healthier sentiment of patriotism and love of country. Men forgot, for the time being, that they were Stalwarts or Conservatives, Republicans or Democrats, Administration or Anti-Administration partisans. They remembered only that they were Americans, and citizens of a common country, children of the same mother, and they came together to shed a tear of sorrow by the sick-bed of their ruling brother.

Is not this a satisfactory answer to your difficulty? Did not God hearken to our petitions by sparing the life and saving the peace of the Republic, by prolonging the President's life till public feeling was quieted, and by inspiring men with a greater abhorrence of the crime of assassination and a deeper love for our country and its institutions? And have not our prayers been profitable, also, in another sense? Have they not been an eloquent rebuke to atheism and infidelity, and a solemn and national profession of faith in God's existence, in His power and wisdom, and in His superintending Providence? Let us remember that the chief object of prayer is not to ask and receive favors from God—that would be a narrow and selfish consideration. God forbid that He should always grant us according to the desires of our heart! This would be abandoning us to our own folly, and the withdrawal of His Providence from us, as happened to the Jews when they importuned God for a king. We are always safe in leaving the result of our prayers to His discretion. The primary motive of prayer is to acknowledge our filial dependence on God and His Fatherly care of us.

Hence, we may judge how inconclusive and revolting to our religious instincts was the prayer-test of Mr. Tyndall, who proposed that the virtue of prayer should be tried by placing in two different wards of a hospital an equal number of patients, afflicted in the same degree with similar maladies, and that the inmates of one ward should pray for their recovery, while those in the other should make no appeal to heaven.

Besides tempting God, the chief fault of the prayer-test lies in the false assumption that prayer is useless, unless the express object of the petition is granted. For my part, while protesting against the blasphemy involved in doubting the efficacy of prayer for temporal blessings, I would infinitely prefer to be a patient in the praying ward through a painful and lingering illness, even though death were to follow, than to be an indevout patient in the other ward, though I were to be restored to health. For I would be placing myself in the loving arms of my Father: "Although He should kill me, I will trust in Him,"[1] and I would expire in the blessed assurance that His mercy would follow me beyond the grave. Immeasurably sweeter to me would be the spiritual consolation, the blissful hope, the solid peace, and the friendship of my Heavenly Father, than the possession of a healthy frame, animated by a soul without God in this world, or the hope of Him in the life to come.

7th. But I may be met here at the end of the discussion by a more subtle objection. I have prayed, you will say, for a spiritual blessing,—the conversion of a friend or relative, or the moral reformation of a wayward son, and my prayer seems to have been thrown away. For what more legitimate blessing could I ask?

I answer, in the first place, that you will very probably obtain the object of your petition, if you pray with perseverance. It was only after sixteen years of earnest entreaty that Monica obtained the conversion of her cherished son Augustine. It was only after persistent solicitations that the Canaanite woman procured the recovery of her

---

[1] *Job* XIII., 15.

daughter's health;[1] and St. Francis de Sales obtained the mastery over his temper only after a prayerful struggle of twenty years.

Secondly. But, perhaps, your friend for whom you constantly prayed, died without manifesting any certain signs of grace and repentance. Be it so. Did God make manifest to you the condition of your friend's soul at the moment of his demise? He may have sanctified that soul by a sudden ray of grace in the moment of dissolution, and concealed from you, for your present humiliation, the blissful fruit of your entreaties, that your joy may be full on the day of the Lord. He may, also, have concealed the conversion of your friend from all who knew him, that they might fully realize the necessity of an early conversion to their Creator, and of securing a happy death by a holy life. Even at the last moment, there is, indeed, hope of salvation; but, then, true conversion of heart after a long life of neglected duties, requires a miracle of grace. Of the conversion of the good thief, St. Augustine said: "*One* was converted at the hour of death, that you might not despair; *only* one was converted, that you might not presume." God's unrevealed mercies are over all His works. Who would have imagined the salvation of the dying thief, if the Evangelist had not recorded the expiring words of our Saviour: "This day thou shalt be with Me in Paradise!"[2]

But, lastly, even admitting that your friend gave

[1] *Matt.* XV., 22-28.
[2] *Luke* XXIII., 43.

manifest evidence of final impenitence and died with a blasphemy on his lips—what then? God compels no man to accept His proffered mercy, neither can your prayers force any one to surrender his will to the influence of divine grace. Nevertheless, your prayer was not offered in vain. If the heavenly waters find no lodgment in his stony heart, they will flow back abundantly into the valley of your own soul, and the words of the Psalmist will be fulfilled in you: "My prayer shall be turned into my bosom."[1]

---

[1] Ps. XXXIV., 13.

CHAPTER X.

Gratitude to God.

Gratitude is another essential element in the worship of God. He is the Author of every perfect gift.[1] He is the Source of every blessing, natural and supernatural, that comes to us.

Gratitude has been justly called the *Respiration of the Soul*. As in every human breast there are two movements: the one that inhales the air, the other that exhales it after it has invigorated the blood; so there should be in every soul two movements: the one receiving the gifts of God, the other pouring forth those gifts in the form of thanksgiving.

1°. God has given us life. How precious is life! How delightful to cross that mysterious boundary which separates nothingness from existence, to leap from darkness to light and life! How great is the boon to breathe the air of heaven, to contemplate the starry firmament above us, to commune with our fellow beings!

Life would be precious in any shape or form. It would be a valuable favor if God had made us birds

[1] *James* I., 17

of the air or beasts of the field or fishes of the sea or even creeping reptiles; for even the creeping reptile shrinks with horror from death, and clings with tenacity to life. But God has made us neither bird nor beast, neither fish nor reptile; for He has given us not merely animal life. He has created us human beings, the noblest of all earthly creatures. He has made us to His own image and likeness. "And God created man to His own image: to the image of God He created him."[1] He has endowed us with a sublime intelligence, with a free will, with an immortal soul, as will be shown in subsequent chapters. "What is man," O Lord, "that Thou art mindful of him, or the son of man that Thou visitest him? Thou hast made him a little less than the angels, Thou hast crowned him with glory and honor, and hast set him over the works of Thy hands. Thou hast subjected all things under his feet, all sheep and oxen: moreover the beasts also of the fields, the birds of the air, and the fish of the sea that pass through the paths of the sea."[2] That universal jurisdiction which He gave to Adam, He imparts also to us. He repeats to us what He said to him: "Rule over all living creatures that move upon the earth."[3]

This universal dominion which God has given us over the earth and all that it contains, is not of a merely nominal and indefinite character. It is to be understood in its strictly literal sense; for all crea-

---

[1] *Gen.* I., 27.   [2] *Gen.* I., 28.
[3] *Ps.* VIII., 5–9.

tures pay tribute to us as our subjects. If they try to escape our hands, it is not because they deny our authority over them, but because they dread our sovereign power.

When we sit down to partake of our daily meals, let us consider how many lands and how many creatures are ministering to our wants and comforts. China and Japan supply us with tea; Arabia and Java, Brazil and Cuba, with coffee. Louisiana and other countries send us sugar. One field yields us bread; another, vegetables. One animal furnishes us with meat; another, with milk and butter. The sea gives up its fish, to contribute to the luxuries of our board. Even the bowels of the earth are invaded to procure fuel for our fires, silver for our table, and iron and other metals for our domestic utensils. One animal affords covering for our hands; another, for our feet; and another, for our head. The sheep is shorn of its fleece, and the silk-worm labors industriously to furnish us with clothing for our body. And yet how many habitually make their toilet and go to their daily meals, without bestowing a thought of thanksgiving on the Giver of all these gifts, as if they were a purchased right, and not a favor granted?

But, some one may say, are we not indebted to human energy, to daring enterprise and skill, for most of the comforts and luxuries just enumerated? I grant it. But was it not God who inspired man with the skill and enterprise necessary for importing or manufacturing these articles of daily use? If, therefore, we admire the engine of the human brain, which exercises such power over inert matter, how much more praise and gratitude are due to the Divine Engineer who has put the brain-engine itself in motion!

The man that studies the famous Moses of Michel Angelo will not waste a thought on the tools with which he wrought, but will concentrate his admiration on the great artist himself. When we reflect on the marvellous enterprise and consummate skill of the nineteenth century, we should rise from the consideration of human genius to the contemplation of the Divine Wisdom, who communicated such talent to men. "Hath not the potter," says the Apostle, "power over the clay of the same lump, to make one vessel indeed unto honor, and another unto dishonor?"[1] And if the Author of our being infuses into human clay the spirit of a Beseleel[2] or of a Columbus, instead of the spirit of an ox, to whom are they indebted for their handicraft or nautical enterprise? "What hast thou that thou hast not received? And if thou hast received it why dost thou glory as if thou hadst not received it?"[3]

We are indebted to God not only for the life that He has given us, but also for the preservation and continuance of that life; for as none but almighty hands could have created us, so none but almighty

---

[1] *Rom.* IX., 21. [3] *I. Cor.* IV., 7.
[2] *Exod.* XXXI.

power can preserve us. Not only must we say with the Royal Prophet: "Thy hands," (O Lord), "have made me and formed me;"[1] but we must add with the same Prophet: "If Thou turnest away Thy face, Thy creatures shall be troubled: Thou shalt take away their breath, and they shall fail and shall return to their dust."[2] Let Him but withdraw His all-sustaining hand, and we not only cease to live, but we lapse into our original nothingness. He is the Life of our life. He is the breath of our nostrils. He is the invisible Sun that illumines our path. Every day we live, every breath we breathe, every pulsation of our heart, is a fresh manifestation of divine power and a new expression of divine mercy.

Our thanks are due to the "Giver of all good gifts" not only for the blessings that we receive directly from His hands, but also for the favors that we receive at the hands of men. What are our parents, what our friends, what our benefactors but the agents of God's mercy, the stewards of His bounty, the channels of His providence? Who was it but God that inspired them with benevolence toward us? Who but God that implanted in the father's and the mother's breast that love stronger than death, that tender solicitude, that spirit of self-sacrifice for their child? So clearly did the Patriarchs and Prophets see the hand of God in all the blessings that came to them by those of creatures, that they lost sight, as it

[1] *Ps.* CXVIII., 73.
[2] *Ps.* CIII., 29.

were, of the secondary agents that ministered to them, and referred all to the Lord of heaven. The Patriarch Joseph is exalted by Pharao from a dungeon to a throne. His chief thanks, however, are bestowed not on Pharao, but on God, who made Pharao the instrument of His mercy.

We should thank God not only for the temporal favors that He vouchsafes to send us, but even for the afflictions and humiliations with which He visits us. We should bless Him not only when as a Father He fondles us, but also when as a Physician He holds to our lips the cup of sorrow and tribulation. We should kiss the hand that strikes, as well as the hand that caresses us; for whether He smites or caresses, He is always our Father. It may seem paradoxical, nevertheless I believe it is true that, when the day of final reckoning will come, when the mysteries of life will be made manifest, we shall very probably discover that we owe a heavier debt of gratitude to God for the trials we have endured than for the comforts we have enjoyed. For how many more are drawn toward Him by sufferings than by consolations! What are those heavy rains of tribulation that fall upon us but the refreshing waters that quicken and revive the seed of faith in our soul, and make it grow into fruit of sanctification! What are afflictions, if righteously borne, but the raw material, out of which we can weave the royal garment that we shall deserve to wear in heaven at the banquet of the great King! "We glory also," says the Apostle, "in tribulations; knowing that tribulation worketh patience: and patience trial; and trial hope. And hope confoundeth not, because the charity of God is poured forth in our hearts by the Holy Ghost who is given to us."[1]

And yet, alas! there are many who, both in propitious and adverse circumstances, fail in this essential act of religion. They do not thank God in prosperity; for in the delirium and intoxication of delight, they become oblivious of their Benefactor. They do not give Him thanks in adversity, for the bitterness of sorrow hardens their heart. The only time that they are disposed to make some pretence of expressing their gratitude, is when they have some favor to ask or some impending danger to escape; so that their gratitude may be defined, "a lively sense of future benefits."

But if we should be grateful to God for the gift of creation, how much more should we be for the supernatural blessing of Redemption! Plato is justly considered the most profound philosopher of Pagan times. He was the light and glory of ancient Greece. He is called "Plato *the Divine*" by his admiring disciples, on account of the sublimity of his writings. He soars aloft on the wings of reason, as John the Apostle on the wings of Revelation. Taught by reason alone, he arrived at the knowledge of the one, true God. This great philosopher was accustomed to thank his Maker for two things: 1st, that he was born in a country so enlightened and culti-

---

[1] *Rom.* V., 3-5.

vated as Greece; 2d, that he had Socrates for his master.

How much more reason have we to be grateful to God that our "lines are fallen in pleasant places;"[1] that we were born not amid the darkness of idolatry, but in a civilized and Christian country; that we were nurtured by Christian parents; and that we live under the benign influence of humane and Christian legislation! Above all, how thankful we ought to be that we have Christ the Lord for our Teacher, who "is the power of God and the wisdom of God,"[2] whose wisdom surpasses that of Socrates immeasurably more than the light of the sun excels that of the flickering lamp! He teaches us not by word only, but also by His example. He preaches to us not only from the pages of the Gospel, but also from the wood of the cross. He is not only our Teacher, but our Saviour and Redeemer as well. He has brought us out of the darkness of idolatry to the admirable light of His Gospel. "Ye were once darkness; but now light in the Lord."[3] He has rescued us from spiritual poverty, that we might be rich in conscience, rich in grace and in good works. "For ye know the grace of our Lord Jesus Christ, that being rich, He became poor for you, that through His poverty, ye might be rich."[4] He rescued us from the bondage of sin, that we might enjoy the glorious liberty of children of God.

[1] *Ps.* XV., 6.
[2] *I. Cor.* I., 24.
[3] *Eph.* V., 8.
[4] *II. Cor.* VIII., 9.

The Prince of the Apostles thus eloquently proclaims our Christian dignity and the duty of adoration and gratitude that it involves. "Ye are," he says, "a chosen generation, a royal priesthood, a holy nation, a purchased people, that ye may declare the virtues of Him who hath called you out of darkness into His admirable light."[1] We are "a chosen generation," chosen from thousands of others that know not God. "He hath not done in like manner to every nation: and His judgments He hath not made manifest to them."[2] "A royal priesthood!" royal, because we are sons of the Most High, the King of kings and Lord of lords; a "priesthood," though laymen, because we were consecrated in baptism to offer to God on the altar of our heart, the sacrifice of praise and thanksgiving. "A holy nation," for in the words of Moses we can truly say: "Neither is there any other nation so great that hath gods so nigh to them as our God is present to all our petitions."[3] "A purchased people"—purchased "not with corruptible gold and silver," but with the Precious Blood of Christ.

If, therefore, we should be thankful for our temporal life, how much more for the supernatural life with which God has endowed us! If in common with our fellow-beings, we should be grateful that He has sent His sun to shine on us, how much more that He has sent His Holy Spirit to illumine our mind and to inflame our heart!

[1] *I. Pet.* II., 9.
[2] *Deut.* IV., 7.
[3] *Ps.* CXLVII., 20.

If we should have a profound sense of the divine goodness in giving us daily food for the support of our animal life, and clothing for the protection of our body, how much stronger should be our obligation for the supersubstantial Bread that our Father gives us for the nourishment of our soul, and for the garments of grace and innocence with which He clothed us in baptism! If we should be thankful to Him for having given us dominion over the birds of the air and the beasts of the field, how much more grateful should we be that He has given us power to subdue those spiritual monsters and birds of prey: namely, our passions! This He has done by teaching us to subject them to reason. If, in a word, we owe a debt of gratitude to our Heavenly Benefactor for having made us lords of His earthly manor, how much greater is our debt for having made us prospective heirs of His everlasting kingdom.

And all these blessings our Saviour has, out of pure love and without hope of reward, vouchsafed to us as the price of His own Blood. Well can He say to each of us: "Greater love than this no man hath, that a man lay down his life for his friends;"[1] for the strongest evidence of human affection is to sacrifice one's life for a friend. But divine love has gone still farther, for Jesus laid down His life even for His enemies. "When we were enemies," says the Apostle, "we were reconciled to God by the death of His Son."[2]

[1] *John* XV., 13.
[2] *Rom.* V., 10.

Now, when we place before our eyes, the manifold gifts of God both in the order of nature and of grace, we may well be astounded at the enormity of the sin of ingratitude. There is no vice more hurtful to ourselves, none more abhorred by men, none more odious to God than the vice of unthankfulness. "Ingratitude," says St. Bernard, "is a parching wind that dries up the fountains of piety, the dew of mercy, and the torrents of grace." "The earth," says St. Paul, "that drinketh in the rain which cometh often upon it and . . . which bringeth forth thorns and briars, is rejected . . . whose end is to be burnt."[1]

And shall not the soul that drinks in the rain of divine grace and that brings forth no first fruits of thanksgiving, but only thorns of ingratitude, be likewise rejected?—for God's grace is too precious to be wasted.

Mankind has a peculiar abhorrence of ingratitude. A man would rather be accused of profanity or of cruelty or of intemperance or of lying than to be charged with an ungrateful sense of obligations towards a benefactor. These sins may sometimes be palliated as resulting from a momentary passion or dread of confusion; but ingratitude always betrays a cold, heartless disposition.

So odious is this sin in the sight of God and so acceptable to Him is the opposite virtue, that He has implanted an instinct of gratitude even in the

[1] *Heb.* VI., 7, 8.

brute creation. When He reproaches the Jews for their ingratitude, He bids them learn a lesson from the dumb beast. "I have brought up children," He says, "and exalted them: but they have despised Me. The ox knoweth his owner, and the ass his master's crib; but Israel hath not known Me, and My people have not understood."[1] The ox recognizes with affection the master that feeds him; and we are indifferent to the Divine Hand that sustains us. The ox submits meekly to the yoke; and we grow impatient of the yoke of the Gospel. The ox ploughs the field, which yields a harvest to its master; and we fail to cultivate in our soul the fruits of sanctification.

All are familiar, I dare say, with the story of Androcles and the lion, a story that is well authenticated.[2] Androcles, who was a slave, fled from his cruel master and buried himself in the forest. One day, a lion approached him and, with piteous moans, held up his paw, which was swollen with corruption. Androcles, at once interpreting the cause of the lion's pain, extracted the thorn and thus relieved the suffering beast. The lion manifested his joy and gratitude by frisking about and, at last, crouching at Androcles' feet. His gratitude and affection did not stop here. He began to share his prey with his benefactor. Some time after, Androcles was recaptured and condemned to be devoured by wild beasts. Imagine the astonishment of the spectators assem-

[1] *Is.* I., 2, 3.
[2] *Aulus Gellius,* L. V., C. XIV.

bled about the arena when they saw that the hungry lion, which proved to be the forest companion of Androcles, after bounding toward his intended victim, instead of seizing and devouring him, gambolled about him and, in every possible manner, manifested his joy on meeting again his benefactor.

O what a lesson this king of the forest teaches us all! When we were groaning under the weight of our iniquities, our Saviour God drew the poison of sin from our heart at the sacrifice of His own life. He healed our wounds with His own Precious Blood. "He was wounded for our iniquities, He was bruised for our sins."[1] He died that we might live. He became a slave that we might be free. How do we repay Him? Like the lion, we are seized with the cravings of hunger. Our hunger is ambition. Our hunger is anger. Our hunger is lust and avarice. Angels look on as spectators, to record the issue of our struggle with our passion. We rush into the arena. We are met by our Divine Benefactor who shows us the Wounds He has received for us. He appeals to our gratitude. Our passions appeal to our personal gratification. We sacrifice our Benefactor to our hungry concupiscence. Gratitude gives way to appetite. We "crucify again the Son of God, and make Him a mockery."[2] "Go to the ant, thou sluggard," says the Wise Man, "and . . . learn wisdom."[3] He could say, likewise: "Go to the dumb

---

[1] *Is.* LIII., 5.   [2] *Prov.* VI., 6.
[3] *Heb.* VI., 6.

beast, thou ingrate, and learn gratitude to thy Redeemer."

The Apostle of the Gentiles is never weary of giving thanks to God. In his Epistle to the Romans, in both of his Epistles to the Corinthians, in his Epistles to the Ephesians, to the Philippians, to the Colossians, in the two to the Thessalonians, in both of those addressed to Timothy, and in his Letter to Philemon, he pours forth his thanks for the spiritual blessings bestowed on himself and his disciples. And in every instance, his expressions of gratitude occur in the opening chapter, as if to admonish us, that all our prayers and good works should be inaugurated by thanksgiving.

The Church is not less zealous than the Apostle in fulfilling this sacred duty. Our Saviour was once sacrificed for our Redemption on the altar of the cross. And, from the rising to the setting of the sun, she daily commemorates this great event on ten thousand altars by the great Eucharistic Sacrifice which, as the very name implies, is a Sacrifice of Thanksgiving.

Every devout Christian should rejoice that the Chief Executive of this nation, as well as the Governors of the different States are accustomed once a year to invite the people of the United States to return thanks to God for His blessings to us. It is a healthy sign to see our Chief Magistrate officially proclaiming the supreme dominion and fatherly supervision of our Creator.

Gratitude is not only a duty we owe for past favors, but it is the best means of attracting fresh ones from the Fountain of Grace; for the prayer of thanksgiving is a heavenly stream that flows into the ocean of divine love, and again returns to us in showers of benediction.

CHAPTER XI.

MAN POSSESSES MORAL FREEDOM.

By moral freedom I mean that, while man is conscientiously bound by law, he is not necessitated by it. Man enjoys moral freedom. He is at liberty to conceive thoughts good or evil; and if no external violence is offered to him, he can speak and act well or ill. He has the inherent power to choose between right and wrong. He can praise or blaspheme his Maker. He is free to honor or despise his parents, to hate or forgive an enemy; to help the poor if the means are at hand, or to reject their petition; to eat and drink, or to decline what is set before him; to entertain deliberately unchaste desires, or to spurn them; to tell the truth or to prevaricate.

If there is any truth which is plain and luminous, which is profoundly rooted in the human heart and universally admitted by the human race, it is the doctrine which proclaims that there is within us an active principle capable of deliberating, choosing, and determining,—which tells us that we are neither machines subject to purely mechanical impulses, nor mere animals led by blind instinct, which masters and controls us.

I have an innate sense or feeling that I am a free agent. Just as I have the evidence of my senses that the sun gives me light, that the fire warms me, that I am now writing in my room; so I have an innate conviction that I possess free-will, that I can speak or be silent, and that, if no coercion is exercised, I can walk out or remain at home. I am not more certain that I feel a sensation of hunger than I am of my ability to accept or reject the food that is set before me. Nay, I am as intimately persuaded of my moral liberty as I am of my very existence; for it is the same interior monitor that makes me conscious of both. This vital principle within me is as worthy of belief when it tells me that I am free, as when it tells me that I exist.

I feel remorse after committing a crime, although it may have been a secret one and not amenable to civil punishment. If I were not free in the commission of the deed, I should not experience this remorse. If in trying to kill a deer, I shot a man by accident, I should indeed be distressed on account of the unfortunate act; but this regret is quite different from the bitter sense of contrition I should experience had I deliberately wounded him, though no one was, nor ever should be privy to the crime.

The denial of human liberty would involve the denial of divine justice and the equity of human tribunals. For the justice of God consists in rendering to every one according to his works, in rewarding merit and punishing demerit. But man could merit neither praise nor blame if, instead of being a free agent, he willed and acted from the necessity of his nature.

The benevolent man who dispenses his charities with a ready hand, would have no more merit before God than the unconscious Nile which, by its overflow, enriches the surrounding country; and the passionate man who allows his impetuous temper to run uncontrolled, would have no more responsibility for his violent conduct than the mighty Mississippi which by its periodical outbreaks, brings ruin and desolation to many families.

An *Evangeline* whose thoughts daily went heavenward, whose soul was pure as the sun's ray, whose outward demeanor was a tribute to virtue and a rebuke to vice; though through life she shed benediction along her pathway,—

"And from the fields of her soul a fragrance celestial ascended,"

—would deserve no more recompense from God for her saintly life than the unthinking rose that bloomed in her garden.

The Sister that voluntarily enters the plague-stricken hospital and, at the risk of her life, ministers to the victim of a loathsome and contagious disease, would be neither better nor worse in the sight of God than the ruthless assassin.

The crime of Guiteau, which excited universal horror and plunged the nation in grief, becomes an irresponsible and guiltless act; the court that tried and condemned him is a usurped tribunal, and his executioner a legalized murderer.

The denial of human liberty would be an impeachment, not only of divine justice, but also of divine goodness. God gives us a law, which we are strictly commanded to observe. He tells us that this law is not only practicable,[1] but that it is easy of fulfilment in view of the aid which He gives us: "This is the love of God that we keep His Commandments: and His Commandments are not heavy."[2] But if man had not free-will and was obliged to follow the bent of his inclinations, the fulfilment of the Divine Law would be not only difficult, but impossible. And would it not be cruel on the part of the Divine Legislator to command impossibilities by imposing on us a burden that we could not bear? Would He not be dealing with us (with all reverence be it said) as harshly as Pharao acted toward the Hebrew people when he commanded them to make bricks without straw?

The Divine Founder of the Christian religion gives us precepts far more sublime and exacting than those of the Old Law. And yet, He tells us, that their observance is by no means above our strength. "Take My yoke upon you," He says, "for My yoke is sweet, and My burden light."[3] But would not this invitation be a delusion and a snare, if we had no free-will, and would not the Son of God be putting a heavier yoke on us than the son of Solomon imposed on his subjects? "My father," said Roboam, "put a heavy yoke upon you, but I will add

---

[1] *Deut.* XXX., 11–14. [3] *Matt.* XI., 29, 30.
[2] *I. John* V., 3.

to your yoke: my father beat you with whips, but I will beat you with scorpions."[1]

Our Saviour says: My Father commanded you not to kill under pain of the judgment. "But I say to you: 'Whosoever is angry with his brother, shall be in danger of the judgment.'" My Father forbade you to commit adultery, but I forbid you to entertain lustful desires in your heart. My Father forbade you to forswear yourself. "But I say to you, not to swear at all." My Father commands you to love your neighbor. "But I say to you: 'Love your enemies.'"[2]

In a word, take away from man his moral accountability, and then conscience becomes a capricious tyrant; the natural law, the divine law proclaimed in the Old and the New Testament, all civil and ecclesiastical law becomes an intolerable burden; moral sermons and instructions are a waste of time; social compacts become as frail and brittle as the paper on which they are written; and all distinction between good and evil, virtue and vice, a life of shame and a life of integrity, at once disappears.

The Holy Scripture not only presupposes the moral liberty of man in the commandments that it enjoins, but it frequently and expressly affirms his power of electing between good and evil: "I call heaven and earth to witness this day, that I have set before you life and death, blessing and cursing.

---

[1] *III. Kings* XII., 11.
[2] *Matt.* V.

Choose therefore life, that both thou and thy seed may live."[1]

"But if it seem evil to you to serve the Lord, you have *your choice* : Choose this day that which pleaseth you, whom you would rather serve. . . . But as for me and my house, we *will* serve the Lord."[2]

"Say not: He hath caused me to err. . . . The Lord hateth all abomination of error. . . . God made man from the beginning, and left him in the hand of his own counsel. He added His commandments and precepts. If thou wilt keep the commandments, . . they shall preserve thee. . . . Before man is life and death, good and evil, that which he shall choose, shall be given him."[3]

These texts that I have grouped together from various parts of Holy Writ, confirm the arguments already adduced that man enjoys moral freedom. They tell us that we cannot ascribe our sins to God, nor to the imperious laws of our own nature. They plainly inform us that we may subdue our passions, or we must be subdued by them; that we may be their master, or we must be their slave; that we have the power to choose between good and evil, blessing and malediction, spiritual life and spiritual death.

There are, it is true, certain causes which influence our will, and which tend to impair and weaken its energy. Some of these causes are inherent, and others are external to us. The interior causes which .

---

[1] *Deut.* XXX., 19.
[2] *Josue* XXIV., 15.
[3] *Ecclus.* XV., 12–18.

act on our will, are our passions and vicious inclinations.

There are, so to speak, two wills in man, the superior and the inferior will. They maintain an irreconcilable warfare with each other, each contending for the mastery. No human being that has arrived at the age of reason, is exempt from this warfare. It is waged in the breast of the saint, as well as in that of the sinner; though ordinarily with different results. There is no place, how secluded or sacred soever, which is not a battle-ground for this domestic strife. The duel is carried on within the hallowed walls of a convent, as well as in the public thoroughfares of the city. The struggle begins with the dawn of reason and ends only with life itself.

The superior will strives to elevate the soul to God, and to act in obedience to the Divine Will. It inspires sentiments of charity, joy, peace, patience, meekness, modesty, continency, chastity.[1] It struggles to obtain the mastery over the flesh.

The lower will endeavors to subject the superior will to its control. It is attended in its train by hatred, malice, envy, lust, intemperance, gluttony, and such like.[2]

The Apostle of the Gentiles, in his Epistles to the Romans and to the Galatians, well describes this internal contest: "The flesh lusteth against the Spirit, and the Spirit against the flesh, for these are

[1] *Gal.* V.
[2] *Ibid.*

contrary one to another."[1] "To will (good) is present with me, but to accomplish that which is good, I find not. . . . For I am delighted with the law of God according to the inward man. But I see another law in my members warring against the law of my mind, and making me captive to the law of sin which is in my members."[2]

But although the struggle between our spiritual and animal nature is fierce and incessant, the result however depends on ourselves. By the grace of God, the superior will can always conquer, if we are only determined that it shall. The flesh may strive to *captivate* and allure us, but it cannot *capture* and enslave us against our will. The most violent and ferocious passions may assail us like hungry wolves eager to devour us; and yet we can escape as unharmed as Daniel in the lion's den.

The Powers of Darkness may afflict us with all the malice with which they pursued Job and St. Anthony. Men may wage against us the most unrelenting persecutions. They may rob us of our civil and religious liberty. They may force us to prostrate ourselves before their idol, but they cannot compel us to worship it. Men may imprison and enchain us, they may assail and take the rampart of the body; but our free-will, dwelling in the citadel of the soul and fortified by the grace of God, is impregnable. We can always say: No surrender!—and with the Royal Prophet exclaim: "The Lord is

[1] *Gal.* V., 17.
[2] *Rom.* VII., 18–23.

my light and my salvation, whom shall I fear? The Lord is the Protector of my life, of whom shall I be afraid?... If armies in camp should stand together against me, my heart shall not fear?"[1] Even the Pagan Poet portrays in language worthy of a Christian the fortitude dwelling in a heart supported by a good conscience: "Not the rage of the people pressing to hurtful measures, not the aspect of a threatening tyrant can shake from his settled purpose a man who is *just* and determined in his resolutions; nor can the South Wind, that tumultuous ruler of the restless Adriatic, nor the mighty hand of thundering Jove. If a crushed world should fall in upon him, the ruins would strike him undismayed."[2]

Look at the unconquerable will of Job. A torrent of temporal calamities cannot force from him a murmur of complaint, nor bend his heart from the path of rectitude. He is covered with ulcers from head to foot. Messenger after messenger hastens to him announcing the loss of all his cattle and herds, the slaughter of his servants, the untimely and vio-

---

[1] *Ps.* XXVI., 1-3.

[2] Justum et tenacem propositi virum
Non civium ardor prava jubentium,
Non vultus instantis tyranni
Mente quatit solida, neque Auster
Dux inquieti turbidus Adriæ,
Nec fulminantis magna manus Jovis;
Si fractus illabatur orbis,
Impavidum ferient ruinæ.
Horace, L. III., Car. III.

lent death of his sons and daughters. His friends accuse him of blasphemy and other crimes; and, to crown his misery, the wife of his bosom turns against him, sneers at his piety, and prompts him to "curse God and die."

But the superior will of Job rises triumphant over all these adversities, and with perfect submission he exclaims: "If we have received good things at the hand of God, why should we not receive evil?"[1] "Naked came I out of my mother's womb, and naked shall I return thither: the Lord gave and the Lord hath taken away: blessed be the name of the Lord. In all of these things, Job sinned not by his lips, nor spoke he any foolish thing against God."[2]

The history of St. Basil, Archbishop of Cæsarea, furnishes us with a notable instance of the superior power of the will over brute force. The Arian emperor Valens was determined to break the will of the great archbishop by forcing him to enter the ranks of the Arian heresy. He sent his prefect Modestus, accordingly, with orders to compel Basil to communicate with the Arians. Modestus, attended by his lictors and surrounded by all the pomp of power, is sitting in his tribunal. Basil is summoned before him, and the following dialogue ensues:

Modestus: "Why dost thou oppose the order of the emperor? Dost thou not know that he can confiscate all thy goods?"

Basil: "He that has nothing to lose, fears not

[1] *Job* II., 10.
[2] *Ibid.* I., 21, 22.

confiscation. All I own are a few books and the clothes I wear."

Modestus: "But he will banish you."

Basil: "I am already an exile. I claim heaven as my true country."

Modestus: "He can inflict torments on you."

Basil: "As for torments, I fear them not. My poor body is already emaciated. The first stroke will despatch me and put an end to my pain. And as for death, I rather covet it, as it will take me sooner to my Creator, for whom alone I live."

Modestus, at last, exclaims: "Never did any man talk to Modestus with such freedom."

"Perhaps," replies Basil, "you never before fell in with a bishop."[1]

It might seem to be a work of supererogation to insist so much on a doctrine so palpable and self-evident as that of free-will. Yet such is the perversity of certain intellects that there is no truth, however luminous, which has not been involved in obscurity, especially when it served as a check to intellectual or moral license; and there is no paradox, how revolting soever, which has not been plausibly defended by the vagaries of eccentric genius.

It is the destiny of truth in this world to have not only its courageous champions, but also its bitter antagonists. Its light, which is grateful to docile minds, is irritating to rebellious spirits. Its voice is melody to the soul that is attuned to virtue, but

[1] Abridged from Gregory of Nazianzus.

discord to the ear of him who is out of harmony with God.

This observation is eminently applicable to the subject of free-will, the absolute impotence of which has been affirmed even by men who in their day were recognized as founders of religious sects, or as leaders in certain schools of thought.

The odious and despairing doctrine of Predestination as expounded by Calvin[1] strikes at the root of moral dignity and responsibility. Luther wrote a special work "On the Slavery of the Will." He maintained as an article of faith, that man is not free, that every act of the will is only apparently free, that all things are ruled by a divine and uncontrollable necessity, and that God is responsible for every human act.[2] David Hume in the last century,[3] and John Stuart Mill in our own time, held views irreconcilable with moral freedom.

Let us briefly examine the principal arguments against free-will, hold them up to the light of reason, and weigh them in the scales of common sense.

Some will say: This event was destined to happen. It was so decreed by the Almighty and, therefore, I could not avert it. Or to put this specious and popular objection in the form of a syllogism: I was not free to avoid doing what God foresaw I would certainly do. But God foresaw that I would com-

---

[1] *Institutes of the Christian Religion.*
[2] *De Servo Arbitrio.*, Tom. III., f. 170.
[3] *Philosophical Essays.*

mit a certain crime. Therefore, I was not free to avoid it. God, indeed, foresaw that you would commit the crime. But He foresaw at the same time that you would commit it not of necessity, but of your own free-will. God foresaw it, because He knew you would perpetrate the deed. You did not commit it *because* He foresaw it. You might as well admit that you were the cause of a man's suicide because, while standing on Victoria Bridge, you saw him plunge into Niagara Falls, as to suppose that God, because He foresaw its occurrence, was the cause of your moral fall.

It is not, indeed, strictly correct to say that God *foresees* at all, since all things are present to Him. God's life is not, like ours, measured by time.

> "Nothing to Him is future, nothing past,
> But an eternal Now doth ever last."

All the actions of our life past, present, and future are simultaneously viewed by the mind of God.

Others contend that our will is as much swayed by our motives as the sword is by the arm that wields it. But certainly this assertion though advanced by such writers as Hume, Herbert Spencer,[1] and the Duke of Argyll,[2] is not borne out by our introspection and personal observation. A motive is an argument or suggestion, presented by the understanding to the will and soliciting its action.

---

[1] *Psychology*, Vol. I., p. 500.
[2] *The Reign of Law.*

But my will is not forced by these motives; it is free to reject them. I act, indeed, from motives, because I am an intelligent being; but I have the power to resist them, because I am free. Motives may guide, but they cannot compel my free-will. They have a moral, but not a necessitating or dominating influence over my action. How often do we commit a deed that is clearly against our better judgment. "I see and approve of the better course," says Ovid, "but I pursue the worse."[1]

Motives, therefore, do not act on my mind with the same imperious necessity that a weight does on evenly balanced scales. A thousand motives cannot coerce my will. They may move, but they cannot control my action.

Whatever may have been the abstract notions of Hume, or Mill, or the Duke of Argyll, regarding free-will, I am sure they would never carry their theory so far as to repudiate the idea of moral responsibility.

There is another and more dangerous class of men who, while religiously maintaining in theory the existence of free-will, are disposed to deny it in practice, since they assert that it is impotent to overcome evil inclinations.

The worst crimes are often palliated and even justified in our days on the false assumption that the criminal under the influence of some pressure, has not the moral power to resist the violence of his passions.

---

[1] "*Video meliora, proboque, deteriora sequor.*" *Metamor.*, LVII.

Thus, one man will say to me: "I am, Sir, the slave of intemperance; and this vice has obtained so dominant a mastery over me that I am powerless to resist. The habit has become a second nature to me." The name of dipsomania is now given to a morbid thirst for drink when it reaches a certain stage. It is a great sedative to a man's conscience when his medical adviser characterizes his criminal propensity by the name of a disease.

Another will excuse his frequent outbursts of anger, of oaths, and profanity on the pretext that his will is impotent to control the habit. A third will avow that he cannot overcome the rebellion of the flesh.

Nay, do we not see the habitual sin of theft often condoned on the plea that it is rather a disease of the mind than a depravity of the will? The old-fashioned sin of shop-lifting is frequently called by the harmless name of kleptomania.

Even the awful crime of suicide is excused on the flimsy pretext that the self-destroyer was laboring under a temporary aberration of mind.

And worse than all, murder itself is extenuated and often pardoned on the dangerous and unwarrantable assumption that a man, under certain impulses, is so far controlled by his animal passions as to be deprived of the use of his free-will. This plea, moreover, has acquired such consistency and strength, as to be admitted even in the courts of justice.

I sometimes read with painful interest the trial of

a murderer whose only defense is temporary aberration of mind. An astute lawyer is employed. He sees at once that the murder cannot be denied, and he accordingly sets up the plea of emotional insanity. The advocate begins by congratulating the cause of justice that the case is to be tried before a jury so enlightened and so impartial as that assembled before him. The jury at once wake up to a sense of their importance, and assume a complacent and attentive air. The lawyer then enters into an elaborate disquisition on the periodical madness of his client. He remarks upon the strange manner in which he was seen to talk and act a few hours before the murder, and declares that this suspension of his moral perception continued until the deed was committed, when his sanity was suddenly restored. The jury vindicate by a verdict of "Not guilty," the character of intelligence given them by the lawyer. This may be called justice in the eyes of men, but in the sight of God it is mockery. Before His tribunal, no crime shall pass unavenged.

It would, indeed, be unwarrantable and unjust in me to accuse the honored professions of law and medicine of magnifying the influence that certain diseases and passions exercise on the will. Science and observation have demonstrated the fact that dipsomania and kindred diseases may sometimes render a man irresponsible for some specific actions which are affected by those distempers. But it cannot be denied that these are much abused terms, which cover a multitude of sins, as an eminent physician once avowed to me. I maintain that many try to soothe a guilty conscience by ascribing to mental or bodily maladies what, by right, is attributable to a perverted will. The man that makes his passions responsible for his crimes, is less excusable than the astrologer whom Shakespeare holds up to ridicule: "We make guilty of our disasters the sun, the moon, and the stars: as if we were villains by necessity; fools, by heavenly compulsion; knaves, thieves, and treachers, by spherical predominance; drunkards, liars, and adulterers, by enforced obedience of planetary influence."[1]

"O liberty!" exclaimed Madam Roland, "how many crimes are committed in thy name!" And just as demagogues sin against their fellow-men by exaggerating the prerogatives of civil liberty, so do men commit crimes against God, by underrating the power and responsibility of moral liberty.

I admit that temperament, natural inclinations, and, above all, force of habit exert a strong influence over our moral actions:

"He that once sins, like him that slides on ice,
Goes swiftly down the slippery ways of vice;
Though conscience checks him, yet those rubs gone o'er,
He slides on smoothly, and looks backs no more."[2]

But this influence is never so dominant as to enslave the will, so long as reason maintains her empire.

[1] *King Lear*, Act I.
[2] *Juvenal, Sat.*, 13, Dryden's Translation.

Besides, as we voluntarily repeat the sins that produce the habit, we become responsible before God for the evil habit itself that we have contracted. But a generous and determined will can always overcome the most vicious temper and the most habitual vices. St. Augustin, Bishop of Hippo, had in his early life been addicted to the most licentious habits, and he continued in them from the age of eighteen till his thirty-second year. From the day of his conversion till the hour of his death, he was a model of austerity.

CHAPTER XII.

How to Exercise our Free-Will.

How sublime is the gift of free-will! It is a faculty that distinguishes us from the brute creation.[1] Man is the only earthly being that enjoys the prerogative of moral freedom. It is a faculty that we possess in common with the angels and that makes us like even to God Himself; for God and angels and men are the only beings that possess free-will.

What a potent instrument for good or for evil is this great gift! If rightly employed, it elevates us to the plane of angelic sanctity; if abused, it degrades us to the level of the demons. The angelic hosts are perpetually happy, because they made a righteous use of their free-will when it was put to the test. The demons are eternally miserable, owing to the perverse use of their will.

It is the exercise of the will that distinguishes the saint from the sinner, the martyr from the apostate, the hero from the coward, the benevolent ruler from the capricious tyrant. The names of Nero, of Diocle-

---

[1] *St. Thomas*, 1ª. Quaest. LXXXIII., 1.

tian, and of Robespierre are execrated by mankind, because of their depraved will. Those of Alfred the Great, Sir Thomas More, and St. Vincent de Paul are held in veneration by posterity, because they employed their will in promoting God's glory, the cause of truth, and the welfare of their fellow-beings.

And even so with us. If we are destined to be saved, we shall, under God, owe our salvation to the good use of our moral liberty. If we provoke the wrath of God, it is our own free-will that shall condemn us. Thy "destruction is thy own, O Israel!"[1] In a word, liberty is a sword with which, like Saul, we can destroy ourselves, by inflicting a deadly wound upon our soul, and ruin our prospects for eternity; or it is a sword with which, like the Archangel Michael, we can conquer the infernal enemy and fight our way to heaven.

> "Choose well, and your choice is
> Brief, but yet endless."[2]

How are we to employ our will? We should exercise our will, 1°. in shunning sin, in resisting temptations, in repressing our passions and vicious inclinations: 2°. we should exercise it in pursuing virtue; in embracing holiness; and, above all, by a perfect and unreserved conformity to the will of God.

[1] *Osee* XIII., 9.
[2] *Goethe.*

"As free," says the Apostle, "and not as making liberty a cloak for malice, but as servants of God,"[1] whom to serve is to reign. "Whosoever committeth sin, is the servant of sin."[2] "Know you not," says St. Paul, "that to whom ye yield yourselves as servants to obey, ye are servants of him, whom ye obey, whether it be sin unto death, or of obedience unto justice."[3] What a degradation to fall from the highest estate of free-born children of God, to become the slaves of Satan! What a degradation to cease to be an heir in our Father's house and to become, like the Prodigal Son, the hireling of a heartless master! "Man when he was in honor, did not understand; he is compared to senseless beasts and is become like to them."[4]

Contemplate Solomon while his heart is right with God. How sublime is his knowledge! how just his judgments! how exalted his sanctity! Who has ever excelled him in wisdom? The wisdom of Solomon has passed into a proverb. He has left us inspired writings, which are the delight and consolation of all succeeding generations.

Now look at Solomon when his will is enslaved by sensuality. See that towering oak bending like a frail reed before the siren breath of wanton females. He who once soared heavenward on the wings of prayer, is now wallowing in the mire of sin. The king that ruled a nation in righteousness, is now ruled by lascivious women. The godly prince who

[1] *I. Pet.* II., 16.
[2] *John* VIII., 34.
[3] *Rom.* VI., 16.
[4] *Ps.* XLVIII., 13.

was the first that ever erected a temple to the living God, is so degraded morally that he builds a temple to obscene divinities and worships them.[1]

Our Saviour told the Jews that the knowledge of His Gospel and the practice of its precepts would deliver them from bondage to true freedom: "You shall know the truth, and the truth shall make you free." The Jews replied to Him: "We are the seed of Abraham, and we have never been slaves to any man."[2] We are freemen. Jesus calmly answered them: "Amen, amen, I say to you: that whosoever committeth sin, is the servant of sin." Do not we sometimes boastingly say like the Jews: We bow to no despotic power; we are free American citizens?

But what will it profit us to enjoy the blessings of civil liberty, if we do not enjoy the glorious liberty of children of God, by which we are rescued from ignorance, and can trample on sin? What will it avail us to be recognized on the streets as free and independent citizens, and to exercise the right of suffrage by voting for the candidate of our choice, if in the circle of our own family or in the sanctuary of our own hearts, we are lashed as slaves by the Man of Sin; if we are slaves to anger and revenge, slaves to lust, intemperance, avarice, pride, and vain glory, slaves to the world, and to public opinion, the most capricious of all tyrants?

---

[1] *III. Kings* XI.
[2] *John* VIII., 33.

Who possessed greater liberty, Herod on his throne or John in his prison? Herod enjoyed civil liberty. His will was law to others. He had the power of life and death over his subjects. He could go whithersoever he chose, but his soul was bound in the chains of sin. John's body was confined in a dungeon, but his soul roamed in unrestrained freedom through the kingdom of God, which was within him.

What will it benefit us to enjoy even religious liberty, if we do not make a righteous and religious use of it? if by our abuse of it, it becomes an occasion of the loss of faith and virtue? No one appreciates more than I do the blessings of religious liberty that we possess in this country. No one would regret more than myself the loss of the religious toleration that here obtains. I am, however, persuaded that religious toleration involves some sacrifices.

An age of religious liberty is not one most fruitful in sturdy heroes of faith. It is not an age most favorable to the growth of a Judas Machabeus, a Cyprian, a Thomas of Canterbury, or a Sir Thomas More. In times of religious persecution, the will is on the alert to resist attacks. In times of religious freedom, the will is off its guard and is easily assailed.

Far better is it to endure the sword of open persecution than to drink the subtle and intoxicating poison of religious indifference, which paralyzes the energies of the will.

While the children of Israel were persecuted in Egypt, they remained faithful to God and steadfast in the practice of their religion; but when they breathed the free air of religious liberty in the desert, they fell into idolatry, and their piety melted away like the manna before the noonday sun.[1]

The Catholics of Ireland during the past three centuries, and those of Germany and Switzerland during the present century, suffered grievous persecutions for the faith with unbroken will and unshaken constancy. How many of their descendants have abandoned their religion in this country where they had nothing to dread from confiscations or fines, or imprisonments or pursuivants or other instruments of religious intolerance.

Where is the religion that once flourished in Northern Africa, in Syria, and in other parts of Asia? Where is the Christianity that once bloomed in Antioch and Alexandria, in Carthage and Constantinople, in Ephesus and Jerusalem? Where is the tree of life that sent its delicious fragrance from the sees of Athanasius and Augustin, of Basil and Chrysostom and Cyprian? That tree has withered and decayed, and its seed has been wafted to other lands more worthy of possessing it; and in its stead is found the Upas tree of Mohammedanism poisoning the atmosphere with its deadly odor. Truly can we say of the once flourishing faith in those countries: "I have seen it exalted and lifted up

---

[1] *Exod.* XXXII.

like the cedars of Libanus. And I passed by, and lo! it was not; and I sought it, and its place was not found."

By what methods was Christianity supplanted by Islamism in those countries? The sword of persecution and the internal dissensions of the Christians themselves were, indeed, powerful factors in the extirpation of Christianity. But I venture to say that the chief cause may be ascribed to the degenerate character of those Eastern Christians. Their will was led captive by the sensual religion of Mohammedanism, which pandered to their animal appetites in this life, and held out to them the promise of voluptuous enjoyment in the life to come.

Had they displayed the determined resistance which has marked their fellow-religionists in Ireland and parts of Germany and Switzerland, they would have been robbed, indeed, of their civil and religious liberty; but their moral freedom and faith, they never would have surrendered.

A man may enjoy not only political and religious liberty, but even supreme dominion over an empire; he may dictate laws to millions, and yet be the most abject slave in the whole realm.

Nothing could surpass the magnificent ovation which Cæsar received in Rome after the series of victories he had achieved. He triumphed successively in Gaul, in Pontus, in Alexandria, and Numidia. The city is filled with strangers to welcome him. A festival of forty days and a four days' triumph are decreed in his honor. He brings with him from the conquered provinces money to the value of twenty-four millions of dollars, and about three thousand golden crowns of immense value.

Cæsar appears in the triumphal march preceded by seventy-two lictors and seated on a chariot drawn by four white horses, that he might have some equality to Jupiter. The entire Forum, the *Via Sacra*, from his own house to the steps of the Capitol are draped with costly silk. His royal prisoners follow him, the famous Gaulish chieftain, Vercingetorix; the Egyptian Queen Arsinoe, sister of Cleopatra; and the son of Juba, King of Numidia. The cities that he has captured, the fifty battles that he has won, are represented in precious wood, in tortoise-shell and ivory.

And yet Cæsar was not free. He was a slave to the exulting shouts of the populace and the soldiery, whom he sought to conciliate by bribes and presents. He was captivated by the glittering crown that his ambition conjured up before him. He was not satisfied with the enormous treasures he had acquired by war, the triumphal honors, and the acclamations of the multitude, so long as the imperial crown was wanting! And whilst seated in repose on the triumphal car, his restless spirit, impelled by the demon of ambition, was rushing headlong to destruction.

Some years later, another hero is conducted to Rome. He is led to the imperial city not amid the acclamations of the people, but laden with chains and exposed to the insults of a brutal soldiery. He enters not in triumph, but as a prisoner sentenced to death. He sees before him not an earthly crown, but the crown of martyrdom. And yet Ignatius is more independent than Cæsar. He rises superior to chains and imprisonment, superior to contempt and humiliations, superior to exile and even to death itself. Cæsar conquered the world. Ignatius conquered himself. "The patient man is better than the valiant: and he that ruleth his spirit than he that taketh cities."[1]

We should exercise our will not only by fleeing from sin, but also by pursuing virtue, and particularly by an entire conformity to the will of God. We should study and "prove what is the good and the acceptable and the perfect will of God."[2]

The perfection of sanctity consists in the love of God; for "Love," says the Apostle, "is the fulfilling of the law." And the perfection of the love of God consists in absolute conformity with His holy will. Union of heart, of sentiment, and of will is the closest bond that can subsist between the soul and its Creator.

Jesus Christ, the Son of God, is the highest ideal of Christian perfection. He is "the way, the truth, and the life." He is the great Model of every virtue. He came to teach us, both by word and

[1] *Prov.* XVI., 32.
[2] *Rom.* XII., 2.

example, the way of righteousness. Now, if there is one virtue that our Saviour inculcates more forcibly than another, it is this: that our heart and will should be in perfect harmony with the will of God. "I came down from heaven," He says, "not to do My own will, but the will of Him that sent Me."[1] "My food is to do the will of Him that sent Me, that I may finish His work."[2] He became subject to the creatures of His own hands, to Mary and Joseph, because He regarded them as His Father's representatives.[3] In His agony in the garden of Gethsemani, He thus prayed to His Father: "My Father, if it be possible, let this chalice pass from Me. Nevertheless not as I will, but as Thou."[4] Every fibre of His sensitive Heart recoiled with terror from the appalling sufferings that awaited Him. But though His feelings revolted, His will remained steadfast, and, after praying again to be relieved, again He added: "If I must drink the chalice, Thy will be done!"

What He practises, He preaches to us. He tells us that, though we prophesy and work miracles in His name, though we convert nations, He will know us not, if our heart is estranged from God. "Not every one that saith to me, Lord, Lord, shall enter into the kingdom of heaven; but he that doeth the will of My Father who is in heaven he shall enter into the kingdom of heaven."[5] He tells us that the

---

[1] *John* VI., 38.
[2] *Ibid.* IV., 34.
[3] *Luke* II., 51.
[4] *Matt.* XXVI., 39.
[5] *Ibid.* VII., 21.

harmony of our will with the will of God, is the key that will unlock the golden gate of the Heavenly Jerusalem, and admit us to the fellowship of the children of God. "Whosoever shall do the will of My Father who is in heaven, he is my brother, and sister, and mother."[1] And in that beautiful prayer which He dictated to His disciples, He bids them ask that they may accomplish the will of God on earth as the blessed do in heaven: "Thy will be done on earth as it is in heaven."[2]

When the Son of God commands us to make the will of God the supreme rule of our actions, He is echoing the voice of His eternal Father: "My son," says God, "give Me thy heart."[3] He does not say: My son, give Me thy riches, thy lands and thy possessions; for these belong to Him already. "The earth is the Lord's and the fulness thereof, the world, and all they that dwell therein."[4] He does not say: My son, give Me thy bodily service, for that also belongs to Him. "Thy hands have made me and formed me."[5] And besides, we readily bestow the service of our brain and hands on one who has already gained our affections. But he says: "Give Me thy heart and the affections of thy will," for this is all that you can call your own; this is the only free, unmortgaged property you can offer Him.

But is it not degrading to our manhood to sur-

---

[1] *Matt.* XII., 50.
[2] *Matt.* VI., 10.
[3] *Prov.* XXIII., 26.
[4] *Ps.* XXIII., 1.
[5] *Ps.* CXVIII.

render our will to any one, even to God Himself? So far from being degrading, there is no act more noble, none more rational, none more in accordance with the higher aspirations of our nature, than a cheerful submission to the will of God. Who are comparable to the angels in dignity? And yet they are unceasingly doing the will of God. "Bless the Lord," says the Psalmist, "all ye His angels: you that are mighty in strength, and execute His word, hearkening to the voice of His orders. Bless the Lord, all ye His hosts, ye His ministers that do His will."[1]

Let us suppose that a Mozart, or a Beethoven, or a Palestrina had the happiness of listening to the heavenly Anthem chanted by the angelic choir on Christmas morning over the Stable of Bethlehem, would it be degrading to those men to employ their musical talents in setting those strains to music? Or if Raphael or Michel Angelo were favored with a vision of the Blessed Mother of our Lord, would it be degrading in them to labor night and day in trying to reproduce on canvass a true copy of the beautiful original? Assuredly not. They could not have consecrated their talents to a higher purpose. And what more sublime use can we make of our will than to attune it to the will of God, and to shape our affections after the Divine Model?

Just as we ennoble our intellect by rejecting falsehood and seizing upon truth, so do we ennoble

[1] *Ibid.*, CII.

our will by combating sin and embracing sanctity.
Now, the will of God is the highest standard of
perfection. But do we not sacrifice our happiness
by surrendering our will to the good pleasure of
God? Quite the contrary. Do not imagine that
they are happy and contented who have their own
way from January till December, who follow their
own inclinations, who are governed by no law but
their caprices and passions. Such persons are the
most wretched and miserable on the face of the
earth. They are continually concocting new schemes
to promote their pleasure, or to advance their interests;
and they are pining and fretting over the result.
They bend all the energies of their will to
realize the object of their desires. They even pray
for a successful issue, though not as our Lord
prayed. They do not say: Not my will but Thine
be done!—but they say: Not Thy will, O Lord, but
mine be done! They will not submit to God. They
want God to submit to them. His providence must
be shaped to their humor. They are like children
intent on making a card house. When their work
is nearly completed, a breath of wind comes and
down the house tumbles. And even so are the
plans of those who follow their own will, frustrated
by the breath of a righteous God:

> "The best laid schemes o' mice an' men,
>   Gang aft a-gley,
> And lea's us nought but grief and pain,
>   For promised joy."[1]

[1] Burns, *To a Mouse.*

They resisted God, and God resists them. "And who hath resisted Him and hath had peace?"[1] "The wicked are like the raging sea which cannot rest, and the waves thereof cast up dirt and mire. There is no peace for the wicked, saith the Lord God."[2]

If there is peace on earth, it is possessed by the man of good will. If we would see a happy and contented person, let us look on the face of a devoted religious who has consecrated her will to God on the altar of obedience, who has taken the Lord for the portion of her inheritance. The light that beams on her face is the reflection of the divine fire that glows in her heart. And strange as the statement may sound, it is yet strictly true that though she has renounced her will, her wishes are always accomplished. And why? Because she has so identified God's will with her own that His desires are her desires, His decrees are her laws. Now, she knows that everything that happens to her, is ordained or permitted by God for her own advantage; therefore she hails every event not only with composure, but with good will and serene satisfaction.

Although God does not communicate with us directly and by special revelation, as He did to the Prophets of old; yet He makes known His mind to us in a clear and positive manner. Dives, in the Parable, thus entreats Abraham: Father, I beseech thee to send Lazarus back to the earth, "to my father's house, for I have five brethren, that he may

[1] *Job* IX., 4.
[2] *Isaiah* LVII., 20, 21.

testify unto them lest they also come into this place of torments. And Abraham said to him: They have Moses and the prophets;" they are all-sufficient. God manifests His will to us by the precepts and counsels contained in Holy Scripture, and particularly in the Gospel of His Son, of whom He says: "This is My beloved Son in whom I am well pleased: hear ye Him."[1] We should study these Gospels, we should meditate on them. God reveals His will to us by the voice of His Church and her ministers, of whom our Lord says: "He that heareth you, heareth Me."[2] We should listen with docility to the voice of those ministers. He declares His will to us by the voice of conscience, which informs us of our duty in every detail of life. Let us hearken to this interior monitor. God manifests His will to us, likewise, by the visitations of His providence.

"Blessed is the man whose delight is in the law of the Lord."[3] Blessed is he who, in every vicissitude and accident of life, preserves in his heart an unalterable adhesion to God's will through honor and dishonor, through evil report and good report, in sickness and in health, in riches and in poverty, in prosperity and adversity, in joy and sorrow, and who sees the loving hand of God and hears His paternal voice through the dense cloud of tribulation that envelops him. Happy, indeed, is he that has this short, but comprehensive prayer often in his

[1] *Matt.* XVII., 5.   [3] *Ps.* I.; 2.
[2] *Luke* X., 16.

heart and on his lips: "Thy will, O Lord, be done!" Thrice happy are they that can say with the confidence of the Apostle: "Who shall separate us from the charity of Christ," and a loyal adhesion to His will? "Shall tribulation, or distress, or famine, or nakedness, or danger, or persecution, or the sword? . . . I am sure that neither death, nor life, nor angels, nor principalities, nor powers, nor things present, nor things to come, nor might, nor height, nor depth, nor any other creature shall be able to separate us from the charity of God"[1] and an abiding conformity to His will.

Whoever are animated by these sentiments are free, indeed. In all their movements they are guided by the Spirit of God. "And where the Spirit of the Lord is, there is liberty."[2] Then, indeed, they may truly be called the children of God. "For whosoever are led by the Spirit of God, they are the sons of God."[3] Then they experience a foretaste of that happy condition and that unalterable peace promised in the life to come— when they "shall be delivered from the bondage of corruption into the glorious liberty of the children of God."[4]

Yes, thanks to God, true liberty will exist in heaven with the power to sin eradicated. In this respect it will differ from liberty in the present life, which involves an unfortunate ability to do wrong. This idea is so well expressed by St. Augustin that

[1] *Rom.* VIII., 35-39.
[2] *II. Cor.* III., 17.
[3] *Rom.* VIII., 14.
[4] *Ibid.*, ver. 21.

I shall conclude with his words: "We are not to suppose that, because sin will have no power to delight them (the blessed in the City of God) free-will must be withdrawn. It will, on the contrary, be all the more truly free, because set free from delight in sinning, to take unfailing delight in not sinning. For the first freedom of will which man received when he was created upright, consisted in an ability not to sin; whereas his last freedom of will shall be superior, inasmuch as it shall not be able to sin. . . . And in this divine gift there was to be observed this gradation, that man should first receive a free-will by which he was able not to sin, and at last a free-will by which he was not able to sin,—the former being adapted to a state of probation, the latter to a state of reward. . . . For as the first immortality which Adam lost by sinning, consisted in his being able not to die, while the last shall consist in his not being able to die; so the first free-will consisted in his being able not to sin, the last in his not being able to sin. And thus, piety and justice shall be as indefeasible as happiness. . . . Are we to say that God Himself is not free because He cannot sin?

"In that city, then, there shall be free-will, one in all the citizens, and indivisible in each, delivered from all ill, filled with all good, enjoying indefeasibly the delights of eternal joys, oblivious of sins, oblivious of sufferings, and yet not so oblivious of its deliverance as to be ungrateful to its Deliverer."[1]

[1] *De Civitate Dei*, Lib. XXII.

CHAPTER XIII.

THE IMMORTALITY OF THE SOUL.

There is but one Being that is absolutely[1] immortal, One alone that is everlasting, that has no beginning, that will have no end—and that Being is God. "In the beginning, O Lord," says the Psalmist, "Thou foundedst the earth, and the heavens are the works of Thy hands. They shall perish, but Thou remainest, and all of them shall grow old like a garment: and as a vesture Thou shalt change them, and they shall be changed. But Thou art always the self-same, and Thy years shall not fail."[2] "I am alpha and omega, the beginning and the end, saith the Lord God, who is, and who was, and who is to come, the Almighty."[3]

Go back in spirit to the twilight of time. Contemplate the early dawn of creation before this earth assumed its present form, when all was chaos. Even then God was in the fulness of life, "and the Spirit of God moved over the waters."[4]

Look forward through the vista of ages to come,

[1] *I. Tim.* VI., 16.
[2] *Ps.* CI.
[3] *Rev.* I., 8.
[4] *Gen.* I., 2.

when the heavens and the earth shall have passed away, even then God will live. He will survive this universal wreck of matter.

Let us now look at man. What a strange contrast is presented by his physical and spiritual natures! What a mysterious compound of corruption and incorruption, of ignominy and glory, of weakness and strength, of matter and mind! He has a body that must be nourished twice or thrice a day, else it will grow faint and languid. It is subject to infirmities and sickness and disease, and it must finally yield to the inevitable law of death.

What is each one of us, but a vapor that rises and melts away, a shadow that suddenly vanishes! A hundred years ago, we had no existence; a hundred years hence, we shall probably be forgotten.

Let us now contemplate man's spiritual nature. In a mortal body, he carries an immortal soul. In this perishable mass, resides an imperishable spirit. Within this frail, tottering temple, shines a light that will always burn, that will never be extinguished. As to the past, we are finite; as to the future, we are infinite in duration. As to the past, we are creatures of yesterday; as to the future, we are everlasting. When this house of clay will have crumbled to dust, when this earth shall have passed away, when the sun and stars shall grow dim with years, even then our soul will live and think, remember and love; for God breathed into us a living spirit, and that spirit, like Himself, is clothed with immortality.

The soul is the principle by which we live and move and have our being. It is that which forms and perpetuates our identity; for it makes us to be the same yesterday, to-day, and forever. The soul has intellectual conceptions and operations of reason and judgment independent of material organs. Our own experience clearly teaches us this important point. Our mind grasps what the senses cannot reach. We think of God and of His attributes, we have thoughts of justice and of truth, we perceive mentally the connection existing between premises and conclusions, we know the difference between good and evil. Such a principle being independent of matter in its operations, must needs be independent of matter also in its being. It is, therefore, of its nature, subject to no corruption resulting from matter. Its life, which is its being, is not extinguished and cannot be extinguished with that of the body.

It is well known that there is a constant waste going on in every part of the human body which has to be renovated by daily nutriment. So steady is this exhaustion that in the judgment of medical science an entire transformation of the physical system occurs every six or eight years. New flesh and bones and tissues are substituted for those you had before. The hand with which you write, the brain which you exercise in thinking are composed of entirely different materials. And yet you comprehend to-day what you learned ten years ago, you remember and love those with whom you were then associated. How is this? You no longer use the identical organic substance you then possessed. Does it not prove that the faculty, called the soul, by which you think, remember and love is distinct from organic matter, that while the body is constantly changing, the soul remains the same, that it does not share in the process of decomposition and renewal through which the human frame is passing and therefore that it is a spiritual substance?

All nations, moreover, both ancient and modern, whether professing the true or a false religion, have believed in the immortality of the soul, how much soever they may have differed as to the nature of future rewards and punishments, or the mode of future existence.

Such was the faith of the people of ancient Greece and Rome, as we learn from the writings of Homer, Virgil, and Ovid, who picture the blessed in the next world as dwelling in the Elysian fields, and consign the wicked to Tartarus and Hades.

This belief in a future life was not confined to the uncultivated masses; it was taught by the most eminent writers and philosophers of those polished nations. Socrates, Plato, Aristotle, Cicero, Seneca, Plutarch, and other sages of Pagan antiquity, guided only by the light of reason, proclaimed their belief in the soul's immortality. "Nor do I agree," says Cicero, "with those that have *lately* begun to advance this opinion, that the soul dies together with the body, and that all things are annihilated by death. The authority of the ancients has more weight with me: either that of our own ancestors who paid such sacred honors to the dead, which surely they would not have done, if they thought those honors in no way affected them; or that of those who once lived in this country and enlightened by their institutions and instructions Magna Græcia (which now, indeed, is destroyed, but then was flourishing); or of him who was pronounced by the oracle of Apollo to be the wisest of men, who did not express first one opinion and then another, as in most questions, but always maintained the same, namely, that the souls of men are divine, and that when they have departed from the body, a return to heaven is opened to them, most speedy in proportion as each has been most virtuous and just."[1]

These eloquent words convey the sentiments not only of Cicero himself, but also of great sages of Greece and Rome.

"This belief which we hold" (in the immortality of the soul), says Plutarch, "is so old that we cannot trace its author or its origin, and it dates back to the most remote antiquity."[2]

The same views were held by the ancient Egyptians, the Chaldeans, and Persians, indeed by all the nations of Asia whose history has come down to us, and by the Germans, Gauls, Britons, and other ancient tribes of Europe.[3] If we question

---

[1] *De Amicitia*, Chap. IV.
[2] *De Consol. ad Apollonium.*
[3] See Grotius, *De Verit. Relig. Christi*, L. I., § 22.

the Indian of North or South America on this point, he will tell us of the happy hunting-grounds reserved in after life for the brave.

We may find nations without cities, without the arts and sciences, without mechanical inventions, or any of the refinements of civilized life; but a nation without some presentiment of the existence of a future state, we shall search for in vain.

Even idolatry itself involved an implied recognition of the immortality of the soul; for how could men pay divine honors to departed heroes, whom they worshipped as gods, if they believed that death is the end of man's existence?

We may, indeed, find a man here and there who pretends to deny the existence of a future state. But like the fool that says in his heart, "There is no God," this man's "wish is father to his thought;" for if there is in the life to come a place of retribution, he feels that it will be so much the worse for him. Or even should we encounter one who really has no faith in a future life, we should have no more right to take him as a type of our intellectual and moral nature than to take the Siamese twins as types of our physical organization. The exception always proves the rule.

Now, whence comes this universal belief in man's immortality? Not from prejudice arising from education; for we shall find this conviction prevailing among rude people who have no education whatever, among hostile tribes, and among nations at the opposite poles of the earth and who have never had intercourse with one another.

We must, therefore, conclude that a sentiment so general and deep-rooted must have been planted in the human breast by Almighty God, just as He has implanted in us an instinctive love for truth and justice, and an inveterate abhorrence of falsehood and injustice.

Not only has mankind a firm belief in the immortality of the soul, but there is inborn in every human breast a desire for perfect felicity. This desire is so strong in man that it is the mainspring of all his actions, the engine that keeps in motion the machinery of society. Even when he commits acts that lead him to misery, he does so under the mistaken notion, that he is consulting his own happiness.

Now God would never have planted in the human heart this craving after perfect felicity, unless He had intended that the desire should be fully gratified; for He never designed that man should be the sport of vain and barren hopes. He never creates any thing in vain; but He would have created something to no purpose if He had given us the thirst for perfect bliss without imparting to us the means of assuaging it. As He has given us bodily eyes to view and enjoy the objects of nature around us, so has He given us an interior perspective of immortal bliss, that we may yearn for it now and enjoy it hereafter.

It is clear that this desire for perfect happiness never is and never can be fully realized in the present life.

Let us take up one by one the various sources of human enjoyment. Can earthly goods adequately satisfy the cravings of the human heart and fill up the measure of its desires? Experience proves the contrary. One might have the wealth of Croesus of old, or of Vanderbilt in our own times, and yet his happiness would be far from complete; for he would still be oppressed by the desire for greater riches, or haunted by the fear of losing what he has acquired, or of being torn from it by death. "O death, how bitter is the remembrance of thee to a man that has peace in his possessions?"[1]

Can honors fully gratify the aspirations of the soul? No. For though the highest dignities were lavished upon a man still, like Aman, the minister of King Assuerus, he would be discontented so long as there was in the Republic one that refused to bend the knee to him. And if he sat upon the most exalted throne on earth and were ruler of kingdoms, he would, like Alexander the Great, sigh for other empires that he might conquer them. Honors bring corresponding cares. The more brilliant and precious the crown, the more heavily it presses on the brow that wears it.

I have seen and contemplated two of the greatest rulers on the face of the earth,—the civil ruler of sixty-five millions and the spiritual ruler of two hundred and fifty millions of people. I have conversed with the President and the Pope in their

---
[1] *Eccles.* XLI., 1.

private apartments; and I am convinced that their exalted position, far from satisfying the aspirations of their soul, did but fill them with a profound sense of their grave responsibility.

Can earthly pleasures make one so happy as to leave nothing to be desired? Assuredly not. They that indulge in sensual gratifications are forced to acknowledge that the deeper they plunge into them, the more they are enslaved and the less they are satiated by them. The keen edge of delight soon becomes blunted.

No one is better qualified than Solomon to express from experience an opinion on the power of the pleasures of sense to promote human happiness. Every creature ministered to his personal gratification, he yielded to every excess, he denied himself nothing that his heart desired; and, as the fruit of all this, he declared that he was weary of life, and that all was vanity and vexation of spirit.[1]

We find great comfort in this life in the society of loving friends and relatives. But how frail is the thread that binds friends and kindred together! The bond *may* be broken by treachery; it *must* be broken by death. This thought haunts like a spectre, and casts its dark shadow over the social and family circle.

Another source of exquisite delight is found in the pursuit of knowledge. And this pleasure is more pure, more solid, and more lasting than sensual

---

[1] *Eccles.* II., 17.

gratifications, because it is rational. Pythagoras was so ravished by the solution of a mathematical problem that he offered to the gods a holocaust in thanksgiving. So deeply was Archimedes absorbed in working out another problem, that he forgot to eat and drink; and when he had made the wished-for discovery, he ran through the streets of Syracuse, crying out: "Eureka! Eureka! I have found it! I have found it!" But the acquisition of knowledge, though attended with great labor, far from satisfying our desires, only sharpens our appetite for more information, and makes us more conscious of our ignorance. The higher we ascend the mount of knowledge, the broader becomes our view of the vast fields of science that still remain uncultivated by us.

Sir Isaac Newton when dying uttered these remarkable words: "I know not what the world will think of my labors; but, as for myself, I feel like a little child amusing itself on the sea-shore, finding here a smooth pebble, and there a brilliant shell, while the great ocean of truth lies unexplored before me." Oh, if Newton was himself made so happy and contributed so much to the delight of others by his discoveries, what must be the bliss of those that, for all eternity, will explore without toil the boundless ocean of Divine Truth!

But the greatest consolation attainable in this life is found in the pursuit and practice of virtue. And if there is any tranquillity of mind, any delight of soul, any joy of spirit, any pure consolation of heart, any interior sunshine, it is shared by those that are zealous in the fulfilment of God's law, that have preserved their innocence from youth, or have regained it by sincere repentance. But this consolation arises from the well-founded hope of future bliss rather than from the actual fulfilment of our desires. The virtuous are happy because they have "a promise to pay," and not because they have received the actual payment of the debt of Divine Justice. They rejoice because, though in exile during this short night of time, they hope to dwell in their true country during the great eternity of to-morrow. They rejoice because they are heirs apparent of God's kingdom. Take from them this hope, and the sunshine in their heart will soon be changed to gloom. "If in this life only we be hoping in Christ, we are more miserable than all men."[1] Why was St. Paul so cheerful in his dungeon in Rome on the eve of his execution? Because, as he tells us, "a crown of justice is laid up for me, which the Lord, the just Judge, will render to me on that day."[2]

Thus we see that neither riches, nor honors, nor pleasures, nor knowledge, nor the endearments of social and family ties, nor the pursuit of virtue, can fully satisfy our aspirations after happiness. Combine all these pleasures as far as they are susceptible of combination. Let each of their sources be augmented a thousand-fold. Let all these inten-

---

[1] *I. Cor.* XV., 19.
[2] *II. Tim.* IV., 8.

sified gratifications be concentrated on one man, let him have the undoubted assurance of enjoying them for a thousand years, yet will he be forced to exclaim: "Vanity of vanities, and all is vanity!" The more delicious the cup, the more bitter the thought that death will dash it to pieces.

Now, if God has given us a desire for perfect felicity, which He intends to be one day fully gratified; and if this felicity, as we have seen, cannot be found in the present life, it must be reserved for the time to come. And as no intelligent being can be contented with any happiness that is finite in duration, we must conclude that it will be eternal and that, consequently, the soul is immortal. Life that is not to be crowned with immortality, is not worth living. "If a life of happiness," says Cicero, "is destined to end, it cannot be called a happy life. . . . Take away eternity, and Jupiter is not better off than Epicurus."[1]

Without the hope of immortality, the condition of man is less desirable than that of the beast of the field.

> "Or own the soul immortal, or invert
> All order. Go, mock majesty! go, man!
> And bow to thy superiors of the stall:
> Through ev'ry scene of sense superior far:
> They graze the turf untill'd; they drink the stream
> Unbrew'd and ever full, and unembittered
> With doubts, fears, fruitless hopes, regrets, despairs."[2]

[1] *De Finibus*, Lib. II., XXVII.
[2] Young's *Night Thoughts*.

We may well exclaim with Augustin: "Thou hast made us, O Lord, for Thyself, and our hearts are restless till they rest in Thee."

> "Hope springs eternal in the human breast:
> Man never Is, but always To be blest:
> The soul uneasy and confined from home,
> Rests and expatiates in a life to come."[1]

Addison clearly portrays the philosophical mind of Cato in the following lines, which are as commendable for sublimity of expression as for depth of reasoning:—

> "It must be so. Plato, thou reason'st well!
> Else whence this pleasing hope, this fond desire,
> This longing after immortality?
> Or whence this secret dread and inward horror
> Of falling into nought? Why shrinks the soul
> Back on herself and startles at destruction?
> 'Tis the Divinity that stirs within us;
> 'Tis heaven itself that points out an hereafter,
> And intimates eternity to man.
> Eternity! thou pleasing, dreadful thought!
> Through what variety of untried being,
> Through what new scenes and changes must we pass!
> The wide, the unbounded prospect lies before me;
> But shadows, clouds, and darkness rest upon it.
> Here will I hold. If there's a power above us,
> (And that there is, all nature cries aloud
> Through all her works) he must delight in virtue;
> And that which he delights in, must be happy.
> * * * * * * * * *
> The soul secure in her existence, smiles
> At the drawn dagger, and defies its point.
> The stars shall fade away, the sun himself

[1] Pope's *Essay on Man*.

Grow dim with age, and nature sink in years.
But thou shalt flourish in immortal youth,
Unhurt amidst the war of elements,
The wreck of matter and the crush of worlds."[1]

But if our unaided reason assures us that our soul will live beyond the grave, how much more clearly and luminously is this great truth brought home to us by the light of Revelation; for the light of reason is but as the dim twilight compared with the noonday sun of Revelation. How consoling is the thought that the word of God comes to justify and sanction our fondest desires and aspirations for a future life!

"The souls of the just," says the Book of Wisdom, "are in the hand of God, and the torment of death shall not touch them. In the sight of the unwise they seemed to die, and their departure was taken for misery. . . . But they are in peace, and their hope is full of immortality."[2]

Man may imprison and starve, may wound and kill the body; but the soul is beyond his reach, and is as impalpable to his touch as the sun's ray. The temple of the body may be reduced to ashes, but the spirit that animated the temple cannot be extinguished. The body, which is from man, man may take away; but the soul, which is from God, no man can destroy. "The dust shall return into its earth from whence it was, and the spirit to God who gave it."[3] "For we know that if our

---

[1] Addison's *Cato*, Act V. [2] *Eccles.* XII., 7.
[3] *Wisdom* III., 1–4.

earthly house of this dwelling be destroyed, we have a building from God, a house not built with hands, everlasting in the heavens."[1]

The Scripture also declares that the blessed shall be rewarded with never-ending happiness, exempt from all pain and misery: "God shall wipe away all tears from their eyes; and death shall be no more, nor mourning, nor wailing, nor sorrow shall be any more, for the former things are passed away."[2]

The beatitude of the righteous will essentially consist in the vision and fruition of God: "Blessed are the clean of heart, for they shall see God."[3] "We know that when He shall be manifested, we shall be like Him, because we shall see Him as He is."[4]

We can form no adequate idea of the felicity of the Saints, for as the Apostle tells us, it is beyond the reach of human experience, as it is above the power of human conception: "Eye hath not seen, nor ear heard, neither hath it entered into the heart of man what things God hath prepared for those who love Him."[5] As well might one born blind attempt to picture to himself the beauty of the landscape, as for the eye of the soul to contemplate the supernal bliss that awaits the righteous in what is beautifully called "the land of the living."

[1] *II. Cor. V., 1.*
[2] *Rev. XXI.*
[3] *Matt. V.*
[4] *I. John III.*
[5] *I. Cor. II.*

Not only shall the soul possess eternal rest, but the body, companion of its earthly pilgrimage, shall rise again to share in its immortal bliss. Fifteen hundred years before Christ, Job clearly predicts the future Resurrection of the dead as he gazes with prophetic eye on the Redeemer to come: "I know," he says, "that my Redeemer liveth, and in the last day, I shall rise out of the earth, and I shall be clothed again with my skin, and in my flesh I shall see my God."[1] And the prophecy of the Patriarch is amply confirmed by our Redeemer Himself: "All who are in the graves shall hear the voice of the Son of God, and they who have done good, shall come forth unto the Resurrection of life."[2]

"The body," says St. Paul, "is sown in corruption, it shall rise in incorruption; it is sown in dishonor, it shall rise in glory; it is sown in weakness, it shall rise in power; it is sown a natural body, it shall rise a spiritual body. . . . For this corruptible shall put on incorruption: and this mortal shall put on immortality. But when this mortal shall have put on immortality, then shall be brought to pass the saying which is written: Death is swallowed up in victory."[3]

Whether our immortality will be happy or miserable, rests with ourselves. It rests with ourselves whether we shall be, as the Apostle Jude expresses it, "wandering stars for whom the storm of dark-

---
[1] *Job* XIX.   [3] *I. Cor.* XV.
[2] *John* V.

ness is reserved forever;"[1] or whether we are destined to be bright stars shining forever in the empyrean of heaven, reflecting the unfading glory of the Sun of Justice. O let us not barter an eternal happiness for a fleeting pleasure! Let us strive by a good life to obtain a blissful immortality. "What things a man shall sow, those also shall he reap. For he that soweth in his flesh, of the flesh also shall reap corruption. But he that soweth in the Spirit, of the Spirit also shall reap life everlasting."[2]

When Sir Thomas More was imprisoned in the Tower of London by Henry VIII. for refusing to take an oath that would sully his conscience, he was visited by his wife, who thus bluntly saluted him: "Why, Mr. More, I marvel much that you who have hitherto been taken for a wise man, will now so play the fool as to lie here in this close, filthy prison, shut up with mice and rats, when you might be abroad at your liberty enjoying the favor of the king and council. You might dwell in peace in your fair house at Chelsea with your library, gallery, and garden, and be merry in company with me, your good wife, your children and household."

"Why, good Alice," said he with a winning smile, "is not this prison as near heaven as my own house?"

[1] *Jude* I.
[2] *Gal.* VI, 8.

"Oh! tilly vally! tilly vally!" she replied with a sneer of contempt.

"Nay, then, Alice," More continued, "how long, think you, one might live to enjoy this house of ours?"

"Perhaps some twenty years."

"Well, now, my good Alice, he were a very bad calculator that, for a hundred or a thousand years, would risk the loss of an eternity."[1]

---

[1] Walter's *Life of Sir Thomas More*, ch. VIII.

CHAPTER XIV.

THE ETERNAL EXCLUSION OF THE REPROBATE FROM HEAVEN NOT INCOMPATIBLE WITH DIVINE JUSTICE AND MERCY.

No article of the Christian creed has been so vehemently assailed as the doctrine of Eternal Punishment. It is denounced even by some professing Christians, as unjust and cruel, and in conflict with our ideas of divine clemency.

That Revelation proclaims the eternal exclusion of the reprobate from the kingdom of heaven, cannot be reasonably questioned, and, therefore, we need not dwell at any length on the subject from a Scriptural point of view.

Our Saviour, contrasting the future retribution of the righteous and of the wicked, says: "These shall go into everlasting punishment, but the just into life everlasting."[1] The duration of punishment and of bliss is declared to be the same. Now, as the eternity of happiness is admitted, so too must the eternity of misery. St. Paul says: "The works of the flesh are manifest, which are fornication, . . .

---

[1] *Matt.* XXV., 46.

murders, drunkenness, and such like, of which I foretell you as I have before said, that they who do such things, shall not obtain the kingdom of God."[1]

My chief aim in the present chapter, is to demonstrate that this doctrine is not incompatible with right reason, or with our ideas of God's justice and clemency.

I might bring forward the following argument commonly urged by divines in vindication of this truth: That penalty, they say, is just which is in proportion to the malice or moral deformity of the offence. But everlasting punishment is in proportion to the malice or moral deformity of sin, which is an offence against God; therefore, the penalty of everlasting punishment is just. The malice of any offence depends chiefly on the dignity of the person offended, and on the special relations that exist between the offender and the offended. So that the greater the dignity of the person offended and the more sacred the duties violated, the greater is the malice of the offence.

Now, the dignity of God, whom man offends by sin, is infinite and the duties that man violates by offending God are the most sacred. They conclude, therefore, that the malice or moral deformity of sin is the greatest that can be conceived; and that consequently, it justly deserves the greatest of all punishments.

As this reasoning, however, may not seem con-

[1] *Gal.* V., 19-21.

vincing to the general reader, I shall pass it over, and content myself with another argument, which I think ought to commend itself to every impartial mind.

The Scriptures declare that nothing defiled shall enter the kingdom of heaven,[1] and that only the clean of heart shall ascend to the mount of the Lord and stand in His holy place.[2] This truth of Revelation is at once approved by our reason: for our conception of the sanctity of God and of His eternal dwelling-place, demands that the citizens of His kingdom should be exempt from moral defilement; that the sinner should be excluded from heaven as long as his defilement remains; and that consequently, should he abide in an eternal habit of sin, he ought to be for ever excluded from the kingdom of heaven.

Let us represent to ourselves a man whose life is given up to the gratification of his sensual desires, "whose god is his belly," whose imagination revels in scenes of debauchery, whose heart is estranged from God and His law. Suppose he dies in one of these orgies; surely, you will admit that in the swift transition from time to eternity, he does not pass through a purifying ordeal to fit him for the kingdom of heaven. The sleep of death does not alter the dispositions of his heart; for just as we are assured that the blessed will bear to the future life, the elevation of soul, the love of God,

---

[1] *Rev.* XXI.
[2] *Ps.* XXIII., 3.

and the aspirations for the good, the beautiful and the true that animated them in their dying moments, so shall the slave of lust awake in eternity encumbered with the passions of an ill-spent life:

"Coelum, non animum mutant, qui trans mare currunt."

Even as they who cross the sea, may change the clime, but not their disposition; so in crossing the sea of life, the sensual man lands on the shores of eternity in the same frame of mind that he had in this world.

Repentance alone can now reconcile him to God. But what is repentance? It does not mean every kind of sorrow. Repentance and sorrow are not convertible terms. Repentance always involves sorrow; but sorrow does not always imply repentance. True repentance does not mean the envious regrets of the wicked who "shall be troubled with great fear, and shall be amazed at the suddenness of the salvation" of the righteous, "saying within themselves, repining and groaning for anguish of spirit: These are they whom we had sometime in derision, and for a parable of reproach. We fools esteemed their life madness, and their end without honor. Behold how they are numbered among the children of God, and their lot is among the saints. Therefore we have erred from the way of truth, and the light of justice hath not shined unto us, and the sun of understanding hath not risen upon us. We wearied ourselves in the way of iniquity and destruction, and have walked through hard ways, but the way of the Lord we have not known. What hath pride profited us? or what advantage hath the boasting of riches brought us? All these things are passed away like a shadow, and . . . we are consumed in our wickedness. Such things as these the wicked said in hell."[1]

The consideration of past iniquity brings some indeed to salutary repentance, as happened to Magdalen, the Prodigal Son, and the thief on the cross; but we know from daily observation that it tends to harden many others.

Again, repentance does not mean the throwing of a mantle over a heart remaining corrupt, just as a foul heap is covered with snow.

Repentance is from within. It signifies a sincere regret for transgressions because they are displeasing to our Creator, a change of heart, a turning to God, by yearning for "holiness, without which no man shall see God."[2]

The heart is not moved without a motive-power. Where will the sinner who has entered into his eternity, find the lever to lift him from the mire in which he wallowed? Where will he find that influence to inspire him with holy aspirations? Not in himself; for the fountain of the heart is poisoned, and no new element of strength has been added to his soul since he passed from time to eternity.

He can find no help in his surroundings, for his companions are on a level with himself.

[1] *Wisd.* V.
[2] *Heb.* XII., 14.

His only hope, then, could be in God. But where is the ground of that hope, when the night of life has passed, and the day of eternity has dawned? Salvation is not an inherent right, but a gift of God: "The grace of God is eternal life in Jesus Christ, our Lord."[1]

Now the giver has a perfect right to prescribe the conditions on which this gratuitous gift may be received, and the term of time beyond which it cannot be obtained. That he has prescribed certain conditions and limitations, is evident from the only authentic Record we possess of His Revelation to man. The condition is that man should present himself as a saint or a supplicant, with the garments of innocence or of repentance. The obdurate sinner has neither, though he could have had them for the asking. He stands at the threshold of eternity, covered with the rags of infamy, without a single claim on divine justice or mercy, without a spark of love in his heart for the Lord who created him through love, nor a single sentiment in harmony with the life of the citizens of heaven. Is it surprising that he is cast into exterior darkness?

God prescribes a term of probation beyond which the door of mercy is to be closed. The very word *probation* implies some limitation. That the time of probation, that is "the acceptable time,"[2] when it is given to us "to do good to all men"[3] and so strive for the mastery that we may receive an incorruptible

---

[1] *Rom.* VI., 23.   [3] *Gal.* VI., 10.
[2] *II. Cor.* VI., 2.

crown,"[1] is limited to this life, is frequently asserted, or insinuated in the New Testament. In the parable of the rich man and Lazarus, Abraham says: "Between us and you a great gulf is *fixed*, so that they who would pass from hence to you cannot, neither can they pass to us that would come from thence."[2] These words intimate not only a local separation between the saints and the reprobate, but also the immutability of their respective conditions. In the parable of the Ten Virgins, five are admitted and five are rejected, never to return. In the parable of the wheat and the chaff, it is declared that our Lord "will gather the wheat into His barn, and the chaff He will burn with unquenchable fire."[3] In the parable of the man who was expelled from the banquet because he came without a wedding garment, we never hear that he was restored to favor. All these parables, undoubtedly, refer to the kingdom of Heaven; and the obvious inference we have to draw from them is, that the sentence of the good and the bad after the separation is final and irrevocable.

But you will say: Is not the punishment *unjust*, since a crime committed in a brief space of time, is visited with eternal retribution?

I answer that, in the criminal jurisprudence of every civilized nation, there is no adequate proportion of time between the offence and its punishment. For a murder or an adultery committed in a moment

[1] *I. Cor.* IX., 25.   [2] *Ibid.* III., 17.
[3] *Luke* XVI., 26.

of passion, our judges not only deprive men during their natural life, of the society of friends and relatives, compelling them to consort with other criminals, but sometimes even condemn them to death. May not this punishment be regarded as eternal, since once the crime is expiated, life can never be recalled? If this code meets with public approval, as a vindication of social order, how shall we declare it unjust in the Supreme Judge to cast out once for all, from the City of God and the society of the Saints, impious men who have sinned against the majesty of the divine law? It is usually malefactors that have defied the law and that are punished for its violation who condemn our criminal code as too severe; and it is only such as choose to be rebels against God that insist upon calling Him a tyrant. Mathematical truths are never controverted, because they do not oppose our passions; but moral and religious truths are denied, because they often conflict with our natural inclinations.

I admit, you will now say, that the punishment may be just, but how can you reconcile it with our ideas of divine clemency?

God is, indeed, infinitely merciful, but His mercy cannot absorb His other attributes; it cannot run counter to His justice, His sanctity, and that moral order He has established in the world. The higher appreciation one has for benevolence, truth, chastity and moral rectitude, the greater is his antipathy to the opposite vices. Now, God whose love for virtue knows no bounds, must by the very nature of His

Being, have an immeasurable aversion for all iniquity, and therefore He can never be reconciled to the sinner, so long as he voluntarily clings to his sin. God exults not in the sufferings of His creatures, but in the manifestation of His eternal attributes.

Again, God is indeed merciful, but He never forces His mercy on any man. He never does violence to our free-will, which is a precious, though a perilous boon. He wishes, indeed, the salvation of all men;[1] but He wishes also that man's will should remain free. He desires, therefore, our eternal happiness by every means short of destroying our freedom of action. He gives grace to *incline* our heart, not to coerce it. God is not willing that any should perish, but that all should come to repentance.[2] But how can we hope to be saved, if repentance be wanting? The humble and contrite heart He will not despise; but if the heart is neither humble nor contrite, what can you expect? To the cry for pardon He ever listens, but what if that cry is never heard? And if a man will persistently rebel against the appeals of paternal love, he has no one but himself to blame for the consequences. If a drowning man refuses to seize the life-preserver within his grasp, he is solely responsible for his unhappy fate. And if a man prefers to be borne down by the tide of passion rather than listen to the inspirations of grace, he alone is to blame. The Prodigal Son never

---

[1] *I. Tim.* II., 4.
[2] *II. Pet.* III., 9.

reproached his indulgent father, but himself for the miseries that followed his dissipated life.

No one has ever presumed to say that God is unmerciful for creating some animals brute beasts instead of human beings. How, then, can He be regarded as cruel in permitting some men to abide in that moral debasement to which they have voluntarily reduced themselves? And if divine mercy is never impugned by the sinner's revolt in this life, why should it be held accountable if that revolt continues in the life to come?

The clemency of God has never been disputed, on account of the eternal reprobation of the fallen angels, though they never had a second trial; why, then, should His mercy be questioned if rebellious man shares a similar fate after repeated ineffectual warnings and a lifelong probation?

It is a great error to suppose that, because the mercy of God has no limits, it should be indiscriminately lavished on every one without regard to his merits or dispositions to receive it. The love of God, though infinite in itself, must be finite in its application. The measure of its communication depends on the capacity of the recipient. The sun can light up ten thousand rooms as easily as a single one. But that the flood of light may enter, it is necessary that the shutters be thrown open. If they are but partially opened, the rooms will admit less light. If the shutters are entirely closed, the rooms will be dark. And if the light is thus excluded, it is not the fault of the sun. In like manner, while

God delights to make all men on the face of the earth bask in the sunshine of His mercy, provided their hearts are open to receive His rays, He cannot force His love through a single heart that is sealed against Him.

I shall now make an assertion, which may seem paradoxical, but which, nevertheless, is true, that if a man of corrupt life were admitted into heaven, he would not be happy there, and, consequently, that it would be no mercy to invite him to remain.

The company surrounding him, the conversation in which they engaged, the praises of God which they sung, the pursuits which occupied them, would be utterly uncongenial and even repulsive to his frame of mind. He would find himself as much in a state of isolation as a profligate woman would be in a circle of pious maidens, or as a licentious youth when compelled by duty or custom to attend divine service in which he had no heart. An essential condition of happiness is to have a heart in the thing enjoyed. Swine feel much happier wallowing in the mire than if allowed to run at large through the chambers of Windsor Castle.

Heaven is indeed a place of infinite delights, but only for the spiritually minded. "The sensual man perceiveth not these things that are of the Spirit of God: for it is foolishness to him, and he cannot understand, because it is spiritually examined."[1] The atmosphere of heaven does not transform a

---

[1] I. Cor. II., 14.

man's moral complexion. It does not impart spiritual life; but rather develops and ennobles it, just as the healthy flower grows and expands under the genial warmth of the summer sun. Expose a diamond to the light, and it will emit brilliant rays: expose a lump of clay, and it remains dark and opaque. Even so "shall the just shine as the sun in the kingdom of their Father,"[1] but the light of God's countenance will not penetrate and illumine a soul that has no principle of spiritual life, but is "of the earth, earthy;"[2] and hence the Apostle adds: "Now this I say, that flesh and blood *cannot* possess the Kingdom of God, neither shall corruption possess incorruption."[3]

Lastly, you will say: If the door of repentance is open to us even to the last breath of life, if one act of genuine sorrow is sufficient to blot out sin, and to reconcile us to God, may we not hope that few are lost and that the great bulk of mankind will be saved?

Happily, neither the Scripture nor the Church has ever authoritatively spoken of the relative number of the elect and the reprobate, though many writers draw conclusions on one side or the other. Far be it from me to interpret unfavorably to the side of mercy. God grant that the great majority of Christians and even of mankind may be ultimately saved!

Meanwhile, prudence imperatively demands that

---

[1] *Matt.* XIII., 43. [2] *Ibid.*, 50.
[3] *I. Cor.* XV., 47.

in a matter affecting our eternal interests, we should pursue the safer course, by "living soberly and justly and piously in this world, waiting for the blessed hope and glorious coming of our great God and Saviour Jesus Christ who gave Himself for all that He might redeem us from all iniquity."[1] Let us blend pious solicitude with filial trust, on the one hand "working out our salvation with fear and trembling,"[2] and on the other, "going with confidence to the throne of grace, that we may obtain mercy and find grace for seasonable aid."[3]

---

[1] *Tit.* II., 12-14.   [3] *Heb.* IV., 16.
[2] *Philip.* II., 12.

CHAPTER XV.

THE DIVINITY OF CHRIST, ATTESTED BY HIMSELF AND HIS DISCIPLES.

The Divinity of Jesus Christ is asserted or at least implied by Himself, as well as by His disciples, in almost every page of the New Testament.

Certain attributes are ascribed in the Gospels and Epistles to our Saviour, which cannot be predicated of human or angelic nature.

1°. His *eternity* is again and again proclaimed. St. John in the opening words of his Gospel, says: "In the *beginning* was the Word, and the Word was with God, and the *Word was God.*"[1] It has never been questioned that the Word here refers to Jesus Christ. "I am Alpha and Omega, the beginning and the end, saith the Lord God, who is, and who was, and who is to come, the Almighty."[2] "I am the first and the last, . . . and I was dead, and behold I am living for ever and ever, and I have the keys of death and of hell."[3] By these words not only His own eternal life, but His Sovereignty

---

[1] *John* I. [2] *Ibid.*
[3] *Rev.* I.

over death is declared. "Amen, amen I say to you, before Abraham was made, I am."[1] He does not say: Before Abraham was made, I was, but *I am*, thus not only claiming pre-existence, but asserting the consciousness of eternal Being by assuming the incommunicable name given to Jehovah in the book of Exodus.

St. Paul says of Christ: "Thy throne, O God, is for ever and ever.... Thou, O Lord, in the beginning, didst found the earth, and the heavens are the works of Thy hands. They shall perish, but Thou shalt remain, and they all shall grow old as a garment. And as a vesture, Thou shalt change them, and they shall be changed; but Thou art the self-same, and Thy years shall not fail."[2]

Our Saviour says of Himself: "Father, I will that where I am, they also whom Thou hast given Me, may be with Me, that they may see My glory which Thou hast given Me, because Thou lovedst Me *before the creation of the world*."[3] And to His disciples He says: "Behold I am with you all days, even to the consummation of the world."[4] It is impossible to express in stronger language, the existence of our Lord before the creation of the world, His survival after its destruction, and His co-eternity with His Father.

2°. The *creation* of the universe is ascribed to Him. "All things were made by Him, and without Him was made nothing that was made.... He

[1] *John* VIII., 58.
[2] *Heb.* I.
[3] *John* XVII., 24.
[4] *Matt.* XXVIII., 24.

was in the world, and the world was made by Him, and the world knew Him not." [1]

"In Him all things were created in heaven and on earth, visible and invisible, whether thrones or dominations, or principalities or powers; all things were created by Him and in Him; and He is before all, and by Him all things subsist." [2]

3°. He is acknowledged to be the Source of all intellectual and supernatural life: "In Him was life, and the life was the light of men." [3] "He was the true light which enlighteneth every man that cometh into this world." [4] "I am," He says, "the way, the truth and the life." [5] "I am the resurrection and the life." [6] "I am the light of the world. He that followeth Me, walketh not in darkness, but shall have the light of life." [7] "My sheep hear My voice; . . . and I give them *life everlasting;* and they shall not perish for ever." [8] St. Peter reproaches the Jews for having killed the Author of life. [9]

4°. He legislates with the conscious power and the absolute independence of Divinity. The people remarked that "He was teaching them as one having authority, and not as their Scribes and Pharisees." [10]

He modestly, yet firmly declares Himself superior

[1] *John* I.
[2] *Col.* I.
[3] *John* I.
[4] *Ibid.*
[5] *Ibid.* XIV.
[6] *John* XI.
[7] *Ibid.* VIII.
[8] *John* X.
[9] *Acts* III.
[10] *Matt.* VII.

to prophets and kings, even to Solomon himself, the wisest and most gifted of royal legislators.[1]

Moses and the Prophets are accustomed to use the phrase: "Thus saith the Lord." Jesus speaks thus: "Amen, *I* say unto you." They are the representatives of a higher name: He speaks in His own name. Keep the Commandments of God, is their exhortation: Keep *My* Commandments, is His injunction. They point out the way; Jesus proclaims Himself as *the* way. They give out some glimpses of truth; He declares Himself to be *the* truth. They bear the torch of light. He presents Himself as the source of all light. They announce the law to one nation; He commands His disciples to teach His truth to *all nations* of the earth.

The legislation of Christ is enforced by the most solemn sanction. He declares that the wilful rejection of His Gospel will be avenged by a more awful retribution than was visited on the licentious inhabitants of Sodom and Gomorrha.[2] Upon the acceptance of it, depends the eternal salvation of mankind.[3]

5°. He claims the divine prerogative of forgiving sins, not as the delegate of a higher Power, but by His own inherent right: "The Son of Man hath power on earth to forgive sins."[4] He exercises this power: "Be of good heart, child," He says to the paralytic, "thy sins are forgiven thee."[5] And as a proof of the healing of the invisible wounds of the

---

[1] *Ibid.* XII.
[2] *Ibid.* X.
[3] *Mark.* XVI.
[4] *Luke* V.
[5] *Matt.* IX.

soul, He cures the visible infirmities of the body. He delegates this power to His disciples: "Whose sins ye shall forgive, they are forgiven them; and whose sins ye shall retain they are retained."[1] The Jews did not misunderstand our Saviour, they knew that the forgiveness of sins was essentially an act of divine clemency, and therefore they exclaim: "Who can forgive sins but God only?"[2]

6°. He is proclaimed to be the Supreme Judge of the living and the dead, giving a final sentence of condemnation or mercy from which there is no appeal: "We shall all stand before the judgment-seat of Christ."[3] "And when the Son of Man shall come in His majesty, and all the angels with Him; then shall He sit on the throne of His majesty. And all the nations will be gathered together before Him . . . and the wicked shall go into everlasting punishment; but the just into life everlasting."[4]

"And every one who hath left house or brethren, or sisters, or father, or mother, . . . or lands for My name's sake, shall receive a hundred fold, and shall possess life everlasting."

7°. He not only pronounces sentence as Supreme Judge, but He recompenses His followers with eternal happiness, as Master of Paradise. "I go," He says, "to prepare a place for you . . . that where I am ye also may be."[5]

"I am the door of the sheep. If any enter through

[1] *John* XX.
[2] *Mark* II.
[3] *Rom.* XIV.
[4] *Matt.* XXV.
[5] *John* XIV.

Me, they shall be saved, and shall find pastures, and I will give them everlasting life, and they shall not perish for ever."[1] He promises heaven to the penitent thief on the cross. He will not only raise the dead to life, but will also endow the bodies of the righteous with the indestructible and glorious qualities of His own risen body.[2] Thus He speaks not as a guest, but as absolute Lord of the kingdom of heaven. He is the Door by which we are to enter its portals, the uncreated Principle of eternal life and bliss, and the Author of our Resurrection. Such language from the lips of any one inferior to God, would sound like madness.

8°. Our Saviour claims to be the Son of God, and He is repeatedly called by that title in the Gospels. In a memorable passage, He puts this question to His disciples: "Who say ye that I am? Simon Peter answered and said: Thou art the Christ, the Son of the living God. And Jesus answered and said to him, Blessed art thou Simon Bar-Jona, because flesh and blood hath not revealed it to thee, but My Father who is in heaven."[3]

It is evident that this Sonship of Christ is not spoken of here in a broad and vague sense. It does not imply that He is the Son of God by adoption and sanctifying grace, such as all good Christians are acknowledged to be, but that He is the Son of God by nature, born of the Father before all ages.

Hence, He is declared to be "the *only-begotten*

---

[1] *John* X.
[2] *Philip* III.
[3] *Matt.* XVI.

Son of the Father, full of grace and truth,"[1] in contradistinction to those who are the children of God by moral union with Him. In the Lord's prayer we are directed to address God as our Father, to indicate our common participation in His sonship by adoption. But it is noteworthy that our Lord, in His prayers as well as in His personal reference to the Father, whenever He employs the possessive pronoun, never uses the phrase "our Father," but invariably He says: *My Father*, as if emphasizing the essential difference between His Sonship and ours.

St. Paul puts in juxtaposition Christ's incommunicable Sonship by generation and our sonship by adoption, thus making manifest the essential distinction between both. "When the fulness of time was come, God sent His Son to redeem those that were under the law, that we might receive the adoption of sons."[2]

In declaring Himself to be the Son of God, Christ affirms that He is one in nature or essence with His Father: "I and the Father are one." The Jews clearly understood His words. They "sought to kill Him, because He made Himself equal to God. We stone Thee for Thy blasphemy, they exclaimed, because Thou makest Thyself God."[3]

Before His judges, Christ made an avowal of His divinity. Caiphas the High Priest pointedly puts this question to Him: "I adjure Thee by the living God that Thou tell us if Thou be the Christ, the Son

---

[1] *John* I. [3] *John* X.
[2] *Gal.* IV.

of God." And Jesus thus adjured openly declares before the court that He is. It was this avowal that led to His death; for he is accused of manifest blasphemy by the Sanhedrim, who say before Pilate: "We have a law by which he ought to die because He made Himself the Son of God." Their language would be meaningless if they had understood Him to speak of the theocratic sonship of their prophets and saints; but they correctly interpret Him as claiming to be consubstantial with His Father.

9°. As Christ is one in essence with His Father, so does He claim to be identical with the Father in honor,[1] identical in power,[2] identical in glory.[3] He insists on being believed by the same faith,[4] trusted by the same hope,[5] and loved with the same intensity of affection as His Father.[6] He is to be invoked and worshipped like His Father. The angel forbids John to worship him.[7] But the angels are commanded to adore our Saviour.[8] Temporal honors when thrust upon Him, He resolutely declines. When a grateful people seek to take Him by force, and make Him King, He flees from them and repairs to the mountain apart,[9] because His Kingdom was not of this world. But when St. Thomas adores our Lord, saying: "My Lord and my God," Jesus far from rebuking him, accepts the title and the

[1] *John* V.
[2] *Matt.* XXVIII.
[3] *John* XVII.
[4] *John* XIV.
[5] *Ibid.* XIV.
[6] *Matt.* X.
[7] *Rev.* XIX.
[8] *Heb.* I.
[9] *John* VI.

homage, and commends the Apostle's faith. When the man who was born blind, had his sight restored, falling down he worshipped Jesus: and the humble Saviour offered no remonstrance, because He was conscious that He received only His due.

He exacts an absolute obedience such as only a God can claim. Earthly rulers can demand only external compliance with the law of the land. But Christ enters the sanctuary of the soul, and becomes absolute Ruler of the human conscience. He requires the submission of our intellect to the teachings of faith; the submission of our will by an interior attachment to His law, as well as an external compliance with it. He must be undisputed Master of the kingdom of our heart.

In a word, He legislates as a God, He pardons as a God, He judges as a God, He punishes as a God, He rewards as a God, He is honored and adored as a God. He exacts obedience as a God, He is to be loved more than father or mother, brother or sister, husband or wife, more than angels or archangels, principalities or powers; in short, more than all that is not God. We can be reconciled to claims so imperious only on the assumption that they are imposed by a God.

Even infidels are unanimous in extolling the moral perfection of Christ. But on due reflection they will find their position untenable, and will be compelled to the alternative of confessing His divinity, or of acknowledging that He was not even an honest man. His words evidently left the im pression on the minds of the multitude that He claimed to be God. He was conscious of this impression, yet He said naught to remove it. On the contrary he accepted the homage of their adoration. If Christ therefore were not a divine Being, He would be guilty of an unpardonable assumption and impiety in usurping divine honors. He would be an untruthful man, nay an arch-hypocrite and impostor; or at least he would be an extravagant, self-deluded enthusiast, a character never ascribed to Him by His most relentless opponents. There is no middle ground to stand upon. We must either deny His moral excellence or declare His divinity.

The first Napoleon was not a theologian; but he was a great man, and a profound observer, whose vast experience had enabled him to judge what forces were necessary to produce a lasting effect on mankind. When chained to the rock of St. Helena, he had ample leisure to measure the greatness of men and to estimate them according to their true value. One day in a conversation with Montholon, he put this question to him: "Who was Jesus Christ?" Montholon having declined to answer, Napoleon proceeded: "I will tell you. Alexander, Cæsar, Charlemagne, and myself have founded great empires. But our empires were founded on force. Jesus alone founded His empire on love, and to this day millions would die for Him. I think I understand something of human nature, and I tell you, all these were men, and I am a man. Jesus Christ was more than man. I have inspired multitudes with a devotion so enthusiastic that they would have died for me. But to do this it was necessary that I should be *visibly* present with the electric influence of my looks, my words, my voice. Who cares for me now removed as I am from the active scenes of life, and from the presence of men? Who would now die for *me?* Christ alone across the chasm of eighteen centuries makes a demand which is beyond all others difficult to satisfy. He asks more than a father can demand of his child, or a bride of her spouse, or a man of his brother. He asks for the human heart. He will have it entirely to Himself. He demands it unconditionally, and forthwith His demand is granted. Wonderful! In defiance of time and space, the soul of man with all its powers and faculties becomes an annexation to the empire of Christ. This phenomenon is unaccountable; it is altogether beyond the scope of man's creative powers. Time, the great destroyer, is powerless to extinguish this sacred flame. This is what strikes me most. This is what proves to me quite convincingly that Jesus Christ is God."

CHAPTER XVI.

Our Lord's Divinity Confirmed by His Miracles, and especially by His Resurrection.

A miracle is an effect which transcends the power and order of all created nature. As God alone is the Author of nature's laws, He alone has power to suspend them.

God, who is truth itself, cannot sanction a lie, nor connive at deceit, nor put the seal of His omnipotence on hypocrisy. But He would be upholding falsehood, if He empowered any man to work miracles in attestation of false doctrines, or in vindication of a pseudo-Messiah.

Hence, miracles have always been justly regarded as the most luminous and convincing evidence in support of the doctrines they confirm.

A mission, therefore, which is authenticated by miracles, is not only furnished with undoubted credentials, but is stamped with the royal seal of divine approbation.

Our Saviour appeals to His miracles in confirmation of His God-head, His divine mission and doctrines. When John sent two of his disciples to ask Jesus whether He was the true Messiah, our Lord gave them this reply: "Go and relate to John what ye have heard and seen. The blind see, the lame walk, the lepers are cleansed, the deaf hear, the dead rise again, the poor have the Gospel preached to them."[1] He quotes the very words of the Prophet Isaiah descriptive of the Redeemer to come, and shows that the prophetic portrait is embodied in Himself.[2]

Again He says: "The works themselves which I do, give testimony of Me, that the Father hath sent Me."[3] If I do not the works of My Father, believe Me not. But if I do, though you will not believe Me, believe the works, that you may know and believe that the Father is in Me, and I in the Father.[4] I perform works before you which transcend the power of man, as the most striking evidence to your senses and reason that I am one in essence with My Father.

He raises Lazarus from the dead, as He expressly declares, to convince the people who surround Him that He is the true Messiah. Before He performs the miracle, He utters these words: "Father, I give Thee thanks that Thou hast heard Me. And I know that Thou hearest Me always, but because of the people who stand about, have I said it: that they may believe that Thou hast sent Me."[5] The disciples accepted those miracles as a proof of Christ's Mes-

---

[1] *Matt.* XI.
[2] *Isaiah* XXXV.
[3] *John* V.
[4] *Ibid.* X.
[5] *Ibid.* XI.

siahship and divinity: "We know," says Nicodemus, "that Thou art come a teacher from God; for no man can do these signs which Thou doest, unless God be with him.[1]

The divine Sonship of Jesus is proclaimed by the Eternal Father Himself, both on the occasion of His baptism, and in the miracle of His Transfiguration, with the view, no doubt, of confirming the faith of the Apostles in the divinity of their Master.

St. John, referring to the wonder-works of Christ, says: "Many other signs also did Jesus in the sight of His disciples, which are not written in this book. But these are written *that you may believe that Jesus is the Christ the Son of God; and* that believing you may have life in His name."[2]

Let us now take some note of the miracles themselves. Our Saviour enters the world by a miracle; He leaves it by another. His whole public life is one continuous series of signs and wonders. If we cut out the miracles from the life of our Saviour, naught will remain of the historical canvass but a few meagre shreds.

As Lord of all creation, He works prodigies on animate and inanimate nature. A word from His lips stills a tempest.[3] He walks upon the sea, as if it were His native element, as does Peter also at His command.[4] He curses the fig-tree, and it is suddenly withered.[5] With a few loaves and fishes, He feeds

[1] *Ibid.* III.
[2] *Ibid.* XX.
[3] *Mark* IV.
[4] *Matt.* XIV.
[5] *Mark* XI.

an immense multitude of people in the desert.[1] He changes water into wine at the marriage-feast of Cana.[2] He gives sight to the blind, hearing to the deaf, the power of walking to the lame, and speech to the dumb. He heals the paralyzed limb, He cures the leper, He dispels fevers and other maladies from the sick. By touching the hem of His garment, the diseased are restored to health.[3] He raises the dead to life, among them Lazarus, who had lain four days in the tomb.

He performs these miracles on the absent, as well as on those around Him.[4] He usually exercises His power before a large number of spectators. His marvellous works are attested by such a cloud of cotemporary and even ocular witnesses, that the denial of them would involve the rejection of all historical facts. They are not only proclaimed by His disciples; but, after a searching investigation, are acknowledged also by His adversaries.[5]

When Lazarus was raised to life, "the chief priests and the Pharisees gathered a council, and said: What do we? for this Man doeth many miracles. If we let Him alone so, all will believe in Him. . . . They designed, therefore, to put Him to death."[6] Confessing their inability to suppress the evidence or deny the truth of these miracles, they resolve to put the Author of them out of the way.

The Resurrection of Christ is the most signal and

[1] *John* VI.
[2] *Ibid.* II.
[3] *Matt.* XIV.
[4] *Luke* VII.
[5] *John* V.
[6] *John* XI.

splendid evidence of His divinity. It is the keystone in the arch of faith, as it is the most brilliant luminary in the constellation of Christian festivals.

A certain religious enthusiast, named Leberaux, once submitted to Talleyrand a project he entertained of founding a new religion, and asked the French statesman's views as to the feasibility of the undertaking. "You will certainly succeed," replied Talleyrand, "and your name will go down with glory to posterity, if you fulfil the conditions which I propose." "And what are they?" eagerly inquired the visitor. "You must first suffer, be scourged and crucified, and then rise on the third day. Do this, and your success is assured." This reply extinguished the zeal of the would-be reformer. The moral of the witty Frenchman's remark is, that as Christ alone, after entering the portals of the tomb, returned by His own power to life, He is without a rival. He alone has made good His claim to found a new religion, and to merit the supreme adoration of mankind.

Our Saviour frequently predicted in attestation of His God-head, that He would rise again the third day after His death. To those that demanded a proof of His divine mission, He answered: "Destroy this temple, and in three days I will raise it up. But He spoke of the temple of His body."[1]

To the Scribes and Pharisees who sought for a miracle as an evidence that He was the Messiah, He replied: "A wicked and adulterous generation

---

[1] *John* II.

seeketh a sign, and a sign shall not be given it, but the sign of Jonas the prophet. For, as Jonas was in the belly of the fish three days and three nights, so shall the Son of Man be in the heart of the earth three days and three nights."[1]

That the chief priests and the Pharisees clearly understood the purport of our Saviour's prediction, is manifest from the words which they addressed to Pilate after the crucifixion: " We have remembered that that seducer said, while He was yet alive: after three days I will rise again."[2]

In His familiar conversation with His disciples, our Lord frequently and without any figure of speech foretold His resurrection. On one of these occasions, " When they abode together in Galilee, He said to them: The Son of Man shall be betrayed into the hands of men, and they shall kill Him, and the third day He shall rise again."[3]

That He rose again in fulfilment of these predictions, is abundantly proved by the most overwhelming testimony: He appears after His Resurrection to Magdalen,[4] also to the women returning from the monument;[5] He manifests Himself to the two disciples going to Emmaus;[6] He appears to Simon Peter alone;[7] then to all the Apostles except Thomas, and again to all of them, Thomas included.[8] Afterwards He shows Himself to several of His disciples at the

[1] *Matt.* XII.
[2] *Matt.* XXVII.
[3] *Ibid.* XVII.
[4] *John* XX.
[5] *Matt.* XXVIII.
[6] *Luke* XXIV.
[7] *Ibid.*
[8] *John* XX.

sea of Tiberias.[1] He appears to the eleven Apostles in Galilee on the mount where He had appointed to meet them.[2] St. Paul testifies that "He was seen by more than five hundred brethren at once."[3] Lastly, He was seen by the eleven Apostles, in whose presence He ascended into Heaven.[4]

It must be here noted that these manifestations of our risen Lord are so palpable and so frequent as to leave no possible room for doubt or cavil about the verity of His Resurrection in the flesh. He does not present Himself before His disciples as a spectral shadow. His visits are not the sudden and transient apparitions of a disembodied spirit. He says to the incredulous Thomas in the presence of his brethren, "Feel with thy fingers the wounds in My hands and in My side." A short time before He had gently reproved the doubting Apostles in these words: "See My hands and My feet that it is I Myself . . . for, a spirit hath not flesh and bones as you see Me to have."[5] He continues to frequent their company for forty days conversing with them, instructing them, eating and drinking with them.

The Resurrection of Christ rests on so solid a foundation that it is proclaimed by every Christian sect and heresy, as well as by orthodox Christians.

The Apostles were the principal witnesses of the Resurrection. It is important, therefore, that we should consider what estimate is to be formed of their

[1] *Ibid.* XXI.
[2] *Matt.* XXVIII.
[3] *I. Cor.* XV.
[4] *Mark* XVI.
[5] *Luke* XXIV.

character, what weight is to be attached to their testimony, what is their standing in the court of public opinion.

The truth of Christ's Resurrection must be tested by the ordinary evidence brought to bear in the examination of any historical fact. For most of our information we depend on the statements of others. The vast majority of the people of the United States know only from hearsay that such cities as Pekin and Paris exist. The whole human race rely on the pages of history for their belief that Cæsar lived and that Tyre once flourished.

We accept the veracity of a narrative when confirmed by a host of witnesses whose calm temperament gives no room to suspect the existence of a fervid imagination, or a credulous disposition; witnesses who are disinterested, who have nothing to gain, but everything to lose by deception. Now, such are the characteristics of the witnesses of the Resurrection.

The Apostles cannot be charged with an overwrought imagination, blind fanaticism, or imbecility. They were plain, blunt men, slow of belief, cautious and calculating. They were, indeed, rude and illiterate, but they were possessed of strong common sense, and were endowed with a temper of mind which best qualified them to judge of a matter of fact like the Resurrection. We are not accustomed to select our juries chiefly or exclusively from the learned professions, but from men of sound judgment, without regard to their literary attainments. We cannot, therefore, suppose that the Apostles were the victims of hallucination or deception in proclaiming the reality of our Saviour's Resurrection.

Nor can they be suspected of imposing on the credulity of their hearers. They had nothing to gain by deceiving the public, and everything to lose; for, their earthly lot was a hard one. They could truly say: "If in this life only we have hope in Christ, we are of all men most miserable."[1] "For, God hath set forth us Apostles, the last, as it were men appointed to death. . . . . Even unto this hour we both hunger and thirst, and are naked, and are buffeted, and have no fixed abode. And we labor working with our own hands: we are reviled and we bless: we are persecuted and we suffer it: we are blasphemed and we entreat: we are made as the refuse of this world."[2]

Now these same men had as strong a belief in the Resurrection of Christ as they had in their own existence. They regarded this event as the crowning miracle and the foundation stone of Christian faith. In their sermons they lay special stress on this fact as an all-sufficient and decisive evidence of the divinity of the Christian religion. They are willing to submit this truth as a crucial test-case, to determine whether Christianity should stand or fall, and whether they are to be pronounced imposters or heaven-sent messengers. "If Christ be not risen again, then is our preaching vain, and vain also is your faith. Yea,

[1] *I. Cor.* XV., 19.
[2] *Ibid.* IV.

and we are found false witnesses of God, because we have given testimony against God that He hath raised up Christ."[1]

They wrought miracles for the express purpose of vindicating the truth of the Resurrection and, consequently, of putting beyond all doubt the claims of Christianity to the acceptance of mankind. Peter and John on entering the beautiful gate of the temple, restore to health a man who had been lame from his birth; and they profess to perform that miracle by the power and in the name of their risen Lord.[2]

If civilized nations accept the verdict of twelve jurymen as the most approved and equitable mode of deciding questions of the greatest moment, how can we dispute the unanimous testimony of twelve Apostolic witnesses who saw with their eyes, heard with their ears, and touched with their hands, the risen Lord; who devoted their life to the promulgation of this miracle; who preached it not in obscure corners, but in Jerusalem itself less than two months after the event had occurred; who converted thousands of hearers that had ample opportunities of testing the correctness of their declaration; who suffered stripes and imprisonment rather than deny it, and, finally, sealed their testimony with their blood!

The two great modern antagonists of the dogma of the Resurrection are Renan and Strauss. Renan, while reluctantly conceding that Jesus actually died on the cross, asserts that Magdalen was the dupe of a

[1] *I. Cor.* XV.
[2] *Acts* III.

fervid imagination in declaring that she saw the Lord. He seems to forget that she was but one witness among hundreds of others who had beheld Him under a variety of circumstances. The faith of Renan's youth and early manhood and the skepticism of his latter years, seem to keep up an unequal struggle in his breast. Hence, his statements and theories are a jumble of contradictions. He blows hot and cold in the same breath. On the same page he elevates and depresses our Saviour. He blasphemes while praising Him; and, like Judas, he betrays his once acknowledged Lord with a kiss of profuse panegyric. While we are admiring the delicious flowers of rhetoric which he lays at the feet of the Messiah, we find them suddenly withered by the breath of his malevolent cynicism.

Strauss, unable to controvert the cumulative evidence of our Saviour's manifestation after His crucifixion, has recourse to the desperate expedient of denying His death on the cross. He pretends that our Lord when taken down from the cross, was in a state of *syncope* from which He afterward rallied. But this objection is scarcely worthy of serious consideration. The death of Christ is minutely described by the four Evangelists including John, who was an eye-witness of the scene.

No one in his senses has ever disputed the fact that Cæsar was slain in Rome nineteen centuries ago. Now, the death of our Saviour is corroborated by human evidence as strong as that which records Cæsar's assassination. It was a public and notorious execution occurring in Jerusalem, which then contained a population of over two hundred thousand inhabitants. It was superintended by Roman officials, and witnessed by an immense concourse of by-standers, Jews and Gentiles, sympathizers and enemies. His death was openly and exultingly acknowledged by His adversaries;[1] it was disputed by none of them. The tomb in which He lay, was guarded by Roman 'soldiers, as well as by the emissaries of the high-priests.

And, surely, those zealots whose minds were sharpened by malice, and who displayed so much ingenuity and vigilant zeal in compassing our Redeemer's arrest and death-warrant, would not allow their friendless Victim to escape their hands, till they were assured that life was extinct.

Thus we see the Resurrection of Christ attested by two incontrovertible facts; namely, the certainty of His death, followed by His living, visible manifestation in the flesh.

---

[1] *Matt.* XXVII.

CHAPTER XVII.

THE DIVINE MISSION OF CHRIST DEMONSTRATED BY THE MARVELLOUS PROPAGATION AND THE PERPETUITY OF THE CHRISTIAN RELIGION.

At the dawn of Christianity, the Roman Empire, after having reached the summit of intellectual culture, had sunk into the lowest depths of moral and religious degradation. When Christ appeared, He called about Him twelve men, His first disciples, and made them the instruments of the mightiest moral revolution that has ever taken place in the annals of time. They were commanded to destroy idolatry the world over, and to establish in its stead the worship of the One, True and Living God; to root out the most inveterate and the stormiest passions from the hearts of men, and to implant therein the reign of the Prince of peace.

Our Saviour lays on them the weighty obligation of preaching His Gospel to all nations, to the end of time, and He strengthens them with a two-fold prophecy, concerning its world-wide dissemination and its enduring stability. He promises that the seed of the word shall take root and spread throughout the world and that His kingdom on earth shall last till time shall be no more. " You shall be witnesses unto Me in Jerusalem, and in all Judea and Samaria and to the uttermost parts of the earth."[1] "And this Gospel of the kingdom shall be preached in the whole world for a testimony to all nations."[2] "I have chosen you and have appointed you, that you should go and bring forth fruit and your fruit shall remain."[3] "The gates of Hell shall not prevail against My Church."[4] "Behold, I am with you all days unto the end of the world."[5]

The Apostles have implicit faith in their Master's words. They know that He is God, for they have been witnesses of the miracles He had wrought in proof of His Divinity. They know that His word is omnipotent; that He who in the beginning said: "Let there be light, and there was light": "Let the earth bring forth fruit" and it was so done,—that He can through their ministry make the light of His truth to shine on the darkened intellects of men and their hearts to yield a rich harvest of good works. And, therefore, they go forth full of courage and full of confidence in the success of their mission. Their only weapon is the Cross; their only credentials the Gospel.

St. Peter begins his Apostolic ministry in Jerusalem, where his first sermon is followed by the con-

[1] *Acts* I., 8.
[2] *Matt.* XXIV.
[3] *John* XV.
[4] *Matt.* XVI.
[5] *Ibid.* XXVIII.

version of three thousand souls. Of these, some had no doubt been witnesses of Christ's death, nay had even perhaps taken part therein. He afterwards carries the Faith to Antioch where he establishes his See, and ends his labors and his life in Rome. St. Paul traverses the Empire from East to West. The history of his journeys and labors, as sketched in the Acts of the Apostles, excites our unqualified astonishment. St. Andrew preaches in Scythia and Greece. St. John evangelizes Ephesus and Asia Minor. St. James the Less exercises the Apostolate in Judea and Galilee. St. James the Greater is said to have penetrated even into Spain. St. Thomas carries the light of truth into India. St. Bartholomew makes Christ known to the people of Armenia, and so on of the other Apostles. Thus they fulfil the command of their Master " to teach all nations," and that with such amazing celerity and in so incredibly short a time that St. Paul could exclaim: "Their sound hath gone forth to all the earth and their words unto the ends of the whole world."[1]

But if we are amazed at the holy audacity of the Apostles and their first disciples in undertaking the tremendous task laid on them, our wonder is increased when we consider the marvellous success which crowned their labors, for it is easier far to preach the Gospel than to persuade men to accept it. The seed of the word soon sprang up and grew into a mighty tree, spreading its branches far and wide,

---

[1] *Rom.* X., 18.

sheltering the nations beneath its ample shade, and feeding them with its life-giving fruit.

In a few years Christianity had secured so strong a foothold in the Roman Empire, as to fill its disciples with joyful enthusiasm, and its enemies with alarm and dismay.

Twenty-five years after the death of Christ, St. Paul, writing to the Romans, congratulates them in that their "faith is spoken of in the whole world,"[1] and of course, spoken of by those who were in sympathy and communion with the faith of Rome.

About thirty years later, Pliny, Proprætor of Bithynia, in a letter to the emperor Trajan, expresses his concern at the growing numbers and influence of the Christians in his own and the neighboring province of Pontus. "The contagion of this superstition," he says, "has spread not only to the cities, but about the villages and open country." He adds that in consequence of the rapid diffusion of Christianity the temples of the gods are almost abandoned and the sale of victims for the sacrifices well-nigh suspended. He asks, therefore, what course he is to pursue in checking the further progress of the evil.

St. Justin Martyr whose death occurred 66 years after that of St. John the Evangelist, declares that "there is not any one race of men, Barbarian or Greek, or of those who are nomads or shepherds in tents, among whom prayers and eucharists are not

---

[1] *Rom.* I., 8.

offered to the Father of the universe through the name of the crucified Jesus.[1]

St. Irenæus, who was born in 120, records with great force the marvellous propagation of Christianity up to his own time: "The Church," he says, "scattered throughout all the world, even unto the ends of the earth, received from the Apostles and their disciples, the faith in one God, the Father Almighty. . . . The Church having received this faith, although it be scattered abroad through the whole world, carefully preserves it, dwelling as in one habitation, and believes alike in these doctrines, as though she had one soul and the same heart. . . . And although there be many diverse languages in the world, yet the power of tradition is one and the same." And he proceeds to illustrate by a beautiful comparison, the cause of this unity. As the light, he says, which illumines this world, is everywhere the same, because it emanates from the luminary of day, so the light of faith is always and everywhere the same, because it proceeds from Jesus Christ, the Sun of justice.[2]

Tertullian, who was born about the year 160, in his *Apologia*, speaks in still more forcible language of the progress of Christianity: "We are but of yesterday," he says, "and yet we have filled every place belonging to you, cities, islands, castles, towns, assemblies, your very camp, your tribes, companies, palaces, senate, forum. We leave you only your temples."

---

[1] *Dial. with Tryphon.*
[2] Lib. I., Ch. X.

Again: "The kingdom of Christ has no limits. Everywhere, there is faith in Him. All peoples honor Him. Everywhere He reigns and receives the tribute of adoration."

Clement of Alexandria at the close of the second century, writes: "The word of our Master did not remain in Judea, as philosophy remained in Greece, but has been poured out over the whole world, persuading Greeks and Barbarians alike, race by race, village by village, every city, whole houses and hearers, one by one, nay not a few of the philosophers themselves."

It is worthy of note that all the writers whom I have quoted, lived in the first or second century, and the latest of them was removed from our Saviour by an interval of only about 150 years.

What a contrast is presented to us between the sanguinary conquests of the great generals of Pagan antiquity on the one hand, and the peaceful victories achieved by the Apostles and their successors, on the other, whether we consider the weapons with which they fought, the battles they won, or the duration of their victories.

Alexander the Great, the most successful perhaps of ancient captains, subdued kingdoms by wading through the blood of his fellow-man. By the sword he conquered, and by the sword he kept his subjects in bondage. But scarcely was he laid in his tomb, when his empire was dissolved, and his subjects shook off the yoke that had been forced upon them.

The Apostles gained nations to Christ not by the

sword, but by the Cross. They conquered not by force, but by persuasion; not by shedding the blood of others, but by shedding their own blood; not by enslaving the bodies of men, but by rescuing their souls from the yoke of ignorance and sin. And the fruit of their victories remains unto this day. The spiritual Republic which they founded is extended and perpetuated not by frowning fortifications and standing armies, but by the divine influence of moral and religious impressions.

The propagation of the Christian religion is the more astonishing when we consider the absolute and enormous disproportion between the means employed and the results obtained. This disparity is manifested in the personal weakness of the men chosen to be the heralds of the new doctrine, the austerity of the message they were to deliver, the pride and sensuality of the world they were sent to subdue, and in the formidable opposition they everywhere encountered.

The Apostles were few in number. They were without wealth or position, without high mental endowments or acquired learning, without the prestige of fame, of obscure origin, and of neither social nor political consequence. They belonged to a race, hated and despised by both Greeks and Romans. They were in fine men quite without those qualifications which are commonly thought to be essential to success in any great enterprise.

Well, indeed, could St. Paul exclaim : "The foolish things of the world hath God chosen, to confound the wise: and the weak things of the world hath

God chosen, to confound the strong: and the base things of the world, and the things which are despised, hath God chosen, and the things that are not, that He might bring to naught those things which are; *that no flesh may glory in His sight,*[1] that the world might clearly see that the Christian religion was not the work of man, but of God.

For, if the Gospel had been propagated by the power of Tiberius Cæsar, and the governors of the Roman Provinces, the world could reasonably say: "There is no miracle here, for Christianity was established not by the finger of God, but by the might and majesty of kings."

Or if armies sword in hand had been sent to force the new religion upon the world, men could say with truth: "There is no marvel here; the Christian faith was propagated, not by the sword of the Spirit, but by the arm of the flesh."

Or if the orators, statesmen and philosophers, the historians and poets had united with voice and pen to champion the cause of the infant Church, the world could say that there was nothing supernatural in all that; that the Gospel was recommended, not by the folly of the cross, but by the "persuasive words of human wisdom." Or again, if money and the hope of temporal advantages had been held out to the Pagan peoples as inducements to join the standard of Christ, it might justly be claimed that these merely natural causes could sufficiently account

---

[1] *I. Cor.* I., 27-29.

for the rapid spread of the Christian religion; that men of all classes and conditions had been drawn thither, not by Divine power, but the greed for gain. Now we know well that the Apostles had on their side neither wealth nor learning, nor the strength of armies, nor the favor of kings, nor any hope of temporal benefit.

Our wonder at the growth of Christianity is enhanced when we consider the doctrines which it offered to a scoffing world. It announced mysteries incomprehensible to human reason and a code of morality which demanded an habitual spirit of self-denial. What truths can be more difficult to reason than that there are three Persons in one divine Being, that the Son of God assumed human nature, that the Man-God died on an infamous gibbet? Hence the Apostle says: "We preach Christ crucified; to the Jews indeed a stumbling-block, and to the Gentiles, foolishness."[1] They preached the resurrection of the flesh which, by the Gentile world, was regarded as impossible.

They enforced moral precepts which waged a relentless war on "the lusts of the flesh, the lusts of the eyes, and the pride of life," which demanded a complete subjugation of our most inveterate and darling passions, and a contempt of wealth and vain-glory.

But when to the personal insignificance of the Apostles, and to the austerity of their doctrine, is

[1] *I. Cor.* I., 23.

superadded the violent opposition which they met at every step from the Jewish and the Gentile world, we are lost in wonder and admiration at the success of their mission. A glance at the Epistles of St. Paul, the Acts of the Apostles, and the History of the early Church, is sufficient to convince us of the systematic hostility they encountered from their own race.

Every element of Pagan society was leagued against the rising Church. The Pagan priests resisted the progress of the Christian religion, because it threatened to put an end to their superstitious calling.

The craftsmen and merchants opposed it, because it was killing their traffic in idols and victims for sacrifice. We learn from the Acts that the silversmiths of Ephesus ran together in hot indignation denouncing the preaching of St. Paul, because it threatened to ruin their trade.[1] Pliny, as we have already seen, complained to the Emperor Trajan that the temples were almost entirely deserted, the sacred rites suspended, and a purchaser of victims hard to be found.

The men of letters denounced Christianity with a bitterness of invective, equalled only by the grace and beauty of their style, because it rejected the gods who had been the inspiration of their labors. They could not endure the insolence that would bring into contempt the divinities whom a Homer, a Virgil and

[1] *Acts* XIX.

an Ovid had celebrated in immortal verse; nor could they brook that despised foreigners from Judea should presume to teach them, polished Greeks and Romans; they forgot what modern writers sometimes forget, that truth though spoken by alien lips, is never an alien, but should find a warm welcome in every heart.

Grave historians even, like Tacitus and Suetonius, condemned the new religion in unmeasured terms. Tacitus calls it "a detestable superstition provoking the just hatred of humanity because of its crimes."[1] And Suetonius speaks of the Christians as "a race of men given up to a new and pernicious superstition."[2] These writers did not think it worth while to inquire into the charges which prejudice and hate had invented against an inoffensive people. They accepted all they had heard against them as true, and thought they could in no better way contribute to the security of the State than by reprehending a religion which aimed at the destruction of its gods.

The conservative element in society opposed the religion of Christ because it was new, and because the worship of the gods had the authority of a venerable antiquity. This was the religion which they and their fathers had followed for generations, and they could not calmly suffer this new sect to disturb the old order of things.

Again, the worship of the gods appealed to the passions of men and pandered to their sensuality.

[1] *Annal.* XV., 44.
[2] *Vita Neronis*, Ch. 6.

They were consequently devout followers of Jupiter, Venus, Bacchus and the rest, in whose example they found the justification of their worst excesses. Christianity, on the other hand, insisted on the subjugation of the passions, and bade its followers "crucify their flesh with its vices and concupiscences."

Lastly, the old religion was upheld by the civil rulers, because it was the religion of the State, and was part of the machinery of government. Its festivals and ceremonies were officially sanctioned by the authorities; its temples were built, and its priests maintained at the public expense; while Christianity was proscribed by the civil law as a dangerous innovation, and an impiety towards the established worship of the State. The Christian religion was denounced as a standing menace to the empire, corrupting the loyalty of the people and provoking by its crimes the vengeance of heaven. The most monstrous misrepresentations were invented with the view of bringing odium on the Christian name. If the Christians assembled for prayer at night, as they were obliged to do in order to elude the vigilance of their persecutors, they were charged with meeting for the basest purposes. If they celebrated the Sacred Mysteries, they were accused of killing an infant at their secret reunions, and of drinking its blood. Such was the way in which Pagans misrepresented the Holy Communion.

If the Christians greeted one another by the endearing title of brother and sister, they were suspected of incest. If they refused to take an oath conflicting with their conscience, they were held up as disloyal to the government. If they refused to offer incense to idols, they were accused of atheism and impiety to the gods.

By a natural consequence the Christians were held responsible for every public calamity that happened to the State. If the Tiber overleaped its banks, or if the Nile did not enrich the land by the annual overflow; if the country was visited by famine or pestilence, or earthquakes, or by war or conflagration, all these visitations were ascribed to the anger of the gods towards the Christians.

All the mighty forces of a great empire were exerted to destroy them. Edicts against them were issued by the emperors and the provincial governors. Everything that official zeal, thirst for blood or gold, or the hope of preferment, could do, was brought to bear against them. A continuous net-work was spread over the land to catch them in its toils. From Nero's time in the middle of the first century, the massacre of Christians was continued with only an occasional lull in the storm till Diocletian's reign at the opening of the fourth century. The storm reached its height under that emperor's rule. So unrelenting was the persecution, so general was the slaughter throughout the empire, so frightful and varied were the tortures inflicted, and so crushing and complete, apparently, was the overthrow of the new religion, that medals were struck and a monument erected in honor of Diocletian, commemorating the utter annihilation of the Christian name. Yet this darkest period of the Church's history, like the hour before dawn was speedily followed by the bright day of freedom, when Constantine, the first Christian emperor, was called to the throne, and proclaimed liberty of worship throughout the land.

Let us now inquire into the cause of the wonderful growth and durability of the Church amid the vicissitudes through which it has passed. This subject is one of profound interest to the friends and foes of Christianity alike, and has engaged the attention of philosophers and statesmen in every age. Can the development and stability of the Church be explained by natural causes, or must it be accounted for upon supernatural grounds?

All human institutions are subject, like man himself, to the law of death. States, Empires and Republics, have their birth, and their periods of growth and development, of decay and dissolution. The Roman Empire of all the states of antiquity was the most conspicuous for strength and duration. It lasted seven hundred and fifty years from its foundation under Romulus, until the zenith of its glory under Augustus. Four hundred years later it was dismembered, so that it lasted altogether eleven hundred and fifty years, after having passed successively through the phases of a Monarchy, a Republic and an Empire.

The Catholic Church has already existed close upon two thousand years, or nearly twice as long as one of the most venerable commonwealths in history.

She appears before the world to-day in unimpaired vigor, with her constitution, laws and government unchanged. So far from betraying any signs of decrepitude and decay, she is instinct with life and displays the missionary spirit and the apostolic zeal which characterized her when she carried the Gospel into France in the fifth century, and to England in the sixth.

Now this grave question confronts us: Why should the Catholic Church, of all institutions, be the sole exception to the law of change and death? The historian Gibbon, unwilling to concede to the Church a divine origin and supernatural protection, endeavors to account for her astonishing growth and perpetuity upon purely natural grounds, and he alleges five causes which, he maintains, are sufficient to explain them. These are, the zeal of the first Christians; the doctrine of the immortality of the soul; the miraculous powers ascribed to the primitive Church; the sublime virtues of the early Christians; and the admirable organization of the Church herself.[1]

The influence of these causes cannot, indeed, be easily overestimated. They were powerful factors in the propagation of the faith. But they were all secondary causes, subordinated to one great controlling Cause. If we come suddenly upon a fair expanse of water, curiosity may impel us to search for the hidden springs that feed it. Our toil may be rewarded by the discovery of several noble streams;

---

[1] *Decline and Fall of the Roman Empire*, Vol. II., Chap. 15.

but we know that they have a common origin in the eternal snows that crown the distant mountains. So with the Church of God. For nineteen centuries the causes enumerated by the English historian have been a principle of perpetual strength and beauty to her. But whence is their peculiar power derived? Are they merely natural? Or is there not behind them the almighty arm of God? We can trace their power and efficacy to the mountain of God, to Jesus Christ Himself, the perennial fountain of everlasting life. It was He who inspired the first disciples with their burning zeal. He opened up to them the luminous perspective of a life to come, "eternal in the Heavens." He gave them miraculous powers. He was the source of their sanctity. He was the living soul that animated the teaching authority in the Church and guided its counsels.

Let us examine more closely the last of these causes assigned by Gibbon. It is the most cogent of them all, comprehending in some measure the others. It is, moreover, the one most frequently alleged by writers unfriendly to the Church, as the secret of her strength and singular continuity.

The Church, say these writers, owes her marvellous vigor and survival to her thorough and skilful organization, her strict discipline and the well-marshalled battalions of her clergy, and to the sagacity and foresight of her popes and prelates.

The reply to this is very plain. 1st. The organization of the Church, admirable as it is, is not an adequate explanation of her strange vitality. Organization is the work of intelligence, but no one has ever imagined that churchmen have a monopoly of human wisdom. Civil rulers have assuredly as high faculties and as much facility to organize as ecclesiastics. 2d. The princes of this world certainly have better means at their disposal for maintaining discipline, than the Church has at her command. There are magistrates to enforce obedience to the laws; and standing armies to coerce refractory subjects. The Church draws no sword to enforce her authority. She relies upon spiritual penalties and moral sanctions alone. Again, civil empires are commonly comprised in one compact and undivided territory. The people speak the same tongue; they are ordinarily of one race, or of races fused into one homogeneous body. The Republic of the Church, on the contrary, is conterminous with the globe itself, embracing people of every race and speaking every language under the sun. Surely it is more difficult to establish and perpetuate among elements so diverse, the unity of faith and discipline, than to secure the political unity of a single nation. 3d. Pontiffs and prelates are not gifted by nature with more judgment and penetration in the art of governing than civil rulers and statesmen. The indestructibility of the Church then cannot logically be referred to the talents and learning of her teachers, or to the far-sighted policy of her rulers. Nay, if the statements of her adversaries are to be admitted, she endures not because of human wisdom, but in spite of human folly.

To the philosophic mind, as well as to the Christian, there remains but one rational conclusion, but one cause entirely adequate to the permanency of Christianity. If the Church has survived the storms of nineteen centuries, it is through Him who promised that "the gates of Hell shall not prevail against her." If she lives, and moves, and has her being to-day, it is to justify the declaration of Christ, who said: "I am with you all days, to the end of the world." Her presence in the world to-day is a palpable proof of the divine mission of Jesus Christ, and every unbiassed mind that calmly reviews her history must admit that "the finger of God is here."

Gamaliel gave the angry Pharisees a true test by which they could discern her true character: "If this work be of men, it will come to naught; but if it be of God, you cannot overthrow it." [1]

Upwards of fourteen hundred years ago, St. Augustin proposed to the cavillers of his time an argument which has greater cogency now than it had even then. Either, he says, the Christian religion was propagated by miracles or without them. If the former is true, the Church is manifestly divine; if, however, the world was converted without miracles, this of itself would be a miracle so stupendous that no other could be compared with it.

It may be objected further, that if rapid growth and protracted existence are to be accepted as proofs of a divinely established religion, Mohammed may lay claim to a divine mission as well as Christ.

[1] *Acts*, V.

Between Christianity and Mohammedanism, however, there is absolutely no parity to warrant any one in asserting for Islam the claims which have been set up in behalf of the Christian religion.

For 1st. Christ was the Founder of a new religion embodying a clearer revelation of God and a new and purer code of morals; Mohammed has enriched mankind with no good thing that was not well known before.

2ndly. Christ confirms his teaching by well authenticated miracles; Mohammed disclaims miraculous gifts, though his credulous followers ascribed miraculous powers to him.

3rdly. The pure and stainless life of Jesus stands out in strong contrast with the voluptuousness of Mohammed. The life of Jesus is in perfect harmony with His sublime precepts, whilst the lessons of moderation, abstinence and almsgiving inculcated by the false prophet, are neutralized by his gross sensuality, his cruelty and imposture.

4thly. Christ propagated His Gospel by an appeal to reason and conscience; Mohammed made proselytes by the sword.

5thly. Christ's system of morals inculcates a relentless war upon the passions; Mohammed's is an incentive to their gratification. Christ stems the torrent of lawless desires; Mohammed floats with their impetuous tide. Even his Paradise is one of sensual delights.

6thly. The Gospel proclaims the unity and indissolubility of marriage. The Koran sanctions polygamy, permitting a man to have four wives and as many concubines as his wealth can maintain, while he may divorce his wives at will. "A special revelation dispensed Mohammed from the laws which he had imposed on his nation; the female sex, without reserve, was abandoned to his desires. . . . Eleven wives enjoyed the favor of his conjugal society."[1] His amorous intrigues are notorious and revolting to Christian modesty.

7thly. Christianity is world-wide and universal, embracing people of every race and nation under heaven. Islamism is limited in territorial extent. In European Turkey, where it is confronted by Christianity, it forms but one-fourth of the population and is fast losing ground. It is racy of the soil from which it sprung. It is a reflex of the people, the country and the climate in which it had its origin.

8thly. Christianity is identified with the intellectual and moral progress of humanity. Mohammedanism is associated with a retrograde and moribund civilization.

9thly. Christianity has abolished slavery wherever its influence dominates. The Mussulman extends and perpetuates it.

10thly. Every thoughtful and impartial mind has for eighteen centuries admired the sublime simplicity of the Gospel. "He will peruse with impatience in the Koran the endless incoherent rhapsody of fable and precept, and declamation which seldom excites

[1] Gibbon's *Decline and Fall of the Roman Empire*, Vol. VI, p. 358.

a sentiment or an idea, which sometimes crawls in the dust, and is sometimes lost in the clouds."[1]

We may therefore conclude that unlike Christianity, Mohammedanism furnishes no evidence of a divine origin or mission in its rapid diffusion, the number of its votaries, or its long duration. These are reasonably accounted for when we consider that it was enforced by the sword, exacts no sacrifice and denies to natural appetite no indulgence.

---

[1] *Ibid.*, Vol. VI, p. 352.

CHAPTER XVIII.

PAGAN SYSTEM OF WORSHIP. ORIGIN AND
DESTINY OF MAN AS VIEWED BY
PAGAN PHILOSOPHY.

Let us imagine ourselves standing on one of Rome's seven hills during the Empire, and let us contemplate in spirit that immense capital teeming with a promiscuous population of about two millions of inhabitants gathered together from every part of the world. We behold at our feet the city dotted with its idolatrous temples, and the public squares and edifices adorned with idols erected to false gods. We see the people paying divine worship to every being in heaven above, on the earth beneath, and in the waters under the earth, excepting to God alone, to whom alone is divine homage due. They worshipped the sun, moon, and stars of heaven. Every sea and river, every grove and forest, every avocation and function of life had its tutelary gods; even every passion and vice was deified. Drunkenness and lust, war and theft, had their patronal divinities. In the words of

St. Paul to the Romans themselves, they "changed the glory of the incorruptible God into the likeness of an image of corruptible man, and of birds, and of four-footed beasts, and of creeping things . . . and worshipped and served the creature rather than the Creator, who is blessed forever."[1]

What I say of Rome must be applied to the Empire also; and what I say of the Empire can be affirmed of the whole world, Palestine excepted. And what is still more remarkable, the most enlightened nations, such as those of Chaldea, Egypt, Phœnicia, and Greece were the most profoundly darkened in regard to religious truth, a fact that conclusively demonstrates man's moral inability to arrive, by his own power, at the knowledge of this truth, and the consequent necessity of a divine revelation.[2]

---

[1] *Rom.* I., 23, 25.

[2] The truth of this assertion is clearly stated by the Vatican Council: "The same Holy Mother, the Church, holds and teaches that God, the beginning and the end of all things, can be known for a certainty from created things by the natural light of human reason; . . . that it pleased His divine wisdom and goodness, however, to reveal to the human race Himself and the eternal decrees in a supernatural manner. . . .

"It is entirely owing to this divine revelation that, even in the present condition of the human race, a knowledge of the things of God, which of themselves are not beyond the reach of human reason, can be acquired easily and without any admixture of doubt or error. It is not for this reason, however, that Revelation is absolutely necessary; but because God, in His infinite goodness, has destined man for a supernatural end, that is, for a participation in those divine blessings that surpass all human understanding." Sess. III., ch. II.

The sanguinary rites of the Gentile world were in keeping with their degraded idea of the Divinity. The practice of immolating human victims prevailed not only in Arabia, Carthage, and Tyre, and in the Druidical worship of Gaul and Britain; but among the Pagan nations generally, even in more enlightened Greece and Rome. Boys and maidens, young men and old, were sacrificed, according as the custom of the place demanded. These sacrifices were offered up chiefly in fulfilment of vows, or to propitiate the gods in time of danger, or in thanksgiving for victories achieved.[1] When Carthage was besieged by Agathocles, fathers moved by paternal instinct immolated to Moloch strange children instead of their own, as they were required to do. To appease the gods, when the deceit was discovered, two hundred of the noblest children were voluntarily offered in sacrifice by their parents.[2]

Instead of invoking the living God and confiding in an overruling Providence, the Pagan nations had recourse to lying oracles and soothsayers, to divination, astrology, and the interpretation of dreams, in order to ascertain their destiny, or to propitiate their passionate and whimsical divinities.

It is true, indeed, that many ancient philosophers, guided by the light of reason, believed in one Supreme God, and ridiculed the host of divinities that were the objects of popular worship. But they were vague and contradictory in their declarations

[1] *The Gentile and the Jew*, Döllinger.
[2] *Diod.*, XX., 14.

which never have the clear ring of the Christian *Credo*. They had not the courage of their convictions, and they feared to run counter to the prevailing belief. They often invoked in their public speeches the gods whom they repudiated in their philosophical writings. And even if they had the will, they could not have succeeded in stemming the widespread torrent of superstition.

Cicero in his orations frequently appeals to the "immortal gods," and expresses himself strongly in favor of the existing system of religion, as in harmony with public sentiment.[1]

Socrates gave as a maxim that every one must follow the prevailing religion of his country;[2] and he disavowed the charge of denying the gods whom the people adored.[3]

Plato, his disciple, says that it would be senseless to change the established religion of the State, and he lays down the order in which the various gods are to be worshipped. He condemns the violation of their sanctuaries, upholds their festivals, and declares it most honorable to offer them sacrifice.[4]

Aristotle believes in one God, but denies His providential supervision of human affairs.[5]

Confused and contradictory in their teachings concerning God, have the Pagan philosophers thrown more light on the origin of the world? They had no knowledge to impart on the subject. They had

---

[1] *De Leg.*, III., 12.
[2] Xen. *Memor.*, L. I.
[3] *Apol. Socrat. apud Plat. et Xenoph.*
[4] *De Leg.*
[5] *The Gentile and the Jew.*

only conjectures to offer; they were hopelessly divided among themselves on this great question.

Some, like Aristotle, taught that the world even in its present form is eternal.

Others, with Plato, approached nearer to the truth by saying that the world as it now exists was formed by God from eternally existing chaos.[1]

Others, with Democritus and Lucretius, imagined that the world was gradually and accidentally formed from imperceptible atoms which had been eternally floating in space, and that life was due to spontaneous generation.[2]

Porphyrius, with other Pantheists, asserted that the universe was an emanation from the Divinity.

The heathen world was as ignorant of man's origin and destiny, as it was of the origin of the works of creation. Man, "know thyself," was the precept of the great Pagan philosopher. But this admonition was more easily given than executed. He knew not whence he came or whither he was going. Man was to himself a profound mystery, which no human philosophy could fathom. He knew only that he was in a state of transition, considering himself the sport of the gods, or driven hither and thither by stern fate, or by chance, or by the influence of the planets.[3]

But the past and the future for him were envel-

---

[1] *Tim.*, pp. 27, *et seq.*
[2] *The Gentile and the Jew*, Vol. I., p. 266; *Hist. of European Morals*, Vol. II., p. 163.
[3] Tacitus, *Hist.* I., 22.

oped in impenetrable darkness. When Edwin, King of Northumbria, England, had, in 627, resolved to become a Christian, he convoked an assembly of his principal counsellors, or Thanes, and required them to state their sentiments on the subject of religion. One of them addressed the king in the following speech: "Often, O king, in the depth of winter, while you are feasting with your Thanes and the fire is blazing on the hearth, you have seen a sparrow pelted by the storm enter one door and escape by the other. During its passage it was visible, but whence it came or whither it went, you knew not. Such seems to me to be the life of man. He walks the earth for a few years; but what precedes his birth, or what is to follow after death, he cannot tell. Undoubtedly, if the new religion can unfold these important secrets, it must be worthy of your attention, and it ought to be followed."[1] This quaint and homely speech strikingly reveals the blindness of the Gentile world regarding the origin and destiny of the human race.

It is no wonder that the Pagans took a gloomy view of life, since they were without God in this world and the hope of Him in the world to come. Their poets, philosophers, and historians proclaimed that man is, of all creatures, the most wretched and unhappy. These maxims were often on their lips: "Not to have been born, were best; the earliest possible death was the next best."[2] "They whom the

[1] *Bede*, B. II., C. 13.
[2] *Lactan.*, III., 18, 19.

gods love, die early." This was said, not in the Christian sense, that they might enter soon into their reward; but that they might cease to suffer by ceasing to exist.

And as their belief in a life to come, with its hopes of future rewards and dread of punishments, was dim and obscure because unaided by revelation, they made the most of their time by plunging into every excess of sensual enjoyment, and by trying to forget their misery in a continued round of intoxicating pleasures. Their philosophy of life was expressed in this brief sentence: "Let us eat and drink and be merry, for to-morrow we die."

And when the cup of pleasure had been emptied to the dregs, they often took refuge in suicide as releasing them from a life no longer endurable. Suicide is, unfortunately, too frequently committed in our own day by men that have emancipated themselves from religious restraint. If self-destruction is so common with us in the face of an enlightened and Christian public opinion, which reprobates it not only as a crime against God and society, but also as an act of moral cowardice, how wide-spread must have been the habit in antiquity, when many of its philosophers and moralists, such as Marcus Aurelius and Pliny,[1] not only declared it to be a lawful deed as a release from mental and physical sufferings, but even enthusiastically applauded it as an heroic act of virtue; and many others, such as Cato and Seneca,

[1] *Epp.* III., 7.

Zeno and Cleanthes,[1] practised what they preached by voluntarily putting an end to their own life.

Some philosophers there were, indeed, who like Plato, Cicero, and Plutarch, had a clearer insight into a future state; but their voice was drowned amid the wail of despair that echoed everywhere around them.

"Since therefore," as Gibbon observes, "the most sublime efforts of philosophy can extend no farther than feebly to point out the desire, the hope, or at most, the probability of a future state, there is nothing except a divine revelation that can ascertain the existence, and describe the condition of the invisible country which is destined to receive the souls of men after their separation from the body."[2]

---

[1] Plutarch, *adv. Stoic*, p. 1063.
[2] *Decline and Fall*, Chap. XV.

CHAPTER XIX.

ORIGIN AND DESTINY OF MAN AS VIEWED BY MODERN UNBELIEF.[1]

Modern scientists, as soon as they close their eyes to the light of Revelation, wander into the most bewildering mazes regarding our common origin. Darwin, Huxley, and Haeckel are the standard-bearers of the modern school of evolutionists. According to their theory, you and I must claim as our primeval father the ape, the monkey, or the gorilla. Our ancestors were dumb beasts. They could speak no articulate tongue. They were without reason, without conscience, without a soul. They had no idea of right and wrong or moral duty. They had no moral freedom, no notion of virtue or vice, of honor or shame.

Mr. Samuel Wainwright exposes the groundlessness of this theory in the following words: "The theory of man's ape-descent is perfect, but it is in the air. It lacks but one thing to give it relevance, and that one thing is reality. Like the 'Chateaux en Espagne,' it exists only in the interested imagination of the pretender. Du Bois Reymond has

[1] See Cardinal Mazella's Treatise, *De Deo Creante, De Hominis Origine.*

incurred the bitter wrath of Haeckel by declaring this genealogical tree to be as authentic in the eyes of a naturalist as are the fabulous pedigrees of the Homeric heroes in those of a historian."[1]

The assertion of man's ape-descent is a gratuitous assumption resting on no scientific foundation. The chief argument in favor of this hypothesis, is taken from the similarity of bodily conformation found to exist between man and some lower animals. A similarity, indeed, there does exist; but that there is an absolute identity in physical construction between man and any other animal, we deny. If there are points of resemblance between the two there are also points of divergence. And this similarity proves nothing; for, as Dr. Albert Stoeckel observes: "If the bodily structure of man shows any similarity to the bodily structure of an ape, does it therefore follow that man has descended from an ape? By no means. Only then such a conclusion could be drawn, if by other empiric facts it could be proved that man could have received such a body *only* by having descended from an ape. But such facts do not exist."[2]

These scientists themselves seem to have only a half-hearted faith in their own theory. They confess to have thus far failed to discover any traces of the missing link necessary to prove man's consanguinity with the ape. "In conclusion, I may say," observes the candid Mr. Huxley, "that the fossil

---

[1] *Scientific Sophisms.*
[2] *Der Materialismus*, p. 65.

remains of man hitherto discovered, do not seem to me to take us appreciably nearer to that lower ape-like form by the modification of which man has, probably, become what he is."[1]

Mr. Haeckel also admits that "of the hypothetical original man who developed himself from anthropoid apes, we are as yet acquainted with no fossil remains."[2]

And Mr. Darwin avows that there exists "the great break in the organic chain between man and his nearest allies, which cannot be bridged over by any extinct or living species known."[3]

The distinguished French naturalist, De Quatrefages, declares: "In the name of scientific truth, I can affirm that we have had for ancestor neither a gorilla, nor an orang-outang, nor a chimpanzee, no more than a seal or a fish, or any other animal whatever."[4]

There is, indeed, an evolution always going on in the world; the oak is evolved from the acorn, and the flower from the seed. But that there is, or that there has been any transmutation from original types, we must deny. No authenticated fact can be adduced to show that one type was ever transmuted into another.

Linnæus, the greatest of botanists, says: "*We reckon on just so many species as there were forms created in*

[1] *Man's Place in Nature.*
[2] L. 6, p. 620.
[3] *The Descent of Man*, Part I., C. VI.
[4] *Natural History of Man*, New York, 1875, p. 87.

the beginning." "All the experiments of breeders and agriculturists and florists," says Sir Charles Lyell, "have never succeeded in giving origin to one new species. . . . The hybrids which result from the union of two distinct species, are always sterile."

If the naked eye could discern the germ as clearly as it does the full-grown body, it would discover the same difference between a human germ and the germ of any brute, as that which exists between them in their developed state.. "The two original germs," says Father Secchi, "of which one produces, for instance, a bird, and the other a fish, must be in the arrangement of their intrinsic parts just as different from each other, as are also the grown and fully-developed animals."[1]

It is a curious illustration of the vagaries of the human mind that, while Darwin refers all living creatures, man included, to one, or at most, to a few original types, another school of philosophers has endeavored to trace the human family not to a single pair, but to different sources. Thus while error runs to both extremes, truth rests between them.

The doctrine of the specific unity of the human race excited the ridicule of the unchristian philosophers of the eighteenth century. Voltaire declared that it could be believed only by blind men, or by those that had never seen people of different races.

Some writers have maintained that the stream of human life descends from two separate sources.

[1] *Die Grösse der Schöpfung.*

Others have enumerated as many as sixteen; while Knox, the head of the American School, insisted that each nation had a distinct origin.

The Holy Scriptures, which, apart from their inspired character, are the oldest, the most authentic and trustworthy historical monuments in existence, repeatedly declare the specific unity of the human family. Now, the dictates of common sense demand that this record should stand until it is disproved by sound investigations.

The chief argument of those that suppose a plurality of the human species, rests upon the great diversity of the human family, chiefly in regard to the color of the skin, the quality of the hair, the shape of the skull, &c. These divergencies appear great in extreme points between individuals of different races. But this is not surprising, since among certain animals manifestly of the same species, there is a greater diversity than even among men.

"As long," says Humboldt, "as attention was directed solely to the extremes in the varieties of color and form, and to the vividness of the first impression of the senses, the observer was naturally disposed to regard races rather as originally different species than as mere varieties. . . . In my opinion, however, more powerful reasons can be advanced for the theory of the unity of the human race; as, for instance, in the many intermediate gradations in the color of the skin and in the form of the skull, which have been made known to us in recent times by the rapid progress of geographical knowledge. . . . The greater number of the contrasts which were formerly supposed to exist, have disappeared before the laborious researches of Tiedemann on the brain of negroes and of Europeans."[1]

The existing difference among some members of the human family is easily accounted for by climate, diet, habits of life, and education.

"Although the existing races of man," says Darwin, "differ in many respects, as in color, hair, shape of skull, proportions of the body, &c., yet if their whole organization be taken into consideration, they are found to resemble one another closely in a multitude of points. Many of these points are of so unimportant and singular a nature that it is extremely improbable that they should have been independently acquired by aboriginally distinct species, or races. The same remark holds good with equal or greater force, with respect to the numerous points of mental similarity between the most distinct races of man. The American aborigines, Negroes, and Europeans differ as much from one another in mind as any three races that can be named; yet I was incessantly struck, while living with the Fuegians on board the 'Beadle,' with many little traits of character showing how similar their minds were to ours; and so it was with a full-blooded Negro with whom I happened once to be intimate. . . . Now,

---

[1] *Cosmos*, Vol. I, p. 352.

when Naturalists observe a close agreement in numerous small details of habits, tastes, and dispositions between two or more domestic races, they use this fact as an argument that all are descended from a common progenitor who was thus endowed."[1]

The anatomical structure and physical constitution of man point decidedly to the unity of the race: in all nations the skin is alike in structure; there is the same general coincidence in respect to the age at which manhood is attained, and to the period in which life begins to decline; all races are subject to similar diseases, modified by climatic influences; and the length of life is, on an average, the same under similar conditions of existence.[2]

The variety of languages, also, was once adduced as an argument against the unity of the descent of the human race. But the best philologists living admit that "no conclusion adverse to the monogenistic doctrine can be drawn from the diversities of speech now existing, or that are known to have existed at any past time."[3] "Nothing," says Max Müller, "necessitates the admission of different independent beginnings for the *material*, or formal elements and grammatical structure of the Turanian, Semitic, and Aryan branches of speech."[4] The same conclusion is reached by Professor W. S. Whiting[5] who, while disclaiming for linguistic

[1] *The Descent of Man*, Part I., Ch. VII.
[2] Cf. Brocklesby, *Elements of Physical Geography*, p. 147.
[3] G. P. Fisher, *Outlines of Univer. History*.
[4] *Lectures on Language*, 1st Series, p. 340.
[5] *Life and Growth of Languages*, p. 267.

science the power to prove that the human race in the beginning formed one society, says that it is "even more demonstrable," and that it can "never prove the variety of human races and origins."

Lastly, the apparent isolation of our American continent from the inhabited portions of the earth, was once considered a formidable objection against the unity of the human family. This error has had but a brief reign, and the objection has long ceased to be seriously entertained by persons of ordinary intelligence. A more familar acquaintance with our globe has shown that our continent is not so far removed from populated countries, as was supposed; and instances are given, by Captain Cook and other navigators, of families in their canoes having been driven by stress of weather from one land to another, a distance of two hundred, and even eight hundred miles. Similar accidents might suffice to transport canoes across the Behring Strait from Asia to North America, or even from Sierra Leone in Africa, to Cape St. Roque in South America.[1] In 1872, a Japanese junk went ashore in Alaska with three live natives on board. Twenty of the crew had perished from hunger. Fifty years ago, a like accident occurred to a Chinese vessel that had drifted ashore to the mouth of the Columbia river with living men on board. Now, it is well known that the junks used at present by the eastern nations are no improvement on those of a thousand years ago.

[1] Cf. Lyell, *Principles of Geology*, Vol. II., p. 472 *et seq.*

We are warranted, therefore, in concluding that neither the difference in color and in the anatomical construction of the human frame, nor the diversity of languages, nor the alleged difficulty in accounting for the original settlement of the American continent, can afford any justification for affirming the plurality of the human species. The dictates of common sense, not to speak of the paramount claims of the inspired Volume, compel us to adhere to the Mosaic narrative, which the cumulative investigations of every succeeding age serve only to corroborate.

Nor are those modern scientists a whit less obscure in regard to our future destiny than in regard to our origin. They have not, any more than the ancient philosophers, a single ray of light to throw across the impenetrable veil that darkens the horizon of the tomb. "Whence come we? whither go we?" asks Mr. Tyndall. "The question dies without an answer, *without even an echo*, upon the infinite shores of the unknown. . . . Having exhausted physics and reached its very rim, the real mystery stills looms up beyond us. We have, in fact, made no step toward its solution. And thus it will ever loom even beyond the bourne of knowledge, compelling the philosophies of successive ages to confess that

> 'We are such stuff
> As dreams are made of, and our little life
> Is rounded with a sleep.'"[1]

[1] Belfast Address.

CHAPTER XX.

Christian Idea of God. Origin and Destiny of Man as viewed by Christian Revelation.

Let us now go with Nicodemus to the Divine Founder of the Christian religion, and ask Him for light on these vital questions. "Master, we know that Thou art come a Teacher from God."[1] "Thou art the way, the truth, and the life." Thou art the light of the world. He that followeth Thee walketh not in darkness, but shall have the light of life.[2] Thou art "a light for the illumination of the Gentiles, and for the glory of Thy people, Israel."[3] Thou didst inspire the Patriarchs and Prophets of the Old Law, and the Apostles and Evangelists of the New. Tell us, then, of God, of the world around us, and of ourselves.

How satisfactory is the answer! How clear and luminous are the pages of Holy Writ regarding God and man and the universe compared with the gropings of Gentile writers! The Christian religion proclaims truths that satisfy the highest aspirations

[1] *John* III.   [3] *Luke* II.
[2] *Ibid.*, VIII.

of the human intellect, and gratify the legitimate cravings of the human heart. The youth furnished with a correct knowledge of his catechism—that admirable compendium of Revelation,—has solved the most momentous questions that ever engrossed the mind of man. He has acquired a knowledge of truths that have baffled the investigation of the most profound philosophers of Pagan antiquity, and even of modern scientists who discard the light of Revelation.

The Christian religion gives us a sublime and beautiful idea of God and His attributes. It tells us of a God essentially one: "Hear, O Israel, the Lord thy God is one God;"[1] a God self-existing, living from eternity unto eternity. It tells us of a God who created all things by His power, who governs all things by His wisdom, whose superintending providence watches over the affairs of nations and of men, who numbers the hairs of our head, and without whom not even a bird falls to the ground. It reveals to us a God infinitely beautiful, the perfect ideal of all created beauty, infinitely holy, infinitely just, merciful, and beneficent. This exalted conception of the Supreme Being, so consonant to our reason, is in striking contrast with the low, grovelling, and sensual attributes ascribed by the Pagans to their divinities.

The knowledge that the Christian religion gives us of God and His attributes, is not of an abstruse

[1] *Mark* XII.

or speculative character; for God never panders to a spirit of vain curiosity: "He that is a searcher of majesty, shall be overwhelmed by glory."[1] The whole Bible contains only a few passages about the Holy Trinity, because the knowledge of that mystery would exercise no influence on our moral life. "What doth it profit thee to discourse profoundly of the Trinity, if thou art wanting in humility and, consequently, displeasing to the Trinity?"[2]

The knowledge disclosed to us is of a practical kind. So much of the veil is uplifted as will enable us to see what is useful and profitable to us, and no more. If some of the divine perfections are made manifest to us, it is that we may endeavor to imitate them. "Be ye perfect even as your Heavenly Father is perfect."[3] "Be ye holy; for I, the Lord your God, am holy."[4] "Be ye, therefore, merciful, as your Father also is merciful."[5] If His infinite justice, truth, and loving-kindness are revealed to us, it is that we may cultivate those virtues, though at an immeasurable distance from our divine Model, and that we may "do according to the pattern which is shown us on the Mount."[6]

The Christian religion teaches us that supreme worship is due to God alone: "The Lord thy God shalt thou adore, and Him only shalt thou serve."[7]

[1] *Prov.* XXV.
[2] *Kempis*, B. I., C. I.
[3] *Matt.* V., 48.
[4] *Levit.* XIX., 2.
[5] *Luke* VI.
[6] *Exod.* XXV.
[7] *Matt.* IV.

It makes no compromise with idolatry or any form of superstition: "I am the Lord thy God. . . . Thou shalt not have strange gods before Me."[1] "Neither let there be found among you anyone that consulteth soothsayers, or observeth dreams and omens; neither let there be any wizard, nor charmer, nor anyone that consulteth familiar spirits, or fortune-tellers, or a necromancer; for the Lord abhorreth all these things."[2]

With regard to the creation of the world and the origin of man, a few strokes of the sacred penman give us more information on this subject than can be evolved from the combined theories of ancient and modern geologists. The Mosaic narrative has never been supplanted by any reasonable system, nor even successfully assailed.

"In the beginning God created heaven and earth. And the earth was void and empty, and darkness was upon the face of the deep: and the Spirit of God moved over the waters. And God said: Let light be, and light was. Let the earth bring forth the green herb, and it was so. And God said: Let the earth bring forth living creatures in their kind. And it was so."[3] Here we have first creation out of nothing, then order out of chaos; next the earth becomes fruitful, it becomes the abode of living creatures, and lastly, of man. As man was destined to be the lord of creation, it was fitting that he

---

[1] *Exodus* XX.   [3] *Gen.* I.
[2] *Deut.* XVIII.

should be created last, and that he should find his palace adorned for him.

"The proper study of mankind is man."

Huxley well observes: "The question of questions for mankind—the problem that underlies all others and that is more deeply interesting than any other—is the ascertainment of the place which man occupies in nature, and of his relation to the universe of things. Whence our race has come—to what goal we are tending—are the problems which present themselves anew and with undiminished interest to every man born into the world."[1] Why are we here? Why do we breathe the breath of life? What is the true aim and purpose of our existence? Is life worth living? It is only in the school of Christ that these questions can be satisfactorily solved.

The Christian religion gives us a rational and ennobling idea of man's origin and destiny, and offers to us also the means of attaining that destiny. It has rescued him from the frightful labyrinth of error in which Paganism had involved him.

The solution of the great problem is found in the first page of the Catechism: "God created us that we might know Him and love Him and serve Him in this world, and be happy with Him forever in the next." This short sentence embodies our divine origin, immortal destiny, and the conditions for fulfilling it.

[1] *Evidence as to Man's Place in Nature.*

The Scriptures tell us that God formed man's body from the earth, that He breathed a living soul into the human form, and gave it life. "God created man to His own image."[1] This living soul of man He endowed with exalted faculties, which distinguish him from the brute creation. He gave him a sublime intelligence capable of knowing his Creator; a memory capable of summoning the past and placing it in review before him; an imagination penetrating into the boundless future. He imprinted on his heart a law to guide him. He gave him a conscience to interpret the law, and free-will to observe or violate it.

I have created this world, He says in Holy Writ, not only for My own glory, but for your use and benefit. The sun, moon, and stars of heaven serve not only to reveal My majesty and power, but also to give you light and to afford you a delightful vision. The earth and all it contains are for your rational enjoyment. In a word, I have made you lord of the earthly creation: "Rule over the fishes of the sea, and the fowls of the air, and all living creatures which move upon the earth."[2]

How well does the Royal Prophet describe the prominent place given to man in nature: "I will behold Thy heavens, the works of Thy fingers: the moon and the stars which Thou hast founded. What is man that Thou art mindful of him, or the son of man that Thou visitest him? Thou

[1] *Gen.* I.
[2] *Gen.* I.

hast made him a little less than the angels, Thou hast crowned him with glory and honor, and hast set him over the works of Thy hands. Thou hast put all things under his feet, the birds of the air and the fishes of the sea that pass through the paths of the sea."[1]

In this exposition of man's dignity, there is not a word about the missing link, not the faintest allusion to our possible descent from the ape, or from any other animal of the brute creation; but man stands forth in the light of Revelation, as the connecting link between the highest and lowest order of creation. He is a world in miniature. By his material body, he is connected with the earth under his feet; by his organic life, he is connected with the vegetable world; by his faculty of sensation, he forms one with the animal world; and by his reason, he is associated with the angels.[2]

There was, indeed, a missing link in the genealogy of man, but philosophers sought for it in the wrong direction. The link was missing not below, but above him. The missing link was the sacred family tie which bound him to God, his Father, and which had been broken by the Fall of Adam. Jesus Christ came to reforge that link, and to add another title to man's dignity. He came to declare man not only the creature of God, but also the child and heir of God. "You were without God in this world," says the Apostle, "but

---

[1] *Ps.* VIII.
[2] *St. Thom.*, 1ª. Quæst., XCVI., 2.

now you who were afar off are made nigh (to Him) by the blood of Christ. . . . For by Him we have access to the Father. Now, therefore, you are no more strangers and foreigners, but you are fellow-citizens with the saints, and of the household of God, built upon the foundation of the Apostles and Prophets, Jesus Christ Himself being the chief corner-stone."[1] Jesus Himself is the link, for He is the Mediator between God and man. When "I am lifted up from the earth," He says, "I will draw all things to Myself,"[2] that is, all that shall truly believe in Me.

"When the fulness of time came, God sent His Son made of a woman . . . that we might receive the adoption of sons."[3] Thus by one stroke of divine clemency, a triple blessing is conferred upon us, the chains of spiritual bondage are stricken from our feet, the sweet yoke of divine fellowship is restored, and we are adopted into the family of God, to enjoy the glorious liberty of children of God.

"Behold," says St. John, "what manner of love the Father hath given us, that we should be called and be the children of God. . . . Beloved, we are now children of God. . . . We know that when He shall appear, we shall be like to Him, because we shall see Him as He is."[4] How different is our intercourse with our God from the relation of even the Jews with Him! They lived under the law of fear. They addressed their Creator by the title

[1] *Eph.* II.
[2] *John* XII.
[3] *Gal.* IV.
[4] *I. John* III.

of God, King, Ruler, or Jehovah, and rarely ever by the endearing name of Father. Not so you, Christian readers! For, as St. Paul says: "You have not received the spirit of bondage again in fear; but you have received the spirit of adoption of sons, wherein we cry: Abba, Father. For the Spirit Himself beareth witness to our spirit that we are the sons of God. And if sons, heirs also: heirs indeed of God, and joint heirs with Christ."[1] By no name is God invoked more commonly than by the tender name of Father, and no prayer is more frequently on our lips than the "Our Father."

Here man is placed before us in his true light, not as the brood of some lower animal, not as a waif tossed about on the ocean of life, the sport of the gods; not as the creature of chance, or the victim of iron fate, but rather as the child of Providence, who takes him by the hand and guides his steps through life even to his eternal destiny in heaven, if he only follow the inspirations of grace.

I am asked to surrender my divine birthright, to renounce my royal origin and my heavenly inheritance, the title of which has been signed and sealed by the hand of God Himself, recorded in the Sacred Book, witnessed by the Apostles with their blood, attested by the greatest intellects of the civilized world, and which has successfully stood the test of nineteen centuries. Instead of it, I am asked to accept an unproven and disproven theory that will

---

[1] *Rom.* VIII.

soon be forgotten to give place to some other phantom of a fertile brain.

The Lord forbid that I should renounce my royal title, and say to the dumb beast what unfaithful Israel said to the stock: "Thou art my father; thou hast begotten me."[1]

Achab, King of Israel, not content with his princely estates, coveted also the vineyard of Naboth. But Naboth said to the king: "The Lord forbid that I should give thee the inheritance of my fathers."[2]

Such is also the ambition of many scientists. Like Achab they are not satisfied with ruling over the territory of science; they are tempted to trespass on the forbidden ground of Revelation. But we must say to them: God forbid that we should surrender to you our inheritance. You have dominion over the empire of science. Be content with its broad domains, explore its fields as you will, develop its rich resources, bring to light its hidden treasures; but do not encroach on the domain of faith. That belongs not to you. Touch it not with profane hands. We are its custodians. God forbid that we should give to you the inheritance of our fathers. Like Naboth, we will die rather than surrender it.

We should hold fast to the inheritance of our Christian faith, which tells us who we are, and what we are to be, and not suffer it to be snatched

[1] *Jer.* II.
[2] *III. Kings* XXI.

from us. It has often been lost by men, and even by whole nations. I have passed through regions now spiritually desolate and strewn with the wrecks of a once vigorous faith.

The history of nations clearly demonstrates that it is much easier to convert a Pagan people to Christianity than to re-convert a nation that has once apostatized. The words of the Apostle contain a profound truth and a fearful warning. It is morally impossible, he says, for those who were once illuminated by faith, who have tasted also the heavenly gift, who were made partakers of the Holy Ghost, and who are fallen away by apostasy, to return once more to the faith of their fathers.[1]

---

[1] *Heb.* VI.

CHAPTER XXI.

CHRISTIANITY AND MODERN SCIENCE. THERE IS NO CONFLICT BETWEEN SCIENCE AND REVELATION.

It cannot be denied that there dwells in many sincere minds a lurking suspicion, amounting in some persons almost to a painful conviction, that antagonism exists between certain dogmas of revelation and the results of scientific investigation. Mr. Huxley, Dr. Draper, and other acknowledged leaders of modern thought, have done their utmost to confirm these sinister impressions and to widen the breach between the teachers of religion and those of physical science. They will tell you that the study of nature leads us away from God and ultimately results in the denial of His existence. They maintain that there is and must be an irrepressible conflict between these two great branches of knowledge; that they cannot coexist; and that, in the long run, theology must surrender to her younger and more progressive rival.

They affect to believe that the champions of Christianity, conscious of the unequal conflict, view with alarm the rapid strides of the natural sciences, and do all in their power to discourage the study of them altogether. You will be told, dear reader, by this modern school of thought, that the more you are attached to the teachings of Christian faith, the more will your judgment be warped—your intellect stunted, and the more you will be retarded in the investigation of scientific truth. They will try to persuade you that, in exploring the regions of science, you will be in constant danger of falling foul of some ecclesiastical ukase warning you away from the poisoned tree of knowledge, just as our primitive parents were forbidden to eat the fruit of a certain tree in Paradise. They will tell you that your path is likely to be intercepted by some Pope's bull, which may metaphorically gore you to death. They will, in a word, contend that, to enjoy full freedom in searching the secrets of the physical world, you must emancipate yourself from the intellectual restraints imposed on you by the Christian religion.

Such are the statements deliberately made in our times against Christian revelation. But though they are uttered by bearded men, we call them childish declamations. We call them also ungrateful assertions, since they are spoken by men who are indebted to Christianity for the very discoveries they have made. Many a Christian Moses has wandered for years through the wilderness of investigation, and died almost in sight of the promised land of scientific discovery. And his successors, guided by the path that he had opened, and who might otherwise have died unknown after vain wanderings, entered the coveted territory and enjoyed its fruits. Even Mr. Tyndall avows that "the nineteenth century strikes its roots into the centuries gone by and draws nutriment from them."[1]

The truth is, that how much soever scientists and theologians may quarrel among themselves, there will never be any collision, but the most perfect harmony will ever exist between science and religion, as we shall endeavor to demonstrate in the following pages.

There are, indeed, and there ever will remain, truths of religion difficult to be reconciled with facts of science. If the ideas of time and space and the relation of soul to body are beyond our comprehension, we cannot be expected with our unaided reason to explain away the apparent incongruities that we find between the unseen and the visible kingdom of the universe. But difficulties do not necessarily involve doubts, still less denials. If we hold the two ends of a chain, we know that the connection is complete, though some of the links may be concealed from us.

Science and Religion, like Martha and Mary, are sisters, because they are daughters of the same Father. They are both ministering to the same Lord, though in a different way. Science, like Martha, is busy about material things; Religion, like Mary, is kneeling at the feet of her Lord.

[1] On the Study of Physics.

The Christian religion teaches nothing but what has been revealed by Almighty God, or what is necessarily derived from revelation. God is truth. All truth comes from Him. He is the Author of all scientific truth, as He is the Author of all revealed truth. "The God who dictated the Bible," as Archbishop Ryan has happily said, "is the God who wrote the illuminated manuscript of the skies." You might as well expect that one ray of the sun would dim the light of another, as that any truth of revelation can be opposed to any truth of science. No truth of natural science can ever be opposed to any truth of revelation; nor can any truth of the natural order be at variance with any truth of the supernatural order. Truth differs from truth only as star differs from star,—each gives out the same pure light that reaches our vision across the expanse of the firmament.

Legitimate inquiries into the laws of nature are, therefore, no more impeded by the dogmas of faith than our bodily movements are obstructed by the laws of physics. Nay, more, we have the highest ecclesiastical authority for declaring that "not only can faith and reason never be opposed to each other, but that they mutually aid each other; for right reason demonstrates the foundations of faith and, enlightened by its light, cultivates the science of things divine, while faith frees and guards reason from errors and furnishes it with manifold knowledge."[1]

[1] Vatican Council.

Revelation teaches us that this material world had a beginning; that it shall have an end; and that God created it to manifest His wisdom and power, and for man's use and benefit. Hence, so far from warping our judgment, stunting our intellect, or retarding us in the prosecution of scientific truth, Christian revelation will be like the sun lighting up our course in the path of science, like a landmark directing us onward in the road of truth, like a beacon-light cautioning us to avoid the quicksands upon which false science has often been shipwrecked.

Science, on the other hand, when studied with humility, reveals to us the intimate relations of the forces of nature with one another, the unity of the laws governing them, and their subordination to a controlling Mind. In all its endeavors to follow up the changes and developments of the earth, it can never get beyond a certain first substance which is under the influence of certain forces, and under the dominion of certain laws.

In contemplating the universe and tracing the effect to the Cause, we are filled with the sentiments of the Royal Prophet: "The heavens show forth the glory of God, and the firmament declareth the work of His hands."[1] No man can view St. Peter's dome without admiring the genius of Michel Angelo; neither can the thoughtful student contemplate the dome of heaven without associating in his mind the great Architect of nature. In beholding

[1] *Ps.* XVIII., 2.

the vast firmament with its countless stars moving through boundless space, he is filled with a sense of God's immensity; for wherever creation is, there also is the Creator.

If from the top of a distant tower, we view a number of trains running in different directions, all arriving on schedule time at their respective stations, we admire the skill of the engineers, although they themselves are beyond the reach of our vision. And what are the numberless orbs of the universe, both stellar and planetary, but vast engines rushing through space with a velocity immeasurably greater than that of the fastest railroad car? Though often crossing one another, they never deviate from their course, never collide, nor are they ever precipitated through the abyss of space. Should we not admire the Divine Intelligence that controls these engines and that leads them with unvarying precision to their appointed destination?

The great luminary of day suggests to us the splendor of that uncreated "Light which enlighteneth every man that cometh into this world."[1] Its rays, illumining our planet and penetrating its hidden recesses, are a fitting type to us of the all-seeing eye of God, of whom the Royal Prophet again says: "Whither shall I go from thy spirit, or whither shall I flee from thy face? If I ascend into heaven, thou art there; if I descend into hell, thou art present."[2]

[1] *John* I., 9.
[2] *Ps.* CXXXVIII., 7, 8.

The earth, yielding its fruits with prolific bounty, proclaims God's merciful providence in supplying man's wants and comforts.

The beauty of the landscape is a mirror dimly reflecting the infinite loveliness of God; for the author must possess in an eminent degree the perfections exhibited in his works. Solomon, who was a close student of nature, was thus impressed.[1] He says, if men are delighted with the beauty of the visible creation, "Let them know how much the Lord of them is more beautiful than they: for the first Author of beauty made all these things. . . . . For by the greatness of the beauty, and of the creature, the Creator of them may be seen, so as to be known thereby."[2] And St. Paul declares that they who will not recognize the power and divinity of God by the contemplation of the works of creation, are inexcusable.[3]

When the thoughtful student reflects that he is a mere atom amid the illimitable space and countless orbs that surround him, he is overawed by a sense of his nothingness; and when he considers how little he has learned after all his labor, in comparison with the treasures of knowledge that still lie hidden in nature's bosom, he is profoundly impressed with his ignorance.

But when he considers the intellectual faculties with which he is endowed and the pre-eminent place he holds in creation, conscious of his dignity,

---

[1] *III. Kings* IV., 33.　　[2] *Rom.* I.
[3] *Wisdom* XIII., 3, 5.

he is filled with gratitude to God, as was David when he said: "What is man that thou art mindful of him! ... Thou hast made him a little less than the angels, Thou hast crowned him with glory and honor, and hast set him over the works of Thy hands."[1]

In a word, every object in creation speaks to him of the wisdom and power of God. He

> "Finds tongues in trees, books in running brooks,
> Sermons in stones, and good in everything."[2]

He rises from nature to nature's God.

The more deeply the student of nature penetrates into her secrets, the more does he admire the wisdom of the Creator. "Small draughts of philosophy," says Bacon, "lead to atheism; but larger ones bring back to God."

It would, therefore, be a great mistake to suppose that the agnostic and unbelieving scientists of the nineteenth century are made such by physical studies. They were already imbued with those ideas when they began their labors, and every phenomenon which they discovered was shaped to suit their preconceived theories.

---

[1] *Ps.* VIII., 5, 6, 7.
[2] *As You Like It.*

CHAPTER XXII.

THE CHURCH IS THE TRUE FRIEND AND PROMOTER OF SCIENCE.

Now, since reason and revelation aid each other in leading us to God, the Author of both, it is manifest that the Catholic Church, so far from being opposed to the cultivation of reason, encourages and fosters science of every kind. The more secrets science will elicit from nature's bosom, the more the Church will rejoice; because she knows that no new revelation of nature will ever utter the words: "There is no God!" Rather will they whisper to the eager investigator, "He made us, and not we ourselves."

Each new discovery of science is a trophy with which religion loves to adorn her altars. She hails every fresh invention as another voice adding its harmonious notes to that grand choir which is ever singing the praises of the God of nature.

At no period of the Church's history did she wield greater authority than from the twelfth to the sixteenth century. She exercised not only spiritual, but also temporal power; and she had great influence with the princes of Christendom. Now, this is the very period of the rise and development of the universities in Europe. During these four centuries, nineteen universities were opened in France, thirteen in Italy, six in Great Britain and Ireland, two in Spain and one in Belgium. At no time did the human intellect revel in greater freedom. No question of speculative science escaped the inquisitive search of men of thought. Successful explorations were made in every field of science and art. The weapons of heathendom were employed in fighting the battles of truth. The principles of Aristotle, the greatest of ancient dialecticians, were used as handmaids to religion and, in the words of Cardinal Newman, "With the jaw-bone of an ass, with the skeleton of Pagan Greece, St. Thomas, the Samson of the schools, put to flight his thousand Philistines."[1]

It is an incontrovertible fact that it is only in countries enjoying the blessings of Christian civilization that science has made any perceptible progress. And the writers who for the last two thousand years have been most conspicuous in every department of physical knowledge, were, with few exceptions, believers in Christian revelation. If we search for light among the followers of Lucretius, Confucius, or Mohammed, we shall find little to reward us for our pains.

In astronomy and geology, mechanics and math-

[1] *The Idea of a University*, Sec. viii.

ematics, in chemistry, physiology, and navigation, Christian scholars hold a pre-eminent place. It is to Copernicus, a priest and canon, that the world is indebted for the discovery of the planetary revolutions around the sun.

It is to the learning and patronage of Pope Gregory XIII. that we owe the reformation of the calendar and the computations which determine with minute accuracy the length of the solar year. Galileo, Kepler, and Secchi, Sir Isaac Newton and Lord Bacon, Leibnitz, Lavoisier, Euler, Cuvier, and Descartes, are recognized leaders in the field of science. They were, moreover, firm believers in revelation, while most of them combined strong religious convictions with scientific erudition. In the study of nature they do not fail to record with devout praise their admiration for the power and providence of the Creator.

The first circumnavigation of the globe, the discovery of the American continent, the doubling of the Cape of Good Hope, as well as the most accurate geographical survey of the earth's surface are events for which we are indebted to Christian navigators and explorers, all actuated by an indomitable spirit of enterprise, and most of them inspired with the higher motive of zeal for the propagation of the Gospel. Marco Polo, Columbus, Amerigo Vespucci, Magellan, and Vasco da Gama, were men of strong religious faith, who embarked on their perilous voyages with the benediction of the Church upon them.

Our own country is largely indebted to Catholic

priests, who were the pioneers, not only of religion and civilization, but also of science. In one hand they bore the torch of science, and in the other the torch of religion. They not only carried the Gospel to the aboriginal tribes of North America, but they explored our rivers, lakes, and mountains; and the charts that they sent to Europe over two hundred years ago are still admired as models of topographical accuracy.

With these facts before us it is difficult to suppress a feeling of indignation when we are told that Christianity is a bar to 'scientific investigation. These maligners of Christianity owe it to the Christian religion that they are able to revile her. Separate them from the universities and schools founded by Christian patronage, withdraw them from Christian traditions and literature, and they would die of intellectual stagnation.

There is no branch of art in which the disciples of Christianity have not excelled. Was not Michel Angelo a devout son of the Church? And who surpassed him in sculpture and architecture? To him we are indebted for St. Peter's basilica, the grandest church ever erected to God by the hand of man. Byron found that

"Power, glory, strength, and beauty,—all are aisled
In this eternal ark of worship undefiled."

And were not Raphael and Domenichino, Fra Angelico and Leonardo da Vinci, members of the Church? And are they not the recognized masters in the exquisite art of painting? Mozart and Haydn, Beethoven and Palestrina were Christian men, and were patronized by Popes and bishops. And are they not acknowledged leaders in the rich and harmonious strains of music? Their masses are as unrivalled in musical composition as our cathedrals are in architecture.

The apparent conflict between the deductions of science and the doctrines of Christian faith is clearly accounted for in the following Decree of the Vatican Council: "There never can be any real discrepancy between reason and faith, since the same God who reveals mysteries, has bestowed the light of reason on the human mind; and God cannot deny Himself, nor can truth ever contradict truth. *The appearance of such a contradiction is mainly due either to the dogmas of faith not having been understood and expounded according to the mind of the Church, or to the inventions of opinion having been taken for the verdict of reason.*"

If these explanations are kept in view, they will serve to demonstrate that the apparent conflict between science and revelation has no foundation upon which to rest.

1. It is often erroneously assumed that the Scriptures propound doctrines which they never professed to teach. The Sacred Volume was not intended by its Divine Author to give us a scientific treatise on astronomy, or cosmogony, or geology, or even a complete series of chronology or genealogy. These matters are incidentally introduced to illus-

trate a higher subject. The purpose of the Scriptures is to recount God's supernatural relations with mankind, His providential government of the world, and man's moral obligations to his Creator.

When, for instance, the Sacred Text declares that the sun stood still in the heavens,[1] it simply gives expression to the miraculous prolongation of the day: and this in popular language such as even now with our improved knowledge of astronomy we employ, for we speak of the rising and setting of the sun as if, according to the Ptolemaic system, we still believed that he revolves around the earth. The Church has no mission to teach astronomy. One may be a bad astronomer and yet be a good Christian.

Again, the results of geological investigation, by which it is claimed that ages must have elapsed between the formation of matter and the creation of man, would seem to conflict with the book of Genesis, which states that all vegetable and animal life was created within the space of six days. But the Church, as is well known, has never defined the meaning to be attached to these *days* of Genesis. We are at liberty, as far as the Church is concerned, and if the deductions of science are incontrovertible, we are compelled to ascribe an indefinite period of years to each day. The context itself insinuates that the day cannot be restricted to twenty-four

---

[1] *Josue* X., 15.

hours, since for the first three days there was no sun to measure their duration; and in the second chapter of Genesis the word *day* is manifestly used to express an indefinite period of time employed in the creation of the material universe.

The Mosaic narrative simply records the creation of matter out of nothing, and the order in which life, both animal and human, came into existence. The chronological order of Moses is borne out by the researches of geologists, who have discovered that vegetable fossils are anterior to animal remains and that those of the lower animals are more ancient than any human skeletons ever found. Our knowledge, moreover, of the laws governing the vegetable and animal kingdoms confirms this arrangement, since vegetable life derives its subsistence from inorganic matter, animal life is nourished by the vegetable kingdom and man himself is sustained by the nutriment he derives from both.

The discovery of human fossils, and of other geological and historical monuments, is sometimes boldly assumed to stamp the human family with a far greater antiquity than appears to be warranted by Scripture genealogies. To this I reply that the Scripture gives no precise data regarding the time intervening between Adam and our Lord. We have only conjectures resting on genealogies. The enumeration of Adam's lineal descendants is not claimed to be consecutive and complete. It is not denied that links may be missing in the chain of generation. There is also a marked discrepancy between the different versions of the Bible in computing the age of man. The Vulgate reckons four thousand years; the Septuagint, five thousand; and the Hebrew six thousand years from Adam to our Saviour. Some Catholic writers, without any reproof from the Church, are disposed to extend the period to over eight thousand years.

On the other hand, some of the ablest scientists have refuted the fabulous ages ascribed by certain writers to the human family. The Egyptian hieroglyphics and the cuneiform inscriptions of western Asia, were triumphantly quoted as demanding for man an antiquity immeasurably more remote than is warranted by Scripture history.

But the patient investigations of Champollion, Rawlinson, and others, prove that Egypt furnishes no authentic record of human government and human life as ancient as is claimed for it by the adversaries of the Bible. The studies of Layard in Assyrian Archæology and the researches of Legge in Ancient Chinese history, concur in dissipating the cloud of legendary fable surrounding the dynasties of these nations.

The presumptive evidence furnished by human fossils is now ruled out of court by the best students of anthropology. When we consider the untiring industry of man and his indomitable tendency to leave a record of his deeds behind him, and since we fail to find any authentic traces of him in pre-Adamite times, we are supplied with an indirect though eloquent confirmation of the substantial correctness of the Mosaic chronology.

Is it not a remarkable fact, which shows the special supervision of God over His Church, that, in her long history, she has never formally interpreted a single text of Scripture which was afterward contradicted by any authenticated discovery of science? Nor were occasions wanting when, in the apparent interests of faith, she was tempted to give a false decision. For centuries the opinion obtained, seemingly supported by Scripture, that the earth was level. St. Boniface, the Apostle of Germany in the eighth century, complained to the Holy See that an Irish bishop named Virgilius had taught that the earth was spherical, as science now demonstrates it to be. But the Holy See prudently abstained from rendering any decision on the subject.

2. Whenever any supposed scientific discovery conflicts with an acknowledged truth of revelation, we may rest assured that the alleged scientific facts have no reality, but are groundless assumptions and mere hypotheses with not even the merit of originality.

For instance, the Scripture declaration affirming the unity of the human species, was for a long time controverted by many scientists. They denied that all men could have sprung from the same stock; first, because the human family is characterized by so many types and colors; secondly, because they speak a variety of tongues having apparently no relation with one another; thirdly, because scientists believed it impossible, for want of adequate means of transportation, that America and other newly discovered countries could have been peopled from any other nation.

But subsequent researches have shown the fallacy of their reasoning and confirmed the truth of the Biblical narrative. It is now admitted that climate, food, and habits of life have a marked influence on the color and physical formation of man. Philologists compute the number of languages and dialects spoken throughout the world to be over three thousand. They tell us that there are common principles governing the constitution of languages, which justify the opinion, if they do not conclusively demonstrate, that all languages can be traced to a single source.

It is now obvious to every one acquainted with geography how easily the aboriginal inhabitants of America could have passed over from Asia by the Behring Strait. A like solution applies to other inhabited places more recently discovered, as has been observed in a preceding chapter.

"Nothing is more strange," observes a recent writer, "than the incessant reproduction of old thoughts under the guise of new and advanced opinions. It would seem as if the human mind, with all its restless activity, were destined to revolve in an endless circle . . . . . Professor Tyndall, addressing the world from the throne of modern science, repeats the thoughts of Democritus and Epicurus as the last guesses of the scientific mind." [1]

---

[1] *Blackwood's Magazine*, November, 1874.

In fact, there is no class of men so dogmatic and so impatient of contradiction as certain modern scientists; and "this dogmatism is the more intolerable, as the so-called 'demonstrations' of one age have sometimes been the butt and ridicule of succeeding generations."[1] Not content with cultivating their own field, they invade the region of theology and politics. They speak as if they had an exclusive diploma to treat of everything in heaven above, on the earth beneath, and in the waters under the earth; and from their infallible judgment there must be no appeal. Mr. Tyndall recently wrote some very angry letters against Mr. Gladstone. The veteran statesman is denounced by the professor as a hoary rhetorician and a desperate gamester, because he presumed to advocate Home Rule for Ireland.

The position of the Catholic Church in reference to modern scientists may be thus briefly summarized: The Church fosters and encourages every department of science. But just because she is the friend of true science she is opposed to all false pretensions of science. There is as much difference between true and false science as there is between authority and despotism, liberty and license. When she hears a man advancing some crude theory at variance with the received doctrines of revelation,— with the existence of God, for example, or His superintending providence or His wisdom or His sanctity; when she hears him advocating some hy-

[1] *Creation's Testimony*, C. V., p. 118.

pothesis opposed to the unity of the human species, to the spirituality and the immortality of the soul, to the future destiny of man, and to those other great doctrines that involve at once the dignity and moral responsibility of the human race, she knows that his assumptions must be false, because she knows that God's revelation must be true. She stands between such a man and the Divine Oracle of which she is the custodian; and when she sees him raise his profane hands and attempt to touch the temple of faith, she cries out, "Thus far shalt thou go and no farther!"

Will you not agree with us that she is right in raising her voice against groundless theories that desecrate the truth and poison its very source? How can we consent to forsake the sacred fountain at which our forefathers slaked their thirst for centuries, to run after some mirage that these modern philosophers have conjured up before our imagination? If God's revelation is at the mercy of every sciolist, what, then, becomes of those great and consoling truths underlying our social fabric? They are no more than shifting sands beneath our feet.

The pathway of time is strewn with the wreck of many an imposing scientific theory that once found favor in the opinion of men. And such will ever be the fate of those wild speculations and unfounded assumptions that impugn the truth of revelation. They may float for a time on the human mind like huge icebergs drifting along the ocean's current, chilling the atmosphere and carrying destruction in their path. But like the false theories before them, they are destined to melt away beneath the effulgent rays of reason and revelation, while "the truth of the Lord remaineth forever."[1]

---

[1] Ps. CXVI., 2.

CHAPTER XXIII.

INFLUENCE OF PAGANISM UPON MORALS.

This and the following chapter treat of the relative influence of Paganism and Christianity upon Morals. In the present chapter, the influence of Paganism, and in the next the influence of Christianity upon Morals, will be considered.

We may form some idea of the moral degradation of the Pagan world when we reflect that they had no heavenly ideal of exalted virtue to follow.

The heathen gods and goddesses were monsters of iniquity. Jupiter and Bacchus, Mars and Mercury, Venus and Circe, were the patrons of some particular passion. Every vice was canonized in the person of some divinity. Lust and drunkenness, violence and theft, had each its respective patron deity. The Pagans had a religious worship; but unlike the Christian worship, it was not intended to exercise, nor did it exercise, any influence on the morals of the people.[1] They had their priests. But what could be expected of a priesthood that offered sacri-

---
[1] Lecky, *History of European Morals*, Vol. I., p. 161.

fice to divinities whose crimes they avowed? The disciples could not be expected to excel their masters; water does not rise above its level. Moreover, moral teaching was not included among the priestly functions. To make man virtuous was no more the business of the priest than of the physician or the tax-gatherer. The priest was a mere state official.

They had festival days, but they were devoted to debauchery and not to moral growth. They had numerous temples, but they were haunts of licentiousness; the voice of exhortation to virtue never resounded within their walls. They offered sacrifices to Mercury from gratitude for his having made known the knavery and artifices of their slaves, and the slaves offered him the first-fruits of their pilferings.[1] On the festivals of Bacchus prizes were given to the deepest drinkers.[2] In Greece and Rome the worship of Aphrodite was characterized by shameless impurity and unnatural crimes. Shrines consecrated to Venus were maintained at the expense of notorious courtesans. Ovid advised women to shun the temples of the gods, that they might not be there reminded of the lasciviousness of Jupiter.[3]

"It is a matter of general notoriety," says Tertullian, "that the temples are the very places where adulteries are arranged, and procuresses pursue their victims between the altars."[4] In the chambers of the priests and ministers of the temple impurity was

[1] Pausanias, V. 24, I.
[2] Döllinger, *The Gentile and the Jew*, II., 191.
[3] *Trist.* 2.   [4] *Apol.* C. 15.

committed amid clouds of incense, and this more frequently than in the privileged haunts of sin.[1] Prostitution was practised as a religious rite in many countries, notably in Syria, Armenia, Babylonia, and Lydia.[2]

If such scenes were enacted in the temples, we may judge of the obscenities of the theatres. The quarrels of the gods, their adulterous gallantries, their robberies and their deeds of violence, were the favorite themes of the plays. The effects of these exhibitions on the impressible hearts of the spectators are vividly described by Juvenal.[3] These representations were witnessed not only by the masses, but also by the Senate and Consuls, and even by the augurs and Vestal virgins, who had special seats assigned to them.

It should also be borne in mind that these popular amusements were regarded as religious acts, forming a part of the public worship. They were intended to appease the wrath of the gods and to propitiate their favor.

What mimic art presented in the theatre, was reproduced in paintings on the walls of temples and private houses. Art was made the handmaid of vice. At every step the Greek and the Roman were confronted by lascivious portraits of their divinities. Religion became associated with lewdness in the mind of youth, and the impure image was stamped upon the imagination, even before the heart was conscious of the poison it was imbibing.

---

[1] Minutius Octavus, C. 25.
[2] *Gentile and Jew,* Vol. I., *passim.*   [3] *Sat.* VI., 67.

INFLUENCE OF PAGANISM UPON MORALS. 325

We need not the pen of a Juvenal or a Tertullian to depict the abomination of Pagan art. A glance at the indecent pictures that have been unearthed from the ruins of Pompeii, reveals a moral depravity which the most prurient imagination can scarcely conceive.

If such were the gods, what must the mortals that worshipped them have been? If such crimes were represented as having been committed in heaven, what infamous deeds must have polluted the earth? If man, by his corrupt nature, has so strong a tendency to glide down the slippery path of vice, what momentum must have been given to his passions by the examples of the gods, of whose excesses he was constantly reminded? "What means," says Seneca, "this appeal to the precedent of the gods, but to inflame our lusts, and to furnish a license and excuse for the corrupt act under shelter of its divine prototype?"[1]

After having feasted their eyes on wanton spectacles in the temples and theatres, the people hastened to the arena to slake their thirst for human blood. The gladiators must show no mercy to their antagonists; the sooner they despatch one another, the more they delight the eager and impatient spectators. As soon as one victim has fallen, a fresh combatant enters the lists, till the amphitheatre runs with human blood. Cæsar once brought six hundred and forty gladiators into the arena.[2] Trajan,

[1] *De Vita Brevi*, 16.
[2] Suet. *Dom.*, 4.

on one occasion, had ten thousand slaves engaged in mortal combat, and prolonged the spectacle for one hundred and twenty-three days.[1] At another time, Agrippa caused fourteen hundred men to fight in the amphitheatre of Berytus in Syria. These sanguinary contests extended over the empire; they were witnessed by multitudes of both sexes and every grade of society; they served to stifle all sentiments of compassion and to inflame the most fierce and brutal instincts of the human breast. It was the special delight of Claudius to watch the countenance of the dying, for he took an artistic pleasure in observing the varying phases of their agony.

The revolting practice of disgorging food by artificial means, in order to gratify the appetite anew, was quite general among the upper classes in Rome. Cicero, in defending King Dejotarus from the charge of having attempted to poison Cæsar while he was his guest, incidentally reminds Cæsar, who was presiding on the bench, of having expressed a wish to dispose of his last meal on a certain occasion. Cicero's remark was not intended as a reproach any more than if he had alluded to Cæsar's having taken a bath or a nap; for he was too dexterous an advocate to irritate the judge.

Juvenal lashes Domitian's gluttony by making the fisherman advise him:

> "Haste to unload your stomach and devour
> A turbot destined for this happy hour."—(*Sat.* IV.)

[1] Dio Cass. LXVIII., 15.

The same poet thus describes the Roman matrons:

> "All glowing, all athirst
> For wine, whole flasks of wine, and swallows first
> Two quarts *to clear* her stomach and excite
> A ravenous, an unbounded appetite."
> —(*Sat.* VI., Gifford's Trans.)

No president or lady of the land, if known to indulge in excesses so unnatural, could retain the respect of the American people.

The only teachers who might be supposed to have the capacity and authority to instruct the people and to check the current of immorality, were the philosophers. Some of them, indeed, guided by the light of reason, inculcated beautiful and sublime moral maxims; but many causes rendered their influence for good scarcely perceptible among the people.

Their audience was generally composed of a narrow circle of literary men. They shrank from proclaiming their doctrines to the masses for fear of exciting public odium against themselves.

They had no well-defined and uniform moral code, and they were often vague and contradictory in their ethical teachings. They suggested no adequate incentives to the practice of virtue. They never employed the great argument of the Apostle: "This is the will of God, your sanctification." The chief, indeed the only motive they had to offer for rectitude of conduct, was the intrinsic excellence of virtue and the deformity of vice.[1] But experience

[1] Cicero, in his admirable moral treatise, *De Officiis*, has no other inducement to offer for the practice of virtue.

proves that the beauty of virtue and the hideousness of vice, unless fortified by higher considerations, afford a weak barrier against the encroachments of passion. If love, as they say, is blind to the defects of the lawful object of its affections, wanton love will little heed the thinly veiled repulsive character of the siren charmer.

There was no sanction attached to their moral precepts. They could not say, with the Christian teacher: "The wicked shall go into everlasting punishment, but the just into life everlasting," for they were in a state of lamentable uncertainty regarding a future life. The ablest moralists among them connived at, and even sanctioned by their example, certain violations of temperance, chastity, and humanity that Christianity reprobates.

Plato, "the divine," condemned drunkenness, but tolerated it on the feasts of Bacchus.[1] In his ideal Republic he recommends infanticide and community of wives, and declares contempt for slaves to be the mark of a gentleman. He advocates the merging of the individual life into the public life of the state, by which personal liberty is lost and man becomes but a part of the great machinery of the state.[2] He congratulates the Athenians on their hatred of foreigners.

The leading philosophers were so much addicted to those unnatural crimes denounced by St. Paul,[3] that parents generally forbade their children to

[1] *De Leg.*, Lib. VI. [3] *Rom.* VIII.
[2] *Rep.* IV., V., VI.

have intercourse with them.¹ And so low was the standard of morals that the indulgence of this passion was not regarded as reflecting any disgrace on the transgressor.

Aristotle was not free from this vice. He also approved abortion and infanticide. He advised the legal destruction of weak and deformed children. While denouncing obscene pictures, he makes an exception in favor of the images of such gods as wished to be honored by indelicate representations.² He taught that Greeks had no more duties to barbarians (foreigners) than to wild beasts.³

Even the wise Socrates, if he is correctly reported by his apologist Xenophon, indulges in a license of speech and conduct that would be tolerated by no Christian teacher of our day.⁴

The elder Cato was noted for his inhumanity to his slaves.⁵ Sallust, who advocated with eloquence an austere simplicity of life, was conspicuous for his rapacity.⁶

Seneca uttered sentiments worthy of the Apostle to the Gentiles. But, unlike St. Paul, "His life was deeply marked by the taint of flattery, and not free from the taint of avarice; and it is unhappily certain that he lent his pen to conceal or varnish one of the worst crimes of Nero."⁷

To sum up: The standard of Pagan morals was

---

¹ Plutarch, *De Educ. Puer.*, 15.
² *Pol.* VII.
³ Lecky, *European Morals*, I., 229.
⁴ *Mem. Socr.* III., 13.
⁵ Plutarch, *Cato Major*.
⁶ Lecky, Vol. I., p. 194.
⁷ *Ibid.*

essentially low, because the Pagans had no divine model held up to them; they had no uniform criterion of right and wrong; the motives presented to them for the practice of virtue were insufficient; no sanction was appended to their moral law; their teachers were limited in their sphere of action; they were often inconsistent in their ethical instructions, and the best of them were stained by some gross vice.

CHAPTER XXIV.

INFLUENCE OF CHRISTIANITY UPON MORALS.

The superior excellence of Christian over Pagan morals is due, first, to the peerless life and example of the Founder of the Christian religion. Our Saviour never inculcates any duty that He does not Himself practise in an eminent degree. No matter how fast we may run on the road to perfection, He is ever before us. No matter how high we may soar, He is still above us, inviting us to ascend higher, as the eagle entices her young to fly. No matter how much we may endure in the cause of righteousness, we find Him laden with a still heavier cross and bearing deeper wounds. He sweetens the most unpalatable ordinances by the seasoning of His example. The beautiful maxims of Plato, Seneca, and Zeno lose much of their savor because their lives were not always conformable to their words. But we have no apology to offer for our Master. He alone is above reproach. He alone can say of Himself: "Which of you shall convict Me of sin?"[1]

"It was reserved for Christianity to present to

[1] *John* VII., 46.

the world an ideal character, which, through all the changes of eighteen centuries, has shown itself capable of acting on all ages, nations, temperaments, and conditions; has been not only the highest pattern of virtue, but the strongest incentive to its practice, and has exercised so deep an influence that it may truly be said that the simple record of three short years of active life has done more to regenerate and soften mankind than all the disquisitions of philosophers and all the exhortations of moralists." [1]

Jesus taught by example before He taught by word. We are drawn toward Him more by the charm of His life than by the sublimity of His doctrine and the eloquence of His speech. The sermons of our Saviour inspire us indeed with esteem for virtue, but His conduct stimulates us to the practice of it. Never did any man speak as Jesus spoke. The most admired discourse that He ever delivered was the Sermon on the Mount. But even the Sermon on the Mount yields in force to the Sermon from the Cross. And if, like the Scribes and Pharisees, our Lord had restricted His mission to the preaching of the word, without illustrating that word by His glorious example, He never would have wrought that mighty moral revolution which has regenerated the world, nor would He be adored to-day by millions of disciples from the rising to the setting sun. When asked by the disciples

[1] Lecky, *European Morals*, II., 8-9.

of John whether He was the true Messiah, He laid more stress on His deeds than on His preaching. "Go," He says, "and relate to John what you have heard and seen. The blind see, the lame walk, the lepers are cleansed, . . . the poor have the Gospel preached to them."[1]

When we hear our Saviour saying on the Mount: "Blessed are the poor in spirit: for theirs is the kingdom of heaven,"[2] we are impressed with the sublimity of His teaching. But when we *see* Him acting out His words: "The foxes have holes, and the birds of the air nests: but the Son of Man hath not where to lay His head,"[3]—oh, then, we are made to feel the blessedness of voluntary poverty; we cherish and embrace our Teacher, who, when He was rich, became poor for our sake. When we hear Him say: "He that exalteth himself shall be humbled, and he that humbleth himself shall be exalted," we admire the virtue of humility. But when we *see* Him at the Last Supper laying aside His upper garments, girding Himself with a towel, pouring water into a basin, and washing the feet of His disciples, then that virtue assumes for us special attractions. When we hear Him say: "Blessed are the merciful: for they shall obtain mercy," we are delighted with His doctrine. But we are more profoundly moved when we *witness* His compassion for the hungering multitude in the desert, and His mercy shown to the erring Magdalen. When He says: "If

---

[1] *Matt.* XI., 4, 5.   [2] *Matt.* VIII., 20.
[3] *Matt.* V., 3.

you will not forgive men, neither will your Father forgive you," He is clothing an old commandment in new words.[1] But when He prays from the cross for His executioners: "Father, forgive them, for they know not what they do," He gives a sublime lesson of forgiveness never before exhibited by sage or prophet.

When we listen to these words: "Blessed are they that suffer persecution for justice's sake: for theirs is the kingdom of heaven. Blessed are ye when they shall revile you, and persecute you, and speak all that is evil against you, untruly, for My sake," we are in admiration at His doctrine. But when we behold the innocent Lamb Himself accused of being a blasphemer, a seditious man, and a disturber of the public peace, we are consoled in our trials and calumny loses its sting.

Beautiful above the sons of men was Jesus in His glorious transfiguration; but far more beautiful is He to us when suspended from the Cross. The crown of thorns is more comforting to us than the halo that encircles His brow on Mount Tabor.

Our Saviour excels the philosophers as well in His moral teaching as in His personal virtues.

There is not a single principle of the natural law, there is not a healthy moral precept of sages or legislators, nor any commandment of the Decalogue, that is not engrafted on the Evangelical Code; for Christ came not to destroy, but to fulfil the law.[2]

[1] See *Ecclus.* XXVIII, 3, 4.
[2] *Matt.* V., 17.

The Christian religion appropriates all that is good, preserving the gold and eliminating the dross.

The moral teachings of our Saviour are as much superior to the Jewish law as the Jewish law itself surpassed all the Gentile moral codes. The Christian religion is more searching, more exacting, more specific in its obligations than the Mosaic legislation. The latter regulated chiefly the exterior conduct, the former guides the movements of the heart; the one forbade the overt act, the other the evil intention; the one condemned the crime of bloodshed, the other prohibits the sin of anger; the one demanded retaliation for injuries received, the other enjoins forgiveness of injuries; the one required us to love our friends, the other bids us love our enemies. "You have heard that it was said to them of old: Thou shalt not kill. And whosoever shall kill, shall be in danger of the judgment. But I say to you, that whosoever is angry with his brother shall be in danger of the judgment. . . . ."

"You have heard that it was said to them of old: Thou shalt not commit adultery. But I say to you, that whosoever shall look on a woman to lust after her, hath already committed adultery with her in his heart. . . . ."

"You have heard that it hath been said: An eye for an eye, and a tooth for a tooth. But I say to you not to resist evil: but if one strike thee on thy right cheek, turn to him also the other. . . . .

"You have heard that it hath been said: Thou shalt love thy neighbor and hate thy enemy. But

I say to you: Love your enemies, do good to them that hate you; and pray for them that persecute and calumniate you: That you may be the children of your Father who is in heaven, who maketh His sun to rise upon the good and the bad, and raineth upon the just and the unjust. For if you love them that love you, what reward shall you have? Do not even the tax-gatherers the same? And if you salute your brethren only, what do you more? Do not also the heathen this? Be ye, therefore, perfect, as also your heavenly Father is perfect."[1]

The intrinsic excellence of the Christian moral code is enhanced by its broad and comprehensive spirit adapting itself to all times and circumstances, to all races and forms of government, and sympathizing with every class of society.

Unlike the *national* religion of the Jews, the Christian religion proclaims the law of universal brotherhood. Unlike the sanguinary religion of Mohammed, which subsists only under despotic rule, and which demands the surrender of one's faith as the highwayman demands the traveler's purse, at the point of the sword, the Christian religion flourishes under every system of government, from an absolute monarchy to the freest republic. Unlike the school of the Pagan philosophers, which was restricted to a narrow circle of disciples, the Gospel of Christ is proclaimed to Jew and Gentile, Greek and barbarian, to bond and free.

---

[1] *Matt.* V., 21-48.

Like the air of heaven, which ascends the highest mountain and descends into the deepest valley, vivifying the face of nature, so has the Christian religion permeated every stratum of society, purifying and invigorating the moral world.

It has a message for the capitalist and the laborer, for the master and the servant, for the rich and for the poor. In the words of St. James, it warns the capitalist against the sin of labor-oppression: "Behold the hire of your laborers who have reaped down your fields, which by fraud has been kept back by you, crieth: and the cry of them hath entered into the ears of the Lord of Sabaoth."[1] It admonishes the laborer to perform his work with fidelity, "not serving to the eye, as it were pleasing men, but doing the will of God from the heart."[2] The most enlightened political economist never formulated a sentence so simple, so comprehensive, so effectual, as is contained in these words: "Thou shalt love thy neighbor as thyself. This principle, if properly applied, would solve every labor problem that perplexes the minds of statesmen.

It charges "the rich of this world not to be high-minded nor to trust in uncertain riches, but in the living God who giveth us all abundantly to enjoy. To do good, to become rich in good works, to give easily, to communicate to others, to lay up for themselves a good foundation for the time to come, that they may lay hold on eternal life."[3]

[1] *St. James* V., 4. [3] *I. Tim.* VI., 17-19.
[2] *Eph.* VI., 6.

It preaches words of comfort to the poor man. It has exploded the false maxim of the world that estimates a man's dignity by his dollars and his degradation by his poverty. It has declared that a man may be scant in this world's goods, and yet be rich and honorable in the sight of God.[1] It cheers him with the old and familiar but always refreshing story of our Lord Jesus Christ, who, being rich, became poor for our sakes, that through His poverty we might be rich.[2]

The exposition of practical duty, as we have seen in the foregoing pages, was wholly unconnected with the life of the Pagan priest and the religious ceremonies of the Pagan temple. Happily, the same cannot be affirmed of our Christian priests and temples. As Mr. Lecky justly observes: "To amalgamate these two spheres (of worship and morals), to incorporate moral culture with religion . . . . was among the most important achievements of Christianity. . . . Unlike all Pagan religions, it made moral teaching a main feature of its clergy, moral discipline the leading object of its services, moral dispositions the necessary condition of the due performance of its rights."[3] The one great aim of our Christian ceremonial worship, of our Sacraments and Sacrifice, our preaching and priesthood, is the development of personal holiness.

The moral power exercised by a good priest in his parish is incalculable. The priest is always a

[1] *James* II. [3] *Hist. of European Morals*, II., 2.
[2] *II. Cor.* VIII., 9.

mysterious being in the eyes of the world. Like his Divine Master, he "is set for the fall and for the resurrection of many in Israel, and for a sign which shall be contradicted."[1] Various opinions are formed of him. Some say of him as was said of our Saviour: "He is a good man. And others say: no, but he seduceth the people."[2] He is loved most by those who know him best. Hated or despised he may be by many that are strangers to him and to his sacred character; but he has been too prominent a factor in the civilization of mankind and the advancement of morality ever to be ignored.

The life of a missionary priest is never written, nor can it be. He has no Boswell. His biographer may record the priest's public and official acts. He may recount the churches he erected, the schools he founded, the works of religion and charity he inaugurated and fostered, the sermons he preached, the children he catechised; the converts he received into the fold; and this is already a great deal. But it only touches upon the surface of that devoted life. There is no memoir of his private daily life of usefulness and of his sacred and confidential relations with his flock. All this is hidden with Christ in God, and is registered only by His recording angel.

"The civilizing and moralizing influence of the clergyman in his parish," says Mr. Lecky, "the simple, unostentatious, unselfish zeal with which he educates the ignorant, guides the erring, comforts

[1] *Luke* II., 34.
[2] *John* VII., 12.

the sorrowing, braves the horrors of pestilence, and sheds a hallowing influence over the dying hour, the countless ways in which, in his little sphere, he allays evil passions and softens manners, and elevates and purifies those around him; all these things, though very evident to the detailed observer, do not stand out in the same vivid prominence in historical records, and are continually forgotten by historians."[1]

The priest is Christ's unarmed officer of the law. He is more potent in repressing vice than a band of constables. His only weapon is his voice; his only badge of authority his sacred office. Like the fabled Neptune putting Eolus to flight and calming the troubled waves, the priest quiets many a domestic storm, subduing the winds of passion, reconciling the jarring elements of strife, healing dissensions, preventing divorce, and arresting bloodshed.

He is the daily depository of his parishioners' cares and trials, anxieties and fears, afflictions and temptations, and even of their sins. They come to him for counsel in doubt, for spiritual and even temporal aid. If he cannot suppress, he has at least the consolation of mitigating the moral evil around him.

We must not overlook the strong inducements that the Christian teacher holds out to his disciples for the practice of virtue in the pressing motives he offers for its due fulfilment. In this respect Christianity has a great advantage over all systems of

---

[1] *European Morals*, I., 152.

religion. The Stoic was incited to a moral life by a sentiment of duty; the Epicurean, by pleasure and self-interest; the Mohammedan, by the hope of sensual delights; the Jew, by servile fear; but the Christian is drawn chiefly by filial love. He is far, indeed, from excluding other motives. He, as well as the Stoic, is influenced by the intrinsic beauty of virtue and by the enormity of sin which he knows could be atoned for only by the blood of his Saviour. He is actuated in the pursuit of virtue by an enlightened self-interest; for he is taught that "Godliness is profitable to all things, having the promise of the life that now is, and of that which is to come."[1] He is moved by a salutary fear of future retribution. But his predominant motive for the practice of piety is love for his Heavenly Father, and love is the strongest of all moral forces. No one can deny that the devotedness of a child to a father is more tender, more profound, more disinterested, and more enduring than the devotedness of a servant to a master, or of a hireling to an employer. A son obeys his father with more alacrity than a servant does his master; and in disobeying his father, he not only transgresses parental authority, but does violence to the instincts of filial affection.

Now, the Christian Church is represented to us as a family whose *Father* is God, and whose members are His adopted children. "You are no more strangers and foreigners," says St. Paul, "but you

---

[1] *I. Tim.* IV., 8.

are fellow-citizens of the saints and of the household of God."[1] It is only in the Christian Church that God is habitually appealed to as Father, and that He admonishes us as His children. We never find the ancient Gentile religions nor the Mohammedan people addressing God by the title of Father. And the same can be affirmed of the Hebrew people. We may search the Old Testament from Genesis to Machabees, and we shall not find the name of Father applied to God a half dozen times. He is called Lord, Omnipotent, Master, King, Judge, and Ruler, titles suggesting the reciprocal relations of authority and fear; not in a solitary instance is a prayer addressed to Him under the endearing name of Father.

Not so you, says the Apostle to the Christians of his time, "for you have not received the spirit of bondage again in fear, but you have received the spirit of adoption of sons, whereby we cry Abba, Father. For the Spirit Himself giveth testimony to our spirit that we are the sons of God, and if sons, heirs also."[2] "Behold," says St. John, "what manner of charity the Father hath bestowed upon us that we should be called and should be the sons of God."[3] In addressing our prayers to heaven, what name is more common on our lips than the name of Father, and what prayer is more familiar to us than that most touching and comprehensive of all prayers, the *Our Father?* The name of Father is applied to God upwards of one hundred times in

[1] *Eph.* II.
[3] *I. John*, III., 1.
[2] *Rom.* VIII., 15-17.

the New Testament, brightening every page and cheering every heart.

What an incentive to virtue is presented to the Christian that recognizes in the moral precepts not only the injunction of his Creator, but also the voice of his loving Father, the Archetype of all sanctity! And what peculiar malice sin should have in his eyes since it is not only an infraction of the law, but also a straining or snapping of those tender ties that bound him to his Father in heaven.

We shall conclude this article by briefly reviewing the moral influence of Christianity on the world at the two extreme stages of its existence—in the first and in the nineteenth century. "It is not surprising," says Mr. Lecky, "that a religious system which made it a main object to inculcate moral excellence, and which, by its doctrine of future retribution, by its organization, and by its capacity of producing a disinterested enthusiasm, acquired an unexampled supremacy over the human mind, should have raised its disciples to a very high condition of sanctity. There can, indeed, be little doubt that for nearly two hundred years after its establishment in Europe, the Christian community exhibited a moral purity which, if it has been equalled, has never for any long period been surpassed."[1]

Some of the early Christians were not exempt from blemishes. There were occasional scandals, divisions, rivalries, envyings, strifes, acts of intem-

---

[1] Lecky, *Hist. of European Morals*, II., 11.

perance, and outbursts of litigious spirit, as is evident chiefly from the first epistle of St. Paul to the Corinthians.[1] The luminous picture of Christian holiness had its shadows, but these shadows were few and far between. They were transient clouds flitting across the moral horizon. Far from dimming, they brought out in bolder relief the brilliant constellation of saints and martyrs that illumined the world.

The Pagans saw with admiration that the Christians, amid the licentiousness and sensuality that surrounded them, preserved their chastity. Like the three children in the fiery furnace, their robes of innocence were not scorched by the impure flames of wantonness that enveloped them. Amid drunkenness and dissipation, they remained temperate and mortified. Amid injustice, rapine, and general self-seeking, they were not only strictly honest and fair-dealing, but they also distributed their goods with a ready hand to their suffering brethren.[*]

While the Pagans fled with horror from the breath of pestilence, the Christians buried their plague-stricken friends, and even their enemies. They surrendered their liberties and their lives that they might ransom or relieve their captive brethren.[2] No wonder that the Pagans exclaimed on witnessing such evidences of heroic charity: "See how these men love one another, how they are ready to die for one another, while we are consumed by mutual hate."[3]

---

[1] *I. Cor.* I. and VI.   [*] *Tertull.* C. 39.
[2] *St. Clem.* I. *Ep. to Corinthians*, St. Cypr. Ep. 51.

In a word, amidst calumnies, contempt, insults, and persecutions, they were calm, patient, and self-possessed. They extorted praise from their enemies by laying down their lives for their faith not only with sublime fortitude, but with unutterable peace.

This peace was not the stern composure of the Stoic philosopher, nor the cold impassibility of the Mohammedan fatalist, nor the intoxicating delirium of the Epicure, but the serene joy of the Christian believer.

The exemplary lives of the primitive Christians served as a powerful auxiliary to the Apostles and their successors in the conversion of souls to Christ, and in swelling the ranks of the Christian family. The observing public were sensible that a religion which bore such celestial fruits must have been planted by the hand of God. They saw and they believed. The preëminent piety of the early Christians and their influence in drawing men to the Christian fold, are attested by one who cannot be suspected of blind partiality toward the Christian religion. "There has probably never existed upon earth," said Mr. Lecky, "a community whose members were bound to one another by a deeper or purer affection than the Christians in the days of persecution. There has probably never existed a community which exhibited in its dealings with crime a gentler or a more judicious kindness, which combined more happily an unflinching opposition to sin with a boundless charity to the sinner, and which was in consequence more successful in reclaiming and transforming the most vicious of mankind."[1]

But does Christianity retain its hold on the public conscience? Most assuredly it does. The name of Christ in the nineteenth century, as well as in the first, is the great battle cry of moral reformation. He has stamped His seal on the laws, the literature, the fine arts of the civilization of Europe and America. His voice is ever ringing among the nations of the earth. He has leavened the social mass. His spirit circulates through the veins of modern society. The precepts of His Gospel continue to regulate public morals. He is the Standard by which we approve or condemn our moral conduct. The number of those whose life is influenced by the teachings of Christ has increased a thousand-fold since the days of the Apostles; and though many have ceased to believe His doctrines of faith, they never cease to admire and praise His transcendent ethical precepts and counsels. The aroma of His sweet life still lingers among many who live outside the pale of the Church.

I have no desire to extenuate the gross vices prevailing among us, which are the more reprehensible, committed as they are in the face of an enlightened conscience. But after making every allowance for this moral depravity, it must be conceded by the most ardent admirer of Gentile civilization that the average morals of a Christian community are of a

---

[1] *Hist. of European Morals*, I., 424.

higher standard than were those of pagan Greece or Rome. The obscenities compelled among us to lurk in dark places, were perpetrated by them openly and without shame. The homage that public opinion pays to virtue is such that vice is not permitted to stalk abroad. Cæsar during his campaigns committed, without detriment to his reputation, unnatural excesses of gluttony and lust that would have consigned any American general to public infamy.[1]

Chastity is held in public esteem in Christendom; it was religiously prostituted in Pagandom.

Lascivious paintings and statues that would not be tolerated in any public hall, and still less in a Christian church, were dutifully exposed in Pagan temples as an homage to the gods.

Unnatural crimes which are severely punished among us, were rarely prohibited by law in ancient Greece.

The profanation of our Christian temples by acts of lasciviousness is unheard of among us; with the Pagans the temples were favorite haunts of lust.

Lascivious dancing is reprobated by Christian ethics; it formed a part of the religious rites among Pagans.

Lucretia was *their* highest type of female chastity. Christianity furnishes innumerable examples of women who suffered tortures and death rather than yield to the aggressor.

The augurs and Vestal virgins could publicly

[1] Sueton., *Cæsar*, 49.

witness the most lascivious plays on the stage, and the butchery of the gladiators in the Flavian amphitheatre, without detriment to their sacred calling.

Imagine our Christian clergy and consecrated virgins frequenting the ballets and low theatres! Could they do so without shocking the moral sense of the people and forfeiting all respect in the community?

It is true, indeed, that the revelations of systematic crime in some Christian communities exhibit a state of moral turpitude hardly surpassed by Rome in the days of Nero. But Paganism was helpless to repair the evil. It had no remedial agencies at its disposal, nor any recuperative power to rise from the slough of sin. Its priests were silent. Its purest philosopher, Seneca, connived at, if he did not participate in, the corruptions of the court, and it sank under the superincumbent weight of its iniquity. The scandals of modern society, on the contrary, are exposed by the press; they are denounced from hundreds of pulpits, and condemned by a healthy public opinion.

CHAPTER XXV.

CONDITION OF WOMAN UNDER PAGAN CIVILIZATION.

The family is the source of society; the wife is the source of the family. If the fountain is not pure, the stream is sure to be foul and muddy. Social life is the reflex of family life.

The history of woman in Pagan countries has been, with rare exceptions, an unbroken record of bondage, oppression, and moral degradation. She had no rights that the husband felt bound to respect. In many of the ancient empires of Asia, notably in Babylon, India and Lydia, the wife was bought, like meat in the shambles, or like slaves in the market-place.[1] Every woman, no matter of what rank, had to submit to be dishonored once in her life by some stranger in the temple of Venus.[2]

Her life was one of abject misery and unrequited toil. Ministering to-day to the capricious passion of her husband, to-morrow she is exposed to all the

[1] Herodot., I., No. 196.
[2] *Ibid.*, No. 199.

revulsions of feeling that follow the gratification of animal appetites.[1] "Among the Indians," says Strabo, "wives are purchased from their parents for a price equal to that of two head of cattle. They are treated as mere servants by their husbands, who have the right to scourge them as their caprices may dictate."[2] To speak to any of the wives of the king of Persia, or even to approach too near her chariot while on a journey, was punished with death. And it is worthy of remark that the same law obtains in that country even to this day.

In Scythia, Tartary, and other countries, the wife who had the misfortune to survive her husband was immolated on his tomb.[3] The same inhuman custom of self-immolation by widows, or *Suttee*, as it was popularly called, prevailed in India, till it was abolished by the English government in 1847. Previously to that period, several ineffectual attempts had been made to put an end to the practice. The Brahmins denounced the humane efforts of the English government as an unwarrantable interference with their religion. We may form some idea of the frequency of these human sacrifices from the fact that, between 1815 and 1826, 7154 cases of Suttee were officially reported to have occurred in Bengal alone.

Another scourge of woman was polygamy. By its baneful influence, her empire over the domestic kingdom was divided, and her conjugal rights were

[1] Lecky, *Hist. of European Morals.* [2] Herodotus, B. I.
[3] L. XV., p. 68.

violated. No one can read Herodotus, the Father of History, without being painfully impressed with the loose ideas of marriage prevailing in Asia. Throughout that vast continent polygamy might be said to have been universal. The Zend-Avesta (or law-book of the Persians) prescribed no rule limiting the number of wives for each household. A maiden, remaining unmarried till her eighteenth year, was threatened with the most severe punishment in the life to come.[1] They regarded the strength of the nation as depending more upon the number of children than upon integrity of morals.

The Medes, according to the testimony of Strabo, were compelled by law to have at least seven wives. The Mongols, the Tartars, and the people of the ancient empire of China legally sanctioned community of wives. The same custom prevailed among the Massagetæ, as Herodotus affirms.[2] Polygamy was regarded as honorable among the ancient Huns and Goths. A man's dignity was estimated by the number of his wives. In no country was the domestic life more grossly dishonored than in Great Britain.[3]

Tacitus represents the domestic life of the Germans in a very favorable light. His honest indignation at the moral corruption of his country-women may have prompted him to embellish the sanctity of marriage among the Germans. He says that, of nearly all barbarous nations, they alone were content

[1] Döllinger, *The Gentile and the Jew*, I., p. 407.
[2] B. I., No. 215.
[3] Cæsar, *Comment.*, I., v.

with one wife, excepting the nobles, who had a retinue of wives, more from a sense of dignity than from luxury. Swift and severe was the punishment meted out to an adulterous wife. Her hair was cut off, and she was lashed naked through the street by her injured husband.[1] "Among the Gauls," says Strabo, "the occupations of the two sexes are distributed in a manner opposite to that which obtains among us. The cultivation of the land and a life of drudgery were imposed on wives, whilst the husbands devoted their time to warlike pursuits."[2]

Aristotle justly boasts that in Greece, woman was not degraded to the level of a slave, as in Asia.[3] But it must be added that, if she was not treated as a slave, she was regarded as a minor. She was under a perpetual tutelage, first to her father, who disposed of her for a price; next to her husband; and, lastly, in her widowhood, to her sons. Even if she had no sons she was not free; for her husband could appoint a guardian to succeed him after death. The Greek wife lived in almost entire seclusion, she and her husband occupying separate parts of the house. She never went abroad unless accompanied by a female slave; she received no male visitors in the absence of her husband; and she was not permitted even to eat at her own table when male guests were present; she was denied the luxury of a polite education, her instruction being usually confined to

[1] *German.*, ch. xix. [3] *Politic.*, I., 1. 5.
[2] B. IV., p. 66.

the most necessary household duties, and to a limited knowledge of music and dancing, which was afforded her, not for the entertainment of herself and family, but to enable her to take part in certain religious festivals.

The domestic life of Greece, it is true, was founded on monogamy. But whilst the law restricted the husband to one wife as his helpmate and domestic guardian, it tolerated and even sanctioned the *hetairai*, who bore to him the relation of inferior wives, and who enjoyed his society more frequently and received more homage from him than his lawful spouse.[1] And whilst the education of the wife was of a most elementary character, the greatest care was lavished in cultivating the minds of the *hetairai*, that they might entertain their paramour by their wit while they fascinated him by their charms. The wife was the beast of burden; the mistress was the petted and pampered animal. These *hetairai* derived additional importance from being legally chosen to offer sacrifice on certain public occasions. This demoralizing system, so far from being deplored, was actually defended and patronized by statesmen, philosophers, and leaders of public opinion, such as Demosthenes, Pericles, Lysias, Aristotle, and Epicurus.

Solon erects in Athens a temple to Venus, the goddess of impure love. Greece is full of such temples, whilst there is not one erected to chaste,

---

[1] *The Gentile and the Jew*, II., 235 *et seq.*

conjugal love.[1] No virtuous woman has ever left a durable record in the history of Greece.

The husband could put away his wife according to his capricious humor, and take a fairer, younger, and richer bride. He could dissolve the marriage bond without other formality than an attestation in writing before the archon; and the wife had practically no power to refuse, as she was completely under the dominion of her husband. She was a mere chattel, marketable at will; nor had she any power to dissolve the marriage without her husband's consent.

Such is the dark but truthful picture of woman exhibited before us in the most polished nation of Pagan antiquity. Now, the sport of man's passions; soon after, she is the victim of his irresponsible hatred. Denied access to her own table in the presence of strangers, she leads a dreary, monotonous life in the society of her slaves. Her very position of wife debars her from a refined education, which is sedulously bestowed on the mistress. She is doomed to a life of domestic bondage; the other enjoys the widest liberty. How can she give her heart to her husband, since she sees his affections divided among usurping rivals? Conjugal love must be reciprocal. She does not reign as queen and mistress of her household, but serves as a tenant at will. Her wishes are not consulted about her marriage or her divorce. Should her husband precede her to the grave, her condition is not improved.

---

[1] Bossuet, *Hist. Univer.*, p. 198.

In a word, the most distinguished Greek writers treat woman with undisguised contempt; they describe her as the source of every evil to man. One of their poets said that marriage brings but two happy days to the husband—the day of his espousals and the day on which he lays his wife in the tomb.

Hesiod calls women "an accursed brood, and the chief scourge of the human race." The daily prayer of Socrates was a thanksgiving to the gods that he was born neither a slave nor a woman. And we have only to glance at the domestic life of Turkey to-day to be convinced that woman fares no better under modern Mohammedanism than she did in ancient Greece.

The Mohammedan husband has merely to say to his wife: "Thou art divorced," and the bond is dissolved. To his followers Mohammed allowed four wives; to himself an unlimited number was permitted by a special favor of Heaven.

The moral standard of the Lacedæmonian wives was far lower than that of the Athenians. They were taught, when maidens, to engage in exercises that strengthened their bodies and imparted grace to their movements, but at the sacrifice of female modesty. The idea of conjugal fidelity was not seriously entertained. Adultery was so common that it was scarcely regarded as a crime. Aristotle says that the Spartan wives lived in unbridled licentiousness.[1]

---

[1] *Apud* Döllinger, *The Gentile and the Jew*, II., 236. Plutarch's *Lives*, Lycurgus.

Passing from Greece to Italy, we find that monogamy was, at least nominally, upheld in Rome, especially during the earlier days of the Republic. But, while the wife was summarily punished for the violation of the marriage vows, the husband's marital transgressions were committed with impunity.

Toward the end of the Republic, and during the Empire, the disorders of nuptial life increased to an alarming extent. There was a fearful rebound on the part of Roman wives, particularly among the upper classes, from the restraints of former days to the most unlimited license. They rivalled the wantonness of the sterner sex. So notorious were their morals, in the time of Augustus, that men preferred the unfettered life of celibacy to an alliance with partners bereft of every trace of female virtue. The strict form of marriage became almost obsolete, and a laxer one, destitute of religious or civil ceremony, and resting solely on mutual agreement, became general. Each party could dissolve the marriage bond at will and under the most trifling pretext, and both were free to enter at once into second wedlock.

Marriage was, accordingly, treated with extreme levity. Cicero repudiated his wife Terentia, that he might obtain a coveted dowry with another; and he discarded the latter, because she did not lament the death of his daughter by the former. Cato was divorced from his wife Attilia after she had borne him two children, and he transferred his second wife to his friend Hortensius, after whose death he married her again. Augustus compelled the husband of Livia to abandon her, that she might become his own wife. Sempronius Sophus was divorced from his wife, because she went once to the public games without his knowledge. Paulus Æmilius dismissed his wife, the mother of Scipio, without any reason whatever. Pompey was divorced and remarried a number of times. Sylla repudiated his wife during her illness, when he had her conveyed to another house.[1]

If moral censors, philosophers, and statesmen, such as Cato, Cicero and Augustus discarded their wives with so much levity, how lax must have been the marriage-bond among the humble members of society, with examples so pernicious constantly before their eyes!

Wives emulated husbands in the career of divorces. Martial speaks of a woman who had married her tenth husband.[2] Juvenal refers to one who had had eight husbands in five years.[3] St. Jerome declares that there dwelt in Rome a wife who had married her twenty-third husband, she being his twenty-first wife.[4] "There is not a woman left," says Seneca, "who is ashamed of being divorced, now that the most distinguished ladies count their years not by the consuls, but by their husbands."[5]

[1] Plutarch's *Life of Sylla.*
[2] *Epig.* VI., 7.
[3] *Sat.* VI., 30.
[4] *Ep.*, 2.
[5] *De Benef* III., 14.

CHAPTER XXVI.

WHAT CHRISTIANITY HAS DONE FOR WOMAN.

The world is governed more by ideals than by ideas; it is influenced more by living, concrete models than by abstract principles of virtue.

The model held up to Christian women is not the Amazon, glorying in her martial deeds and prowess; it is not the Spartan woman, who made female perfection consist in the development of physical strength at the expense of feminine decorum and modesty; it is not the goddess of impure love, like Venus, whose votaries regarded beauty of form and personal charms as the highest type of female excellence; nor is it the goddess of imperious will, like Juno. No; the model held up to woman from the very dawn of Christianity is the peerless Mother of our Blessed Redeemer.

She is the pattern of virtue alike to maiden, wife, and mother. She exhibits the virginal modesty becoming the maid, the conjugal fidelity and loyalty of the spouse, and the untiring devotedness of the mother.

The Christian woman is everywhere confronted by her great model. Mary's portrait gazes down upon her from the wall. Her name is repeated in the pages of the book before her. Her eulogy is pronounced from the pulpit. Altars and temples are dedicated in her honor. Festivals are celebrated in her praise. In a word, the Virgin Mother is indelibly stamped on the intellect, the heart, the memory, and the imagination of the Christian daughter.

The influence of Mary, therefore, in the moral elevation of woman can hardly be overestimated. She is the perfect combination of all that is great, and good, and noble in Pagan womanhood, with no alloy of degradation.

Hers is exquisite beauty, but a beauty more of the soul than of the body; it delights without intoxicating. The contemplation of her excites no inward rebellion, as too often happens with Grecian models. She is the mother of fair love devoid of sickly sentimentality or sensuality.

In her we find force of will without pride or imperiousness. We find in her moral strength and heroism without the sacrifice of female grace and honor—a heroism of silent suffering rather than of noisy action. What Spartan mother ever displayed so much fortitude as Mary exhibited at the foot of the cross?

It seems to me that some writers are disposed to lay undue stress on the amiable and tender qualities of Mary and of holy Christian women without dwelling sufficiently on the strong and robust points of their character. The Holy Scripture in one place pronounces a lengthened eulogy on woman. What does the Holy Ghost especially admire in her? Not her sweet and amiable temper or her gentle disposition, though of course she possessed these qualities, for no woman is perfect without them. No; He admires her valor, courage, fortitude, and the sturdy virtue of self-reliance. He does not say: "Who shall find a gentle woman?" but rather: "Who shall find a valiant woman? As things brought from afar and from the uttermost coasts is the price of her."[1] It is only heroic virtues or virtues practised in an heroic degree that the Church canonizes.

In every age the Church abounds in women immeasurably surpassing in sturdy virtue the highest types of Pagan female excellence. What woman of ancient Greece or Rome can exhibit evidences of moral strength so sublime as have been manifested in the lives of an Agnes, an Agatha, or a Cecilia, who suffered death rather than tarnish their souls? of a Felicitas and a Symphorosa, who encouraged their sons to endure torments and death rather than renounce their faith, and who shared also in their glorious martyrdom? Pagan history furnishes no instance of motherly devotedness comparable to the strong and tender love of Monica, who traversed land and sea that she might restore her son to a life of virtue.

[1] *Prov.*, **XXXI.**

Every impartial student of history is forced to admit that woman is indebted to the Catholic religion for the elevated station she enjoys to-day in family and social life.

We may recall in what contempt woman was held by the leading minds of Greece. She was kept in perpetual bondage or unending tutelage; she was regarded as the slave and the instrument of man's passions, rather than his equal and companion, by nearly every nation of antiquity; and she is still so regarded in all countries where Christianity does not prevail.

The Catholic Church, following the maxims of the Gospel and of St. Paul, proclaims woman the peer of man in origin and destiny, in redemption by the blood of Christ, and in the participation of His spiritual gifts. "Ye are all," says the Apostle, "the children of God by faith which is in Christ Jesus. . . . There is neither Jew nor Greek; there is neither servant nor freeman; there is *neither male nor female.*"[1] The meaning is that in the distribution of His gifts God makes no distinction of person or sex. He bestows them equally on bond and free, on male and female. And as woman's origin and destiny are the same as man's, so is her dignity equal to his. As both were redeemed by the same Lord and as both aspire to the same heavenly inheritance, so should they be regarded as of equal rank on earth; as they are

---

[1] *Gal.* III., 26-28.

partakers of the same spiritual gifts, so should they share alike the blessings and prerogatives of domestic life.

In the mind of the Church, however, equal rights do not imply that both sexes should engage promiscuously in the same pursuits, but rather that each sex should discharge those duties which are adapted to its physical constitution and sanctioned by the canons of society.

To some among the gentler sex the words *equal rights* have been, it is to be feared, synonymous with *similar* rights. It was no doubt owing to this misapprehension of terms that the attempt was made, not so very long ago, by some of the strong-minded fair, to introduce the glories of the Bloomer costume. But though the attempt proved a failure, the spirit that impelled it still survives, as may be seen by the various masculine modifications that have crept into female dress during the past few years. Where is the flowing and graceful drapery of former days that jealously shielded the modest wearer from gaze on the public street? Is it because the woman of to-day has laid aside what she looks upon as the cumbersome style of her grandmother's time that she aims at dauntlessly presenting herself at the ballot-box to cast in her suffrage for *A* or for *B?* Only a few years ago it provoked laughter to hear that Miss Jemima Snarl was to lecture on "Woman's Rights," or that Dr. Mary Walker had appeared on Broadway in male habiliments *cap-à-pie*. But now it is quite ordinary to hear of ladies, gentlewomen, daughters of some of our country's best men, not, indeed, imitating Dr. Mary Walker's exceptionable attire, but mounting the rostrum to harangue their audiences on the power of the "Faith Healers" or the merits of the "Salvation Army." Is it any wonder that a feeling of sadness creeps over one that such things should be?

To debar woman from such pursuits is not to degrade her. To restrict her field of action to the gentler avocations of life is not to fetter her aspirations after the higher and the better. It is, on the contrary, to secure to her not *equal* rights so-called, but those supereminent rights that cannot fail to endow her with a sacred influence in her own proper sphere; for as soon as woman trenches on the domain of man, she must not be surprised to find that the reverence once accorded her has been in part, or wholly, withdrawn.

But it was by vindicating the unity, the sanctity, and the indissolubility of marriage that the Church has conferred the greatest boon on the female sex. The holiness of the marriage-bond is the palladium of woman's dignity, while polygamy and divorce involve her in bondage and degradation.

The Church has ever maintained, in accordance with the teachings of our Saviour, that no man can lawfully have more than one wife; and no woman more than one husband. The rights and obligations of both consorts are correlative. To give to the husband the license of two or more wives would be an injustice to his spouse and destructive of domestic peace. The Church has also invariably taught that the marriage compact, once validly formed, can be dissolved only by death; for what God hath joined together man cannot put asunder. While admitting that there may be a legitimate cause for separation, she never allows any pretext for the absolute dissolution of the marriage-bond. For so strong and violent are the passion of love and its opposite passion of hate, so insidious is the human heart, that once a solitary pretext is admitted for absolute divorce, others are quickly invented, as experience has shown; thus a fearful crevice is made in the moral embankment, and the rush of waters is sure to override every barrier that separates a man from the object of his desires.

It has, again and again, been alleged that this law is too severe, that it is harsh and cruel, and that it condemns to a life of misery two souls who might find happiness if permitted to have their marriage annulled and to be united with more congenial partners. Every law has its occasional inconveniences, and I admit that the law absolutely prohibiting divorce *à vinculo* may sometimes appear rigorous and cruel. But its harshness is mercy itself when compared with the frightful miseries resulting from the toleration of divorce. Its inconvenience is infinitesimal when contrasted with the colossal evils from which it saves society and the solid blessings it secures to countless homes. Those exceptional ill-assorted marriages would become more rare if the public were convinced, once for all, that death alone can dissolve the marriage bond. They would then use more circumspection in the selection of a conjugal partner. Hence it happens that in Catholic countries where faith is strong, as in Ireland and the Tyrol, divorces are almost unheard of.

The enforcement of this law has been maintained by the Church against fearful odds, and has caused her many a mortal struggle. For if the strong government of the United States, with military forces at its command, with the sympathy of public opinion and Christian traditions on its side, is successfully resisted by a colony of Mormons, how violent must have been the opposition to the Church and how hopeless her task, humanly speaking, when physical force and inveterate custom were arrayed against her, and when she had on her side only moral power and spiritual penalties.

In vindicating the sanctity of marriage, the Church had to contend with a triple enemy—the fierce passions of barbarous tribes, the arbitrary power of princes, and the compromising spirit of rebellious churchmen.

From the fifth to the eighth century Europe was periodically visited by warlike tribes from the shores of the Baltic, from Asia, and from Africa. They threatened the overthrow of the Christian religion, and, in the general upheaval of society, the landmarks of Christian civilization were well-nigh swept away. The invading hosts were utter strangers to monogamy and the restraining maxims of the Gospel. But when the storm subsided, the voice of religion was heard in defence of female honor and the sanctity of marriage, and the triumphant barbarians voluntarily submitted to the yoke of the Gospel.

Virginal and conjugal chastity found still more formidable opponents among many of the petty princes and barons of the Middle Ages. Fortified in their castles and surrounded by submissive vassals, they recognized no power that thwarted their lust; they set the laws of the land at defiance; they intimidated the local clergy; they disregarded even the authority of the bishops. The only voice before which they trembled and which compelled them to surrender their prey, was the anathema of Rome.

What a sorry figure the so-called Reformers presented when the honor of woman was at stake, and what little protection she had to expect from them in the hour of trial! Luther, in his commentary on Genesis, says that he does not decide whether a man is or is not permitted to have several wives at once; yet we all know that he did decide the question by permitting the Landgrave of Hesse to have two wives at the same time, his brother reformer Melanchthon concurring in the decision. We know, also, how obsequious Cranmer was to Henry VIII. in sanctioning his divorce from Catherine. How different was the conduct of Pope Innocent III., who compelled the French king, Philip Augustus, to dismiss Agnes de Méranie, whom he had unlawfully married, and take back his lawful wife, Ingelburga of Denmark, whom he had discarded! And all know with what firmness Pius VII., in the present century, refused to dissolve the marriage of Jerome Bonaparte with Elizabeth Patterson.

The Protestant Bishop of Maine makes the following candid avowal: "Laxity of opinion and teaching on the sacredness of the marriage bond and on the question of divorce *originated among the Protestants* of Continental Europe in the sixteenth century. It soon began to appear in the legislation of Protestant States on that Continent, and nearly at the same time to affect the laws of New England. From that time to the present it has proceeded from one degree to another in this country, until, especially in New England and in States most directly affected by New England opinions and usages, the Christian conception of the nature and obligations of the marriage bond finds scarcely any recognition in legislation or in the prevailing sentiment of the community."[1] In confirmation of this statement, it may be remarked that, according to the latest census, there was one divorce to every eight marriages in Ashtabula County, Ohio, which is the focus of the Western Reserve, a colony founded by New England settlers. Had the indissoluble character of the marriage bond not already taken so deep and firm a

[1] Quoted from *The Calling of a Christian Woman*, by Rev. Morgan Dix.

hold upon the heart and conscience of Europe at the time of the "Reformation," it would have been uprooted by the storm of licentiousness aroused by the teaching and practice of the "Reformers."

What woman can calmly reflect on these facts without blessing the Catholic Church as, under God, the saviour of her sex? If virginal and conjugal chastity is held to-day as the brightest gem in the diadem of woman; if the wife is regarded as the peer of her husband, and not as his slave, the toy of his caprice and passion, as are the wives of Asiatic nations; if she is honored as the mistress of her household, and not looked upon as a tenant at will, as were the wives of Greece and Rome; if she is respected as the queen of the domestic kingdom, to be dethroned only by death, and not treated as the victim of rival queens, like the Mohammedan and Mormon wives, she is indebted to the Church which always held inviolate the unity and indissolubility of marriage, and especially to the Roman Pontiffs who never failed to enforce those fundamental laws.

And if woman has been elevated and ennobled by the Gospel, she has not been ungrateful for the boon conferred; she merits the eternal gratitude of the Christian world for the influence she has zealously exerted and is still exerting in behalf of religion and society. It is fearful to contemplate what would have become of our Christian civilization without the aid of the female sex. Not to speak of the grand army of consecrated virgins who are fanning the flame of faith and charity throughout the world, how many thousands of homes are there in our country from which God withholds His avenging hand, and to which He shows mercy, solely on account of a pious mother or daughter, just as He was willing to show mercy to Sodom for the sake of a few righteous souls, and as He restored life to the young man borne to the tomb, for the sake of his mother, the widow of Naim! How many brothers, who had been long since buried in the grave of sin, are brought back to a life of virtue through the intercession of a pious sister, just as Lazarus was raised from the dead by the prayers and tears of Mary and Martha! How many daughters keep alive the spark of religion, which otherwise would be utterly extinguished, in many a household! How many are in their families angels of expiation, atoning by their prayers and mortification for the sins of fathers and sons!

Women, it is true, are debarred from the exercise of the public ministry and the celebration of the Sacred Mysteries, for they are commanded by the Apostle to "keep silence in the churches."[1] But if they are not apostles by preaching, they are apostles by prayer, by charity, and by good example. If they cannot offer up the Sacrifice of the Mass, they are priests in the broader sense of the term; for they offer up in the sanctuary of their own

[1] *I. Cor.* XIV., 34.

homes and on the altar of their hearts the acceptable sacrifice of supplication, praise, and thanksgiving to God. Viewing, then, woman's dignity and her work in the cause of Christ, well may we apply to her these words of the Prince of the Apostles: "You are a chosen generation, a royal priesthood, a holy nation, a purchased people."[1]

The noblest work given to woman is to take care of her children. The most important part of her apostleship should consist in instructing them in the ways of God. The education of the young should begin at the mother's knee. The mind of a child, like softened wax, receives with ease the first impressions, which are always the deepest and most enduring. "A young man, according to his way, even when he is old, he will not depart from it."[2] A child is susceptible of instruction much earlier in life than parents generally imagine. Mothers should watch with a jealous eye the first unfolding of the infant mind, and pour into it the seed of heavenly knowledge.

For various reasons the mother should be the first instructor of her children:

1st. As nature ordains that the mother should be the first to feed her offspring with her own substance, so does God ordain that she should be the first to impart to her little ones the "rational milk" whereby they "may grow unto salvation."[3]

2d. Those children that are nurtured by their

[1] *I. Peter*, II., 9.   [3] *I. Peter*, II., 2.
[2] *Prov.* XXII., 6.

own mother are usually more healthy and robust than those that are nursed by strangers. In like manner they that are instructed by their own mother in the principles of Christian piety, are usually more robust in faith than those that have been guided exclusively by other teachers.

3d. It cannot be doubted that maternal and filial affections are mutually nurtured by the closer and intimate relations that mother and child have with each other, while these affections are chilled by a prolonged separation.

4th. The more confidence a child has in its preceptor, the more he is apt to advance in learning. Now, in whom does a child confide more implicitly than in his mother? In every danger he flies to her as to an ark of safety; he will place the utmost reliance on what she says. The mother should not lose the golden opportunity of instructing her children in faith and morals while their hearts are open to receive her every word.

5th. Lastly, the mother occupies the same house with her children, frequently the same apartment, and eats at the same table with them. She is the visible guardian-angel of her children. She is therefore the best calculated to instruct them, as she can avail herself of every little circumstance that presents itself to draw from it a moral lesson.

Let Christian mothers recognize their sublime mission. Let them bear in mind that to them is confided the most tender portion of the flock of Christ, which on that account should be watched with the greater care. On them devolves the duty of directing the susceptible and pliant minds of their children, and of instilling into their youthful hearts the principle of piety. It is theirs to plant the seed of the word of God in the virgin soil, and when a more experienced hand is required to cultivate it, the ministers of God will not be wanting in developing its growth.

We would exhort mothers in the name of the holy religion they profess; in the name of their country, which expects them to rear not scourges of society, but honorable and law-abiding members; in the name of God, who requires them to have their offspring fed with the nourishment of sound doctrine; in the name of their own eternal salvation and that of the souls committed to their charge, to provide for their children *at home* a healthy, moral, and religious education. "If any one have not care of his own, and especially of those of his house, he hath denied the faith, and is worse than an infidel." [1]

And, then, what a source of consolation it will be to them in their declining years when they reflect that they will leave after them children who will inherit not only their name, but also their faith and virtues! They will share in the beautiful eulogy pronounced by the Holy Ghost on the mother of the family: "Who shall find a valiant woman? . . . . She hath opened her mouth to wisdom, and

---

[1] *Tim.* V., 8.

the law of clemency is on her tongue. She hath looked well to the paths of her house, and hath not eaten her bread idle. Her children rose up and called her blessed: her husband, and he praised her. Many daughters have gathered together riches; thou hast surpassed them all. Favor is deceitful and beauty is vain: the woman that feareth the Lord, she shall be praised." [1]

---

[1] *Prov.*, XXXI.

CHAPTER XXVII.

PAGANISM AND CHRISTIANITY COMPARED IN THE PRACTICE OF SOCIAL VIRTUES—ABORTION—INFANTICIDE—NEGLECT OF THE POOR AND THE SICK IN HEATHEN COUNTRIES—COMPASSION OF JESUS CHRIST FOR SUFFERING HUMANITY IMITATED BY THE PRIMITIVE CHURCH—HER ABHORRENCE OF FOETICIDE—HER CARE OF THE POOR AND THE SICK IN PRIMITIVE TIMES.

In the old Gentile world, the individual was absorbed in the commonwealth; the man was lost in the citizen. He was a part and parcel of the machinery of the State; he was a hinge or a screw or a wheel in the engine of the government. As soon as his usefulness was at an end, he was cast aside to rust like worthless iron, and replaced by another. The Stoics, a leading sect of philosophers, regarded compassion for suffering humanity as a moral weakness, a disease, instead of a virtue. Human life was esteemed only so far as it contributed to the welfare of the State.

The practice of abortion was almost universal in Greece and Rome. It prevailed alike among the poor and the rich. It was forbidden by no law of Greece or Rome, except toward the close of the Empire, and then by legislation feeble and inoperative. Aristotle even recommended that abortion should be enforced by law when the population exceeded certain limits.[1] The moral sense was so blunted by the frequency of the practice, that it was scarcely considered a crime.

Infanticide was another dark stain on Pagan civilization; and as an evidence that human nature does not improve with time and is everywhere the same unless leavened by Christianity, the wanton destruction of infant life is probably as general in China and other heathen countries to-day as it was in ancient Greece and Rome. Infanticide was universal in Greece, with the possible exception of Thebes. It was sanctioned, and sometimes even enjoined by such philosophers and jurists as Plato and Aristotle, Lycurgus and Solon.

The exposure and destruction of new-born children was also very common among the Romans. Up to the days of the Empire, there was no legal check to this inhuman crime, except by a law framed in the twilight of Roman history, and which soon became obsolete. The father had entire discretion to preserve or destroy his child. Paulus, the jurist, admits that fathers had this right. Augustus, who made some efforts to check the evil, not from motives of humanity, but alarmed at the decrease of population, set the bad example of exposing the child

[1] Lecky, *Hist. of Europ. Morals*, Vol. II., 21.

born to his granddaughter Julia. Tertullian thus addresses the Romans of his time: "How many are there among you, and they too in the magistracy, who put an end to your children! You drown them, or you suffer them to die of cold and hunger, or to be eaten by dogs."[1] "I see you," says Minutius Felix to the Romans, "I see you expose your children to beasts and birds of prey, or even wretchedly choke to death your own offspring."[2] We may judge how general was the custom of exposing infants throughout the Roman Empire, when Tacitus mentions with honor the Jews and Germans as the only people that considered it a crime not to rear all their children.[3]

The number of poor in Rome in the days of Augustus exceeded half a million, in a population of about two millions of inhabitants.[4] And yet there is no instance recorded in the history of Rome of any asylum for the poor, or hospital for the sick having ever been founded, either by the bounty of the State or by private munificence. The same utter disregard for the indigent and afflicted, prevailed in Greece and in every ancient nation with which we are acquainted. Some philosophers, like Crates, showed their contempt for wealth by throwing it into the sea; others, like Democritus, gave up their riches that they might be free from care. But the idea never occurred to any of them of founding a charitable institution. Seneca says that most men

[1] Apol. 9, *ad Nationes*, 15.   [2] Chap. 30.
[3] *Hist.* V. 5., *Germ.* 19.
[4] Döllinger, *The Gentile and the Jew*, Vol. I., p. 5.

fling an alms to a beggar with repugnance, and solely to get rid of him.¹ It was superstitiously regarded as a bad omen to meet a mendicant. "What is the use," says Plautus, "of giving a beggar anything? One loses what one gives away, and only prolongs the miserable existence of the receiver." How different is the old Spanish Christian maxim: "What I give away, I keep; what I keep, I lose." Even the gentle Virgil includes among the features of the wise man's happiness his apathy for the indigence of others.² The highest beneficence granted by Roman ethics to the indigent, was to bestow upon them what one could give without inconvenience to one's self.³

How strange and revolting these sentiments seem to us, accustomed as we are to the contemplation of works of benevolence everywhere existing around us! How much soever Christians may be unhappily divided among themselves on questions of religious faith, there is no disagreement among them on the great law of charity to their fellow-beings. Whatever may be their practical conduct, both Catholics and non-Catholics agree, that it is meet and proper to relieve helpless infancy and feeble old age, to aid the widow and the orphan. This is a common platform on which Christians of all denominations stand united.

Of all the virtues that shine forth in the life of our Blessed Redeemer, there is none so prominent or conspicuous as His mercy to suffering humanity. This might be called His characteristic virtue, if the

¹ *De Clem.* V., 6. ³ Cicero, *De Officiis*, I., 16.
² *Geor.* 11. 499.

term could be applied to One who was perfect in every virtue. On every leaf of the Gospel, that golden word *compassion* shines forth, brightening every page and cheering every heart.

Take, for instance, the miracles of our Saviour. They are far more remarkable for their utility and beneficence than for their splendor or terror-producing effect. There is as much difference between the miracles of Jesus Christ and those of Moses, as there is between the thunder and lightning that ushered in the Old Law and the lambent tongues of fire that heralded the New Law of grace. We never hear of our Saviour's exercising His divine power as Moses did, by changing rivers into blood and by destroying the first-born of the land. We never hear of His commanding the sun to stand in the heavens, as Josue did; nor do we read of Him as we do of Elias, that He called down fire from heaven to consume an offending city, though he was once importuned to do so by His disciples while they were as yet but imperfectly instructed in the spirit of the Gospel. We remember His reply in language so worthy of Himself: "Ye know not of what spirit you are. The Son of man came not to destroy souls, but to save."

No, the miracles of our Lord were wrought to lessen the sufferings and to lighten the burdens of men. He manifested His power in going about doing good.[1] He gave sight to the blind,[2] speech to

[1] *Acts* X., 38.
[2] *Matt.* XV., 30.

PAGANISM AND CHRISTIANITY COMPARED. 379

the dumb and hearing to the deaf,[1] the power of walking to the lame,[2] strength to the paralyzed limb.[3] He gave health to the sick;[4] He cleansed the leper;[5] He fed the hungry;[6] He raised the dead to life;[7] and, what is more, He raised to the life of grace those that had lain buried in the grave of sin;[8] He blessed the little ones that gathered around Him,[9] and comforted the heart of the afflicted widow.[10]

But nothing is more manifest in the Gospel than the sympathy of Jesus for the poor. He wished to stamp with condemnation the spirit of the world, that estimates a man's dignity by his wealth and his degradation by his poverty. To render His mission to the poor more effective, He chose to be born of humble parentage, in an obscure town, in a wretched stable. He led a life of poverty, not from necessity, but from choice. He could say of Himself: "The foxes have burrows and the birds of the air nests; but the Son of man hath not where to lay his head."[11] He selected His twelve Apostles from the lower walks of life, men without wealth or human learning or social or family influence. When He entered the synagogue of Nazareth in the first days of His public life, He gave as a proof of

[1] *Mark* VII., 35.
[2] *Matt.* XXI., 14.
[3] *Ibid.* IX., 6.
[4] *Luke* VII., 10.
[5] *Matt.* VIII., 3.
[6] *John* VI., 11.
[7] *Ibid.* XI., 43.
[8] *Luke* VII., 14.
[9] *Mark* X., 16.
[10] *Luke* VII., 14.
[11] *Matt.* VIII., 20.

His divine mission that in Him were fulfilled the words of the Prophet Isaiah who foretold that the Messiah was to preach to the poor and afflicted: "The Spirit of the Lord is upon Me. Wherefore, He hath anointed Me. He hath sent Me to preach the Gospel to the poor, to heal the broken-hearted."[1] And when John the Baptist in prison sent two of his disciples to our Lord to ask Him if He was the true Messiah, Jesus returned this answer: "Go and relate to John what ye hear and see. The blind see, the lame walk, lepers are cleansed, the deaf hear, the dead rise again, *the poor have the Gospel preached to them.*"[2] In other words, tell him that My mission is especially to the poor. His miracles were wrought more frequently in behalf of the lowly; and the blessings of eternal life are promised especially to the meek and poor in spirit.[3]

The Catholic Church, guided by this beautiful example of our Redeemer, has always proclaimed the sanctity of human suffering and of human life. Ever since He bore His cross for mankind, His sorrows have sanctified the sorrows of humanity and shed a halo around them.

The Church has also proclaimed the sanctity of human life. She sets no mercenary price on man. Great in her eyes is the dignity of the citizen, but greater is the dignity of the man. Though he is bound to contribute to the welfare of the State, according to the best of his ability, yet his moral

---

[1] *Isaiah* LXI., 1; *Luk.* IV., 18.   [3] *Matt.* V., 3, 4.
[2] *Matt.* XI., 4, 5.

grandeur is independent of the service he may be able to render it. The infant born yesterday into the world; the old man tottering toward the grave; the deformed creature that can give no present or prospective aid to his country,—all are precious in the sight of God and His Church. For within that body, whether of helpless infancy, or decrepit old age, or deformed humanity, there dwells an immortal spirit. The Christian religion regards man as a child of God, a brother of Christ, an heir of heaven.

This recognition of man's dignity and of the sanctity of human suffering, is the secret of that quickening spirit of benevolence which always animates the Church wherever she gains a firm foothold.

For my part, were I investigating the respective claims of the various systems of religion that have sprung up in the course of centuries, much as I would be attracted to the Catholic Church by her admirable unity of doctrine, the sanctity of her moral code, her world-wide Catholicity, and by that unbroken chain of Apostolic succession, which binds her inseparably to the primitive Church, I should be still more irresistibly drawn to her by that organized system of charity which she has established throughout the world in behalf of suffering humanity. As the unity of the Church's faith is secured by the principle of authority, so are the works of charity fostered and perpetuated by her organized system of benevolence. Montesquieu, who cannot be suspected of partiality to the Church, well remarks that the Catholic religion, which was established to provide for man's happiness in the life to come, in reality succeeds better than any other institution in contributing to his happiness even in this life.

The Church declares sinful the wanton destruction of human life in any stage of its existence. She pleads for the life of the yet unborn infant, whether assailed by the mother to hide her shame; or by the physician, who wishes to sacrifice the life of the child, to save the mother. She denounces abortion not only as an inhuman act, but as murder. In the penitential discipline of the Church, abortion was visited with the same penalties as infanticide. In the Council of Ancyra, the guilty mother was excluded from the Sacraments till the hour of death; and according to the present discipline of the Church, absolution from the crime of procuring abortion, is always reserved to the Bishop of the diocese.

From the earliest days of Christianity, the custom was established of taking up on Sunday after Communion, a collection among the faithful in behalf of "orphans, widows, the sick, the needy, those who are in chains, pilgrims, and all the indigent of the flock."[1]

At the breaking out of the Decian Persecution, A. D. 249, the Church supported more than fifteen hundred widows, poor, and suffering persons in

---

[1] St. Justin, *Apology to Antoninus Pius.*

Rome.[1] As soon as liberty was restored, institutions of charity, unknown to Paganism, sprang up throughout the Roman Empire.

Fabiola, a Roman lady, founded a hospital in Rome in the fourth century. St. Basil established in Cæsarea a great hospital, and also an asylum for lepers. The Council of Nice directed that Xenodochia, or asylums for indigent pilgrims, should be erected in every city. When St. Chrysostom ruled the church of Antioch, that city supported three thousand poor widows and maids, besides caring for the sick. St. Ephrem founded and superintended a hospital at Edessa. The monk Thalaleseus organized an asylum for the blind on the banks of the Euphrates. So conspicuous were the charities of the Church to friend and to foe that Julian the Apostate, in his letter to Arcacius, avows that it is shameful that "the Galileans," as he called the Christians, should support not only their own, but also the heathen poor.

The Hotel Dieu of Paris, the finest and most capacious hospital in the world, was founded in the seventh century; and the erection of the Hotel Dieu of Lyons is ascribed to Childebert, the son of Clovis, the first Christian king of France. As early as the ninth century, Rome had not fewer than nine hospitals.

In the next chapter we shall see that the Christians of our own times are emulating the zeal of the early disciples in works of charity, particularly in organized systems of benevolence.

[1] *Eusebius* VI., 43.

CHAPTER XXVIII.

Benevolent Institutions Founded and Fostered by Christianity in Modern Times.

There is no phase of human misery and affliction for which the Catholic religion does not provide some antidote, some alleviations. She has Foundling Asylums to receive and shelter helpless infants that are either abandoned by unnatural mothers, or bereft of their parents before they knew a mother's love. These unconscious victims of sin or misery are rescued from spiritual and temporal death by consecrated virgins, who become their nursing mothers.

As the Church provides homes for those yet on the threshold of life, so too does she secure Retreats for those on the threshold of death. She has asylums in which the aged, men and women, find at one and the same time a refuge in their old age from the storms of life, and a novitiate to prepare them for eternity. Thus from the cradle to the grave she is a nursing mother. She rocks her children in the cradle of infancy, and she soothes them to rest on the couch of death.

Louis XIV. erected in Paris the famous *Hôtel des Invalides* for the veteran soldiers of France who had fought in the service of their country. And so has Religion provided for those that have been disabled in the battle of life, a home in which they are tenderly nursed in their declining years by devoted Sisters.

The *Little Sisters of the Poor*, whose Congregation was founded in 1840, have now charge of two hundred and fifty establishments in different parts of the globe; the aged inmates of those houses numbering thirty thousand, upwards of seventy thousand having died while under their care, up to 1889.

To these asylums are welcomed not only the members of the Catholic religion, but those also of every form of Christian faith, and even those without any faith at all. The Sisters make no distinction of persons or nationality or color or creed; for true charity embraces all. The only question proposed by the Sisters to the applicant for shelter, is this: Are you oppressed by age and penury? If so, come to us and we will provide for you.

Mr. Lecky[1] and other distinguished writers have asserted that some forms of Catholic charity, though dictated by most praiseworthy motives, have a pernicious tendency to encourage idleness and increase poverty whilst attempting to relieve the latter; and that the most effectual way to suppress it, is to foster trade and commerce along with habits of industry.

[1] *Europ. Morals*, Vol. II., 93 *et seq.*

It cannot be denied that great abuses often arise from indiscriminate mendicancy and that it should be kept within certain bounds. Promiscuous almsgiving is not always charity. Instead of supplying a real want, it often ministers to the passions of the unworthy applicant. The sturdy man who habitually begs instead of working for a livelihood, is justly open to suspicion. He loses self-respect, imposes on the charitable public, and defrauds the deserving poor. He is a drone in the social beehive. Unlike the steward in the Gospel, who said: "To dig I am not able; to beg I am ashamed,"[1] he is able to dig and not ashamed to beg.

This language coming from a Christian prelate may appear unfeeling. But I believe that genuine charity is best promoted by exposing and discountenancing the pernicious counterfeit.

Everyone will admit that habits of industry should be encouraged; and that the best way to serve the poor man, is to put him on his feet.

But after exhausting all his resources for the extinction of poverty, the political economist will still be confronted by it, and he will realize the truth of our Saviour's words: "The poor ye have always with you."[2] You can no more legislate penury than you can legislate vice out of existence. In the hard struggle of life, especially in great centres, there will always be found willing hands that cannot get employment. Some are impoverished by

---

[1] *Luke* XVI., 3.
[2] *Matt.* XXVI., 11.

a life of sin; others, by improvident habits; and others still, by the mysterious dispensation of God.

London is to-day not only the most populous, but the richest city in the world. It is the poorest also.

According to official statistics for 1886, Berlin with a population of a million and a half, has 197,000 persons living from hand to mouth on the verge of poverty, whilst 46,000 receive regular aid from the poor fund. These figures have a profound signification when we reflect that all the appliances of political economy are employed in the administration of these two cities; that the Church has no voice in their municipal government; and that her children form but an insignificant fraction of the entire population.

Unequal distribution of goods is the law of divine economy. In every nation you will find men occupying the two extremes of bodily and intellectual stature, of towering height and diminutive size, of gigantic strength and physical impotency, of luminous intellect and dulness of comprehension; and so, also, will be met the two extremes of fortune's gifts and social life.

This law of inequality is decreed by a wise dispensation of Providence for the exercise of social virtues, that the strong may aid the weak, the learned instruct the ignorant, the rich help the poor. God has given you wealth, that you may practice beneficence toward the needy. He has permitted others to live in indigence, that they might exercise patience and self-denial, and manifest gratitude to their benefactors.

Were all men in equal conditions of fortune, the benevolent affections, which add a charm to life, would grow torpid, and there would be little room left for the discharge of those reciprocal duties that strengthen the bonds of society.

The most efficient way to relieve the wants of the poor, is through organizations like that of the Little Sisters, of which I have already spoken, and of the St. Vincent de Paul Society. The members of this admirable association visit personally the poor in their homes, inquire into their condition, and distribute aid where it will do the most good. They thus avoid the danger of being imposed upon by unworthy applicants. They give their services gratuitously. The system is, therefore, more economical than one that is controlled by salaried officials. Their offerings are doubly blessed, because they fulfil their errands of mercy from motives of religion and charity, greeting the indigent as brothers, and not in the patronizing tones of an official working for pay.

The Church has Orphan Asylums for the moral and industrial training of boys and girls, whom she teaches to become worthy and useful members of society. She has hospitals where every form of human disease is healed or assuaged. Her consecrated daughters do not shrink from nursing the sick and wounded on the battle-field and in the plague-stricken city. During the Crimean War, I remember having read of a Sister who was killed by a ball as she was bending over a bleeding soldier and bandaging his wounds. Much praise was deservedly bestowed in those days on Florence Nightingale for her noble charity in tending the sick and wounded of the camp hospitals. But within the breast of every Sister, there breathes the spirit of a Florence Nightingale with this difference that, like the ministering angels, the Sister moves noiselessly through life; and, like the angel Raphael, who concealed his name from Tobias, she hides her name from the world.

While I was bishop of Richmond, Governor Kemper, of Virginia, was pleased on one occasion to attend the Commencement at the Academy kept by the Sisters of Charity. At the close of the exercises, he made a touching address, in which he narrated the following personal incident: "In the battle of Gettysburg, there was a soldier wounded and, as it was thought, to death. When restored to consciousness, he saw beside him on the battle-field a deal coffin ready to receive his mortal remains. But he also saw a Sister of Charity, who bound up his wounds, cooled his fevered brow, moistened his parched lips, and nursed him till he was able to be removed from the field.—And now that soldier stands before you!"

A Sister of my acquaintance, a daughter of a U. S. Naval officer, happened to be in charge of an Orphan Asylum in Detroit, when the yellow fever broke out in 1878. In the following letter addressed to her Superior at Emmittsburg, she begged permission to devote herself to the victims of the plague: "Hearing that you are about to send Sisters to the relief of our dear and suffering Sisters of the South, I cannot resist the feeling that urges me to tell you how my soul longs to go to their aid. Should it cost this poor life, it shall be freely given. I have no fear of the fever, and I should love to fall in so noble a cause, should our dear Lord so will it. One word more, which I feel your kind heart will understand. My mother is not in the Church. What would be a few short days given in exchange for her eternal happiness, should our Lord hear the cry of my heart!"—Her services were accepted. She arrived in Vicksburg on September 15th and the next morning entered on her duties. On the 21st she was prostrated by the contagion and on the 27th she expired. Almighty God, who accepted the sacrifice of her life, deigned also to hear her prayer; for since her death, her mother has embraced the Catholic religion.

Here is an example of sublime charity, not culled from the musty pages of hagiology, but happening before our eyes. Here is heroism, not roused by the emulation of brave comrades on the battle-field or by the clash of arms or the sound of martial music or the lust of fame, but inspired by filial piety and by a love of God and her fellow beings.

I shall relate one more instance of Christian devotedness that fell under my own observation. During the war I accompanied eight Sisters of Charity from Baltimore to New Orleans. They had been sent to reinforce the ranks of their heroic companions that had fallen during the yellow fever at the post of duty. Their departure was not marked by public announcement or applause. They silently rushed into the jaws of death, not bent on deeds of destruction like the famous "Six Hundred," but aiming at the fulfilment of a mission of mercy. They had no Tennyson to sound their praises. Their only ambition was (and how lofty is that ambition!) that their good deeds should be inscribed by the recording angel in the Book of Life; and that they might receive their reward from Him who said: "I was sick and you visited Me... for, as long as ye did it to one of the least of My brethren, ye did it to Me."[1] Within a few months after their arrival, six of the eight Sisters fell victims to the epidemic.

Of all the diseases that have ever afflicted the human family, leprosy has justly been regarded as the most loathsome and appalling. It is a universal cancer preying on the whole body with insatiable appetite. The malady is incurable. The skill of the physician may retard, but it cannot prevent the fatal progress of the disease.

In ancient times, as soon as the distemper declared itself, the victim was removed from the society of his fellow-beings. He dragged out a miserable existence in some secluded place with the companions of his sufferings depending on his labor, or on an alms for his subsistence. He had no hospital to shelter him, for such institutions were unknown among the nations of antiquity.

[1] *Matt.* XXV., 36.

When the Church was yet in her infancy, lepers began to share in the beneficent spirit of Christianity. At a very early age, pious confraternities were organized for the care of lepers. The Council of Orleans, in 549, and that of Lyons, in 583, prescribe to the Church authorities the duty of clothing and supporting lepers. The ravages of leprosy were most fearful in the eleventh and the twelfth centuries, having been spread by the Christian troops on their return from the East after the first Crusade. But works of charity kept pace with the disease, and leper hospitals were erected in great numbers over the continent of Europe.

Thanks to judicious sanitary laws, this terrible scourge is now well-nigh banished from civilized centres, though it still lingers on their confines. It prevails to a fearful extent in Molokai, one of the Sandwich Islands, whither the patients are consigned from the other islands of the group, and where from six to eight hundred are usually congregated.[1]

In 1873, Father Damien, a young Belgian priest, volunteered to consecrate his life to the care of these lepers. After thirteen years of unremitting labor, he contracted the fatal malady to which he succumbed in 1889. His place was promptly supplied by Rev. Lambert Conrady who for several years had labored as a missionary priest in Oregon. A sacrifice more heroic than this can hardly be conceived;

[1] Numerous victims of leprosy may also be found in India, China, Japan and Palestine.

for on entering this island, these apostles could apply to themselves the words of Dante: "You who enter here, leave hope behind." Agathocles, king of Syracuse, lives in history because, when he carried the war into Africa, he burned his ships on reaching the coast of Carthage, that his army, having no means of escape, should determine to conquer or die. These soldiers of Christ, also, burned their ships, and voluntarily cut themselves off once for all from their kindred, their country, and the world.

Perhaps in the whole range of human wretchedness, there is no class of persons that should appeal more strongly to our sympathy than those whose reason is dethroned; since, possessing as they do an imbecile mind in a developed body, there are none so helpless as they.

History does not record that any nation outside of Christendom had institutions for the custody or care of the insane, or laws for their protection. But now every nation enlightened by the genius of Christianity regards special provision for the insane as a sacred duty; and in this humane work, the government is often aided by private corporations.

The Christian religion labors not only to assuage the physical and mental distempers of humanity, but also to reclaim the victims of moral disease.

The redemption of fallen women from a life of infamy, was never included in the scope of heathen philanthropy; and man's unregenerate nature is the same now as it was before the birth of Christ. He worships woman so long as she has charms to fascinate; but she is spurned and trampled upon, as soon as she has ceased to please. It was reserved for Him who knew no sin to throw the mantle of protection over sinning woman. There is no page in the Gospel more touching than that which records our Saviour's merciful judgment on the adulterous woman. The Scribes and Pharisees, who had perhaps participated in her guilt, ask our Lord to pronounce sentence of death upon her in accordance with the Mosaic Law. "Hath no one condemned thee?" asked our Saviour. "No one, Lord," she answered. "Then," said He, "neither will I condemn thee. Go, sin no more."

Inspired by this divine example, the Catholic Church shelters erring females in Homes not inappropriately called *Magdalen Asylums* and *Houses of the Good Shepherd.* Not to speak of other Institutions established for the moral reformation of women, the Congregation of the Good Shepherd at Angers, founded in 1836, has charge to-day of one hundred and fifty Houses, in which upward of four thousand Sisters devote themselves to the care of over twenty thousand females, who had yielded to temptation, or were rescued from impending danger.

But there is no good work, how benevolent and disinterested soever, that escapes the shafts of adverse criticism. And Magdalen Asylums and Foundling Hospitals are no exceptions to the rule. They have been vehemently assailed by Lord Brougham in the *Edinburgh Review,* as well as by other writers, who assert that the very protection which these

Institutions afford to fallen women, are an incentive to sin. A more unjust or uncharitable statement could hardly be made. We have life-saving stations scattered along the Atlantic coast. No one will have the hardihood to maintain that sea-captains, from the knowledge they have of these humane establishments and from the hope of being rescued by them, are less vigilant for the safety of their vessels.

It would be equally unreasonable to suppose that the consciousness of the existence of Magdalen Asylums influences females in making a wreck of their virtue. I am convinced that ninety-five per cent. of the unfortunate women who enter them, never heard of these institutions till after their fall, and that not one of them was in the slightest degree influenced by the hope of finding shelter for her lost innocence. People do not launch on the sea of vice with all the foresight and calculation they exhibit when embarking on a voyage. They usually plunge into the tumultuous waves of pleasure reckless of consequences. It is only after the moral wreck that their eyes are opened. Like Eve, they become sensible of their condition; and filled with shame, hasten eagerly to hide their guilt in the asylums which religion provides.

CHAPTER XXIX.

WARFARE IN PAGAN AND CHRISTIAN TIMES—
CHRISTIANITY HAS DIMINISHED THE NUMBER,
AND MITIGATED THE ATROCITIES OF WARS.

I.

Christianity has conferred another signal blessing on society by lessening the number and frequency of wars. Prior to the advent of the Prince of Peace, war was the rule; peace, the exception. So regular was the recurrence of military strife before the Christian era, that the sacred writer designates a certain season of the year as the usual time for the reopening of hostilities; and seems to regard war as the habitual occupation of kings: "And it came to pass at the return of the year, at the time when kings go forth to war."[1]

The temple of Janus in Rome was opened in time of war, and closed in time of peace. From the accession of Tullus Hostilius, the second successor of Romulus, till the reign of Augustus Cæsar,

[1] *II. Kings* XI.

embracing a period of nearly six hundred and fifty years, the temple was closed but once, and then for only six years, which implies that Rome was engaged during that long period in an almost uninterrupted series of military operations.

It had been a maxim among the Greeks that no more acceptable gifts can be offered in the temples of the gods than the trophies won from an enemy in battle.[1] Such a sentiment could not fail to be a powerful incentive to aggressive warfare. History, in fact, exhibits the various Grecian communities engaged in incessant wars. Among them not less than among the Romans, a citizen and a soldier were synonymous terms; and with the exception of, perhaps, Egypt alone, this is equally true of all the nations of antiquity of which we have any record.

The Prophet Isaiah, in portraying the life of the coming Redeemer, enumerates among His distinguishing traits, His pacific character and mission: "A Child is born to us, . . . and His name shall be called Wonderful, Counsellor, God the mighty, the Father of the world to come, *the Prince of Peace*."[2] The song of the angelic choir at the birth of Jesus in Bethlehem foreshadowed His twofold mission on earth: "Glory to God in the highest, and on earth peace to men of good will."

And these predictions of the prophet and the angels are fully borne out by the example and precepts of our Saviour. The Gospels and Epistles

---
[1] Dion Chrysostom, Or. II. *De Regno*.
[2] *Isaiah* IX., 6.

habitually inculcate peace and good will, charity and benevolence, patience and self-denial, forgiveness of injuries and the returning of good for evil. They condemn with equal force, hatred, resentment and retaliation, enmities and warfare. They recommend the settlement of difficulties by peaceable arbitration rather than by recourse to arms or litigation.

"Blessed are the meek; for they shall possess the land. Blessed are the peace-makers; for they shall be called the children of God."[1]

"Ye have heard that it was said: An eye for an eye, and a tooth for a tooth. But I say to you not to resist evil: but if one strike thee on thy right cheek, turn to him the other also."[2]

"Ye have heard that it was said: Thou shalt love thy neighbor, and hate thine enemy. But I say to you: Love your enemies, do good to those who hate you, and pray for those who persecute and calumniate you: that ye may be the children of your Father who is in heaven, who maketh His sun to rise on the good and the bad, and raineth on the just and the unjust."[3]

"James and John said: Lord, wilt Thou that we command fire to come down from heaven and consume them? And turning, He rebuked them, saying: Ye know not of what spirit ye are. The Son of man came not to destroy souls, but to save."[4]

"Jesus answered: My Kingdom is not of this

[1] *Matt.* V. [2] *Ibid.*
[3] *Ibid.* [4] *Luke* IX.

world. If My Kingdom were of this world, My servants would certainly strive that I should not be delivered to the Jews; but now My Kingdom is not from hence."[1]

"The works of the flesh are manifest which are ... enmities, contentions, rivalries, wrath, quarrels, disputes, sects, envying, murders, ... and the like; of which I forewarn you that they who do such things, shall not obtain the Kingdom of God. But the fruit of the Spirit is charity, ... peace, patience, mildness, goodness, long-suffering. ... Against such there is no law."[2]

"Whence are wars and contests among you? Is it not hence, from your lusts which war in your members? Ye covet and ye have not: ye kill and envy, and ye cannot obtain: ye fight and war, and ye have not, because ye ask not."[3]

Indeed war and enmities are so strongly deprecated in these and other passages of the New Testament, that a few of the early Fathers regarded all war as unlawful for Christians, and some of the primitive converts to Christianity conscientiously abstained from military service as intrinsically wrong. While the Church never considered a military life as incompatible with the profession of the Christian religion, and while admitting that war may be sometimes necessary, she declares that hostilities undertaken even in a just cause, are always to be deplored because they involve great calamities, and are rarely

[1] *John* XVIII.   [3] *James* IV.
[2] *Gal.* V.

exempt from acts of injustice and inhumanity. She forbids churchmen to take up arms, applying to them the words addressed by Christ to Peter: "Put thy sword into its place, for all they that take the sword, shall perish by the sword."[1]

In advocating the reign of peace, the Church has always labored at a great disadvantage. From the foundation of Christianity till the peace of Constantine in the beginning of the fourth century, the Church herself was pursued with unrelenting fury, and was obliged to struggle for her very existence:

"Oft doom'd to death, though fated not to die."

She had, consequently, no voice in the councils of the nations; and her influence for peace was confined to individuals and to the secretly-assembled congregations of the faithful.

The incursions of the barbarians preceding and following the extinction of the Roman Empire in 476; the rise of Mohammedanism in the seventh century; the warlike spirit and rapid invasions of the Saracens, were all disturbing elements on the face of Europe, and they hampered the ministers of religion in proclaiming the Gospel of peace. But if Christianity could not at once subdue, it tempered the fierce spirit of the invaders of Europe. The sons of St. Benedict converted swords into ploughshares in many country districts of Italy, France, Germany and England, and diverted the minds of thousands

---

[1] *Matt.* XXVI.

from warlike pursuits to the peaceful occupations of agriculture and manufacture.

And during the middle ages, especially in the turbulent period of the eleventh century, when civil war broke out so frequently between the princes and their vassals, and among the feudal lords themselves, the Church, while unable to stop bloodshed, succeeded at least in checking the ardor of strife by establishing the "Truce of God." By this Truce it was decreed that from Wednesday evening till Monday morning of each week, and during the whole season of Advent and Christmas Tide, and also from the beginning of Lent till the octave of Pentecost, all military contests should be suspended under pain of excommunication. By this pacific compact, reason had time to assert its sway, and habits of amity and good-will were gradually engendered. And later on we find the Roman Pontiffs one after another laboring incessantly for the preservation or the restoration of peace. "They rebuked the passions and checked the extravagant pretensions of sovereigns; their character as the common fathers of Christians, gave to their representations a weight which no other mediator could claim; and their legates spared neither journey nor fatigue to reconcile the jarring interests of courts, and interposed the olive of peace between the swords of contending armies."[1]

By proclaiming the universal brotherhood of mankind and by fostering social and friendly relations

---

[1] Lingard, *Edward III.*, Vol. III.

among nations, Christianity has contributed to reduce the number of wars in modern times.

It is a subject of profound concern to the friends of the Gospel of peace that Christian Europe presents to-day the spectacle of a great military camp. All the nations of the continent are armed to the teeth in mutual distrust, devoured by an insatiable lust for dominion and territory, or by a dread of invasion. When heavy clouds, surcharged with the electricity of war are hanging over these nations, the thunder-clap may come at any moment. Armed nations, like armed individuals, are a constant menace to one another, and are easily provoked to fight. And these military forces are unhappily increasing; for as soon as one nation augments its armament, its neighbor seems impelled to do likewise. According to a report compiled in 1887 from official documents, the army list of Europe on a war footing comprises nearly fourteen millions of men, and the annual cost of maintaining the military establishments in time of peace, exceeds six hundred millions of dollars.[1]

When we consider the immense number of men torn in the bloom of life from the bosom of their families, withdrawn from active and industrial pursuits, condemned to a monotonous existence and exposed to the temptations incident to such a career, we can form some estimate of the material, moral and social evils resulting from this system. In contem-

---

[1] *Amer. Almanac* for 1887, edited by Spofford, Librarian of Congress.

plating these standing armies, the calm observer might have the conviction forced upon him that European governments were primarily established to instruct men in the tactics of military rather than in the duties of civil life, and to teach them to destroy life rather than to develop the resources of the country.

This fearful condition of things is in a great measure attributable to the revival of Paganism, which, after the conquest of Constantinople, in 1445, invaded the arts, literature and philosophy of Western Europe under the name of *Renaissance*, and poisoned the intellectual and moral life of many sovereign houses, and of a large proportion of the aristocracy both of birth and of wealth. Thus it happened that the governments of Christian nations, one after another, have betrayed a spirit and pursued a policy indifferent if not unfriendly to Christianity. The European nations as such, are indeed Christian to-day just as well as the people of the United States; but they do not enjoy the political advantages which Providence has granted to us. Our government has always been conducted on Christian principles, because its vigorous youth is periodically renewed by the suffrages of the people who have ever proved faithful to the maxims and sentiments of Christianity.

Even with this dark picture confronting us, it would be unjust to infer that Christianity has failed in her mission of peace to the nations. It should be borne in mind that the Christian religion enforces her humane precepts not by the sword, but by moral and religious sanctions; and that in contending for peace, she has to struggle against the most formidable of earthly forces, and the most imperious of human passions.

While deploring the fierce conflicts which have agitated Christendom for centuries, it must be admitted that even the most martial nation of Europe does not exhibit a war record so sanguinary and protracted as that of heathen Rome, or of the petty States of Greece, or of the ancient monarchies of the East.

A comparison between the war history of the Roman Empire and that of the United States will result vastly in favor of our country, and will forcibly illustrate the pacific tendencies of our Christian civilization. During the six centuries and a half which elapsed from the death of Numa to the reign of Augustus, as already observed, with the exception of six years, Rome was engaged in continuous warfare. The United States has existed as an independent government for over a century. Since our independence we have been involved in only three wars,—with England from 1812 to 1815; with Mexico from 1845 to 1848; and in our civil war from 1861 to 1865. Thus while Rome enjoyed but six years of peace during six hundred and fifty years, the United States has had but a little over ten years of war in upwards of a century.

It is also a gratifying fact that, with a population of over sixty millions, the army of the United States does not exceed twenty-five thousand men, who are scattered for the most part along the frontiers of the country. This force while sufficiently strong to preserve our domestic peace, is too insignificant to excite the fear or provoke the jealousy of our neighbors. Our best security lies in the supremacy of the law, in the loyalty of our citizens, in their strong attachment to our free institutions, and in abstention from entangling alliances.[1]

That the cause of international peace is gaining ground, is evident from the fact, that war is no longer precipitated among Christian nations, as in former times, at the whim of the sovereign; but the

[1] There is one chapter in our early history which, I deeply regret to say, does not reflect credit upon us when viewed by the light of the Gospel. I refer to the treatment of the Indian tribes by the North American colonists. The Indians were too frequently regarded as enemies to be exterminated or slain, rather than as brethren to be conciliated.

It may be alleged as an extenuating circumstance that this aggressive warfare was carried on by individuals without the sanction of the government, which had not the ability to protect the aboriginal tribes extending over so vast a territory. At all events the responsibility rests somewhere.

The Spanish and Portuguese settlers of South America, whatever may have been their faults, have pursued toward the Indians a more humane policy. They have not only preserved the race, but they have endeavored, also, to civilize and christianize them.

It is pleasing to record that, in recent times, our government is atoning for the sins and shortcomings of past generations by its efforts not only to rescue from extinction the remnant of those once flourishing tribes, but by instructing them in the principles of the Christian religion, and in the industries of civilized life.

voice of the people is heard through their representatives and the press, at least, in constitutional governments. Commercial interests and fraternal and social relations between the nations of the earth, are now becoming so intertwined, that one country can hardly inflict an injury on another without having the blow recoil upon itself.

Christianity has created and is daily developing international law throughout the civilized world. Courts of arbitration are growing in favor among Christian nations. Alexander VI. was chosen by Spain and Portugal to arbitrate regarding their respective claims to the newly-discovered territory in the western world. The decision of the Pontiff was very probably the means of averting a sanguinary and protracted conflict between these two rival nations. Instances of arbitration are multiplying in our own day. The dispute between Germany and Spain in reference to the Caroline Islands, was adjusted by Pope Leo XIII. in 1886. The Samoan difficulty between the United States and Germany in 1889, was referred to a friendly conference held in Berlin. At the close of President Cleveland's administration, an arbitration treaty between Mexico and the United States was signed in Washington. By an act of Congress passed in 1888, the President is authorized to invite Representatives of the governments of South America, Central America, Mexico and Hayti to an international Conference in Washington. The very first proposition to be discussed has reference to the adoption of "measures that shall tend to preserve the peace and promote the prosperity of the several American States."

With the view also of promoting the blessing of international concord, a society has been organized in this country. It was fitting that Philadelphia should be chosen as the seat of this society, for its very name signifies brotherly love. Its founder was an illustrious member of the Society of Friends, whose distinguishing characteristic is aversion to strife, and the cultivation of peace and fraternal relations among mankind.

In well-ordered society the disputes of individuals are settled not by recourse to a duel, but to the law. Would it not be a blessing to humanity if national controversies were composed on the same principle, and that the just cause of a nation should be vindicated by a court of arbitration rather than by an appeal to arms? Then to rulers, as well as to private litigants, could be applied the words:

"Thrice is he armed that hath his quarrel just."

And this amicable system, while protecting the rights of the weak, would not humiliate or wound the national pride of the strong, since it does not attempt to trench on the sovereignty or autonomy of any power.

Let us cherish the hope that the day is not far off when the reign of the Prince of Peace will be firmly established on the earth, when the spirit of the Gospel will so far sway the minds and hearts of rulers, that standing armies will yield to permanent courts of arbitration, that contests will be carried on in the council-chamber instead of the battle-field, and decided by the pen instead of the sword.

II.

Christianity has not only diminished the number, but has also mitigated the horrors of wars. In Pagan times the conqueror rarely showed mercy to the conquered. *Vae victis*, woe to the vanquished, was his usual motto. The cities were laid waste. The wives and daughters of the subdued nation became the prey of the victorious soldiery. The defeated kings and generals were obliged to grace the triumph of the conqueror. They were led away in chains and doomed to hopeless captivity. So sure was the enslavement of captured kings and queens to follow from defeat, that we find prince Hector of Troy thus feelingly addressing his wife Andromache:

"The day shall come when some mailed Greek shall lead thee
    weeping hence,
And take from thee thy day of freedom.
Thou then in Argos shalt, at another's bidding,
Ply the loom, and from the fountain of Messeis draw water."[1]

Sometimes the captives were destined for a more summary fate; for they were often sacrificed on Pagan altars to appease the gods. In many instances they were executed without regard to age or sex; and the commander who ordered the

[1] Homer's *Iliad*, B. VI.

execution was not supposed to exceed his rights, nor did he shock the public conscience. In fact, Pagan commanders assumed the same proprietary rights over human beings, including non-combatants, that Christian generals exercise over cattle and beasts of burden in an enemy's country. They were enslaved or put to the sword, as the policy of war dictated.

When Salmanasar, King of Assyria, subdued Samaria (722 B. C.), the people of Israel with Osee their king were all carried into captivity, and Assyrian colonists planted in their stead.

When Nabuchodonozor, King of Babylon, one hundred and thirty-four years later, destroyed Jerusalem, Sedecias, King of Juda, beheld his children slaughtered by his side; his own eyes were torn out, and he was exiled into Chaldea with the princes and officers and the rest of the inhabitants.

Alexander the Great, after the capture of Tyre, ordered two thousand of the inhabitants to be crucified, and the remainder of the population were put to death, or sold into slavery. Nor was his treatment of Gaza less cruel. At the storming of that city, all the surviving defenders were killed on the spot, and their wives and children sold as slaves. How different was the conduct of General Scott after his successful siege of the Mexican capital! As soon as the enemy surrendered, not a single soldier or citizen was sacrificed to the vengeance of the victorious army, and not a single family was exiled from their native land.

Annibal on one occasion slew five thousand captives.[1] His father Hamilcar, on the occasion of a revolt of the Carthagenian mercenaries, did not sheathe his sword so long as a single rebel survived, —an act extolled by Polybius as most just.[2] The Romans, though perhaps the most generous of ancient nations, punished military prisoners in a manner which to us appears absolutely heartless and revolting. Jugurtha, king of Numidia, after being borne in chains from his native country to Rome, was cast into the Mamertine prison, a living tomb hewn out of the rock, the contemplation of which, even at this day, excites a shudder. He died after struggling for six days with cold and hunger.

Julius Cæsar avows without apology or scruple of conscience, that in the siege of Avaricum, in Gaul, forty thousand of the inhabitants, including the young and the old of both sexes, were by his command put to the sword. Nor did he hesitate on several occasions to strike terror by acts of cruelty still more revolting. Thus at Uxellodunum (Captenac), in south-western Gaul, he cut off the hands of all that had borne arms against him, and turned the maimed wretches adrift as a warning to their countrymen. And the valiant Gaulish chieftain, Vercingctorix, had his agony prolonged for six years that he might grace the conqueror's triumph, and was then put to death. How humane and magnanimous was Washington's

[1] See Grotius, Lib. III., Chap. IV., where this and several other acts of cruelty are recorded.
[2] See Vuibert's *Ancient History*, p. 407.

treatment of Cornwallis after his surrender at Yorktown, compared with Cæsar's conduct toward the Gaulish king! While the latter was expatriated, imprisoned and slain for defending his country against a foreign invader, Cornwallis was permitted to return unharmed to England with his defeated troops.

In the year 70 of the Christian era, upwards of a million of Jews perished by war or famine in the siege of Jerusalem under Titus, and ninety-seven thousand were carried into captivity from their native land. Thousands of the more robust captives were sent in chains to work at the Egyptian mines; thousands of others were thrown to wild beasts or reserved to slaughter one another for the amusement of the populace in the Roman and provincial amphitheatres. Of the Jews two thousand five hundred were immolated in honor of the birthday of Domitian, the brother of Titus; and his father Vespasian's birthday was solemnized by the sacrifice of a multitude of others. The aged and infirm were slain, while the young of both sexes were sold as slaves. The hallowed vessels of the sanctuary of Jerusalem were borne in triumph by the blood-stained hands of Gentiles, followed by Simon, the captive chief, and the flower of the Jewish race, amid the gaze of the Roman populace. Simon, after gracing the triumph of the conqueror, had a rope thrown around his neck, and was dragged to the Forum, where he was cruelly tortured and put to death.[1]

---

[1] Josephus, *Wars of the Jews*, B. V. and *seq.*

Yet Titus far from being condemned for exceptional cruelty, was applauded by his contemporaries as a most benevolent ruler. He was called *the Delight of the Human Race*, and the monument commemorating his victories and triumphant entry into Rome, exists to this day. The author of the "Decline and Fall of the Roman Empire,"[1] with his usual bias, concurs in this favorable verdict, remarking that "under the mild administration of Titus, the Roman world enjoyed a transient felicity," and that his memory was beloved by his subjects. But in the light of the atrocities sanctioned or tolerated by Titus, it is difficult to explain why even Gibbon should pass so warm a eulogy on the Roman general. A Christian leader with a similar record would surely have been painted in more sombre colors by the English historian.

Contrast the treatment of the Jews under Titus with the conduct of General Grant toward the conquered Confederate States. Both generals were engaged in a civil war. Judea was as much an integral part of the Roman Empire as the Southern States were of the Federal Union. Its inhabitants appealed to the clemency of Titus as forcibly as the vanquished States appealed to the magnanimity of the Northern general. Yet Grant in allowing the Southern leader with his officers and men to return home after the surrender at Appomattox Court House, was not particularly praised for his humanity.

---

[1] Vol. I., Chap. 3.

Imagine General Lee with his surrendered army led in chains through the streets of Washington, and the victorious troops bearing aloft the confiscated treasures of Southern homes and sanctuaries! Imagine also a monument erected in Washington by the enslaved prisoners of the Confederacy to commemorate the victories of General Grant! Would not such a spectacle be revolting to the feelings of the whole country, and would not the American people protest against such a humiliation inflicted on their conquered brethren?

The Roman and the American general each acted up to the spirit of the time in which he lived. Titus in exterminating a race, was obeying the sentiment of Pagan cruelty. Grant in sparing the vanquished, was reflecting the humanity of Christian civilization.

But it is by comparing the conduct of the same nation towards its enemies before and after its conversion, that we can form a more correct idea of the restraining influence of the Gospel. The moderation with which the newly-converted English used their victories in Wales, is in pleasing contrast with their former inhumanity towards the people of that country, and is an eloquent tribute to the humanizing influence of Christianity: "The evangelical precepts of peace and love," says Freeman, "did not put an end to aggressive conquests, but they distinctly humanized the way in which war was carried on. From this time forth the never-ending wars with the Welsh cease to be wars of extermination. The heathen English had been satisfied with nothing short of the destruction and expulsion of their enemies; the Christian English thought it enough to reduce them to political subjection. . . . The Christian Welsh could now sit down as subjects of the Christian Saxon. The Welshman was acknowledged as a man and a citizen and was put under the protection of the law."[1]

Under the benign influence of Christianity, not only are conquered nations shielded from the penalty of death and from the degradation of slavery, but every contrivance which humanity and science can invent, is employed to mitigate the sufferings of the sick and wounded and prisoners of war. Hospitals, hospital-nurses, medical purveyors, ambulance corps, and exchange of prisoners are expressions familiar to modern warfare. I do not think that such terms are ever met in the military annals of Paganism.

Montesquieu pays the following just tribute to the successful efforts of Christianity in mitigating the barbarities of war: "When we place before our eyes the massacres committed by Greek and Roman chieftains, the populations and cities destroyed by them, the ravages of Timur, and Genghiskhan, who devastated Asia, we shall see that we owe to Christianity, for the right of nations in war, a debt of gratitude which human nature cannot sufficiently repay."[2]

[1] *Hist. of the Norman Conquest*, Vol. I., pp. 33–34.
[2] *Esprit des Lois*, Liv. XXIV., Chap. III.

Candor compels us to admit that Christian generals have too often been guilty of deeds of cruelty and inhumanity to a fallen foe. But these instances are exceptions to the rule. These cruelties were perpetrated in contests usually aggravated by religious strife, and they have been condemned by the judgment of Christendom. We may well conclude in the words of Thomas Arnold, of Rugby: "Wars between independent states in the ancient world were far more frequent than now, and produced a far greater amount of human misery."[1]

---

[1] *History of Rome*, Appleton, p. 450.

CHAPTER XXX.

THE INFLUENCE OF PAGANISM ON HUMAN SLAVERY.

At the dawn of Christianity, slavery was universal.[1] Although some Pagan philosophers, like Seneca, declared that all men are by nature free and equal, still by the law of nations slavery was upheld in every country on the face of the earth; and it was an axiom among the ruling classes that "the human race exists for the sake of the few." Aristotle maintained that no perfect household could exist without slaves and freemen, and that the natural law, as well as the law of nations, makes a distinction between bond and free.[2] Even Plato avowed that every slave's soul was fundamentally corrupt, and that no rational man should trust him.[3]

The proportion of slaves to freemen varied, of course, in different countries, though usually the former were largely in excess of the free population. In Rome, for three hundred and sixty-six years, from the fall of Corinth to Alexander Severus, the

---

[1] *The Gentile and the Jew*, II., 265.   [3] *Legg.* VI., p. 277.
[2] *Polit.* I., 3.

slaves, according to the testimony of Blair, were three to one. Her bondmen were recruited from Britain, Gaul, Germany, Scandinavia, in fact from every country into which her army or traders could penetrate. At one time, they became so formidable in Rome that the Senate, fearing that, if conscious of their own numbers, the public safety might be endangered, forbade them a distinctive dress.

In Greece, also, the number of slaves was far greater than that of the free population. Attica had 20,000 citizens and 400,000 slaves, females not included. Sparta contained 36,000 citizens and 366,000 bondmen. The number of slaves in Corinth was 460,000, and in Egina, 470,000.[1] In Tyre, they were so numerous at one time that they succeeded in massacring all their masters. The Scythians, on returning from a hostile invasion of Media, found their slaves in rebellion, and were compelled for a while to abandon their country. Herodotus remarks with quaint humor that, after vainly attempting to conquer the slaves with spears and bows, the Scythians cast these weapons aside, and armed themselves with horse-whips. The slaves, who fought like heroes when confronted with warlike arms, lost heart and fled before the lash.[2]

By far the greatest number of slaves were acquired by military conquest, perpetual bondage being the usual fate of captives. Many others were purchased in the slave-market, or obtained by

[1] *The Gentile and the Jew*, II., 227.
[2] Bk. IV, No. 3.

kidnapping. Children were frequently sold by impoverished or sordid parents, men were sold for debt or for the non-payment of taxes, and certain crimes were punished by perpetual servitude.

The head of the family was absolute master of his slaves, having over them the power of life and death. This atrocious law was modified by Hadrian, the Antonines, and Alexander Severus in the latter days of the Empire. But the imperial clemency was rendered almost nugatory by a provision which declared that the master could not be indicted for the murder of his slave, unless the intention to kill could be proved. Mr. Lecky thinks that barbarity to slaves was rare in the earlier days of the Republic; but the reasons which he assigns for his assertion are hardly conclusive.[1]

When a slave gave testimony in a court of justice, his deposition was always acompanied by torture, a practice approved by Demosthenes, Lycurgus, and other Attic orators. What the oath was to the freeman, the torture was to the slave. Female slaves when giving testimony were subjected to the same inhuman treatment.

An atrocious law ordained that if a master was murdered, all the slaves of his household, excepting those in chains and helpless invalids, should be put to death.[2] On one occasion, four hundred slaves of Pedanius, the Prefect of Rome, were ruthlessly executed, to avenge their master's assassination.

[1] *History of Europ. Morals*, I., 301.
[2] Tacit. *Annal.* XIII., 32 *et seq.*

INFLUENCE OF PAGANISM ON SLAVERY. 419

Aged and infirm slaves were habitually exposed to perish on an island in the Tiber. The elder Cato, who lived under the Republic and who may be regarded as a type of the Roman nobility of his time, considered slaves simply as machines for acquiring wealth, to be cast aside in decrepit old age like worthless lumber. And, indeed, freedom would be but a poor boon to them in sickness and infirmity, since they had neither hospital nor asylum to receive them, nor self-sacrificing nurses to assuage their sufferings. Death was, therefore, a merciful relief to them.

When condemned to execution for a crime, their last moments were embittered by the most excruciating tortures, the usual death penalty being crucifixion until, out of reverence for our Saviour, it was abolished by Constantine.

The marriage of slaves was not recognized by law. Their union was regarded only as a concubinage or a contubernium; hence, they had no parental rights over their offspring, who belonged exclusively to their master. The words adultery, incest, polygamy, had no meaning for them.

Roman fugitive slaves were usually branded on the forehead, and the punishment due their offence redoubled. Sometimes they were thrown to the wild beasts in the amphitheatre.[1]

The wretched condition of slaves in Pagan times was often rendered more intolerable by aggravating

---

[1] Gell. V., 14.

circumstances. Many of them had once enjoyed the blessings of freedom, but had been reduced to bondage by the calamities of war. Unlike the negro slaves of America, they were usually of the same color as their masters; and, in some instances, better educated, more refined, and of a more delicate frame than those whom they served. Epictetus, one of the ablest of the Stoic philosophers, was a slave. Horace and Juvenal were the sons of freedmen.

Slavery exercised, also, a most injurious influence on the free population. It degraded labor, increased idleness, and fostered immorality. Contempt for work and a propensity to idleness formed a characteristic vice among the ancients, because they associated toil with slavery and idleness with freedom. "The Germans," says Tacitus, "cannot endure repose, and yet are fond of inactivity. They consider it dishonorable to earn by the sweat of their brow what they can win by the sword."[1] The Gauls, also, looked upon all labor, agriculture included, as degrading. Hatis, the first lawgiver of Tartessus, in Spain, forbade citizens to perform any kind of manual labor, which was reserved for slaves.[2] The Lusitanians and Cantabrians subjected their wives and slaves to incessant drudgery, living themselves by plunder.[3] Herodotus says: "The Greeks, Thracians, Persians, Lydians, and almost all barbarous nations hold in less honor than their other citizens

[1] *Germ.* XIV, 15.   [2] *Ibid.*
[3] Justin, XLIV., 4.

those that learn any trade, but deem such as abstain from handicrafts noble."[1] In Sparta and other States tradesmen were excluded from political privileges. The free laborer was lowered in the eyes of his fellow-citizens by having slaves for competitors. Even the Romans did not regard any labor, agriculture excepted, as respectable. Cicero declared all mercenary trades to be sordid and dishonorable, and pronounced the workshop unworthy of the dignity of a freeman.[2]

The obvious result of this unhealthy sentiment was, that mechanical and manual labor, agriculture, artistic work, the practice of medicine, and the instruction of youth, were relegated to slaves. Even trade and commerce were carried on by them under the supervision of their masters.

Slavery engendered idleness and poverty among the free citizens. Thousands were daily congregated in the streets of Rome, occupying their time in frequenting the baths; in discussing politics; in selling their votes to the highest bidder during the days of the Republic; in paying homage to their patrons during the Empire, when they had no votes to sell; and in witnessing the slaughter of their fellow-beings in the amphitheatre, depending on the public distribution of money and corn for their support.

In Julius Cæsar's time 320,000 persons in Rome derived their support from imperial largesses.[3] And notwithstanding all the efforts of Augustus to reduce

---

[1] Vol. II., 167.
[2] *De Officiis*, I., 42.
[3] Sueton. XLI., 421.

the number of idle citizens, he was obliged to admit 200,000 of them, along with their wives and children, to share in the sportula.[1] Under the Antonines, the recipients of public aid increased to the number of half a million.

Many others, shrinking on the one hand from a life of idleness, and debarred on the other, from honest toil by the stigma cast upon it, betook themselves to corrupting professions, such as pantomimes, hired gladiators, political spies, panders, astrologers, and religious charlatans.

The debauchery of morals was the worst feature of slavery. Reinforced from various parts of Europe, Africa, and Asia, the slaves contributed each his favorite vice to swell the common tide of depravity. All soon became indoctrinated in the iniquity of their companions. Denied the privileges of lawful wedlock, they plunged into the lowest depths of sensuality. Mothers had ceased to train their own children. They had neither inclination nor capacity for such duties—the race of Cornelias had disappeared. The instruction of youth of both sexes was confided to slaves.[2] For the social degradation to which they were subjected, they were amply avenged by the moral degradation in which they involved their pupils. Excluded from civic honors and preferment, they wielded their brief authority over the youths committed to their care with terrible effect by initiating them into every species of vice. Denied

[1] Dio Cass. LV., 10.
[2] *The Gentile and the Jew*, II., 281.

INFLUENCE OF PAGANISM ON SLAVERY. 423

the privilege of bearing arms, the bondmen used with consummate skill the weapons of lying, deceit, and treachery. Taught from childhood, by their accommodating teachers, to regard no law but that of their own whims, the Roman youth of both sexes grew up proud, insolent and overbearing; and the first victims of their caprice were often the slaves themselves. Many a bondwoman received on her naked breast the sharp point of the stilletto, darted at her by her haughty and imperious mistress.[1] In a word, the homes of the rich and noble were hotbeds of moral corruption.

Nor do the Mohammedans in Africa exhibit less greed in our day in reducing their fellow-beings to the yoke of slavery, nor less cruelty in the treatment of them than did the Romans in Pagan times.

Livingstone,[2] Cameron,[3] and still more recently Cardinal Lavigerie, Archbishop of Carthage,[4] who is furnished with information by his missionaries, declare that at least 400,000 negroes are annually carried into bondage in Africa by Mussulman traders, and that fully five times that number perish either by being massacred in the slave-hunt, or from hunger and hardship on the journey. Thus the lives or liberty of upwards of two millions of the human race are each year sacrificed on the altars of lust and mammon.

[1] See Cardinal Wiseman's *Fabiola*, Ch. IV.
[2] The last journals of Dr. Livingstone. London, 1874.
[3] *Across Africa.*
[4] Conference delivered in Paris, 1888.

The line of march taken by the caravans bearing their human freight from Equatorial Africa to the slave-markets, can be easily traced by the bleaching bones of the unfortunate victims who succumbed to famine and fatigue on the way.

In consequence of this iniquitous commerce, entire villages in the interior of Africa are depopulated, and extensive districts are made desolate by the organized incursions of these traffickers in human flesh.

CHAPTER XXXI.

THE INFLUENCE OF CHRISTIANITY ON HUMAN SLAVERY.

Among the many social blessings conferred by Christianity, her successful efforts in the mitigation of the excesses of slavery and in the gradual emancipation of the slave, will justly hold a conspicuous place.

The Church did not deem it a part of her mission hastily to sever, or rudely to disturb, the relations that she found subsisting between master and man. She encountered slavery in every land. The bondmen were, in most places, largely in excess of the free population. They were regarded rather as chattels than as human beings, and were looked upon as an indispensable element of family life. With such ideas ruling the world, a violent crusade against slavery would cause a universal upheaval of society; it would involve the commonwealth in bloodshed, and would be disastrous to the slaves themselves. The Apostles and their successors pursued a policy that, without injustice, violence or revolution, led to the gradual emancipation of slaves.

They succeeded in lightening the chain, in causing it to relax its hold day by day, till it fell harmless from the limbs of the captives.

Their first step toward manumission was to Christianize the slave, to emancipate him from the thraldom of his passions and the darkness of error, and to admit him to the glorious liberty of a child of God. Before his elevation to the Papacy, and while yet a monk, Gregory the Great, in walking through the streets of Rome, observed a number of slaves exposed for sale in the market-place. Struck by their fair complexion and long flaxen hair, he heaved a deep sigh and remarked: "What a pity that persons of such exterior beauty should not be interiorly enlightened with the illumination of faith and adorned with the gifts of grace!" He then asked who they were and whence they came. "They are Angles" (or English), was the reply. "They are well-named," he quaintly added, "for they have the faces of angels. They must become the brethren of the angels in heaven."[1] This anecdote shows that their conversion was the first and dominant desire of Gregory's heart. He wished them to enjoy "the liberty wherewith Christ hath made us free;"[2] for he well knew that spiritual bondage is far more galling than chains of iron, and that Christian liberty is the best preparation for civil emancipation. But while solicitous for the conversion, Gregory was equally zealous for the enfranchisement

[1] Bede, II., 1.
[2] *Gal.* IV., 31.

of the slave, as his history beautifully demonstrates. The conduct of Gregory outlines the policy of the Pontiffs that have succeeded him.

In the next place the Christian missionary cheered the heart of the converted slave by giving a prominent place to those virtues that had hitherto been deemed mean, contemptible and unworthy of a freeman. The virtues appreciated and extolled by the Pagan world as the ideal of human perfection were courage, fortitude, magnanimity, self-reliance, and all such as are calculated to excite the admiration and win the applause of the populace. But poverty of spirit, humility and meekness under contempt, patience and resignation under affronts, forgiveness of injuries and love of enemies, a spirit of obedience and long-suffering, were despised by them as servile virtues, or rather as no virtues at all, but the base characteristics of an enslaved and ignoble caste.

The founder of the Christian religion set His royal seal on these despised virtues and proclaimed their true value, so that henceforth they passed current among the faithful as the most precious medium of communication, enriching souls and purchasing the kingdom of heaven. He taught them these virtues by word and example from Bethlehem to Calvary.

The wretched hovel of the slave was no longer degrading to him when he reflected that the Son of Man had not where to lay His head. He had comfort in his bondage seeing that the Lord of heaven humbled Himself, "taking the form of a slave."

How could manual labor be degrading to him when he learned that his Divine Master had for several years worked as an artisan? How could obedience be any longer intolerable to him, since his Lord had become for his sake "obedient unto death, even the death of the cross!" Neither could chains nor stripes rob him of his peace of mind, when he remembered that his Master bore them at the pillory. It is a great alleviation to a captive people for a prince voluntarily to share their miseries; and, above all, are they consoled when conscious that their future recompense will be proportioned to their present sufferings if borne with Christian patience.

The Apostle of the Gentiles frequently comforts the Christian slave by reminding him of the real source of moral grandeur. He tells him that true dignity does not depend on the accident of birth, or wealth, or civil freedom, or social station, but that virtue is the sole standard of moral excellence in the sight of God, as well as the sole test of future retribution. He informs the slave that he has a soul as well as Cæsar; that he is the child of God by adoption, the brother of Christ, and a member of His mystical body; and that he has equal privileges with the freeman to a participation in the Divine Spirit. "In one spirit were we all baptized into one body, whether Jews or Gentiles, whether bond or free."[1]

In the family of Christ to which they belong "there is neither Gentile nor Jew, circumcision nor

---

[1] *I. Cor.* XII, 13.

uncircumcision, barbarian nor Scythian, bond nor free, but Christ is all and in all."[1] No wonder that the slave took heart on listening to revelations so cheering.

Again the Church contributed largely to the moral elevation of the slave by levelling all distinctions between bond and free in her temples and religious assemblies. As soon as the slave entered the place of worship he breathed the air of liberty. He possessed every privilege accorded to the freeman. He was admitted to an equal participation in the Sacraments of the Church. He was baptized at the same font. He sat side by side with his master at the Agape, and joined with him in the public prayers.[2] In the penitential discipline of the Church there was no class distinction. The Christian master who had no punishment to fear from the State for scourging his slave to death, was, if guilty of such a crime, debarred by the ecclesiastical law from Holy Communion.[3] The slave was admitted into the ranks of the clergy, though before taking orders he was redeemed from bondage, as none but freemen served at the altar. In a council held in Rome, in 597, under Pope Gregory, it was decreed that freedom should be granted to slaves that wished to embrace the monastic state. The applicants, however, were not indiscriminately received, for wise precautions were taken to ascertain the sincerity of their vocation.

[1] *Colloss.* III., 11.   [2] *Ibid.*, p. 67.
[3] *Hist. of Europ. Morals*, II., 66.   [4] Balmez, pp. 109 and 437.

Not only were slaves permitted to join in the public offices of the Church and in the reception of the Sacraments, not only were they raised to the ranks of the clergy, but many of them who had died for Christ were honored in Christian sanctuaries as saints and martyrs, and even had temples erected to their honor. The names of Blandina, Potamiena, Eutyches, Victorinus, Nereus, and numerous others, are enrolled in our Martyrology. The most stately Byzantine church in Ravenna is dedicated to a martyred slave.[1]

The Church taught the slave and the master their reciprocal duties, prescribing laws that exercised a salutary restraint on the authority of the one, and sanctified the obedience of the other. "Servants," says St. Paul, "be obedient to your masters according to the flesh, with fear and trembling, in the simplicity of your heart as to Christ. Not serving to the eye as pleasing men, but as the servants of Christ, doing the will of God from the heart. . . . Knowing that whatsoever good thing any man shall do, the same shall he receive from the Lord, whether he be bond or free. And you, masters, do the same things to them, forbearing threatenings, knowing that the Lord both of them and you is in Heaven; and there is no respect of persons with Him."[2]

In his touching letter to Philemon, while fully recognizing the claims of the master, the Apostle

[1] Lecky, II., 69.
[2] *Eph.* VI., 5-9.

exhorts him to receive Onesimus not only as his slave, but also as his brother in Christ; and while pleading for the slave he does not exempt him from the lawful service he owes to his master.

This brief Epistle of twenty-five verses has served as a guiding principle to the Church in her solution of the slave problem; and it has contributed more to alleviate the miseries of humanity than all the moral treatises of the most philanthropic of Pagan philosophers.

Perhaps the most substantial service rendered by the Church to the slaves was the recognition of their marriage-tie as valid and indissoluble, and not as mere concubinage such as Paganism regarded it. Pope Adrian I., in the eighth century, uses the following language: "According to the words of the Apostles, as in Jesus Christ, we ought not to deprive either slaves or freemen of the Sacraments of the Church, so it is not allowed in any way to prevent the marriage of slaves; and if their marriages have been contracted in spite of the opposition of their masters, they ought nevertheless not to be dissolved in any way."[1] And St. Thomas maintains that slaves are not bound to obey their masters in regard to the contracting of marriage.[2]

In upholding the moral dignity and prerogatives of the slave, the Church was striking a blow for his civil freedom. Though she was not charged with the framing of the civil laws, she moved the hearts of

[1] De Conjug. Serv., lib. IV., tom. 9, c. 1.
[2] 2ª, 2ᵃᵉ, Quæs. 104, art. 5.

the slave-owners by moral suasion, and she moulded the conscience of the legislators by an appeal to the innate rights of man. Thus, as snow melts before the sun, slavery yielded to the genial rays of the Gospel.

As a pious incentive to emancipation, it was ordained that the ceremony of manumission should be celebrated in the church on festival days, especially on Easter Sunday, and the slave-owners were admonished that the manumission of the slave was an act well calculated to conciliate the clemency of Heaven.

A brief review of the relative influence of Paganism and Christianity on slavery will bring out in bold relief two important facts of history which shed glory on the Christian religion.

1st. No Pagan government of ancient times ever framed any law aiming at the immediate or gradual extinction of slavery. The same remark is true of modern nations outside the pale of Christendom. Slavery in its most odious form is still upheld in Persia, Arabia, and Turkey, among the idolatrous worshippers of Africa, and wherever Mahommedanism holds sway. It exists, also, in China[1] and Japan, and had continued in India until it was abolished by British influence in the present century.

2d. Christianity, from its birth to the present time, has labored in mitigating and extirpating this social evil. Slavery practically ceased to exist in Christian

---

[1] Huc, *Travels in Tartary*, etc., I., ch. VIII.

Europe from the thirteenth century, and it has since been abolished in all European colonies. It was extinguished in the British possessions in 1833, chiefly through the influence of Wilberforce and Clarkson; and ten years later, more than twelve millions of slaves were set free in the East Indies by the government of Great Britain. France abolished slavery in her West India colonies in 1793. Spain emancipated her slaves in Porto Rico in 1873, and in 1886 the institution ceased to exist in Cuba. It has passed away from all the Spanish-American Republics. A decree of emancipation was promulgated in 1888, in Brazil, by virtue of which slavery is absolutely extinguished in the Empire.

Slavery was abolished by President Lincoln in 1863 in the States or parts of States then in rebellion. Although the Emancipation Proclamation was designed as a war measure in the interests of the Union, slavery would have eventually disappeared independently of the war; for it was confined to the South in whose border States it was gradually dying out, and it was opposed by the public sentiment of the Christian world. The thirteenth amendment to the Constitution adopted by Congress January 31, 1865, and ratified December 18, the same year, totally abolished slavery in the United States.

In a word, the consoling fact can be recorded to-day that, at the present moment, *a single slave is not to be found on a solitary foot of Christendom.*

To what cause are we to ascribe this happy result? Not to intellectual culture, for Pagan Greece and

Rome were as cultured as France and England; nor to an enlightened self-interest, for the immediate interests of the slave-owner demanded its retention; nor to the free intercourse of nations and the march of commerce, for the slave-trade was one of the most lucrative branches of business. The result is due to the humanizing influence of the Gospel alone.

Among the forces enlisted in the cause of freedom, the most potent came from the Papacy. In every age the voice of the Popes resounded clearly throughout the world in the interests of human freedom. Gregory the Great in the sixth century, Pius II. in the fifteenth, Paul III. in the sixteenth, Urban VIII. in the seventeenth, Benedict XIV. in the eighteenth, and Pius VII. in the nineteenth—all raised their voice either in commending the slaves to the humanity of their masters, or in advocating their manumission, or in righteous condemnation of the slave trade. Gregory XVI., in 1839 published a memorable Encyclical in which the following energetic language occurs: "By virtue of our Apostolic office, we warn and admonish in the Lord, all Christians of whatever condition they may be, and enjoin upon them that for the future no one shall venture unjustly to oppress the Indians, negroes, or other men whoever they may be, to strip them of their property, or reduce them into servitude, or give aid or support to those who commit such excesses, or carry on that infamous traffic by which the blacks, as if they were not men, but mere impure animals reduced like them into servitude, contrary to the laws of justice and humanity, are bought, sold, and devoted to endure the hardest labor. Wherefore, by virtue of our Apostolic authority, we condemn all these things as absolutely unworthy of the Christian name."

And, lastly, Leo XIII.[1] denounces in emphatic terms the infamous slave-trade now systematically carried on in Africa by Mohammedan invaders.

He declares such a traffic to be in violation of the natural and the divine law. He proclaims this commerce in man the most infamous and inhuman that can be conceived. He exhorts Christian rulers and all true friends of humanity to rise in their might and, by concerted action and every righteous means, "to repress, forbid, and put an end once for all" to this violent and unholy abduction of human beings. He calls upon all Apostolic men in Africa to bring the weight of their moral influence toward securing the safety and liberty of the slaves; and he heartily commends the Emperor of Brazil for his recent decree by which all the slaves of the Empire are emancipated.

How different is the record of the following lines condensed from Cardinal Lavigerie's Discourse! Slave-hunting is carried on in every independent Mussulman State in Africa; and yet no Mufti, Ulema, or any other expounder of the Koran, has ever protested against so atrocious a practice.

---

[1] Letter of Leo XIII. to the Bishops of Brazil, May 5, 1888.

The redemption of captives was another work which engaged the pious solicitude of the Church. From the fourth to the fourteenth century, Europe was periodically a prey to northern barbarians and Mohammedan invaders. The usual fate of the vanquished was death or slavery. They who escaped the sword were carried into bondage. A more wretched fate awaited the female sex, for they were reserved to gratify the caprices of their conquerors.

"In no form of charity," says Mr. Lecky, "was the beneficial character of the Church more continually and more splendidly exercised than in redeeming captives from servitude."[1]

When the Goths invaded Italy in the fourth century, St. Ambrose sat on the chair of Milan. After disposing of his private means for the redemption of captives, he melted down the golden vessels of the Church, that he might ransom his brethren in bondage. The Arians affected to be scandalized at his course. They charged him with atrocious sacrilege for thus disposing of the sacred vessels. Ambrose replied to them in language worthy an Apostle, that the liberty of man was of more value than gold or silver, that the salvation of souls was more precious than chalices, and that no sacrifice should be spared to rescue woman from a life of dishonor and degradation.

Instances of similar deeds of charity are recorded of St. Cyprian, St. Augustin, and St. Gregory the Great.

---

[1] *History of European Morals*, II., 72

But the Church exerted herself not only in rescuing Christians from captivity in Pagan lands, she also labored to ransom Pagan captives in Christian realms, and restored them to their native country. When seven thousand Persians were held in durance by a Roman general, Acacius, Bishop of Amida, sold all the rich plate of his church and sent these captives redeemed to their country, saying that God had no need of plates and dishes.[1]

Few men have rendered more signal service in behalf of captives than St. John of Matha in the twelfth century. On the morning that he celebrated his first Mass, he made a vow at the altar to consecrate his life to the redemption of the slaves who were held captive in Morocco and other parts of Africa. To render his labors more effectual and permanent he formed a congregation of men animated by his own spirit, who made a solemn vow to consecrate their life and liberty to the redemption of slaves. They made frequent incursions into Africa, and purchased the liberty of hundreds of their brethren. If it is a virtue to give to others out of the abundance of our own means, if it is a greater virtue to give away all that we possess, what shall we say of him who devotes his life and liberty to the redemption of his fellow-beings? "Greater love than this no man hath, that a man lay down his life for his friends."[2]

---

[1] *Ibid.*
[2] *John* XV., 13.

CHAPTER XXXII.

THE DIGNITY, RIGHTS AND DUTIES OF THE LABORING CLASSES.

The Redeemer of mankind has never conferred a greater temporal blessing on the human race than by ennobling and sanctifying labor, and by rescuing it from the stigma of degradation that had been branded upon it. He is ushered into the world not environed by the splendor of imperial majesty, nor attended by the force of mighty legions. He comes rather as the reputed child of an artisan, and the days of His boyhood and early manhood are spent in a mechanic's shop; "Is not this the carpenter, the Son of Mary?"[1]

The primeval curse attached to labor has been obliterated by the toilsome life of Jesus Christ. He has shed a halo around the workshop, and has lightened the mechanic's tools by assuming the trade of an artisan. If the profession of a general, a jurist, a statesman and a prelate is adorned by the example of a Washington, a Taney, a Burke and a Carroll, how much more is the calling of a workman ennobled by the example of Christ!

[1] *Mark* VI.

I cannot conceive any thought better calculated to ease the yoke and to lighten the burden of the Christian toiler than the reflection that the highest type of manhood had voluntarily devoted Himself to manual labor.

Labor is honorable on other grounds. It contributes to the prosperity of the country, and whatever conduces to a nation's welfare, is most worthy of commendation. It is not the office or occupation that dignifies the man, but it is the man that dignifies the office.

> "Honor and shame from no condition rise;
> Act well your part—there all the honor lies."[1]

Cincinnatus lent dignity to agriculture by working at the plow! Caligula, by an infamous life, degraded his crown and imperial purple.

De Tocqueville could not pay a juster and more beautiful tribute of praise to the genius of our country than when he wrote in 1835 that every honest occupation in the United States was honorable. The honest, industrious man is honored among us, whether he work with his hands or with his brains, because he is an indispensable factor in the nation's progress. He is the bee in the social hive; he is the benefactor of his race, because he is always producing something for the common weal.

> God bless the noble working men
> Who rear the cities of the plain,

---

[1] Pope's *Essay on Man*.

> Who dig the mines and build the ships,
> And drive the commerce of the main.
> God bless them! for their swarthy hands
> Have wrought the glory of our lands.

As an evidence of the esteem in which the thrifty son of toil is held among us, we see from daily observation that the humblest avocations of life are no bar whatever to the highest preferment in the Commonwealth, when talent and ability are allied to patient industry. Franklin was a printer; President Lincoln's youthful days were spent in wielding the axe and in handling the plow on his father's farm. President Johnson in his boyhood was apprenticed to a tailor. Grant was the son of a tanner, and Garfield once drove a canal boat. These examples are given not to excite a morbid and feverish ambition in the heart of the laborer or the artisan, but to illustrate the truth that no stain is affixed to the lowliest pursuits of life.

In honoring and upholding labor, the nation is strengthening its own hands as well as paying a tribute to worth. For a contented and happy working class are the best safeguard of the Republic, while ill-paid and discontented laborers, like the starving and enslaved populace of Rome in the time of Augustus Cæsar, would be a constant menace and reproach to the country.

Labor has its sacred rights as well as its dignity. Paramount among the rights of the laboring classes, is their privilege to organize, or to form themselves into societies for their mutual protection and benefit.

It is in accordance with natural right that those who have one common interest, should unite together for its promotion. Our modern labor associations are the legitimate successors of the ancient guilds of England.

In our days there is a universal tendency towards organization in every department of trade and business. In union there is strength in the physical, moral and social world; and just as the power and majesty of our Republic are derived from the political union of the several States, so do men clearly perceive that the healthy combination of human forces in the economic world, can accomplish results which could not be effected by any individual efforts. Throughout the United States and Great Britain there is to-day a continuous network of syndicates and trusts, of companies and partnerships, so that every operation from the construction of a leviathan steamship to the manufacture of a needle is controlled by a corporation.

When corporations thus combine, it is quite natural that mechanics and laborers should follow their example. It would be as unjust to deny to workingmen the right to band together because of the abuses incident to such combinations, as to withhold the same right from capitalists because they sometimes unwarrantably seek to crush or absorb weaker rivals.

Another potent reason for encouraging labor unions suggests itself to my mind. Secret societies lurking in dark places and plotting the overthrow of existing governments, have been the bane of continental Europe. The repressive policy of these governments and their mistrust of the intelligence and virtue of the people, have given rise to those mischievous organizations; for, men are apt to conspire in secret, if not permitted to express their views openly. The public recognition among us of the right to organize, implies a confidence in the intelligence and honesty of the masses; it affords them an opportunity of training themselves in the school of self-government, and in the art of self-discipline; it takes away from them every excuse and pretext for the formation of dangerous societies; it exposes to the light of public scrutiny, the constitution and laws of the association and the deliberations of the members; it inspires them with a sense of their responsibility as citizens and with a laudable desire of meriting the approval of their fellow-citizens. "It is better," as Matthew Arnold observes, "that the body of the people with all its faults, should act for itself, and control its own affairs, than that it should be set aside as ignorant and incapable, and have its affairs managed for it by a so-called superior class."[1]

God forbid that the prerogatives which I am maintaining for the working classes should be construed as implying the slightest invasion of the rights and autonomy of employers. There should not and need not be any conflict between labor and

[1] *Discourses in America.*

capital, since both are necessary for the public good, and the one depends on the coöperation of the other. A contest between the employer and the employed is as unreasonable and as hurtful to the social body, as a war between the head and the hands would be to the physical body. Such an antagonism recalls the fabled conspiracy on the part of the members of the body against the stomach. Whoever tries to sow discord between the capitalist and the laborer, is an enemy of social order. Every measure should therefore be discountenanced that sustains the one at the expense of the other. Whoever strives to improve the friendly relations between the proprietors and the labor unions by suggesting the most effectual means of diminishing and even removing the causes of discontent, is a benefactor to the community. With this sole end in view I venture to touch this delicate subject, and if these lines contribute in some small measure to strengthen the bond of union between the enterprising men of capital and the sons of toil, I shall be amply rewarded.

That "the laborer is worthy of his hire," is the teaching of Christ as well as the dictate of reason itself. He is entitled to a fair and just compensation for his services. He deserves something more, and that is kind and considerate treatment. There would be less ground for complaint against employers if they kept in view the golden maxim of the Gospel: "Whatsoever you would that men should do unto you, do ye also to them." [1]

[1] *Matt.* VII., 12.

Our sympathies for those in our employ, whether in the household, the mines, or the factory, are wonderfully quickened by putting ourselves in their place, and asking ourselves how we would wish to be treated under similar circumstances. We should remember that they are our fellow-beings, that they have feelings like ourselves, that they are stung by a sense of injustice, repelled by an overbearing spirit, and softened by kindness, and that it largely rests with us whether their hearts and homes are to be clouded with sorrow, or radiant with joy.

Surely men do not amass wealth for the sole pleasure of counting their bonds and of contemplating their gold in secret. No, they acquire it in the hope that it will contribute to their rational comfort and happiness. Now there is no enjoyment in life so pure and so substantial as that which springs from the reflection that others are made content and happy by our benevolence. And I am speaking here not of the benevolence of gratuitous bounty, but of fair-dealing tempered with benignity. Considerate Kindness is like her sister Mercy:

> "It droppeth as the gentle rain from heaven
> Upon the place beneath; it is twice bless'd;
> It blesseth him that gives, and him that takes;
> 'Tis mightiest in the mightiest; it becomes
> The throned monarch better than his crown."[1]

I am happy to say that commercial princes answering the description of the English bard do not

---

[1] *The Merchant of Venice.*

wholly belong to an ideal and imaginary world, but are easily found in our great centres of commerce; and if the actual condition of the average wage-worker in this country is a safe criterion by which we are to estimate the character and public spirit of American employers, I believe that an impartial judgment will concede to the majority of them the honorable title of just, fair-dealing and benevolent men. In my visits to England, Scotland, Ireland and the continent of Europe, I have studied the condition of the laboring classes, and I am persuaded that the American workman is better paid and fed, better clothed and housed, and usually better instructed, at least in the elements of useful knowledge, than his brethren across the Atlantic.

Instances of genuine sympathy and beneficence exercised by business concerns toward those in their employ, could be easily multiplied. Some time ago, the head of a Baltimore manufacturing company received a message announcing the total destruction by a flood, of his uninsured mills, involving a loss of $365,000. On receiving the news, his first exclamation was: "What a loss to—so many families! Here are 200 men thrown out of employment!" Of the personal injury he sustained, he uttered not a word.

But while applauding the tender feelings and magnanimity of so many capitalists, I am constrained in the interests of truth, humanity and religion, to protest against the heartless conduct of others whose number, for the honor of our country, is, I hope, comparatively small.

When men form themselves into a business corporation, their personality is overshadowed, and their individual responsibility is lessened. And for this reason, many will assent in their corporate capacity, to measures from which the dread of public opinion, or the dictates of conscience would prompt them as individuals to shrink. But perhaps the injury is all the more keenly felt by the victims of oppression when inflicted by a corporation, as it is easier to obtain redress from one responsible proprietor than from a body of men, most of whom may be unknown or inaccessible to the sufferers.

No friend of his race can contemplate without painful emotions, those heartless monopolists exhibiting a grasping avarice which has dried up every sentiment of sympathy, and a sordid selfishness which is deaf to the cries of distress. Their sole aim is to realize large dividends without regard to the paramount claims of justice and Christian charity. These trusts and monopolies, like the car of Juggernaut, crush every obstacle that stands in their way. They endeavor, not always it is alleged, without success, to corrupt our national and state Legislatures and municipal councils. They are so intolerant of honest rivalry as to use unlawful means in driving from the market all competing industries. They compel their operatives to work for starving wages, especially in mining districts and factories, where protests have but a feeble echo, and are easily stifled by intimidation. In many places the corporations are said to have the monopoly of stores of supply, where exorbitant prices are charged for the necessaries of life; bills are contracted which the workmen are unable to pay from their scanty wages, and their forced insolvency places them entirely at the mercy of their task-masters. To such Shylocks may well be applied the words of the Apostle: "Go to now ye rich men; weep and howl for your miseries which shall come upon you . . . you have stored up to yourselves wrath against the last days. Behold the hire of the laborers, . . . which by fraud hath been kept back by you, crieth, and the cry of them hath entered into the ears of the God of Sabbath."[1]

In the beginning of the present century, Mr. Pitt uttered in the House of Commons the following words which reveal the far-seeing mind of that great statesman:

"The time will come when manufactures will have been so long established, and the operatives not having any other business to flee to, that it will be in the power of any one man in a town to reduce the wages; and all the other manufacturers must follow. Then, when you are goaded with reductions and willing to flee your country, France and America will receive you with open arms; and then farewell to our commercial state. If ever it does arrive to this pitch, Parliament (if it be not then sitting) ought to be called together, and if it cannot redress your grievances, its power is at an end. Tell me

---

[1] *St. James* V.

not that Parliament cannot; it is omnipotent to protect."[1]

How forcibly this language applies now to our own country, and how earnestly the warning should be heeded by the constituted authorities! The supreme law of the land should be vindicated and enforced, and ample protection should be afforded to legitimate competing corporations as well as to the laboring classes against unscrupulous monopolies. It would be also a humane measure if the government interposed its authority in forbidding both capitalists and parents to employ children under a certain age, and at a period of life which ought to be devoted to their physical, intellectual and moral development.

But if labor organizations have rights to be vindicated and grievances to be redressed it is manifest that they have also sacred obligations to be fulfilled and dangers to guard against.

As these societies are composed of members very formidable in numbers, varied in character, temperament and nationality, they are, in the nature of things, more unwieldy, more difficult to manage, more liable to disintegration than corporations of capitalists, and they have need of leaders possessed of great firmness, tact and superior executive ability, who will honestly aim at consulting the welfare of the society they represent, without infringing on the rights of their employers.

[1] Pitt's speech on the Arbitration Act, quoted in Vol. 23, p. 1091. Hansard.

They should exercise unceasing vigilance in securing their body from the control of designing demagogues who would make it subservient to their own selfish ends, or convert it into a political engine.

They should be also jealous of the reputation and good name of the rank and file of the society as well as of its chosen leaders. For while the organization is ennobled, and commands the respect of the public by the moral and civic virtues of its members, the scandalous and unworthy conduct of even a few of them is apt to bring reproach on the whole body, and to excite the distrust of the community. They should therefore be careful to exclude from their ranks that turbulent element composed of men who boldly preach the gospel of anarchy, socialism and nihilism; those land-pirates who are preying on the industry, commerce and trade of the country; whose mission is to pull down and not to build up; who instead of upholding the hands of the government that protects them, are bent on its destruction, and instead of blessing the mother that opens her arms to welcome them, insult and defy her. If such revolutionists had their way, despotism would supplant legitimate authority, license would reign without liberty, and gaunt poverty would stalk throughout the land.

I am persuaded that the system of boycotting by which members of Labor-unions are instructed not to patronize certain obnoxious business houses, is not only disapproved of by an impartial public sentiment, but that it does not commend itself to the more thoughtful and conservative portion of the guilds themselves. Every man is free indeed to select the establishment with which he wishes to deal, and in purchasing from one in preference to another, he is not violating justice. But the case is altered when by a mandate of the society he is debarred from buying from a particular firm. Such a prohibition assails the liberty of the purchaser, and the rights of the seller, and is an unwarrantable invasion of the commercial privileges guaranteed by the government to business concerns. If such a social ostracism were generally in vogue, a process of retaliation would naturally follow, the current of mercantile intercourse would be checked, every centre of population would be divided into hostile camps, and the good feeling which ought to prevail in every community, would be seriously impaired. "Live and let live" is a wise maxim, dictated alike by the law of trade and by Christian charity.

Experience has shown that strikes are a drastic, and, at best a very questionable, remedy for the redress of the laborer's grievances. They paralyze industry, they often foment fierce passions, and lead to the destruction of property, and above all, they result in inflicting grievous injury on the laborer himself by keeping him in enforced idleness, during which his mind is clouded by discontent while brooding over his situation, and his family not unfrequently suffers from the want of even the necessaries of life.

From official statistics furnished by Bradstreet and Carroll D. Wright, United States Commissioner of Labor for eight years ending December, 1888, the following summary is condensed:[1]

Number of strikes in the United States for 8 years, 5,453
Number of employed involved in the strikes, . 1,879,292
Loss to employed in wages, ... $77,538,324

The loss inflicted by the strikes on the employers was but a little over half the amount sustained by the employed, who could much less afford to bear it.

It would be a vast stride in the interests of peace and of the laboring classes, if the policy of arbitration which is now gaining favor for the settlement of international quarrels, were also availed of for the adjustment of disputes between capital and labor. Many blessings would result from the adoption of this method, for, while strikes, as the name implies, are aggressive and destructive, arbitration is conciliatory and constructive; the result in the former case is determined by the weight of the purse, in the latter by the weight of argument.

And now permit me to address to you, hardy sons of toil, a few words of friendly exhortation solely inspired by a sincere affection for you, and an earnest desire for your temporal and spiritual welfare.

1°. Cultivate a spirit of industry without which all the appliances of organized labor are unavailing.

[1] The statistics for the six years ending December, 1886, are compiled by Mr. Wright, and those for the two following years, are supplied by Mr. Bradstreet.

Activity is the law of all intellectual and animal life. The more you live in conformity with that law, the happier you will be. An active life, like the purling rivulet, is an unfailing source of gladness, health and contentment, while an indolent life, like the stagnant pool, breeds discontent, disease and death. No man enjoys with a keener relish the night's repose and the Sunday and holiday rest than the son of toil.

A life of patient industry is sure to be blessed with a competence, if it is not crowned with an abundant remuneration. The great majority of our leading men of wealth are indebted for their fortunes to their own untiring industry. Take an active, personal, conscientious interest in the business of your employer; be as much concerned about its prosperity as if it were your own. And are not your employer's affairs in a measure yours? For, your wages come from the profits of the concern, and the more you contribute to its success, the better he can afford to compensate you for your services. He will be impelled by an enlightened self-interest, as well as by a sense of justice, to requite you for your services with a generous hand.

2°. Foster habits of economy and self-denial. No matter how modest your income may be, always live under it. You will thus protect your liberty and business integrity, and guard yourself against the slavery and humiliation of debt, which is too often the precursor and the incentive to commercial dishonor. Most of the alleged wants of mankind are purely artificial, and contribute little or nothing to the sum of human happiness. Rather do they add to the sum of human misery; for, what are our earthly desires but so many links in our chain of bondage?

3°. While honestly striving to better your condition, be content with your station in life, and do not yield to an inordinate desire of abandoning your present occupation for what is popularly regarded as a more attractive avocation. Remember that while the learned professions are over-crowded, there is always a demand for skilled and unskilled labor, and that it is far better to succeed in mechanical or manual work, than to fail in professional life. Be not over eager to amass wealth, for, they who are anxious "to become rich, fall into temptations and into the snares of the Devil, and into many unprofitable and hurtful desires which drown men in destruction and perdition."[1] A feverish ambition to accumulate a fortune, which may be called our national distemper, is incompatible with peace of mind. Moderate means with a contented spirit are preferable to millions without it. If poverty has its inconveniences and miseries, wealth has often greater ones. A small income is suggestive of abstemious habits, and abstemious habits are conducive to health, while wealth is a powerful incentive to excessive indulgence which is the fruitful source of complicated diseases.

[1] *I. Tim.* VI.

A poor peasant who was roaming one morning through his landlord's demesne in the hope of catching some game to appease his hunger, was suddenly confronted by its owner, and asked what induced him to be out so early. And pray, what brings you out so early? interposed the peasant. I am trying to find an appetite for my breakfast, replied his lordship. And I, added the peasant, am hunting to find a breakfast for my appetite. Of these two men, the pampered landlord was perhaps the greater sufferer; a long and severe regimen would be necessary to restore his health, while a hearty meal would suffice to relieve the pain of the peasant.

4°. Sobriety will be an angel of tranquillity and comfort to yourself and family. While this virtue should be cultivated by all men, it ought to be especially cherished by the laboring class who are so much exposed to the opposite vice. Intemperance has brought more desolation to homes than famine or the sword, and is a more unrelenting tyrant than the grasping monopolist.

5°. Above all, let religion be the queen of your household. It will be a sacred bond uniting all the members in the ties of domestic love. It will be the guardian of peace and contentment: it will season the bread of labor: "Not by bread alone doth man live but by every word that proceedeth from the mouth of God."[1] It will be to you an unfailing

---

[1] *Matt.* IV.

source of wealth; for, "godliness with sufficiency is great gain."[1] "It is profitable to all things, having the promise of the life that now is, and of that which is to come."[2] When the evening of life has come, and your earthly labors are drawing to a close, it will cheer you with the bright prospect of an eternal Sabbath.

---

[1] *I. Tim.* VI.
[2] *Ibid.* IV.

CHAPTER XXXIII.

RELIGION THE ESSENTIAL BASIS OF CIVIL SOCIETY.

Religion is the bond that unites man with his Creator. It is a virtue by which due honor and worship are paid to God. It embraces all those fundamental truths that involve God's sovereignty over us and our entire dependence on Him. I employ the term *religion* here in its broadest and most comprehensive sense, as embodying the existence of God; His infinite power and knowledge; His providence over us; the recognition of a divine law; the moral freedom and responsibility of man; the distinction between good and evil; the duty of rendering our homage to God, and justice and charity to our neighbor; and finally, the existence of a future state of rewards and punishments.

I hold that religion is the only solid basis of society. If the social edifice rests not on this eternal and immutable foundation, it will soon crumble to pieces. It would be as vain to attempt to establish society without religion as to erect a palace in the air, or on shifting sands, or to hope to reap a crop from seed scattered on the ocean's surface. Religion is to society what cement is to the building; it makes all parts compact and coherent. "He who destroys religion," says Plato, "overthrows the foundations of human society."[1]

The social body is composed of individuals who have constant relations with one another; and the very life and preservation of society demand that the members of the community discharge toward one another various and complex duties.

What does society require of your rulers and magistrates? What does it require of you? It demands of your rulers that they dispense justice with an even hand. It demands of you that you be loyal to your country, zealous in her defence, faithful in the observance of her laws, conscientious in the payment of imposts and taxes for her maintenance and support. It demands that you be scrupulous in observing your oaths and vows, just in the fulfilment of your contracts and obligations, honest in your dealings, and truthful in your promises. It demands that you honor and respect your lawful superiors, that you be courteous towards your equals, condescending to your inferiors, faithful to your friends, magnanimous to your enemies, and merciful to the poor and the oppressed. It demands of the married couple conjugal fidelity, of parents provident vigilance, of children filial love. In a word, it demands that you "render to all men their dues; tribute, to whom tribute is due; custom, to whom

---

[1] Lib. X., *De Legibus*.

custom; fear, to whom fear; honor, to whom honor;"[1] and that you "render to Cæsar the things that are Cæsar's, and to God the things that are God's."[2]

How can these social virtues be practised without sufficient motives? These motives must be strong and powerful, because you have passions and self-interest to overcome. They must be universal, because they are binding on all members of society. They must be permanent, because they apply to all times and places.

What motives, religion apart, are forcible enough to compel legislators, rulers, and magistrates to be equitable and impartial in their decisions? What guarantee have we that they will not be biassed by prejudice and self-interest? Will a thirst for fame and a desire for public approbation prove a sufficient incentive for them to do right? How often has not this very love of glory and esteem impelled them to trample on the rights and liberties of the many, in order to win the approbation of a few sycophants, just as Roboam oppressed his subjects that he might be admired and praised by his young courtiers, and as Alexander enslaved nations to receive the applause of the fickle Athenians.

Would you vote for a presidential candidate that avowed atheistic principles? I am sure you would not. You would instinctively mistrust him; for an unbelieving president would ignore the eternal laws of justice, and the eternal laws of justice are the basis of civil legislation.

[1] *Rom.* XIII., 7.
[2] *Mark* XII., 17.

What principles without religion are binding enough to exact of you that obedience which you owe to society and to the laws of your country? Is it the dread of civil punishment? But the civil power takes cognizance only of overt acts. It has no jurisdiction over the heart, which is the seat of rebellion, the secret council-chamber where dark schemes are concocted. The civil power cannot enter the hidden recesses of the soul, and quell the tumults raging there. It cannot invade the domestic circle to expel the intemperance and lewdness that enervate and debauch both mind and body. It cannot suppress those base calumnies, whispered in the dark, which poison the social atmosphere with their foul breath, and breed hatred, resentment, and death. You might as well expect to preserve a tree from decay by lopping off a few withered branches whilst allowing the worms to gnaw at the roots, as to preserve the social tree from moral corruption by preventing some external crimes whilst leaving the heart to be worm-eaten by vice.

Besides, if you are so disposed, can you not in many instances escape the meshes of the law by resorting to gifts, bribes, and ingenious frauds?

If the civil sword, even with the aid of religion, can scarcely restrain public disorders, how futile would be the attempt to do so without the coöperation of moral and religious influence!

Still less do you fear the judgment that posterity may pronounce on your conduct. For if you believe neither in God nor in a life to come, the condemnation of after-ages will not disquiet you, the censures of future generations will not disturb your ashes reposing in the tomb.

Nor can you suppose the emoluments of office an adequate incentive to induce you to be an upright and law-abiding member of society. The emoluments of office are reserved for the privileged few; the great bulk of society will always be consigned to private life.

Do not imagine, because you happen to be a man of irreproachable private life, integrity of character, and incorruptible justice, that your fellow-citizens will seek you out, as the Romans sought Cincinnatus, at the plow, that they will cordially embrace you, force you from your cherished seclusion, and bestow upon you some office of trust and distinction.

"The office should seek the man, not the man the office," is a beautiful, but Utopian maxim,—a maxim so antiquated as to deserve a place in the cabinet of national curiosities. The most successful office-holder usually has been and usually will be the most industrious office-seeker; and his chances of success are not always improved by a delicate sense of honor and an inflexible adhesion to principle.

The esteem of your fellow-men will not be a sufficient inducement to make you a virtuous citizen; for the great mass of virtues, even of those virtues that influence the well-being of society, are practised in private, and are hidden from the eyes of men, like the root which gives life and bloom to the tree, or the gentle dew of heaven which silently sheds its blessings on the labors of the husbandman.

Nor should you be surprised if your good actions, instead of winning the applause of your fellow-citizens, will sometimes even draw upon you their suspicion, their jealousy, their odium, and their calumny. The wisdom and integrity of Aristides were such that the Athenians surnamed him "The Just;" yet they condemned him to exile. On the day on which the people were to vote upon the question of his banishment, an illiterate burgher, who did not know him personally, requested him to write the name of *Aristides* upon his ballot. "Has that man done you any injury?" asked Aristides. "No," answered the other, "nor do I even know him. But I am tired of hearing him everywhere called 'The Just.'"

The case of the Founder of the Christian religion is still more familiar to the reader. Who was so great a benefactor to society as He? He went about doing good to all men. He gave sight to the blind, and hearing to the deaf, and walking to the lame, and strength to the paralyzed limb, and comfort to the afflicted, and even life to the dead. He promulgated the most sublime and beneficent laws that were ever given to man, He invariably inculcated respect for ruling powers and obedience to their authority; and yet He was branded as a seditious man, an enemy of Cæsar, and He was put to death by the very people whom He had sought to deliver from spiritual bondage.

But, perhaps, you will say that a natural sense of

justice, independently of religion, can exercise sufficient influence in inducing you to practise the duties of an upright citizen. But to discard religion and yet profess to believe in natural justice, is self-contradictory. It is grasping at the shadow, and rejecting the substance. It is unconsciously clothing oneself in the garment of religion, whilst rejecting its spirit, "having, indeed, an appearance of godliness, but denying the power thereof."[1] If you seriously reflect, you will discover that natural justice has no solid foundation unless it rests on religion. Natural justice may sound well in theory, but it is a feeble barrier against the encroachments of vice.

Tell me, what becomes of your natural love of justice, or what influence does it exert on your conduct, when it stands in the way of your personal interests, pleasures, and ambition?

It is swept away like a mud-bank before the torrent, because it has not the strong wall of religion to support it.

Would your love of justice lead you to give a righteous decision against your friend and in favor of a stranger, though you were persuaded that such a decision would convert your friend into a life-long enemy? Would it prompt you to disgorge ill-gotten wealth, and thus to fall in a single day from affluence into poverty? Would your natural sense of duty inspire you with patience and resignation, if you were defrauded of your property by the treachery

---

[1] *II. Tim.* III., 5.

of a friend? Would a mere natural sense of duty or propriety restrain a Joseph or a Susanna from defiling his or her conscience, and violating the sacred laws of marriage? Would a natural love of truth and honor compel a guilty man to avow his secret crime, that he might vindicate the innocent falsely accused? Such acts of justice, patience, and truth are not uncommon in the Christian dispensation; but they would have been deemed prodigies of virtue in Pagan times.

There are many that consider mental culture a panacea for every moral disorder. "Let knowledge," they say, "be diffused over the land. Social order and morality will follow in its track."

The experience of other nations, as well as that of our own, shows it to be a very great illusion to suppose that intellectual development is sufficient of itself to make us virtuous men, or that the moral status of a people is to be estimated by the widespread diffusion of purely secular knowledge.

When the Roman Empire had reached the highest degree of mental culture, it was sunk in the lowest depths of vice and corruption. The Persian Empire, according to the testimony of Plato, perished on account of the vicious education of its princes. While their minds were filled with knowledge, they were guided by no religious influences. The voice of conscience was drowned amid the more eager and captivating cries of passion, and they grew up monsters of lust, rapine, and oppression, governed by no law save the instincts of their brutal nature.

It does not appear that vice recedes in the United States in proportion as public education advances. Statistics, I fear, would go far to prove the contrary to be the fact. The newspapers published in our large cities are every day filled with startling accounts of deep-laid schemes of burglary, bank defalcations, premeditated murders, and acts of refined licentiousness. These enormities are perpetrated for the most part, not by unlettered criminals, but by individuals of consummate address and skill; they betray a well-disciplined mind uncontrolled by morality and religion. How true are the words of Kempis: "Sublime words make not a man holy and just, but a virtuous life maketh him dear to God."

If neither the vengeance of the civil power, nor the hope of emoluments, nor the esteem of our fellow-men, nor the natural love of justice, nor the influence of education and culture, nor all these motives combined, can suffice to maintain peace and order in society, where shall we find an adequate incentive to exact of us a loyal obedience to the laws of the country? This incentive is found only in religious principles. Religion, I maintain, is the only sure and solid basis of society. Convince me of the existence of a Divine Legislator, the Supreme Source of all law, by whom "Kings reign, and lawgivers decree just things;"[1] convince me of the truth of the Apostolic declaration that "there is no power but from God, and that those that are, are ordained

---

[1] *Prov.* VIII., 15.

of God, and that, therefore, he who resisteth the power resisteth the ordinance of God;"[1] convince me that there is a Providence, who seeth my thoughts as well as my actions, that there is an incorruptible Judge, who cannot be bought with bribes nor blinded by deceit, who has no respect of persons, who will render to every man according to his works, who will punish transgressions and reward virtue in the life to come; convince me that I am endowed with free-will and the power of observing or of violating the laws of the country,—and then you place before me a Monitor, who impels me to virtue without regard to earthly emoluments or human applause, and who restrains me from vice without regard to civil penalties; you set before my conscience a living Witness, who pursues me in darkness and in light, and in the sanctuary of home, as well as in the arena of public life.

Religion teaches me that we are all children of the same Father, brothers and sisters of the same Redeemer, and, consequently, members of the same family. It teaches me the brotherhood of humanity.

Religion, therefore, is the fostering mother of charity, and charity is the guardian of civility and good-breeding, and good-breeding is one of the essential elements of the well-being of society. Worldly politeness, devoid of religion, is cold, formal, and heartless; it soon degenerates into hollow ceremony. Good-breeding, inspired by religion and charity,

[1] *Rom.* XIII.

inculcates a constant self-denial. It is sincere and unaffected, it has the ring of the genuine coin, it passes current everywhere, and it is easily distinguished from the counterfeit. A stranger, who would feel oppressed by the rigid mannerism which rules in the *salons* of Paris, would be charmed by the quiet dignity and genial warmth with which he would be received by the simple and religious people of the Tyrolese mountains.

The Christian religion is all-pervading. It influences the master and the servant, the rich and the poor. It admonishes the master to be kind and humane toward his servant by reminding him that he, also, has a Master in heaven who has no respect to persons. It admonishes the servant to be docile and obedient to his master; "not serving to the eye as it were pleasing men, but, as the servants of Christ, doing the will of God from the heart."[1]

It reminds him that true dignity is compatible with the most menial offices, and is forfeited only by the bondage of sin.

It charges the rich not to be high-minded, nor to trust in uncertain riches, but in the living God, who "giveth us abundantly all things to enjoy."[2] It counsels the poor to bear their privations with resignation, by setting before them the life of Him who, in the words of the Apostle, "being rich, became poor for your sake, that, through His poverty, you might be rich."[3]

[1] *Eph.* VI., 6.
[2] *I. Tim.* VI., 17.
[3] *II. Cor.* VIII., 9.

In a word, religion is anterior to society and more enduring than governments; it is the focus of all social virtues, the basis of public morals, the most powerful instrument in the hands of legislators; it is stronger than self-interest, more awe-inspiring than civil threats, more universal than honor, more active than love of country,—the surest guarantee that rulers can have of the fidelity of their subjects, and that subjects can have of the justice of their rulers; it is the curb of the mighty, the defence of the weak, the consolation of the afflicted, the covenant of God with man; and, in the language of Homer, it is "the golden chain which suspends the earth from the throne of the eternal."

Every philosopher and statesman who has discussed the subject of human governments, has acknowledged that there can be no stable society without justice, no justice without morality, no morality without religion, no religion without God. "It is an incontrovertible truth," observes Plato, "that if God presides not over the establishment of a city, and if it has only a human foundation, it cannot escape the greatest calamities. . . . If a State is founded on impiety and governed by men who trample on justice, it has no means of security."[1]

The Royal Prophet, long before Plato, had uttered the same sentiment: "Unless the Lord built the house, they labor in vain that build it. Unless the

---

[1] *De Leg.*, tom. VIII.

Lord keep the city, he watcheth in vain that keepeth it."[1] And Isaiah says: "The nation and the kingdom that will not serve Thee shall perish."[2]

Xenophon declares that "those cities and nations which are the most devoted to divine worship have always been the most durable and the most wisely governed, as the most religious ages have been the most distinguished for genius."[3] "I know not," says Cicero, "whether the destruction of piety toward the gods would not be the destruction also of good faith, of human society, and of the most excellent of virtues, justice."[4]

"If you find a people without religion," says Hume, "rest assured that they do not differ much from the brute beasts."[5]

"Never," says Rousseau, who had his lucid intervals of strong sense, "never was a state founded that did not have religion for its basis."[6]

Machiavel, who was not an extremist in piety, avows that good order is inseparable from religion. He brands the enemies of religion as "infamous and detestable men, destroyers of kingdoms and republics, enemies of letters and of all the arts that do honor to the human race and contribute to its prosperity."[7]

---

[1] *Ps.* CXXVI., 1.
[2] *Isaiah* LX., 12.
[3] *Memor. Socrat.*
[4] *De Nat. Deor.* I., 2.
[5] *Natural History of Religion.* (Not having the original at hand, I quote from a French translation.)
[6] *Contrat Social*, L. IV., ch. VIII.
[7] L. I., *De' Discorsi.*

Even Voltaire admits that "it is absolutely necessary for princes and people, that the idea of a Supreme Being, Creator, Governor, Rewarder, and Avenger, should be deeply engraved on the mind."[1]

Legislators and founders of empires have been so profoundly impressed with the necessity of religion as the only enduring basis of social order, that they have always built upon it the framework of their constitution. This truth must be affirmed of Pagan as well as of Jewish and Christian legislators. Solon of Athens, Lycurgus of Lacedæmon, and Numa of ancient Rome, made religion the corner-stone of the social fabric which they raised in their respective countries.

So long as the old Romans adhered to the religious policy of Numa, their commonwealth flourished, the laws were observed, their rulers governed with moderation and justice, and the people were distinguished by a simplicity of manners, a loyalty to their sovereign, a patient industry, a quiet contentment, a spirit of patriotism, courage, and sobriety which have commanded the admiration of posterity. "The vessel of state was held in the storm by two anchors, religion and morality."[2]

It must be observed, however, that these virtues were too often marred by harshness, cruelty, ambition, and other vices, which were grave defects when weighed by the standard of the Gospel. But a righteous God, who judges nations by the light that is given

[1] *Diction. Philos.*, art. *Athéisme.*
[2] *Esprit des Lois*, L. VIII.

them, did not fail to requite the Romans for the civic virtues which they practised, guided solely by the light of reason. The natural virtues they exhibited were rewarded by temporal blessings, and especially by the great endurance of their republic.[1]

Montesquieu traces the downfall of Rome to the doctrines of Epicurianism, which broke down the barrier of religion and gave free scope to the sea of human passions.

Lust of power and of wealth, unbridled licentiousness, and the obscenities of the plays, corrupted the morals of the people. The master had unlimited power over his slaves. The debtor was at the mercy of his creditors. The father had the power of life and death over his children. The female sex was degraded, and the sanctuary of home desecrated by divorce. The poison that infected the individual invaded the family, and soon spread through every artery of the social body.

Toward the close of the last century, an attempt was made by atheists in France to establish a government on the ruins of religion, and it is well known how signally they failed. The Christian Sabbath and festivals were abolished, and the churches closed. The only tolerated temple of worship was the criminal court, from which justice and mercy were inexorably banished, and where the judge sat only to condemn. The only divinity recognized by the apostles of anarchy was the goddess of reason; their

---

[1] *Cfr.* St. Augustin's *City of God*, Bk. V., ch. 15.

high priests were the executioners; the victims for sacrifice were unoffending citizens; the altar was the scaffold; their hymns were ribald songs; and their worship was lust, rapine, and bloodshed.

The more exalted the rank, the more sacred the profession, the more innocent the accused, the more eagerly did the despots of the hour thirst for their blood. They recognized no liberty but their own license, no law but their own wanton and capricious humor, no conscience but their own insatiate malice, no justice but the guillotine. At last, when the country was soaked with blood, suspicion and terror seized the tyrants themselves, and the executioner of to-day became the victim of to-morrow.

In a few months, as De Lamennais says: "They accumulated more ruin than an army of Tartars could have left after a six years' invasion."[1] They succeeded in a few weeks in demolishing the social fabric which had existed for thirteen centuries.

---

[1] *Essai sur l'Indifférence*, p. 431.

CHAPTER XXXIV.

THE RELIGIOUS ELEMENT IN OUR AMERICAN CIVILIZATION.

The subject treated in the foregoing chapter would not be adequately discussed unless some application of it be made to our own country. It may be interesting and instructive for us to consider in this place whether the dictum of the Holy Scripture, "Righteousness exalteth a nation,"[1] is as applicable to the United States as it has been to ancient empires; whether the founders of our government and their successors, down to our time, have been indebted to religion as an indispensable element for establishing and maintaining the Republic on a solid basis; what blessings we owe to our Christian civilization; and what dangers are to be averted that the Commonwealth may be perpetuated.

At first sight it might seem that religious principles were entirely ignored by the Fathers of the Republic in framing the Constitution, as it contains no reference to God, and makes no appeal to religion.

[1] *Proverbs* XIV., 34.

It is true, indeed, that the Constitution of the United States does not once mention the name of God. And even the first article of the amendments declares, that "Congress shall make no law respecting an establishment of religion, or prohibiting the free exercise thereof." And so strongly have certain religious sects been impressed with this fact, that they have repeatedly tried to get the name of God incorporated into the Constitution.

But the omission of God's holy name affords no just criterion of the religious character of the Founders of the Republic or of the Constitution which they framed. Nor should we have any concern to have the name of God imprinted in the Constitution, so long as the Constitution itself is interpreted by the light of Christian Revelation. I would rather sail under the guidance of a living captain than under that of a figure-head at the prow of a ship. The adorable name of God should not be a mere figure-head adorning the pages of the Constitution. Far better for the nation that His Spirit should animate our laws, that He should be invoked in our courts of justice, that He should be worshipped in our Sabbaths and thanksgivings, and that His guidance should be implored in the opening of our Congressional proceedings.

If the authors of the Constitution did not insert the name of God in that immortal instrument, they did not fail however to recognize Him as the essential source of wisdom, as is evident from the following memorable words recorded of one of their most illustrious members: "The small progress we have made after four or five weeks of close attendance and continued reasonings with each other, our different sentiments on almost every question, is, methinks, a melancholy proof of the imperfection of the human understanding. We indeed seem to feel our own want of political wisdom, since we have been running about in search of it. We have gone back to ancient history for models of government, and examined the different forms of those republics which, having been formed with the seeds of their own dissolution, now no longer exist. In this situation of this assembly, groping as it were in the dark to find political truth, and scarce able to distinguish it when presented to us, how has it happened, sir, that we have not heretofore once thought of humbly applying to the Father of Light to illuminate our understandings? I have lived for many years, and the longer I live, the more convincing proofs I see that God governs in the affairs of men, and if a sparrow cannot fall without His notice, is it probable that an empire can rise without His aid? We are told in the sacred writings that except the Lord build a house, they labor in vain that build it. This I firmly believe, and I believe that without His concurring aid we shall succeed no better in this political building of ours than did the builders of Babel."[1]

The Declaration of American Independence is one of the most solemn and memorable professions of

[1] Parton's *Life of Benjamin Franklin*, Vol. II., pp. 573-4.

political faith that ever emanated from the leading minds of any country. It has exerted as much influence in foreshadowing the spirit and character of our Constitution and public policy as the Magna Charta exercised on the Constitution of Great Britain. A devout recognition of God and of His overruling providence pervades that momentous document from beginning to end. God's holy name greets us in the opening paragraph, and is piously invoked in the last sentence of the Declaration; and thus it is at the same time the corner-stone and the keystone of this great monument to freedom.

The illustrious signers declared that "when, in the course of human events, it becomes necessary for one people to dissolve the political bands that have connected them with another, and to assume among the powers of the earth the separate and equal station to which the laws of nature *and of nature's God* entitle them, a decent respect for the opinions of mankind requires that they should declare the causes that impel them to the separation."

They acknowledge one Creator, the source of life, of liberty, and of happiness. They "appeal to the Supreme Judge of the world" for the rectitude of their intentions, and they conclude in this solemn language: "For the support of this declaration, with a firm reliance on the protection of Divine Providence, we mutually pledge to each other our lives, our fortunes, and our sacred honor."

The inaugural address of the Father of his country, to both houses of Congress, is pervaded by profound religious sentiments. He recognizes, with humble gratitude, the Hand of Providence in the formation of the government, and he fervently invokes the unfailing benediction of heaven on the nation and its rulers.

"It would," he says, "be peculiarly improper to omit, in this first official act, my fervent supplication to that Almighty Being, who rules over the universe, who presides in the councils of nations, and whose providential aid can supply every human defect, that his benediction may consecrate to the liberties and happiness of the people of the United States, a government instituted by themselves for these essential purposes, and may enable every instrument employed in its administration to execute with success the functions allotted to his charge. In tendering this homage to the great Author of every public and private good, I assure myself that it expresses your sentiments not less than my own: nor those of my fellow citizens at large, less than either. No people can be bound to acknowledge and adore the invisible Hand, which conducts the affairs of men, more than the people of the United States. Every step, by which they have advanced to the character of an independent nation, seems to have been distinguished by some token of providential agency. And, in the important revolution just accomplished in the system of their united government, the tranquil deliberations and voluntary consent of so many distinct communities, from which the event has resulted, cannot be compared with the means by which most governments have been established, without some return of pious gratitude, along with an humble anticipation of the future blessings which the past seems to presage."

Referring again, at the close of his address, to his sense of dependence on Almighty God, he used this language:

"Having thus imparted to you my sentiments, as they have been awakened by the occasion which brings us together, I shall take my present leave; but not without resorting once more to the benign Parent of the human race, in humble supplication that, since He has pleased to favor the American people with opportunities for deliberating in perfect tranquillity, and dispositions for deciding with unparalleled unanimity on a form of goverment for the security of their union, and the advancement of their happiness; so His divine blessing may be equally conspicuous in the enlarged views, the temperate consultations, and the wise measures on which the success of this government must depend."

His devout trust in God is affirmed with equal emphasis in his farewell address:

"Of all the dispositions and habits which lead to political prosperity, Religion and Morality are indispensable supports. In vain would that man claim the tribute of patriotism who should labor to subvert these great pillars of human happiness, these firmest props of the duties of men and citizens. The mere politician, equally with the pious man, ought to respect and cherish them. A volume could not trace all their connections with private and public felicity. Let it simply be asked: Where is the security for property, for reputation, for life, if the sense of religious obligation desert the oaths, which are the instruments of investigation in courts of justice? And let us with caution indulge the supposition that morality can be maintained without religion. Whatever may be conceded to the influence of refined education on minds of peculiar structure, reason and experience both forbid us to expect that national morality can prevail in exclusion of religious principle."

I may add that Washington's successors, in deference to public sentiment, and also, no doubt, in obedience to their own religious convictions, have followed his example, by imploring the Divine protection in their inaugural addresses.

The laws of the United States are so intimately interwoven with the Christian religion that they cannot be adequately expounded without the light of Revelation. The common law of this country is derived from the common law of Great Britain. "The common law," says Kent, "is the common jurisprudence of the people of the United States, and was brought with them as colonists from England and established here, *so far* as it was adapted to our institutions and circumstances. It was claimed by the Congress of the United Colonies, in 1774, as a branch of those 'indubitable rights and liberties to which the Colonies are entitled.' . . . Its principles may be compared to the influence of the liberal arts and sciences: 'Adversis perfugium ac solatium præbent; delectant domi; non impediunt foris; pernoctant nobiscum, peregrinantur, rusticantur.' To use the wonds of Duponceau: 'We live in the midst of the common law; we inhale it at every breath, imbibe it at every pore; we meet with it when we awake and when we lie down to sleep, when we travel and when we stay at home, and it is interwoven with the very idiom that we speak.'"[1]

Now, it is an incontrovertible fact that the common law of England is, to a great extent, founded on the principles of Christian ethics; the maxims of the Holy Scripture form the great criterion of right and wrong in the civil courts. Hence blasphemy and perjury are punished as crimes against the commonwealth, *because* they are crimes against religion. The Chancellors of England, who were "the keepers of the king's conscience," have ever been, for succeeding generations, professing Christians, and, until the Reformation, they were even churchmen.

"The best features of the common law," says an American jurisconsult, "if not derived from, have at least been improved and strengthened by, the prevailing religion and the teachings of the Sacred Book, especially those that regard the family and social relations." The Church left the impress of the Divine Law so indelibly on the common law that Sir M. Hale was moved to assert that Christianity was a part of the laws of England, and that to reproach the Christian religion "was to speak in

---

[1] *Commentaries*, p. 336 *et seq.*

subversion of the law," and that it was the judgment of the English people and their tribunals that "he who reviled, subverted and ridiculed Christianity did an act which struck at the foundation of civil society."

The oath that is taken by the President of the United States before he assumes the duties of his office, and that is administered in our courts of justice, not only to the witnesses, but also to the judge, jury, lawyers, and officers of the court, in accordance with the Constitution, implies a belief in God and forms an act of religious worship. It is a national tribute of homage to the universal sovereignty of our Creator. By the act of taking an oath a man makes a profession of faith in God's unfailing truth, absolute knowledge, and infinite sanctity. He also acknowledges God as Supreme Judge, who, in the life to come, will reward righteousness and punish iniquity.

The Bible, which is placed in the hands of the witness and is reverently kissed, involves a recognition of divine Revelation.

The Christian Sabbath is revered as a day of rest and public prayer throughout the land. The halls of Congress and of our State legislatures are closed on that day. The proceedings of our courts of justice —Federal, State, and municipal—are suspended. The din of commerce is hushed; the looms in our factories are silent; the fires burn low in our foundries; and every city, town, and hamlet resounds with the peal of the joyous bell inviting men to prayer. This is a national homage to the Christian religion.

Again, the Chief Magistrate of the nation and the Governors of the States issue their annual proclamations, inviting the people to offer their thanksgiving to "the Giver of all good gifts" for the blessings He has vouchsafed to the land.

There is another national custom which proclaims God's sovereignty and superintending providence. I refer to the practice prevailing in this country of opening the proceedings of Congress and of State legislatures, of inaugurating other important measures with prayer, and of invoking the blessing of God on the work about to be commenced.

I do not pretend to excuse or palliate the bad taste and irreverent familiarity which characterize some of those prayers. But the holiest practices may be perverted. And I cannot fail to express my admiration for a custom which, in principle, recognizes God's mercy and moral government, and which confides in Him as the Fountain of all light and wisdom.

The original settlers of the American colonies, with very rare individual exceptions, were all professing Christians, who inaugurated and fostered that Christian legislation and those religious customs to which I have referred.

The Puritans who founded New England, the Dutch who settled in New York, the Quakers and Irish who established themselves in Pennsylvania, the Swedes in Delaware, the English Catholics who colonized Maryland, the English Episcopalians who colonized Virginia, Georgia, and North Carolina, the Irish Presbyterians who also emigrated to the last-named State, the French Huguenots and the English colonists who planted themselves in South Carolina, the Spanish settlers of California and New Mexico, the French and Spaniards who took possession of Louisiana and Florida—all these colonists made an open profession of Christianity in one form or another, and recognized religion as the basis of society.

The same remark applies with equal truth to that stream of population which, from the beginning of the present century, has been constantly flowing into this country from Ireland and Germany and extending itself over the entire land.

In one century we have grown from three millions to sixty millions. We have grown up, not as distinct, independent and conflicting communities, but as one corporate body, breathing the same atmosphere of freedom, governed by the same laws, enjoying the same political rights. I see in all this a wonderful manifestation of the humanizing and elevating influence of Christian civilization. We receive from abroad people of various nations, races and tongues, habits and temperament, who speedily become assimilated to the human mass, and who form one homogeneous society. What is the secret of our social stability and order? It results from wise laws, based on Christian principles, and which are the echo of God's eternal law.

What is the cohesive power that makes us one body politic out of so many heterogeneous elements?

It is the religion of Christ. We live as brothers because we recognize the brotherhood of humanity— one Father in heaven, one origin, one destiny.

We shall appreciate our Christian civilization all the more by considering the aboriginal tribes of North America, with whom war was the rule and peace the exception; or by casting our eyes on the numerous tribes of Africa, who, though living side by side for ages, enjoy no friendly intercourse, but are habitually at war with one another. And had our country been colonized, developed and ruled by races hostile to religion, we should seek in vain for the social order and civic blessings that we possess to-day.

CHAPTER XXXV.

The Dangers that Threaten our American Civilization.

If our government and legislation are permeated and fortified by divine Revelation and Christian traditions, we cannot ignore the fact that they are assailed by unbelief, impiety and socialism. We have our moral Hell-Gate, which threatens our ship of state, and which it requires more than the genius of a Newton to remove. If we have strong hopes for the future of our country, we are also not without fears. The dangers that threaten our civilization may be traced to the family. The root of the commonwealth is in the homes of the people. The social and civil life springs from the domestic life of mankind. The official life of a nation is ordinarily the reflex of the moral sense of the people. The morality of public administration is to be gauged by the moral standard of the family. The river does not rise above its source.

We are confronted by five great evils—Mormonism and divorce, which strike at the root of the family and society; an imperfect and vicious system of education, which undermines the religion of our youth; the desecration of the Christian Sabbath, which tends to obliterate in our adult population the salutary fear of God and the homage that we owe Him; the gross and systematic election frauds, and lastly the unreasonable delay in carrying into effect the sentences of our criminal courts, and the numerous subterfuges by which criminals evade the execution of the law. Our insatiable greed for gain, the coëxistence of colossal wealth with abject poverty, the extravagance of the rich, the discontent of the poor, our eager and impetuous rushing through life, and every other moral and social delinquency, may be traced to one of the five radical vices enumerated above.

Every man that has the welfare of his country at heart cannot fail to view with alarm the existence and the gradual development of Mormonism, which is a plague-spot on our civilization, a discredit to our government, a degradation of the female sex, and a standing menace to the sanctity of the marriage bond. The feeble and spasmodic attempts that have been made to repress this social evil, and the virtual immunity that it enjoys, have rendered its apostles bold and defiant. Formerly they were content with enlisting recruits from England, Wales, Sweden and other parts of Scandinavia; but now, emboldened by toleration, they send their emissaries throughout the country and obtain disciples from North Carolina, Georgia, and other States of the Union.

The reckless facility with which divorce is procured is an evil scarcely less deplorable than Mormonism; indeed, it is in some respects more dangerous than the latter, for divorce has the sanction of the civil law which Mormonism has not. Is not the law of divorce a virtual toleration of Mormonism in a modified form? Mormonism consists in simultaneous polygamy, while the law of divorce practically leads to successive polygamy.

Each State has on its statute books a list of causes, or rather pretexts, which are recognized as sufficient ground for divorce *a vinculo*. There are in all twenty-two or more causes, most of them of a very trifling character, and in some States, as in Illinois and Maine, the power of granting a divorce is left to the discretion of the judge.[1]

[1] Afghanistan has the questionable honor of presenting a new plea for divorce, which, if applied to this country, might fill with dismay many unfortunate husbands uncongenial with their spouses. "A Lahore newspaper states that an Afghan lady recently applied to the Ameer Abdul Rahman for a separation from her husband on the ground that he was becoming bald. The defender and savior of Afghan unity, recognizing the importance of vindicating the sanctity of domestic as well as governmental authority, decided, after due reflection upon the demoralizing tendency of feminine disrespect for intellectual men, to make an example of the presumptuous plaintiff. His first step was to order a vial of sour milk to be poured on the husband's head, whether as an 'invigorator' or 'tonic' the eastern journalist does not say. Then, abandoning curative for punitive measures, the Ameer next commanded the wife to lick the milk off with her tongue, and when that was done, and the husband's head shone like a billiard ball, his highness directed that the unsympathetic woman should be 'placed on the back of

From the special Report on the statistics of marriage and divorce made to Congress by Carroll D. Wright in February, 1889, we condense the following startling facts:

DIVORCES IN THE UNITED STATES BY YEARS.

Year.	Divorces.	Year.	Divorces.
1867	9,937	1877	15,687
1868	10,150	1878	16,089
1869	10,939	1879	17,083
1870	10,962	1880	19,663
1871	11,586	1881	20,762
1872	12,390	1882	22,112
1873	13,156	1883	23,198
1874	13,989	1884	22,994
1875	14,212	1885	23,472
1876	14,800	1886	25,535
	122,121		206,595

From this table it will be seen that there was a total of 328,716 divorces in the United States in the twenty years 1867–1886. Of these there were 122,121 in the first half of the period and 206,595 in the last half. That is to say the divorces in the latter half were 69 per cent. more than those in the

a donkey with her face to the tail, and thus be forced to ride through the bazaar.' After that she knew better, it is reported, than to jeer heartlessly at the misfortune of the head of the house. A humane silence, if not respectful commiseration, was the least that a proper respect for the marriage vow dictated. To the ladies of America, the Ameer's conduct will perhaps savor of oriental despotism, but it is possible that not a few of their worse halves will envy the position of honor that Eastern law secures to the bald-headed husband."

first half. The population between 1870 and 1880 increased only 30 per cent. The divorces in 1870 were 10,962, and in 1880, they were 19,663, and as the table shows they are in 1886 more than two and one-half times what they were in 1867.

Our neighbor Canada presents a far more creditable attitude on this subject than we do. From 1867 to 1886 inclusive, only 116 divorces were granted in the Dominion of Canada, or an average of less than six every year in a population of four millions. During the same period of twenty years, there had been only eleven divorces in all Ireland.

From the figures quoted above it is painfully manifest that the cancer of divorce is rapidly spreading over the community, and poisoning the fountains of the nation. Unless the evil is checked by some speedy and heroic remedy, the very existence of family life is imperiled. How can we call ourselves a Christian people, if we violate a fundamental law of Christianity? And if the sanctity and indissolubility of marriage does not constitute a cardinal principle of the Christian religion, we are at a loss to know what does.

Let the imagination picture to itself the fearful wrecks daily caused by this rock of scandal, and the number of families that are cast adrift on the ocean of life. Great stress is justly laid by moralists on the observance of the Sunday. But what a mockery is the external repose of the Christian Sabbath to homes from which domestic peace is banished by intestine war, where the mother's heart is broken, the father's spirit is crushed, and where the children cannot cling to one of their parents, without exciting the jealousy or hatred of the other! And these melancholy scenes are followed by the final act in the drama when the family ties are dissolved, and hearts that had vowed eternal love and union, are separated to meet no more.

This social plague calls for a radical cure; and the remedy can be found only in the abolition of our mischievous legislation regarding divorce, and in an honest application of the teachings of the Gospel. If persons contemplating marriage were persuaded that once united, they were legally debarred from entering into second wedlock, they would be more circumspect before marriage in the choice of a life partner, and would be more patient afterwards in bearing the yoke and in tolerating each other's infirmities.

The second evil that bodes mischief to our country and endangers the stability of our government, arises from our mutilated and defective system of public school education. I am persuaded that the popular errors now existing in reference to education spring from an incorrect notion of that term. *To educate* means *to bring out*, to develop the intellectual, moral, and religious faculties of the soul. An education, therefore, that improves the mind and the memory, to the neglect of moral and religious training, is at best but an imperfect system. According to Webster's definition, to educate is "to instil into the mind principles of art, science, *morals, religion,* and behavior." "To educate," he says, "in the arts is important; in religion, indispensable."

It is, indeed, eminently useful that the intellect of our youth should be developed, and that they should be made familiar with those branches of knowledge which they are afterward likely to pursue. They can then go forth into the world, gifted with a well furnished mind and armed with a lever by which they may elevate themselves in the social scale and become valuable members of society. It is also most desirable that they should be made acquainted in the course of their studies with the history of our country, with the origin and principles of its government, and with the eminent men who have served it by their statesmanship and defended it by their valor. This knowledge will instruct them in their civic rights and duties, and contribute to make them enlightened citizens and devoted patriots.

But it is not enough for children to have a secular education; they must receive also a religious training. Indeed, religious knowledge is as far above human science as the soul is above the body, as heaven is above earth, as eternity is above time. The little child that is familiar with the Christian catechism, is really more enlightened on truths that should come home to every rational mind, than the most profound philosophers of Pagan antiquity, or even than many of the so-called philosophers of our own times. He has mastered the great problem of life. He knows his origin, his sublime destiny, and the means of attaining it, a knowledge that no human science can impart without the light of Revelation.

God has given us a *heart* to be formed to virtue, as well as a *head* to be enlightened. By secular education we improve the mind; by religious training we direct the heart.

It is not sufficient, therefore, to know how to read and write, to understand the rudiments of grammar and arithmetic. It does not suffice to know that two and two make four; we must practically learn also the great distance between time and eternity. The knowledge of bookkeeping is not sufficient, unless we are taught, also, how to balance our accounts daily between our conscience and our God. It will profit us little to understand all about the diurnal and annual motions of the earth, unless we add to this science some heavenly astronomy. We should know and feel that our future home is to be beyond the stars in heaven, and that, if we lead a virtuous life here, we shall "shine as stars for all eternity."[1]

We want our children to receive an education that will make them not only learned, but pious men. We want them to be not only polished members of society, but also conscientious Christians. We desire for them a training that will form their heart, as well as expand their mind. We wish them to be not only men of the world, but, above all, men of God.

---

[1] *Dan.* XII., 3.

A knowledge of history is most useful and important for the student. He should be acquainted with the lives of those illustrious heroes that founded empires,—of those men of genius that enlightened the world by their wisdom and learning, and embellished it by their works of art.

But is it not more important to learn something of the King of kings who created all these kingdoms, and by whom kings reign? Is it not more important to study that Uncreated Wisdom before whom all earthly wisdom is folly, and to admire the works of the Divine Artist who paints the lily and gilds the clouds?

If, indeed, our soul were to die with the body, if we had no existence beyond the grave, if we had no account to render to God for our actions, we might more easily dispense with the catechism in our schools. Though even then Christian morality would be a fruitful source of temporal blessings; for, as the Apostle teaches, "Piety is profitable to all things, having promise *of the life that now is*, and of that which is to come."[1]

But our youth cherish the hope of becoming one day citizens of heaven, as well as of this land. And as they cannot be good citizens of this country without studying and observing its laws, neither can they become citizens of heaven unless they know and practise the laws of God. Now, it is only by a good religious education that we learn to know and to fulfil our duties toward our Creator.

[1] *I. Tim.* IV., 8.

The religious and secular education of our children cannot be *divorced* from each other without inflicting a fatal wound upon the soul. The usual consequence of such a separation is to paralyze the moral faculties and to foment a spirit of indifference in matters of faith. Education is to the soul what food is to the body. The milk, with which the infant is nourished at its mother's breast, feeds not only its head, but permeates at the same time its heart and the other organs of the body. In like manner, the intellectual and moral growth of our children should go hand in hand; otherwise, their education is shallow and fragmentary, and often proves a curse instead of a blessing.

Piety is not to be put on like a holiday dress, to be worn on state occasions, but it is to be exhibited in our conduct at all times. Our youth must put in practice every day the Commandments of God, as well as the rules of grammar and arithmetic. How can they familiarize themselves with these sacred duties, if they are not daily inculcated?

Guizot, an eminent Protestant writer of France, expresses himself so clearly and forcibly on this point that I cannot forbear quoting his words: "In order," he says, "to make popular education truly good and socially useful, it must be fundamentally religious. . . . It is necessary that national education should be given and received in the midst of a religious atmosphere, and that religious impressions and religious observances should penetrate into all its parts. Religion is not a study or an exercise, to be restricted to a certain place or a certain hour; it is a faith and a law, which ought to be felt everywhere, and which, after this manner alone, can exercise all its beneficial influence upon our mind and our life."

In this country, the citizen happily enjoys the largest liberty. But the wider the liberty, the more efficient should be the safeguards to prevent it from being abused and degenerating into license. The ship that is destined to sail on a rough sea and before strong winds, should be well ballasted. To keep the social planet within its proper orbit, the centripetal force of religion should counterbalance the centrifugal motion of free thought. The only effectual way to preserve the blessings of civil freedom within legitimate bounds, is to inculcate in the mind of youth while at school, the virtues of truth, justice, honesty, temperance, self-denial, and those other fundamental duties comprised in the Christian code of morals.

The catechetical instructions given once a week in our Sunday-schools, though productive of very beneficial results, are insufficient to supply the religious wants of our children. They should, as far as possible, breathe every day a healthy religious atmosphere in those schools in which not only is their mind enlightened, but the seeds of faith, piety and sound morality are nourished and invigorated. By what principle of justice can you store their mind with earthly knowledge for several hours each day, while their heart, which requires far more cultivation, must be content with the paltry allowance of a few weekly lessons?

Nor am I unmindful of the blessed influence of a home education, and especially of a mother's tutelage. As she is her child's first instructor, her lessons are the most deep and lasting. The intimate knowledge she has acquired of her child's character by constant intercourse, the tender love subsisting between them, and the unbounded confidence placed in her by her pupil, impart to her instructions a force and conviction which no other teacher can hope to win.

But how many mothers have not the time to devote to the education of their children! How many mothers have not the capacity! How many, alas, have not the inclination!

And granted even that the mother has done her duty, the child's training does not end with the mother, but it will be supplemented by a curriculum in other schools. And, of what avail is a mother's toil, if the seeds of faith that she has planted, attain a sickly growth in the cheerless atmosphere of a schoolroom from which the sun of religion is rigidly excluded?

The remedy for these defects would be supplied if the denominational system, such as now obtains in Canada, were applied in our public schools.

The desecration of the Christian Sabbath is the third social danger against which it behooves us to set our face, and take timely precautions before it assumes proportions too formidable to be easily eradicated.

The custom of observing religious holidays has prevailed, both in ancient and modern times, among nations practising a false system of worship, as well as among those professing the true religion. They have set apart one day in the week, or at least certain days in the month or year, for the public and solemn worship of their Creator, just as they have instituted national festivals to commemorate some signal civic blessing obtained by their heroes and statesmen.

The Mohammedans devote Friday to public prayer and special almsgiving, because that day is appointed by the Koran.

The Parsees of Persia and India have four holidays each month consecrated to religious worship.

The Hebrew people were commanded by Almighty God to keep holy the Sabbath Day, or Saturday, because on that day God rested from His work.[1] He wished to remind them by this weekly celebration that He was their Creator and Master, and the Founder of the universe. He desired that they should be moved to worship Him by the contemplation of His works, and thus rise from nature to nature's God.

The Sabbath was marked also by a beneficent character, which admirably displays God's tender mercy toward His creatures and appeals with touching pathos to the compassion of the Hebrew master in behalf of his servant and beast of burden. "The

---

[1] *Exod.* XX., 8.

seventh day is the Sabbath of the Lord, thy God. Thou shalt not do any work therein, thou, nor thy .... bondman and bondwoman, ... nor any of thy beasts, nor the stranger that is within thy gates. . . . Remember that thou also wast a slave in the land of Egypt, and the Lord thy God brought thee out from thence with a strong hand and a stretched-out arm."[1]

The prophet Isaiah attaches abundant blessings to the due observance of the day: "The children of the stranger that adhere to the Lord to worship Him, and to love His name, to be His servants: every one that keepeth the Sabbath from profaning it, and that holdeth fast My covenant; I will bring them into My holy mount, and will make them joyful in My house of prayer; their holocausts and their victims shall please Me upon My altar. For My house shall be called the house of prayer for all nations."[2]

The prophet Ezekiel declares the profanation of the Sabbath foremost among the national sins of the Jews, and the chief cause of their national calamities. "I lifted up My hand upon them in the wilderness, to disperse them among the nations, and to scatter them through the countries: because they had not done My judgments, and had cast off My statutes, and had violated My Sabbaths."

It is the opinion of Grotius and of other learned commentators that the Sabbath was held sacred for

[1] *Deut.* V., 14, 15.
[2] *Isaiah* LVI., 6, 7.

generations prior to the time of Moses, and its observance, according to Lightfoot and other writers, dates even from the creation, or, at least, from the Fall of Adam. Hence they maintain that the Jewish lawgiver, in prescribing the Sabbath, was not enacting a new commandment, but enforcing an old one.

This inference is drawn from the words of Genesis: "And He blessed the seventh day and sanctified it,"[1] which plainly means that He then instituted it as a day of rest and prayer for Adam and all his posterity. It is manifest also from the significant fact that the Hebrew people, for some time before they received the Law on Mount Sinai, were enjoined in the desert to abstain on the Sabbath Day from gathering manna, and to rest from all servile work.[2] The same conclusion is obvious from the very words of the precept: *Remember* to keep holy the Sabbath Day, by which God recalls to their mind an already-existing ordinance which had grown well-nigh obsolete during their bondage in Egypt. This inference is, moreover, warranted by the fact that the Sabbath was kept sacred by the Egyptians, as Herodotus testifies. We cannot suppose that a people, so tenacious of their traditions, would adopt from their own slaves a religious custom that was rarely, if ever, practised by the slaves themselves, owing to their wretched condition. We are, therefore, justified in asserting that it was derived from the primitive law given to Adam.

[1] *Gen.* II., 3.
[2] *Exod.* XVI., 23.

With what profound reverence, then, should we view an ordinance instituted to draw man closer to his Maker, and to inculcate on him humanity toward his fellow-beings and compassion for even the beast of burden; an ordinance, whose observance was requited by temporal blessings, and whose violation was avenged by grievous calamities; which was first proclaimed at the dawn of human life, reëchoed on Mount Sinai, and engraved by the finger of God on the Decalogue; an ordinance, which applies to all times and places, and which is demanded by the very exigencies of our nature!

Sunday, or the Lord's Day, is consecrated by the Christian world to public worship and to rest from servile work, in order to commemorate the Resurrection of our Saviour from the grave, by which He consummated the work of our Redemption, and to foreshadow the glorious resurrection of the elect and the eternal rest that will be theirs in the life to come. "We who have believed," says the Apostle, "shall enter into rest." "There remaineth, therefore, a day of rest for the people of God."[1] Yea, an everlasting day of rest and supreme felicity prefigured by the repose of the ancient Sabbath. Most appropriately, indeed has Sunday been chosen. If it was proper to solemnize the day on which God created the world, how much more meet to celebrate the day on which He consummated its redemption.

As the worship of our Creator is nourished and

---

[1] *Heb.* IV., 9-11.

perpetuated by religious festivals, so does it languish when they are unobserved, and become paralyzed when they are suppressed. Whenever the enemies of God seek to destroy the religion of a people they find no means so effectual for carrying out their impious design as the suppression of the Sabbath. Thus, when Antiochus determined to abolish the sacred laws of the Hebrew people and to compel them to conform to the practice of idolatry, he defiled the Temples of Jerusalem and Garizim, he put an end to the Jewish sacrifices, and, above all, he forbade, under pain of death, the *observance of the Sabbath and the other religious solemnities*, substituting in their stead his own birthday and the Feast of Bacchus as days of sacrifice and licentious indulgence.[1]

The leaders of the French Revolution of 1793 adopted similar methods for the extirpation of the Lord's Day in France. The churches were profaned and dedicated to the *goddess of Reason;* the priests were exiled or put to death. The very name of Sunday, or Lord's Day, was abolished from the calendar, that every hallowed tradition associated with that day might be obliterated from the minds of the people.

And it is a well-known fact that, in our own times, the enemies of religion are the avowed opponents of the Christian Sabbath. I have seen Sunday violated in Paris, in Brussels and in other capitals of Europe.

[1] *II. Mac.*, VI.

And even in Rome I have seen government workmen engaged on the Lord's Day in excavating and in building, a profanation which grieved the Holy Father, as he himself acknowledged to me. Who are they that profane the Sunday in those cities of Europe? They are men lost to all sense of religion, who glory in their impiety and who aim at the utter extirpation of Christianity.

A close observer cannot fail to note the dangerous inroads that have been made on the Lord's Day in our country within the last quarter of a century. If these encroachments are not checked in time, the day may come when the religious quiet, now happily reigning in our well-ordered cities, will be changed into noise and turbulence, when the sound of the church-bell will be drowned by the echo of the hammer and the dray, when the Bible and the prayer book will be supplanted by the newspaper and the magazine, when the votaries of the theatre and the drinking saloon will outnumber the religious worshippers, and salutary thoughts of God, of eternity, and of the soul will be choked by the cares of business and by the pleasures and dissipation of the world.

We cannot but admire the wisdom of God and His intimate knowledge of the human heart in designating one day in the week on which public homage should be paid Him. So engrossing are the cares and occupations of life, so absorbing its pleasures, that it is difficult, if not impossible, to direct the thoughts of mankind to the higher pursuits of virtue and religious worship, unless a special time is set apart for these spiritual exercises. We have certain hours assigned to the various functions of daily life. We have stated hours for retiring to rest and for rising from sleep, for partaking of our meals, and for attending to our regular avocations. If we attended to these ordinary pursuits only when inclination would prompt us, our health would be impaired and our temporal interests would suffer. And so, too, would our spiritual nature grow torpid if there were no fixed day for renovating it by the exercise of divine praise and adoration. We might for a time worship God at irregular intervals, but very probably we would end by neglecting to commune with Him altogether.

The Christian Sabbath is a living witness of Revelation, an abiding guardian of Christianity. The religious services held in our churches each successive Sunday are the most effective means for keeping fresh in the minds and hearts of our people the sublime and salutary teachings of the Gospel. Our churches exercise on the truths of Revelation an influence analogous to that exerted by our courts of justice on the civil law. The silence and solemnity of the court, the presence of the presiding judge, the power with which he is clothed, the weight of his decisions, give an authority to our civil and criminal jurisprudence and invest it with a sanction which it could not have if there were no fixed tribunals.

In like manner, the religious decorum observed in our temples of worship, the holiness of the place, the sacred character of the officiating ministers, above all, the reading and exposition of the Sacred Scriptures, inspire men with a reverence for the Divine Law and cause it to exert a potent influence in the moral guidance of the community. The summary closing of our civil tribunals would not entail a more disastrous injury on the laws of the land than the closing of our churches would inflict on the Christian religion.

How many social blessings are obtained by the due observance of the Lord's Day! The institution of the Christian Sabbath has contributed more to the peace and good order of nations than could be accomplished by standing armies and the best organized police force. The officers of the law are a terror, indeed, to evil doers, whom they arrest for overt acts; while the ministers of religion, by the lessons they inculcate, prevent crime by appealing to the conscience, and promote peace in the kingdom of the soul.

The cause of charity and mutual benevolence is greatly fostered by the sanctification of the Sunday. When we assemble in church on the Lord's Day, we are admonished by that very act that we are all members of the same social body, and that we should have for one another the same lively sympathy and spirit of coöperation which the members of the human body entertain toward one another. We are reminded that we are all enlivened and sanctified by the same spirit. "There are diversities of graces," says the Apostle, "but the same spirit; and there are diversities of ministries, but the same Lord. And there are diversities of operations, but the same God who worketh all in all."[1] We all have divers pursuits and avocations; we occupy different grades of society, but in the house of God all these distinctions are levelled. The same Spirit that enters the heart of the most exalted citizen, does not disdain to descend also into the soul of the humblest peasant. We all profess our faith in the same Creator, and we are all regenerated by the waters of baptism. We hope for the same heaven. We meet as brothers and sisters of the same Lord whose blood was shed on the Cross not only to cleanse our soul from sin, but to cement our hearts in love. We are, in a word, taught the comforting lesson that we all have one God and Father in heaven. "One body," says the Apostle, "one Spirit, as you are called in one hope of your vocation. One Lord, one faith, one baptism, one God and Father of all, who is above all, and through all, and in us all."[2]

If, indeed, the observance of the Sunday were irksome and difficult, there would be some excuse for neglecting this ordinance. But it is a duty which, so far from involving labor and self-denial, contributes to health of body and contentment of mind. The Christian Sunday is not, to be confounded with the Jewish or even the Puritan Sabbath. It prescribes the golden mean between rigid sabbatarianism on the one hand, and lax indulgence

---

[1] *I. Cor.* XII., 4–6.
[2] *Ephes.* IV., 4–6.

on the other. There is little doubt that the revulsion in public sentiment from a rigorous to a loose observance of the Lord's Day, can be ascribed to the sincere but misguided zeal of the Puritans, who confounded the Christian Sunday with the Jewish Sabbath, and imposed restraints on the people which were repulsive to Christian freedom, and which were not warranted by the Gospel dispensation. The Lord's Day to the Catholic heart is always a day of joy. The Church desires us on that day to be cheerful without dissipation, grave and religious without sadness and melancholy. She forbids, indeed, all unnecessary servile work on that day; but as "the Sabbath was made for man, not man for the Sabbath," she allows such work whenever charity or necessity may demand it. And as it is a day consecrated not only to religion, but also to relaxation of mind and body, she permits us to spend a portion of it in innocent recreation. In a word, the true conception of the Lord's Day is expressed in the words of the Psalmist: "This is the day which the Lord hath made, let us be glad and rejoice therein."

A word must be added on two other pregnant evils: The ballot is the expression of the will of a free people, and its purity should be guarded with the utmost jealousy. To violate that purity is to wound the State in its tenderest point.

The repeated cry of "election frauds" is one full of warning. In many instances, undoubtedly, it is the empty charge of defeated partisans against the victors: yet enough remain, of a substantial character, to be ominous. In every possible way—by tickets insidiously printed, by "stuffing" the box, by "tissue ballots," by "colonizing," "repeating" and "personation"—frauds are attempted, and too often successfully, upon the ballot. It is the gravest menace to free institutions.

Defective registration laws and negligence to secure the ballot-box by careful legal enactments, in part account for such a state of affairs; but a prime cause is that the better class of citizens so often stand aloof from practical politics and the conduct of campaigns. It is one result of universal suffrage that elections very frequently turn upon the votes of that large class made up of the rough and baser sort. To influence and organize this vote is the "dirty work" of politics. Gentlemen naturally shrink from it. Hence it has gotten, for the most part, with the general political machinery, into unreputable hands; and from these hands issue the election frauds, which thicken in the great cities, and gravely endanger our institutions. The ballot is the ready and potent instrument which registers the will of a free people for their own government, and the violation of its purity leads directly to the point where there is either loss of liberty or revolution to restore it. We all remember what happened in 1876, when alleged tampering with election returns affected the Presidential succession, and a great cloud arose and for weeks hung, dark and threatening, over the land. It was a tremendous crisis, and perhaps only the memories of recent war averted disastrous strife.

The privilege of voting is not an inherent or inalienable right, but a solemn and a sacred trust to be used in strict accordance with the intentions of the authority from which it emanates. When a citizen exercises his honest judgment in casting his vote for the most acceptable candidate, or for a measure that will best subserve the interests of the community, he is making a legitimate use of the prerogatives confided to him.

But when he sells or barters his vote, and disposes of it to the highest bidder like a merchantable commodity, he is clearly violating his trust, and degrading his citizenship. The enormity of this offence may be readily perceived by pushing it to its logical consequences. If one man may sell his vote, so may the multitude. Once the purchase of votes is tolerated, or condoned or connived at, the obvious result is that the right of suffrage will become a mere farce, money and not merit will be the test of success, and the election will be determined not by the personal fitness and integrity of the candidate, but by the length of his purse.

We hail it with satisfaction, that a more healthy public opinion on this subject seems developing, that reputable citizens appear more disposed to bear an active part in practical politics, and that "reform," "a free ballot," "a fair count," are becoming, under the pressure, more and more party watchwords. It is a purifying tendency in a vital direction.

Yet, another crying evil is the wide interval that so often interposes between a criminal's conviction and the execution of the sentence, and the frequent defeat of justice by the delay. Human life is, indeed, sacred, but the laudable effort to guard it has gone beyond bounds. Of late years the difficulty to convict (in murder trials, especially) has greatly increased from the widened application of the pleas in bar,—notably, that of insanity. When a conviction has been reached, innumerable delays generally stay the execution. The many grounds of exception allowed to counsel, the appeals from one court to another, with final application to the Governor, and the facility with which signatures for pardon are obtained have combined to throw around culprits an extravagant protective system and gone far to rob jury trial of its substance and efficacy. A prompt execution of the law's sentence, after a fair trial had, is that which strikes terror into evil doers and satisfies the public conscience. The reverse of this among us has brought reproach upon the administration of justice and given plausible grounds for the application of lynch-law.

INDEX.

ABEL and Cain, contrast between, 100.
Abortion, 374.
　Condemned as murder by the Church, 382.
Abraham, example of, 195, 222.
Achab and Job, contrast between, 100.
　Example of, 299.
Addison's interpretation of Cato, 210.
Address of author to workingmen, 451.
Adrian I. Pope, on marriage of slaves, 431.
Adversaries acknowledge Christ's miracles, 243.
Afflictions, cause of gratitude to God, 153.
Africa, state of religion in, 186.
African races not without vague ideas of God, 33–4.
Agathocles, example of, 275.
Age of the world, 315.
Alaska, reference to, 288.
Alexander the Great, reference to, 257, 409.
Alexandria, Cæsar's triumphs in, 187.
　State of religion in, 186.
Alfred the Great, example of, 182.
All actions present to God, 175.
Amalecites conquered by David, 124.
Aman, example of, 205.

American civilization and religion, 472.
Ammonites conquered by David, 124.
Anatomical structure, proof of unity, 287.
Androcles, example of, 159.
Angel, symbol of prayer, 121.
Animal kingdom, equilibrium in, 95.
Anthem of angels at Bethlehem, 192.
Anthony, St., example of, 170.
Antichristian schools, methods of counteracting, 9.
Antioch, state of religion in, 186.
　St. Peter in, 254.
Antiochus Epiphanes, example of, 103.
Antiquity of man, 315.
Apostacy, difficulty of conversion from, 300.
Apostles, and Pagan generals, contrast between, 257.
　Confidence of, in Christ's promises, 253.
　Estimate of character of, 247.
　Hard earthly lot of, 248.
　Influence of prayer on, 122.
　Not guilty of imposture, 248.
　Not victims of deception, 248.
　Miracles of, 249.
　Success of, 254.
Aquinas, St. Thos., mind and writings of, 119.

510 INDEX.

On utility of prayer, 132.
Arabia, example of, 275.
Arbitration, international, 407.
  Should take the place of strikes, 451.
Arch of Titus, 8.
Archimedes, example of, 207.
Argyll, Duke of, errors concerning will, 175, 176.
  On poisons, 94.
Aristides, anecdote about, 461.
Aristotle, on existence of God, 25.
  Belief of, in immortality, 201.
  Quoted, 276, 277.
  Errors taught by, 329.
  Taught that slavery existed by the law of nature, 416.
Arnold, Matthew, on popular rights, 442.
Arnold, Thomas, quoted, 415.
Arsinoe, prisoner of Cæsar, 188.
Art, favored by the Church, 312.
Ashantees, no tribe of, without some notion of Supreme Being, 34.
Aspirations of man, satisfied by Christianity, 291.
Assuerus, example of, 205.
Assyrian antiquities and scripture, 316.
Astrology, among Pagans, 275.
  Ridiculed by Shakespeare, 179.
Asylums, created by Christianity, 14.
  Foundling and other, 384.
Athanasius, see of, 186.
Atheistic government, failure to establish it in France, 470.
Atheists, as feeble in argument as small in number, 44.
  Not types of man's moral nature, 44.
  Four reasons of, to explain belief in God, 45.

Atom-theory of Epicurus, refuted, 20.
Atrocities of Pagan war, 12.
Attraction and repulsion, whence? 22.
Augustin, St. and Monica, example of, 145.
  On conversion, 146.
  On free-will, 197.
Australian aborigines, belief of, in Supreme Being, 33.
Aztecs believed in Supreme Being, 35.

BACON on atheism, 46.
Ballot, purity of, demanded, 505.
Bancroft on religion of aborigines, 35.
Basil, St., firmness of, 172.
Beatitude of the righteous, 213.
Belief in God's presence influences moral conduct, 70.
  In God not due to prejudices of early education, 46.
  In God not due to fear, 45.
  In God not due to ignorance, 45.
  In God not due to legislation, 48.
Beliefs of mankind classified, 27.
Benedictines, influence of, on barbarians, 400.
Bernard, St., on ingratitude, 158.
Bismarck, letter of, to wife, 43.
Body to rise again, 213.
Borromeo, St. Charles, and plague of Milan, 137.
Boycotting by labor unions, 449.
Brahminism not atheistic, 31.
Brazil, slavery abolished in, 435.

INDEX.

Britons, ancient, belief of, in immortality, 202.
Brougham, Lord, on Foundling Hospitals, 394.
Brue, on belief of Africans in God, 34.
Buddhism not atheistic, 28.

CÆSAR, triumphal march of, 187–8.
Cairn, testimony about Buddhism, 29.
Calvin on predestination, 174.
Canada, divorce in, 488.
  School system of, 495.
Capital not endangered by recognition of rights of labor, 442.
Captives, redemption of, 436–7.
Carthage, state of religion in, 186.
Cato, favored slavery, 419.
  Soliloquy of, by Addison, 210.
Chaldeans, believed in immortality, 202.
Chance does not account for universe, 19.
Chapman on belief of Bechuanas in God, 33.
Charitable asylums among Christians, 384.
Charity among Christians, 377 *et seq.*
  Among Christians in modern times, 384.
  Its obligation among Christians, 387.
  A note of the true religion, 381.
  Catholic, no encouragement to idleness, 385–394.
Chevalier on Egyptians' belief in God, 27.
Children, condition of Pagan, 11.
Chinese not atheists, 30.

Christ predicts His resurrection, 244–5.
  The Mediator between God and man, 297.
  His death a public fact, 250.
  And natural morality, 334.
  His example a solace to the slave, 427.
  Judge of living and dead, 233.
  Claims to be Son of God, 234.
  Claims to be identical with the Father, 236.
  Avows His divinity, 236.
  Shuns temporal honors, 236.
  Exacts absolute obedience, 237.
  Either divine or an impostor, 238.
  Appeals to His miracles, 240.
  His miracles examined, 241.
  His miracles acknowledged by adversaries, 243.
Christian civilization, blessings of, 13 *et seq.*
Christian and Jewish law contrasted, 298–335.
Christians, number of, 27.
  Virtues of early, 343.
Christianity, moral revolution wrought by, 250.
  Disparity between means and results in establishment of, 258.
  Not propagated by armies, 259.
  Not spread by human wisdom, 259.
  A peacemaker to nations, 14.
  Persecution of, 264.
  Stability of, how explained, 265.
  A practical religion, 292.
  Favors science, 309.
  Favors art, 312.
  Influence of, on morals, 331 *et seq.*

And charity, 337 *et seq.*
Ennobles servile virtues, 427.
Cicero, belief of, in immortality, 201.
　On future life, 209.
　Testimony of, concerning God's existence, 25, 27, 37.
Civil allegiance, motives of, 457.
Civilization, Christian superior to Pagan, 10.
Clarkson, influence of, on emancipation, 433.
Coercion does not convert, 9.
Communism, errors of, 98.
Confucius, number of followers of, 28.
Conscience, a witness to God, 51 *et seq.*
　Demands absolute jurisdiction, 52.
　Echo of voice of God, 53.
　Proves God to be all-seeing, 55.
　Proves God to be holy, 55.
　More acute by exercise, 58.
　Revelation of God's will, 195.
Constantinople, state of religion in, 186.
Constitution of the United States and religion, 473.
Controversies, religious, avoided, 1.
Cook, Capt., testimony of, 288.
Corporations, dangers from, 446.
Creation of world explained by Christianity, 293.
　In six days, 314.
Creator recognized by His works, 49.
Criminal procedure, delays in, a danger, 508.

DAHOMEY, inhabitants of, believe in Supreme Being, 34.

Damien, Father, and the lepers, 392.
Dangers threatening our civilization, 484.
Darwin, belief of, in Divine Creator, 37.
　On origin of species, 284.
　On evolution, 281.
　Testimony of, 286.
David, example of, 123.
Declaration of Independence appeals to religious motives, 475.
Democritus, doctrine of, 277.
Destiny of man according to Revelation, 294 *et seq.*
De Tocqueville, quoted, 439.
Divination among Pagans, 275.
Divinity of Christ (see Christ).
Divorce, 486 *et seq.*
　Among Pagans, 354, 356 *et seq.*
　Among Mohammedans, 355.
　In Canada, 488.
　Facility in obtaining, 486.
　Statistics of, 487.
Dogmatism of scientists, 319.
Du Bois Reymond, quoted by Wainwright, 281.

EDUCATION no remedy adequate against vice, 464.
　Unreligious, a danger to the country, 489.
　Definition of the term, 489.
　Denominational, a remedy, 495.
Egypt, persecution of Israelites in, 186.
Egyptian antiquities and Scripture, 316.
Egyptians, doxology of, 26.
　Belief of, in immortality, 202.
　Testimony of, concerning God's existence, 26.
Elect, number of, not known, 227.

Election frauds, 505–6.
Electoral commission, example of, 115.
Emancipation of slaves made gradually, 425.
Emerson, testimony of, to God's existence, 39, 40.
Emotional insanity, plea of, 178.
Empire of Rome, condition of, 271.
Ephesus, state of religion in, 186.
Epicurus, atom-theory of, refuted, 20.
Epiphanes, Antiochus, cruelty and death of, 103.
Epistles of St. Paul full of gratitude, 161.
Equilibrium in animal kingdom, 95.
Esther, example of, 123.
Euler on duty of prayer, 133.
Evolutionists, theory of, 281.
Existence of God, recognized by every age and country, 24.
   Acknowledged by modern scientists, 37.
   Belief in, not caused by fear, 46–7.

FABIOLA, dialogue between Syra and, 75.
Family, the, is the foundation of the social life, 484.
Faraday, testimony of, to God's existence, 42.
Farrar, Canon, comparison by, of words of Seneca and St. Paul, 61.
Fatalism defined, 105, 106.
Fatherhood of God, 341.
Fellowship among Christians, 1.
Fetichism involves idea of Supreme Being, 33.

Foreknowledge of God no obstacle to free-will, 174–175.
Forgiveness of sins exercised by Christ, 232.
Fossils, human, their antiquity, 315, 316.
Francis de Sales, St., example of, 146.
Franklin, Benj., address of, in favor of religion, 474.
   Belief in Divine Providence, 43.
Freeman, the historian, on influence of Christianity, 413.
Free-will affirmed by Scripture, 167.
   Not against divine foreknowledge, 174, 175.
   Right exercise of, 181 *et seq.*
Fuegians, example of, 286.

GALEN, words of, 26.
Gamaliel, example of, 269.
Garfield, President, example of, 141, 142.
Gaul, Cæsar's triumphs in, 187.
Gauls, belief of, in immortality, 202.
Gentile world, blindness of, 276.
Geological formations and the Bible, 314.
Germans, belief of, in immortality, 202.
Gibbon, on future state, 280.
Gibbon's five causes, 266.
Gladiatorial exhibitions, 325.
God reveals Himself as Creator, Lawgiver and Judge, 50.
   His presence fills all space, 63.
   Type and Model of earthly parents, 80.
   His justice often vindicated in this life, 103.

Not excluded from His own works, 136.
Always our Father, 152–3.
Desires salvation of all, 224.
His existence and attributes, shown by universe, 305.
Goethe, personal belief of, in God, 41.
Good Shepherd, Sisters of, 394.
Gratitude, essential element in worship, 148.
In Christians, special causes for, 155.
Even in brutes, 159.
Gregory the Great, St., on prayer, 132.
And the Anglo-Saxon slaves, 426.
Gregory XVI., Pope, on slavery, 434.
Grotius, on the antiquity of Sabbath observance, 497.
Guizot, in favor of religious education, 493.

HABIT, force of, influences action, 179.
Hades, belief of Pagans in, 201.
Haeckel, admissions of, 283.
Hale, Sir M., on Christianity and English law, 479.
Happiness, not fully realized in present life, 204.
Heaven, true liberty in, 197.
A reward, 212.
Delights of, for spiritually minded, 226.
Heliogabalus, example of, table of, 99.
Hell, eternity of, taught by Revelation, 216.
Compatible with reason, 216.
Its eternity does not affect divine clemency, 224.
Herodotus, on existence of God, 25.

Holidays, religious, universally observed, 496.
Holmes, profession of faith in God, 40.
Home-training often insufficient, 495.
Homer, words of, concerning Supreme Being, 36.
On prayer, 114.
Testimony of, respecting future life, 201.
Horace, on strength of will, 171.
Hospitals, created by Christianity, 12.
Antiquity of, among Christians, 383.
Hübner, testimony of Baron, concerning Chinese Theism, 31.
Huc, testimony of Abbé, concerning Buddhism, 28.
Human family, differences in, explained, 286.
Unity of, proved by anatomy, 287.
Race, its unity, 317.
Sacrifices, examples of, 275.
Wisdom, not a factor in spread of Christianity, 259.
Humboldt, on unity of human race, 285.
Hume and the basis of civil government, 468.
Avows belief in God, 43.
On free-will, 174 *et seq.*
Huxley, not an Atheist, 38.
On human destiny, 294.
Admissions of, 282.

IDLENESS among Pagans, 421.
Idolatry, of Pagan worship, 11 *et seq.*
No compromise of Christianity with, 293.

INDEX.

Ignatius Loyola, St., example of, 121.
Immortality of soul, 198 *et seq.*
  Universal belief in, 201.
  Assured by Revelation, 212.
Improvidence reproved by God, 106.
Indians unjustly treated, 405.
Inequality in human condition compatible with Providence of God, 95.
  Essential to order, 96.
  Incentive to emulation, 96.
  Effects of, exaggerated, 98.
Infanticide legalized in Paganism, 375.
Infidels, untenable position of, 237.
Ingratitude, enormity of sin of, 158.
Insane, their care among Christians, 393.
Insanity, plea of emotional, 178.
International law a Christian institution, 406.
Ireland, persecutions in, 186, 187.
Irenæus, St., testimony of, 256.
Isaac and Rebecca, example of, 105.
Islamism (see Mohammedanism).

JEHOVAH, incommunicable name of, 230.
Jeremias on God's covenant, 67.
Jewish people, number of, 28.
  Opposition to Christianity, 261.
Job and Achab, contrast between, 100.
  Example of, 171.
  Words of, on resurrection, 213.

John Baptist, St., example of, 241.
Jonas, prophet, example of, 245.
Jones, Sir William, digest of Vedas, 31.
Joseph, patriarch, example of, 104.
Josue, example of, 120, 123.
Judas Machabeus, example of, 123.
Judith, example of, 123.
Juries, example of, 247, 249.
Justin Martyr, testimony of, 255.
Juvenal, on force of habit, 179.

KANG-HI, inscription of, on church in Pekin, 30.
Kemper, Gov., of Virginia, anecdote by, 389.
Kent, on the Gospel interwoven with our laws, 478.
Kleptomania, example of, 177.
Knowledge, no security for happiness, 206.
Knox, quoted, 285.
Koran, contrasted with Gospel, 271.

LABOR, dignity of, proclaimed by Gospel, 14.
  Ennobled by Christ, 439.
  Its rights and duties, 439 *et seq.*
  Paramount right to organize, 440.
  Its rights not in conflict with those of capital, 442.
  Entitled to just wages, 443.
  And capital, and the Golden Rule, 443.
  Entitled to kind treatment, 443.
  Better paid, etc., in America than in Europe, 445.

Summary of qualities most essential to success of, 451.
Labor-Unions, in danger from demagogues, 448.
Laborers, address to, 451.
Languages, all traced to one source, 318.
Lavigerie, Cardinal, on slavery, 423.
Law, tyranny of just, denounced only by wicked, 223.
Laws of nature, constant, 19.
Subject to divine control, 135.
Attraction and repulsion, whence? 22.
Lazarus, example of, 194, 222, 241, 243.
Lecky, on Christ as a moral teacher, 332.
Legislation, founded on religion, 48.
Of Christ, solemn sanctions of, 231.
Leo XIII, on slavery, 435.
Liberty of children of God, 184.
Life, Pagan view of, 277.
Principle of, in soul, 200.
Light of reason reveals moral law, 50.
Demonstrates God, 49.
Lightfoot, on the antiquity of the Sabbath, 498.
Lincoln, President, and emancipation, 433.
Linnæus, testimony of, 283.
Little Sisters of the Poor, 385.
Livingstone, testimony of, concerning African belief in God, 34.
On slavery, 423.
Livy, on equality of riches, 97.
Lord's day (see Sabbath).
Love of God, perfection of sanctity, 189.
Lucretius, example of, 277.

Luther, on slavery of will, 174.
Lycurgus, founded legislation on religion, 48.
Lyell, Sir Charles, testimony of, 284.

MACHIAVEL, on the basis of civil government, 468.
Magdalen, example of, 220.
Appearance of Christ to, 245.
Malice of offence proportionate to dignity offended, 218.
Man, possesses moral freedom, 163 et seq.
Condition of, without hope of immortality, 209.
His origin and destiny, according to modern unbelief, 281.
His origin and destiny, viewed by Revelation, 294.
His place in nature, 295.
Manhood, its sanctity among Christians, 380 et seq.
Marcus Aurelius, example of, 279.
Marriage, among Pagans, 350 et seq.
Lax doctrines and practices of Protestants at the present day, 367.
Christian, 363 et seq.
Mary, the model of Christian womanhood, 358.
Materialists, theories of, refuted, 20.
Material world, beauty of, in variety, 98.
Maury, testimony of, concerning deserts, 91.
Mercy of God, revealed by Christianity, 291.
Michael, Archangel, example of, 182.
Miracle, definition of, 240.

INDEX. 517

Miracles, credentials of mission, 240.
  Evidence of doctrine, 240.
  Appealed to by Christ, 241.
  Of Christ examined, 242.
  Accepted by disciples as proofs of divinity, 242.
  Of Apostles, 249.
  Vindicate truth of resurrection, 249.
Mill, views on free-will, 174, 176.
Minos, founded legislation on religion, 48.
Mivart, testimony of, concerning Buddhism, 29,
Moabites conquered by David, 124.
Modestus, dialogue between Basil and, 172.
Mohammed *versus* Christ, 270, 271, 272.
Mohammedanism, spread of, 186.
  Methods of, 187.
Mohammedan morality compared with Christian, 336.
Mohammedans and slavery, 423.
  Believe in one God, 28.
  Number of, 28.
Monica and Augustin, example of, 145.
Monogamy a Christian institution, 363.
Monopolies and trusts, 446.
Montesquieu on primitive religion, 48.
  Tribute to Christianity, 414.
Moral cowardice often cause of unbelief, 5.
Moral freedom self-evident, 163.
  Proved by Scripture, 168.
  Revolution wrought by Christianity, 252.
  World, charm of, in distinctions created by God, 98.

Morality and Paganism, 322.
  Fundamental motive of Christians, 340.
  Parallel between Christian and Pagan, 347.
More, Sir Thos., example of, 182, 185.
Mormonism, 485.
Mosaic and Gospel legislation compared, 232.
  Narrative, purpose of, 315.
  Narrative, sustained, 289.
Mothers, right and duty of instructing children, 370 *et seq.*
Motion of planets demonstrates Supreme Being, 21.
Motives do not force the will, 176.
Müller, Max, on existence of God, 40, 41.
  On language, 287.

NABOTH, example of, 299.
Napoleon, conference of, with his physician, 43.
  On Divinity of Christ, 238.
Natural religion basis of supernatural, 5, 6.
Nature's laws under Divine control, 135.
Nero and St. Paul, contrast between, 100.
Newman, Cardinal, quoted, 310.
Newton, Sir Isaac, anecdote of, 207.
  Testimony of, 23.
Nicodemus, words of, 290.
Numa, founded legislation on religion, 48.
Numidia, Cæsar's triumphs in, 187.

OMNIPRESENCE of God by essence, 62.
  In His works, 62.

By His intelligence, 64.
By His superintending power, 66.
Oracles among Pagans, 275.
Order, St. Augustin's definition of, 96.
Organic matter, distinct from soul, 201.
Organization, right of workingmen to, 440.
Origin and destiny of man, according to modern unbelief, 281 *et seq.*
Of man, according to Revelation, 293.
Orphans sheltered by Christianity, 13.
Ovid on free-will, 176.
Testimony of, 201, 262.

PAGAN world, splendor and wickedness of, 8.
Civilization inferior to Christian, 10.
And Christian systems contrasted, 10.
Family, condition of, 11.
Generals and the Apostles, contrast between, 257.
Opposition to Christianity, 261.
View of life gloomy, 278.
View of suicide, 279.
Idea of future life obscure, 279.
Paganism, influence of, on morals, 322.
And manhood, 374.
And pauperism, 376.
Palmerston's objection to prayer, 137.
Pantheists, theories of, 277.
Parsees not atheists, 32.
Pasteur, on existence and majesty of God, 41.
Patriotism, infused by prayer, 143.

Paul, St., and slavery, 428, 430.
Pauperism among Pagans, 376.
Peace of heart, through Christianity, 13.
Peace possessed by the man of good-will, 194.
Perpetuity of Christianity, prophecy of, 253.
Persecution of Christians, 264.
Persians, belief of, in immortality, 202.
Pharisees, example of, 243.
Philistines, conquered by David, 124.
Philosophers, Christian, view of prayer, 137.
Feeble influence of, among Pagans, 327, 329.
Pagan, uncertain of immortality, 328.
Philosophy, Pagan, on destiny of man, 277.
Phœnicia, condition of, 274.
Pitt, William, prophetic words of, as to oppression of labor, 447.
Planetary motion demonstrates Supreme Being, 21.
Plato, testimony of, concerning God's existence, 25.
His belief in God, 154.
Belief of, in immortality, 201.
On State religion, 276.
On future state, 280.
Errors taught by, 328.
Favored slavery, 416.
On basis of society, 457.
On the basis of civil government, 467.
Pliny, example of, 255.
On future state, 280.
Plutarch, testimony of, concerning God's existence, 24.
Belief of, in immortality, 201, 202, 280.

INDEX.

Poison, Duke of Argyll on, 94.
Polygamy, 350.
Polytheism, demonstrates necessity of revelation, 37.
Pope, lines of, on Supreme Being, 45.
Popes, influence of the, for peace, 401, 406.
The, and slavery, 434.
Popular objections against Divine Providence, 90 et seq.
Porphyrius, example of, 277.
Prayer, dignity and efficacy of, 110 et seq.
  Example of power of, 113.
  Essential element of divine worship, 113.
  Channel of illumination and comfort, 118.
  Enlarges mental vision, 118.
  Strengthens the will, 122.
  Influence of, on Apostles, 122.
  Inspires heroic deeds, 123.
  Efficacy of, promised, 125.
  Obligation of, imperative, 126.
  Duty of, inculcated, 126.
  Most exalted function of man, 129.
  Objections against, 130 et seq.
  Efficacy of, no infringement on decrees of God, 131.
  Does not disregard human prudence, 137.
  Encouraged by our Lord, 140.
  Never unanswered, 142.
  Test of, Tyndall, 144.
  Necessity of perseverance in, 145.
  At opening congress and legislatures, 481.
Predestination, Calvin's theory of, 174.
President's oath of office a tribute to religion, 480.

Priest, moral influence of, 338 et seq.
Priests, explorers and discoverers, 311.
Prisoners of war, treatment of, by Pagans and Christians compared, 409 et seq.
Providence of God proved a ruler, by conscience, 57.
  Of universal extent, 77.
  In natural order, 82.
  Objections to, 90 et seq.
  Revealed by Christian religion, 289.
Public conscience and Christian principles, 346.
Pythagoras, on prayer, 114.
  Example of, 207.

QUATREFAGES, on evolution, 283.

READE, Charles, description of solitary prisoner, 74.
Reason can demonstrate fundamental truths underlying Christianity, 7.
  Demonstrates God, 49.
  Reveals moral law, 50.
Reformers, the, and marriage, 366.
Religion, the basis of legislation, 48.
  Antecedent to civil society, 48.
  And science, harmony between, 303.
  The basis of civil society, 456.
  Gives motives for civil virtues, 458 et seq.
  Social influences of, 465 et seq.
  Guardian of good breeding, 465.
  And American civilization, 472.

And the American Constitution, 472.
In the Declaration of Independence, 475.
Constantly appealed to by Washington, 476.
The Christian, embodied in our laws, 478.
In education, 489 *et seq.*
Religious beliefs of mankind, 27.
Communities founded in prayer, 123.
Persecution sometimes salutary, 185.
Renan, assertions of, 249.
Repentance, nature of, 220.
Door of, always open, 227.
Reptiles, usefulness of, 90, 93.
Republic of Church universal, 268.
Resurrection, of dead, 213.
Attests Christ's divinity, 243.
Predicted by Christ, 244 *et seq.*
Proofs of, 245.
Examined as historical fact, 247.
Revelation, necessity of, demonstrated by Polytheism, 37.
Assures immortality, 212.
Necessity of, 274.
Rich and poor, relation between, according to Christian morals, 337.
Righteous, beatitude of the, 212.
Robespierre, example of, 182.
Roboam, example of, 166, 167.
Roland, Madam, on liberty, 179.
Roman Empire, state of, at Christ's coming, 252.
Rousseau's objection to prayer, 138.
And the basis of civil government, 468.

SABBATH, the Christian, revered throughout the land, 480.
The Christian, desecration of, a danger, 495 *et seq.*
In the old law, 496 *et seq.*
Its antiquity, 497–98.
Kept by the ancient Egyptians, 498.
Result of suppression, 499, 500.
And the French Revolution, 500.
Threatened profanation of, 501.
Wisdom of God in establishing, 501–2.
A living witness of Revelation, 502.
Social blessings of, 503.
Charity promoted by observance of, 503–4.
Contrast between Catholic and Puritan observance of, 504–5.
Saints, felicity of, 212.
St. Vincent de Paul Societies, 388.
Salvation a boon, 221.
Of all desired by God, 221.
Schiller, personal acknowledgment of God, 41.
Science and Religion, harmony between, 303, 317, 319.
Science favored by Christian spirit, 309.
Scientists, their dogmatism, 319.
Scoffers, described by St. Jude, 2.
Scott, Gen., 409.
Scriptures, affirm free-will, 167.
Not a scientific treatise, 313.
Secchi, testimony of, 284.
Secret societies, causes and evils of, 441.
Self-will, misery of, 193.

INDEX. 521

Seneca, testimony of, concerning God's existence, 25.
   Resemblance of expressions of, compared with those of St. Paul, 61.
   Letter of, to Lucilius, concerning God's omnipresence, 61.
   On virtuous life, 103.
   Belief of, in immortality, 201.
   Example of, 279.
   Testimony to Pagan immorality, 325.
Settlers, American, were Christians, 481 *et seq.*
Shakespeare, on astrology, 179.
Shintos not atheists, 31.
Signal service, example from, 133.
Sins, forgiveness of, exercised by Christ, 231.
Sister in hospital, example of, 165.
Sister of Charity, 388, 390.
Six days, creation of world in, 314.
Slavery, in Pagan times and countries, 416 *et seq.*
   Its degrading influence on the free, 420 *et seq.*
   Among the Mohammedans, 423.
   And Christianity, 425 *et seq.*
   Not abolished by the Church recklessly or by bloodshed, 425.
   St. Paul and, 428.
   Parallel between Pagan and Christian, 432.
   Mitigated and abolished only by Christianity, 432 *et seq.*
Slaves, awarded equal religious privileges with freemen, 429.
   Who are canonized saints, 430.
   Validity of their marriages, 431.
   Their manumission made a religious ceremony, 432.
Sobieski, example of, 124.
Social virtues, motives of, 458.
Socialism, errors of, 98.
Societies, secret, causes and evils of, 441.
Society, religion basis of, 456.
   Of Jesus, example of, 121.
Socrates, belief of, in immortality, 201.
   On religious worship, 276.
Solomon, example of, 206.
Solon, words of, quoted by Herodotus, 25.
   Founded legislation on religion, 48.
Soothsayers among Pagans, 275.
Soul, immortality of, 198 *et seq.*
   Distinct from organic matter, 200.
   Principle of life, 200.
Spencer, Herbert, errors concerning will, 175.
Stoeckel on evolution, 282.
Strauss, assertions of, 250.
Strikes, a questionable remedy, 450.
   Should be replaced by arbitration, 451.
   Statistics of, 451.
Suetonius, testimony of, 262.
Suicide, a virtue among Pagans, 279.
Sun, the, standing still at Josue's command, 314.
Sunday (see Sabbath).
Sunday-School insufficient, 494.
Supreme Being, universal belief in, 24 *et seq.*
Susanna, example of, 73.
Switzerland, persecutions in, 186, 187.
Syria, state of religion in, 186.

TACITUS, testimony of, 262.
Talleyrand's witty sayings, 244.
Tartarus, Gentile belief in, 201.
Tennyson, quotation from, 110.
Tertullian, testimony of, 256.
  Testimony of, to Pagan immorality, 323.
  Witnesses to infanticide among Pagans, 376.
Thanes of Northumbria, example of, 278.
Thanksgiving Day, a healthy sign, 161.
  A tribute to religion, 481.
Thomas, St., of Canterbury, example of, 185.
  On marriage of slaves, 431.
Tiedemann, researches of, 286.
Trajan, emperor, example of, 255 and 261.
Transfiguration of Christ, 242.
Truce of God, 401.
Trusts and monopolies, 446.
Turkey, example of, 271.
Tyndall's prayer-test, 144.
Tyndall, on destiny of man, 289.
  Not an atheist, 38.
Tyre, example of, 275.

UNHAPPINESS of unbelievers, 4.
Unions, labor, dangers from demagogues, 448.
United States and Pagan Rome compared as to wars, 404, 412.
Unity of human race declared by Scripture, 285.
  Confirmed by anatomy, 287.
Universal consent of mankind an overwhelming argument, 44.
  Belief in God, 49.
  Belief in immortality, 201.
Universality of Christianity, 271.

Universe, creation of, ascribed to Christ, 230.
  The, witnesses to God's existence and attributes, 305.

VALENS, Emperor, example of, 172.
Variety, in material world, source of beauty, 98.
Vatican Council, on Revelation, 274.
  Teaches faith and reason not opposed, 304, 313.
Vaughan, testimony of Archbishop, concerning Australian aborigines, 33.
Vedas, doctrine of the, 31.
Vercingetorix, prisoner of Cæsar, 188.
Vice not remedied by education, 464.
Vienna besieged by Turks, 124.
Vincent de Paul, St., example of, 182.
Virgil, testimony of, 201.
  Example of, 261.
Virtuous, hope and happiness of, 103, 208.
Vitality of Church not due to organization, 267.
Voltaire, abhorrence of atheists, 42.
  On human unity, 284.
  On the basis of civil government, 469.
Vote, to, not a right but a trust, 507.

WAINWRIGHT, on evolution, 281.
War the universal rule before Christ, 12, 396.
Ward, on laws of nature, 135.
Wars, number and horror of, diminished by Christianity, 14.

Washington appealed to religious motives, 476.
Wealth, no security for happiness, 205.
Whiting, Prof., on language, 287.
Wife, condition of Pagan, 11, 349 *et seq.*
Wilberforce, influence of, on emancipation, 433.
Will of God revealed to us, 195.
Blessedness of submission to, 196.
Will, human, strengthened by prayer, 122.
Influenced by certain causes, 168.
Not forced by motives, 176.
Not a slave, 179.
Woman and Christianity, 348.
Condition of, in Pagan civilization, 349.
Equal rights of, with men, 362.
Her mission according to Christianity, 368 *et seq.*

World, created or eternal? 16 *et seq.*
Governed by Divine Wisdom, 77.
Worship, prayer essential element of, 113.
Gratitude essential element in, 148.
Of Christ commanded, 236–237.

XENOPHON and the basis of civil government, 468.

YOUNG'S Night Thoughts, quoted, 107.

ZEND-AVESTA, testimony of, to Monotheism, 32.
Zeno, example of, 280.
Zimmerman, on belief of Dahomey in God, 34.

www.ingramcontent.com/pod-product-compliance
Lightning Source LLC
Chambersburg PA
CBHW031947290426
44108CB00011B/709